The Catastrophe of Modernity

The Bucknell Studies in Latin American Literature and Theory
Series Editor: Aníbal González, Pennsylvania State University

The literature of Latin America, with its intensely critical, self-questioning, and experimental impulses, is currently one of the most influential in the world. In its earlier phases, this literary tradition produced major writers, such as Bartolomé de las Casas, Bernal Díaz del Castillo, the Inca Garcilaso, Sor Juana Inés de la Cruz, Andrés Bello, Gertrudis Gómez de Avellaneda, Domingo F. Sarmiento, José Martí, and Rubén Darío. More recently, writers from the U.S. to China, from Britain to Africa and India, and of course from the Iberian Peninsula, have felt the impact of the fiction and the poetry of such contemporary Latin American writers as Borges, Cortázar, Garcia Márquez, Guimarães Rosa, Lezama Lima, Neruda, Vargas Llosa, Paz, Poniatowska, and Lispector, among many others. Dealing with far-reaching questions of history and modernity, language and selfhood, and power and ethics, Latin American literature sheds light on the many-faceted nature of Latin American life, as well as on the human condition as a whole.

The aim of this series of books is to provide a forum for the best criticism on Latin American literature in a wide range of critical approaches, with an emphasis on works that productively combine scholarship with theory. Acknowledging the historical links and cultural affinities between Latin American and Iberian literatures, the series welcomes consideration of Spanish and Portuguese texts and topics, while also providing a space of convergence for scholars working in Romance studies, comparative literature, cultural studies, and literary theory.

Titles in Series

Robert Ignacio Díaz, *Unhomely Rooms: Foreign Tongues and Spanish American Literature*

Mario Santana, *Foreigners in the Homeland: The Latin American New Novel in Spain, 1962–1974*

Ronald J. Friis, *José Emilio Pacheco and the Poets of the Shadows*

Robert T. Conn, *The Politics of Philology: Alfonso Reyes and the Invention of the Latin American Literary Tradition*

Andrew Bush, *The Routes of Modernity: Spanish American Poetry from the Early Eighteenth to the Mid-Nineteenth Century*

Santa Arias and Mariselle Meléndez, *Mapping Colonial Spanish America: Places and Commonplaces of Identity, Culture, and Experience*

Alice A. Nelson, *Political Bodies: Gender, History and the Struggle for Narrative Power in Recent Chilean Literature*

Julia Kushigian, *Reconstructing Childhood: Strategies of Reading for Culture and Gender in the Spanish American Bildungsroman*

Silvia N. Rosman, *Being in Common: Nation, Subject, and Community in Latin American Literature and Culture*

Patrick Dove, *The Catastrophe of Modernity: Tragedy and the Nation in Latin American Literature*

James J. Pancrazio, *The Logic of Fetishism: Alejo Carpentier and the Cuban Tradition*

The Catastrophe of Modernity

Tragedy and the Nation in Latin American Literature

Patrick Dove

Lewisburg
Bucknell University Press

© 2004 by Rosemont Publishing & Printing Corp.

All rights reserved. Authorization to photocopy items for internal or personal use, or the internal or personal use of specific clients, is granted by the copyright owner, provided that a base fee of $10.00, plus eight cents per page, per copy is paid directly to the Copyright Clearance Center, 222 Rosewood Drive, Danvers, Massachusetts 01923. [0-8387-5561-5/04 $10.00 + 8¢ pp, pc.]

Associated University Presses
2010 Eastpark Boulevard
Cranbury, NJ 08512

The paper used in this publication meets the requirements of the American National Standard for Permanence of Paper for Printed Library Materials Z39.48-1984.

Library of Congress Cataloging-in-Publication Data

Dove, Patrick, 1967–
 The catastrophe of modernity : tragedy and the nation in Latin American literature / Patrick Dove.
  p. cm.—(The Bucknell studies in Latin American literature and theory)
 Originally presented as the author's thesis (doctorate—State University of New York at Binghamton).
 Includes bibliographical references and index.
 ISBN 0-8387-5561-5 (alk. paper)
 1. Spanish American literature—20th century—History and criticism. 2. Literature and society—Latin America. 3. Tragic, The, in literature. 4. Borges, Jorge Luis, 1899– Sur. 5. Rulfo, Juan. Pedro Páramo. 6. Vallejo, César, 1892–1938. Trilce. 7. Piglia, Ricardo. I. Title. II. Series.
PQ7081 .D64 2004
860.9′98′0904—dc22   2003015422

PRINTED IN THE UNITED STATES OF AMERICA

Contents

Acknowledgments	7
Introduction	11
1. The Idea of Tragedy: Form and Institution of Modernity	30
2. Visages of the Other: On a Phantasmatic Recurrence in Borges' "El Sur"	53
3. *Exígele lo nuestro*: Transition and Restitution in Rulfo's *Pedro Páramo*	98
4. The Catastrophe of Modernity: Vallejo's *Trilce* Between Indigenism and the Avant-garde	161
5. Heterotopic Memory and the Narration of Disaster in Piglia	222
Notes	253
Bibliography	286
Index	296

Acknowledgments

THIS BOOK FIRST BEGAN TO TAKE SHAPE AS A DOCTORAL DISSERTATION at the State University of New York at Binghamton. It was supported in the early stages by a dissertation-year fellowship from the Department of Comparative Literature, and it could not have been completed without generous subsequent support from both the Social Science Research Council and the Andrew Mellon Foundation in conjunction with Department of Spanish and Portuguese at the University of Southern California.

One of the major challenges in this book's development has been the problem of how to incorporate two distinct intellectual and cultural traditions—Latin American literature and what is often simply called "theory"—while doing justice to the specific concerns, perspectives, and experiences of these fields. To whatever extent I have been able to establish a dialogue between the two traditions, I am indebted to Brett Levinson for his spirited questioning and his incisive criticism as a mentor and dissertation director. I have learned from Brett not only through exchanging ideas in seminars, conversations and written work, but likewise by observing his intellectual ethic, or his unique way of engaging with Latin Americanist concerns in new academic contexts. I also express my gratitude to Alberto Moreiras for his intellectual and moral support. Alberto's work has been an inexhaustible source of challenge and inspiration, and has in many ways helped to make this book possible. To Chris Fynsk, Horacio Legrás, and Carlos Riobó, I give my thanks for their comments and criticism on early drafts of the manuscript, and likewise to Aníbal González for his helpful guidance as the manuscript was taking its final form. I would also like to thank Christine Retz at Associated University Presses for all of her help during the editing process.

To my parents, Bill and Alexandra Dove, I owe an immeasurable debt for their generous support and encouragement. And finally, my most heartfelt appreciation and admiration go to my lovely wife, Deborah, for her patience, her support and her sense of humor throughout this project. This book is dedicated to our winsome son, Samuel.

Abbreviated versions of chapters 2 and 3 have already appeared in print: "Visages of the Other: On a Phantasmatic Recurrence in Borges' Fictions" (*Latin American Literary Review* 28:56 [July-Dec 2000]:61–88), "Exígele lo nuestro: Deconstruction, Restitution and the Demand of Speech in Juan Rulfo" (*Journal of Latin American Cultural Studies* 10:1:25–44), and "Reflections on the Origin: Tragedy and Transculturation in *Pedro Páramo*" (*Angelaki: Journal of the Theoretical Humanities* 6:1:91–110). I thank both the Latin American Literary Review Press and Taylor & Francis Ltd (http://www.tandf.co.uk) for permission to republish these articles in revised form.

The Catastrophe
of Modernity

Introduction

EVER SINCE THE PUBLICATION OF DOMINGO SARMIENTO'S *FACUNDO* IN 1845, literature has been viewed as playing a fundamental role in the historical emergence of the modern Latin American nation-state. The value accorded the written or poetic word by the generation of Sarmiento, Bello, and Echeverría is similarly reflected in subsequent generations of Latin American thinkers, including Rubén Darío, José Martí, Octavio Paz, and many of the "Boom" writers. In each case, and despite the possibility of considerable ideological differences, literary expression is regarded as offering an alternative, supplementary path to modernity in circumstances where the project of social and economic modernization otherwise remains unfulfilled. Recent work in Latin American cultural studies has contributed significantly to our understanding of how literature participates in the consolidation of the modern nation-state by acting as a pedagogical device, helping to secure consensus for the economic, political and military projects associated with nation-building. This book takes a different but related approach to the question of literature and nation, beginning with the premise that the thought of "nation" and "modernity" is marked in advance by catastrophe. With regard to the question of national origins, the idea of catastrophe in fact evokes two distinct facets or moments: it describes the fact of annihilation, or the process of violent clearing and reordering that paved the way for the modern nation-state, and it names a new beginning associated with the promise of the Enlightenment project, in which modernity equals the advance of the spirit of political and cultural autonomy and social justice.

The central argument of this book is that the use of tragedy as a theoretical index affords new ways of understanding how literary expression reflects on and seeks to come to terms with societal catastrophe in Latin America. It would perhaps be more precise to say that tragedy offers a certain key or *attunement* for reading Latin American cultural production, while providing a new interpretive frame for viewing the relation between literature and modernity in

Latin America. As the terms "key" and "attunement" suggest, a consideration of tone and mood will be fundamental to this discussion of tragedy and modernity. For, whatever we understand by tragedy, and however we define its form, its idea and its ends, what is at stake in the tragic is never simply and exclusively conceptual and theoretical. My use of tragedy as an interpretive model seeks to engage critically a recurrent theme present in Western thinking: the notion or belief that the aesthetic, removed in principle from the concrete particular concerns and interests of everyday life, is uniquely able to reconcile political conflict, heal social antagonism and foment a sense of group unity or identification. While tragedy is by no means the only possible basis for examining the idea of aesthetic reconciliation in Latin America (the confessional *relato* or the modern novel could just as easily serve as models), my claim is that no matter what the literary form, the thought and the sense behind aesthetic reconciliation is *essentially tragic*—even when we no longer have to do with tragedies per se. This is in part because the basis for such a view of literature and its possibilities is indebted to a long history of interpreting tragedy.

Modern interest in classical tragedy has more than once led to attempts to transpose or translate ancient works into a modern context, and has similarly provided the occasion for critical explorations of the aporetic origins of European modernity.[1] For late-eighteenth- and early-nineteenth-century Germany, this interest in classical tragedy coincides with a search for a cultural form that would be adequate to the task of representing or constituting (the ambiguity between the constative and the performative is unavoidable) a new sense of national unity, in a social arena that had previously seen itself as nothing more than an array of autonomous and potentially-conflicting states devoid of a single organizing principle. In the liminal context of German unification, the turn to tragedy can be understood within a broader attempt to present national culture as the self-defining work of a people (*Volk*). In its appropriation for a modern context, tragedy thus assumes the form of a universal: a signifier that would constitute the unifying point for a totality of discrete and conflicting particularities, by virtue of embodying or making visible a vital aspect of each.[2] It would constitute the self-projecting representation of a people in its contemporaneity. Tragedy, which since its emergence at the origin of Athenian democracy has always embodied the sense of a foundational work, provides an important aesthetic or identificatory mechanism through which the modern state will justify its tutelary and disciplinary functions, i.e. as mediator through which a people realizes itself as such. Tragedy exemplifies an "aesthetic promise" that underwrites the formation of the modern nation-state.

The interest that guides my exploration of Latin American literature and tragedy is in fact twofold. On one hand, I argue that a similar tragic determination of literature as "aesthetic promise" is at work, explicitly or secretly, throughout the Latin American tradition, and that it can be found in both the self-critical commentaries of renowned nineteenth- and twentieth-century authors and in a number of prominent hermeneutic schools of thought. Well-known examples can be found in the essays of Domingo Sarmiento and Octavio Paz, as we shall see in chapters 2 and 3. For Sarmiento and Paz, literature does not merely represent an order of truth or reality that precedes writing: more importantly, it supplements and perfects what nature and history are unable to accomplish by themselves. The ideological basis of this determination of literature as compensatory modernity is, I argue, essentially tragic—regardless of the presence or absence of "tragedy" as a theme. This idealized view of literary aesthetics makes its way into Latin America in the early- to mid-nineteenth century, and plays an important role in orienting nation-building projects during the ensuing decades.[3] Recent groundbreaking work in cultural studies has shown how, during the Argentine nation-building process, the written word is treated as the avatar of a number of traits essential to the modern nation-state: the word is a sign of universal culture and of the language of law, but it is likewise seen by Sarmiento and others as a means to mobilize support for the liberal vision of a centralized and well-ordered republic.[4] In its literary form, writing helps to mobilize ideological support for the political, economic, and military operations through which properly national spaces are delimited, cleared, and cultivated. Moreover, it is literature that gives shape to the *idea* of the state—as a pedagogical and orthopaedic mechanism, and as a space of neutral, disinterested and universal representation—at a time when the institutional bases of the state are in large part lacking. In this sense, the tragic tone that resonates throughout a text such as Domingo Sarmiento's *Facundo* expresses a foundational intention: the *Facundo*, whose form is that of the essay rather than tragedy, nonetheless derives its prevailing tone and logic from tragedy—or from a certain reading of tragedy. With the assistance of this foundational tragic tone, the text hopes to provide a sufficient symbolic basis for orienting the project of modernity.

My primary concern is not that of identifying specific thematic resonances between Latin American cultural production and classical tragedy. It is not a question of influence or "imitation" (at least not in the ordinary sense) that interests me here. Instead, I focus on the relations that link literary aesthetics to questions about politics and history—a connection first made and exemplified in interpretations of Greek tragedy. An analogy can be found in one of the central premises of David Lloyd and Paul Thomas's *Culture and the State*: namely, that modern Europe has since its beginnings sought to define itself as a continuation or recovery of classical Greek culture, and that the aesthetic has in this context come to be regarded as a neutral and ideal means of grounding the modern state. Accordingly, the tragic aesthetic is considered to provide a tropological blueprint for the state's claim to reconcile sociopolitical conflict. It reproduces and institutionalizes the process of sociopolitical mediation through the pedagogical work of the example. Above and beyond the particular content of a given work of art, the aesthetic by its very nature instructs us on how to be good citizens, teaching us to cultivate good judgment and to desire (political) representation.

On the other hand, this book also examines the idea of tragedy in a handful of twentieth-century authors—namely Jorge Luis Borges, Juan Rulfo, César Vallejo, and Ricardo Piglia—who (except in the case of Piglia) are all writing in the decades immediately following the culmination of national modernization. For each of these writers, the untimely end of the modernization project—or the exhaustion of its promise in Latin America—threatens the imminent, catastrophic collapse of an entire epochal or ideological framework. In light of this crisis of national ground, the thought of tragedy provides a point of departure for critical reexaminations both of the nation-building project and of the history of literature's participation therein. For these writers, certain formal and tonal dynamics borrowed from tragedy help to call into question two of the principle roles assigned to literature in modern times: that it be a faithful reflection of local reality and a palliative or an antidote for the violent contradictions in society. For Borges, Rulfo, and Vallejo, the thought of tragedy helps to destabilize the ideologeme of "high literature," and thereby exposes the limits of the idea that literature can or should provide the cultural basis of national hegemonic projects. At the same time, tragedy also helps set the tone for exploring new possibilities for literary aesthetics in Latin America. For these writers, tragedy offers a *counter-foundational* perspective: it at once expresses the hope of an *other* foundation (one that would be less violent, less barbaric, more democratic) and it attempts to think the limits of all foundational discourse, or the sense in which every foundationalism is marked by a traumatic origin whose meaning precisely escapes it.

In the first chapter, "The Idea of Tragedy: Form and Institution of Modernity," I describe a scenario that will help to clarify my use of tragedy as an interpretive frame. The chapter traces a long history of relation between the philosophical and theoretical tradition and Greek tragedy, beginning with commentaries by Plato and Aristotle and again as tragedy becomes important for post-Kantian philosophical projects. It is a negative reference to tragedy that first defines philosophy's central mission for Plato: to organize the Greek *polis* and to legislate its social space. In the *Republic*, tragic poetry serves as the bad example or scapegoat for philosophy's endeavor to arbitrate and regulate the poetic use of language, or mimesis. Plato views tragedy as alien to the polis; it is an outsider in need of classification and domestication, an array of tropes and affects that must be brought under control or expelled if social space is to be maintained in good order.[5] However, the philosophical tradition also has a long history of celebrating Greek tragedy as a pinnacle of human creation, and has frequently sought to "borrow" from tragedy in order to inaugurate new bearings for critical thinking. For a number of post-Kantian thinkers, tragedy functions as a kind of mirror for philosophy as it attempts to define for itself a regulatory role among the sciences. For such disparate thinkers as Hegel, Nietzsche, and Heidegger, tragedy affords a glimpse of philosophy's own mechanisms and possibilities. However, the suspicion and ambivalence regarding tragedy that was present at the beginning of Western metaphysics in Plato is also—and somewhat surprisingly—at work in the post-Kantian speculative tradition. Friedrich Schelling describes the inauguration of speculative philosophy as substituting Aristotelean poetics (a theory of tragedy's effects on the spectator) with a theory of tragic form (based exclusively on the formal logic of the work).[6] Regardless of the professed intentions of speculative philosophy, however, the project of classifying and regulating mimesis, and of distinguishing between the "good" and the "bad" uses of representation, remains a fundamental if unstated concern.

The first chapter offers a contingent definition of tragedy that is established through reference to Hegel's view of the form as essentially a political narrative. In tentatively adopting the Hegelian reading for this project, I am not implying that it is superior to other views of tragedy, nor for that matter do I wish to suggest that *any* particular definition could account for the entirety (or what remains to us) of Greek tragedy. A certain privilege is accorded to Hegel's reading because it has been highly influential (if not always recognized as such) in shaping the imaginary processes at work in both nation-building and literary aesthetics in Europe and the Americas during the past two centuries. As a representation of conflict between individuals, tragedy also attests to strife between distinct and seemingly incommensurable social orders, epochs, or "worlds." According to Hegel, tragedy as a formal composition stages an encounter between the antithetical domains of family and civil society. This juxtaposition, a crossing of incompatible codes, engenders violent misunderstanding. Tragedy in turn, understood as work of art rather than historical event, seeks to reconcile this antagonism through symbolic production. In other words, the aesthetics of tragedy as envisioned by Hegel aims to make meaningful an encounter or event that would otherwise exceed our understanding.

However, the works upon which Hegel bases his theory of tragedy also reveal certain facets that are not easily assimilated into the final tally of aesthetic reconciliation. Tragedy also presents a thought of "difference" that eludes the dialectical dream of producing a systematic account of the relation between identity and difference. In recent decades, poststructuralism and psychoanalysis have each turned to tragedy in order to shed new critical light on the claims of the metaphysical tradition. For contemporary thinkers such as Jacques Lacan, Jacques Derrida, and Philippe Lacoue-Labarthe, the tragic form provides an important point of departure for questioning philosophical principles such as the transparency of self-consciousness and the self-sufficiency of logical systems. Whereas modern philosophy conceives of self-consciousness as a unifying power operating over the myriad objects and realms of experience, both deconstruction and psychoanalysis maintain that consciousness is in fact structured around certain gaps, elisions or a kind of forgetting. While neither deconstruction nor psychoanalysis claims in turn to provide an alternative, comprehensive "theory" of tragedy, each uses tragedy to call attention to the limits of philosophy's engagement with literature. For these contemporary interventions, tragedy commemorates a loss whose traces are in danger of being eroded by the dominant sway of reconciliation and progress. In a highly paradoxical sense, tragedy would be a "memory" of the impossibility of founding an adequate and total memory of the past. Moving both with and against the prevailing spirit of reconciliation, these contemporary readings of tragedy reflect on the trace of catastrophe that haunts every articulation of history. In Walter Benjamin's words, "the concept of progress has to be grounded in the idea of catastrophe. That things continue to 'go on' *is* the catastrophe."

In the central chapters, I redirect this somewhat abstract discussion of tragedy and philosophy to an examination of nineteenth- and twentieth-century Latin American literature. It is not my intention to apply uncritically a theoretical debate to a literary scenario, nor do I wish to imply that these (primarily European) theoretical reflections enjoy a privileged interpretive position for Latin American literature. The intent is to create a dialogue between two academic "worlds," while at the same time paying heed to the problems, tensions, and misunderstandings that invariably attend such encounters. In this respect, it is worth considering several related points regarding the impossibility of "applying" theory to literature. For one, it should be noted that consideration of some of contemporary theory's most important questions and insights had already been initiated in Latin American literary texts prior to their emergence in the academic discourses of the metropolis. This critical production *avant la lettre* does not mean that we should be content with simply inverting the Eurocentric paradigm and taking Latin America to be the true source of contemporary theoretical innovation rather than its passive recipient. Indeed, one of the important Latin American contributions in this respect is precisely to have destabilized the cultural opposition between "original" and "copy." Furthermore, the relation between theory and literary text can never be guaranteed in advance, as the notion of "application" would require. When undertaken thoughtfully, theoretical analysis does not follow a preestablished route or lead to preformed conclusions. On the contrary, it must continually be produced anew on uncertain ground. The relation between text and theory is both inimitable and uncategorizable: the encounter with a text is both the beginning of theory (there is no general theory of deconstruction, for instance, outside of specific readings) and the limit of theory (every literary text, insofar as it is a text, constitutes an unprecedented occasion for theory, an encounter for which previously established terms and methods might not be adequate). Similarly, my readings of these texts remain attentive to the particular time and place of writing. If, when considering a given historical moment, it is possible to imagine similar ideas, sentiments and moods taking shape in different parts of the world and through distinct modes of expression, comparative studies must also take into account the crucial differences that are conferred by a particular locus of enunciation. While one can argue that Jorge Luis Borges "anticipates" many of the insights of deconstructive literary theory, Borges' oeuvre is also marked by questions specific to the experience of writing at the so-called "margins" of Western culture (and this marking may well include a number of *unexpressed* or *disavowed* contradictions pertaining to Argentine tradition in Borges). In other words, Borges' text grapples with—and is concurrently shaped by—Latin American questions that by and large have yet to be seriously addressed by theoretical discourses such as deconstruction.

Certain texts in the Latin American tradition reveal a concern with what Hegel would term the "vanishing mediator" of the historical present. But if the perspective of these works could be described as tragic insofar as they attend to experiences of tyranny, destruction, and radical loss at the origin of the modern nation-state, the tragic emphasis in these works is nonetheless not a strictly thematic issue. On the contrary, the tragic sense of a work often emerges through literary phenomena that challenge our attempts to describe and categorize them: for instance, through variations in literary tone, tropological distortions, and repetitions, strategic recourse to silence and dissimulation, and so on. The mnemonic traces that circulate in these works could be loosely described as manifestations of *literary affect*, in contradistinction to literary meaning or signification. The term "affect" should be understood in manner akin to the "psychosomatic" occurrence described by Freud under the same name: as a material (corporeal) warning signal that announces the uneasy proximity of the unpresentable. These insistent "remainders," resistant to assimilation into relations of equivalence, substitution, or progression, are not simply representatives of an alternative memory that had at some point been repressed or silenced by a dominant discourse. In many cases, they in fact mark the site of literature's encounter with the limits of memory and representation. Unable to incorporate all, literary memory discovers the traces of loss, forgetting and erasure in its own foundations. Literature encounters what could be termed "originary absence" as a necessary condition for the formation of particular memories.

While examining a selection of key figures in the national literary traditions of Argentina, Mexico and Peru, the difficulties that accompany such a seemingly self-evident category as "Latin American literature" also bear emphasizing here. Although the idea of a unified Latin American cultural tradition is as old or older than the name "Latin America" itself, the texts examined here attest to a heterogeneous character that complicates the premise of a general literature of the continent. As we will see, in each of the central chapters it is the dual thought of nation and modernity that gives rise to literary reflection on heterogeneity and singularity. This is not only for the simple reason that what is "Argentine" is defined in part by what is not Chilean or Peruvian, but moreover because these texts are also considerations of the violence at work (and often concealed) within the nation-building processes themselves. Nation is a sign around which conflicting significations and values tend to accumulate. For a writer such as Juan Rulfo, the Mexican nation names the hope of vanquishing violence through speech and shared memory, while at the same time it is a mask covering an archaic loss. Literary consideration of Latin American singularity can be viewed as seeking to convey what Peter Fenves calls the *topicality* of an event: that is, literary expression is shaped by both the place, the timeliness and the distinct tones involved in the emergence of the modern nation.[7] While in Latin America "the nation" is invariably associated with a more or less abstract or negative determination of modernity (modernity as "promise," announcing the end of colonialism, barbarism, dependency, underdevelopment, etc.), literature's treatment of nation is determined by the specific texture of each particular scene. The general, abstract question of modernity is thus always already transcribed and hence *marked*: for instance, as the domestication of the Argentine Pampa, the taming of the gaucho, along with the vast waves of immigration into cosmopolitan Buenos Aires; and as the image of the Mexican revolution, celebrated as absolute break with Porfirian oligarchy and also acknowledged as renewed conflict between popular interests, bourgeois interests and the modern state, and so on. For a number of Argentine, Mexican, and Peruvian writers, reflection on nation-building is shrouded in a tone of mourning. Literature laments and struggles to remember violence and loss that accompany the founding of the modern nation-state. Developing this connection between origin and loss, I suggest that "the nation" can be understood as a fundamentally tragic thought, seeking to bring forth, through the universality of language, an object that can only be experienced as partially absent, either as the promise of a community to come or as belated recognition of a possibility that has already been foreclosed.

Taking the intersection of literature and nation as a point of departure, this book performs close readings of three literary texts whose publications postdate the consolidation of the nation-state in Latin America by several decades or more. These primary texts are Jorge Luis Borges' short story "El Sur," Juan Rulfo's novella *Pedro Páramo,* and the lyrical poetry of César Vallejo's *Trilce.* Although these authors do not belong to a common literary school or movement, the texts occupy a similar juncture in their respective national or regional traditions, a "reflective" moment in the aftermath of nation-building and modernization. By way of conclusion, I then turn to two contemporary novels by Ricardo Piglia. While Piglia's work actively engages with the Argentine tradition, his writing is also marked by an awareness that recent events in the Southern Cone have called into question the tradition's capacity to respond to the exigencies of present moment. If, since the Renaissance, Western thinking has always held a special regard for ancient tragedy, frequent endeavors to incorporate or transcribe tragedy into a modern context necessarily involve the appropriation or translation of something both fundamental *and* irreducibly foreign to modern Western thinking. It is my belief that this ambiguous juxtaposition of origin and alterity affords a productive tension for examining Latin American cultural production as a self-consciously peripheral enterprise, as a tradition that feels itself to be both marginal to and inseparable from the metropolitan culture of Europe. As an interpretive frame, tragedy offers new ways of understanding how Latin American literature participates both in the development of foundational narratives of national identity, and likewise in what Alberto Moreiras terms "critical regionalism," or diverse literary strategies for marking the limits of these institutional and identitarian forms of thinking. Each of the central chapters of this book examines a particular national tradition in Latin America under the hypothesis that the idea of tragedy, or what I have described as the tragic sense of the literary aesthetic, plays an important role in the development of a self-critical perspective within these national traditions. But my use of tragedy as an interpretive frame is not an attempt to define a common aesthetic or political ground. On the contrary, in each of the works explored here the idea of tragedy emerges in a different way and yields markedly different consequences.

My discussion of how these authors relate to and intervene in their repsective traditions is influenced by previous Latin Americanist work on literature and nation, including books by Josefina Ludmer (*El género gauchesco*, 1988), Antonio Cornejo Polar (*Formación de la tradición literaria en el Perú*, 1989), Néstor García Canclini (*Culturas híbridas*, 1989), Julio Ramos (*Desencuentros de la modernidad*, 1989), Roberto González Echevarría (*Myth and Archive*, 1990) and Beatriz Sarlo (*Jorge Luis Borges: A Writer on the Edge*, 1993). Each of these critics has helped in one way or another to reshape our understanding of how cultural production, and especially literature, works to generate popular consensus for the consolidation of the modern Latin American nation-state. While the literary traditions of the late-nineteenth and early-twentieth centuries frequently celebrate a diversity of long-standing popular traditions, they also portray the desirability of establishing homogeneous national institutions and modern forms of citizenship. In arguing that Borges, Rulfo, and Vallejo occupy "reflective" moments in their respective traditions, meanwhile, I maintain that their writing is defined in part by an emerging distance separating them from both modernization and the literary counterparts of this process. With the decline of nineteenth-century liberalism under which the nation was first conceived in Latin America, and in the emergence of new political forms such as nationalism, populism, and indigenism, the interrelated questions of nation and modernity begin to reveal new and previously unanticipated possibilities and risks. The texts I examine here not only offer critiques of the specific ideological mechanisms at work in nation-building; at the same time, each in its own way calls into question any attempt to secure an adequate representation of nation. All four writers reflect on the nation as a conjunction of heterogeneous interests and incommensurable registers. "Nation" at once names an irreducible multiplicity of particular interests and it functions as a transcendental—and hence unpresentable—order of signification, which, at least in principle, would organize the aforementioned constellation of competing partial interests.

My understanding of these issues also owes a considerable debt to the recent work of Alberto Moreiras (*Tercer espacio*, 1999) and

Idelber Avelar (*The Untimely Present*, 1999), and to their questioning of some of the fundamental assumptions operating in contemporary Latin Americanist discourse. In particular, this book is influenced by the borrowing of the psychoanalytic concepts of "mourning" and "melancholia" for the interpretation of twentieth-century Latin American cultural production. To a large degree, the use of tragedy as a theoretical device here complements the work done by Moreiras in seeking to unravel the complex and often ambiguous relation between foundational and counterfoundational literary tendencies in canonical twentieth-century Latin American writers. Of course, one of the important contributions brought forth in discussions of "mourning" and "melancholia" as indices of Latin American cultural production is that of introducing *emotion* and *affect* as crucial terms for the analysis of twentieth-century symbolic production. In this light, I concur with Moreiras's observations concerning the ends of theory itself: an interpretive tool such as "mourning" or "tragedy" is not a ready-made, stable concept waiting to be applied indiscriminately. Nor is it the purpose of theory to aid in constructing metaphysical systems that could account for a particular work, author, or historical moment in its entirety (although a certain slippage and complicity between theory and metaphysics may indeed be unavoidable, as Paul de Man has suggested). Theory only works—if and when it works—when it exposes itself to the enigmatic singularity of the text, or to what is both *in* and *more than* the text's intentional, metaphorical signifying economy. Theoretical concepts as such are inherently and notoriously unstable, and the turn to literature does not present an opportunity for theory to finally colonize and secure for itself a firm ontological ground. On the contrary, the engagement with literature constitutes a *chance*—and it is perhaps theory's only chance—to say something that would not merely serve to buttress metaphysical system-thinking. As theoretical topoi, mourning and tragedy no doubt have a good deal in common; indeed, mourning has often been described as the proper mood of tragic drama. At the same time, there are subtle but important differences between "mourning," which emphasizes the paradoxical dual labor of "introjection" and "expulsion" in the recuperation of personal and collective libidinal investments, and "tragedy," understood as a mode of representing an unsuspected identity between distinct epochs and their respective codes, ontotheological premises, and attunements, as well as a purging of the particular emotions of fear and empathy. As interpretive frames, then, let us grant that tragedy and mourning potentially lend support to similar theoretical perspectives. Yet these indices also give rise to subtle but important differences in literary tone, pitch, and rhythm. And, for both tragedy and mourning, it is perhaps such minor differences, which border on the incalculable, that truly matter.

As an object of academic study, "literature" has been subject to increasing scrutiny in Latin Americanist and other circles in recent decades, and has undoubtedly suffered a loss of prestige in relation to other indices of personal and collective expression such as *testimonio*. In Latin Americanist circles, the consensus seems to be that we are now witnessing the definitive demise of literature as a privileged medium of cultural production. In selecting four more or less canonical authors for study, I am neither ignoring these recent debates nor attempting reactively to recuperate literature's former preeminence. Rather, I believe that it is in fact a *certain understanding of "literature"*—and not this or that literary text—that has recently entered into crisis: the idea that literature offers a compensatory form of modernity, or that it functions as the purveyor, arbiter or exemplar of the proper, of more or less permanent national or universal cultural values. However, I also feel that recent Latin Americanist attempts to challenge and demystify this idealized, monolithic view of literature at times run the risk of simply replacing one unquestioned cultural standard with another. In this sense, the critique of "literature" must be expanded to include a far-reaching reassessment of traditional assumptions about the transmission of "cultural values" in general. Tragedy can assist in this critical reassessment of "culture" by revealing another dimension of literary aesthetics, a facet that has frequently been ignored or suppressed by traditional theories of literature. Instead of relying on a presumably stable opposition between literature and other forms of cultural production—a presumption that governs both the culturalist idealization of literature and many cultural studies-oriented critiques of culturalism—this project seeks to underscore a difference that arises within literature and divides literature from itself. This difference could be described, somewhat schematically, as a contrast between literature in its *representative* functions—for instance, as exemplar of national or universal cultural values—and literature as moving toward the *limits of representation*, as causing the signifying bonds of representative to begin to tremble. In pointing to the limits of representation (for instance, that of a particular political image of a nation), literature brings to the fore a certain kind of forgetting or effacement that accompanies the institutionalization of sociocultural norms. But it reflects on these limits as a productive site, a juncture where relation takes place and new alliances and meanings are formed. The topos of tragedy is thus shared by dominant national discourses and various attempts to think the limits of prevailing representations of nation. Like literature itself, the notion of tragedy is neither essentially conservative nor necessarily subversive or contestatory. Tragedy's potential for either reinforcing or questioning predominant views about art and society is determined in the final instance by reading: by the relation between text and reader, an event of particular and perhaps unrepeatable contact.

Each of the book's central chapters (2–4) performs a close analysis of a particular twentieth-century text, while also discussing how this text engages with its respective regional or national tradition. The first of these central chapters, "Visages of the Other: On a Phantasmatic Recurrence in Borges' 'El Sur'," examines how the "civilization and barbarism" debate has shaped Argentine letters. The chapter begins by looking at Domingo Sarmiento's *Facundo* (1845), in which the nation-building project is construed as the process of "civilizing" a "barbaric" national topography (of course, these assignations are also codified justifications of the domination and annihilation of Argentina's indigenous populations). I then turn to Leopoldo Lugones's *El Payador* (1916), an inversion of Sarmiento's elitist hierarchy that transforms the "barbaric" gaucho into a national hero. Literature's role at both ends of this debate goes beyond the mere reflection of a reality that precedes it. More importantly, literary language is charged with transforming the meaning of this reality, or with bringing into view a new possibility—and thus Argentine literature reveals the utopian kernel at work in its conception, as an attempt to present *being* where previously there was only barbarism. For Sarmiento, poetry is charged with conveying an ideal image of the nation's future and thereby forging consensus for the incipient nation-building project. For Lugones, on the other hand, literature is invested with recuperating a national "purity" or "essence" that had been diluted and contaminated by modernization. I then turn to a text by Jorge Luis Borges that illustrates a blind spot in the claims of both liberalism and nationalism. The short story "El Sur" (1953) is an incisive intervention in the debate over national destiny and the conflicting assignations of "civilization" and "barbarism." The text unfolds as a brilliant critique of the unexamined assumptions of both foundational discourses, but at the same time it offers a new way of thinking about nation, identity, and modernity. Borges asserts elsewhere that Argentine literature derives its most radical possibilities from what we might call a thought of its constitutive impossibility, or of the nation's inability ever fully to become One. "El Sur" can be read as an allegory of this impossibility. The story in fact closely resembles a "translation" of tragedy into prose form, in which the protagonist embodies the limit of what both Sarmiento and Lugones envisioned as the proper destiny or essence of the nation. Yet the deconstruction in "El Sur" of both Sarmiento's founding opposition and its nationalist critique does not mean that the text discards history in favor of relativism. On the contrary, through tragedy it also gives shape to a different thought of agency, or to an attempt to think freedom from *within* an awareness of human mortality or limits. I describe this as a shift from the sovereign subject of metaphysics to the subject of heteronomy. While the tragic representation of the nation in "El Sur" parodies both nationalism and Eurocentrism, it likewise presents a potential incongruity with some of Borges' own infamous political statements. This tension between the literary and the metaliterary, or between the critical potential of Borges' writing and the deeply conservative position of the author himself, constitutes an unsurpassed and perhaps unresolvable difficulty for Borges criticism.

Chapter 3, "*Exígele lo nuestro*: Transition and Restitution in Rulfo's *Pedro Páramo*," examines Juan Rulfo's novella *Pedro Páramo* (1955) as both an important event in Mexican literature and as a supposed precursor of the Latin American "boom" novel. On one hand, Rulfo's writing brings to a close the regionalist tradition popularized by Mariano Azuela, Augustín Yáñez, and others; it does so by entombing the idea of literature as mimesis or faithful reflection of local reality. At the same time, *Pedro Páramo* presents difficulties that readers such as Octavio Paz and Carlos Fuentes appear to have overlooked. Both Paz and Fuentes would like Rulfo's work to herald a national passage into the realm of "universal culture." But while these cultural ambassadors of modern Mexico envision modern Latin American literature as a compensatory mode of production, substituting high culture for the Revolution's failure to successfully institute socioeconomic modernization, Rulfo's writing casts a very different light on the themes of revolution and modernity. His text reveals an irreducible dissymmetry between aesthetic modernism and the idea of modernization as progression toward socioeconomic emancipation. Rulfo's work points to an antinomy that haunts the idea of modernity, understood as the simultaneity of social emancipation and creative autonomy. Not surprisingly, however, the tragic motif in *Pedro Páramo* also differs considerably from that of Borges' "El Sur." Tragedy is evoked in Rulfo's writing through the protagonist's search for a father he never knew, in which he is in fact bound to discover a primordial crime associated with the paternal name. But the allegorical link between filial and national histories in Rulfo's novella does not open the door for literature to become the purveyor of a new national identity.

The first half of Rulfo's novel is brought to a close with the narrator's enigmatic testimony: "Me mataron los murmullos" ("The murmurs killed me"). This "death" announces a rupture in the culture of national identity or *mexicanidad* promoted by the postrevolutionary state. In contrast to the patrilineal narrative parodied in the first half of Rulfo's novella, the second half is comprised of myriad fragmentary memories of tyrannical *caciquismo*. Although Rulfo's literary treatment of these problems at times closely resembles what has since come to be known as *testimonio* narrative, his text continually destabilizes the idea that speech constitutes a compensatory measure that could symbolically rectify experiences of loss or suffering. Instead, Rulfo's writing situates literary restitution at the limits of sovereignty and propriety. These limits offer new possibilities for thinking about community in the context of the subaltern, albeit in ways that do not turn to myths of communion and immanence for support. Tragedy and *anagnorisis* in Juan Preciado's narrative do not pretend to reconcile two opposing perspectives, the dominant and the subaltern. Instead, this tragic encounter with the traces of the subaltern yields a different kind of knowledge, which could be better described as the apocalypse of reconciliation.

From the prose writing of Borges and Rulfo, I then turn to the lyric poetry of César Vallejo's *Trilce* (1922) in the penultimate chapter, entitled "The Catastrophe of Modernity: Vallejo's *Trilce* between Indigenism and the Avant-garde." My reading takes issue with a tendency to reduce this work to a supposed vanguard aestheticism. I argue that the experimental style of *Trilce*, while responding to stylistic innovations of some of Vallejo's Latin American contemporaries, also gives shape to a far-reaching confrontation with the problem of Peruvian modernity. Vallejo's aesthetic innovation contributes a critical assessment of the role that literature has traditionally played in sustaining and naturalizing social, ethnic, and economic contradictions in the Andes. As opposed to the idealized images of *mestizaje* as assimilation popularized by nineteenth-century writers such as Ricardo Palma, in Vallejo's poetry the aforementioned dissymmetries are made to "return" as disturbances in the grammar and syntax of the poetry itself. Thus the critical tendency to situate *Trilce* at the forefront of the Latin American avant-garde only tells part of the story. Peter Bürger and others have described the European avant-garde as a self-reflective critical phase in modernist artistic practices. Vanguard aesthetic experimentation attempts to counteract art's (perceived) tendency to serve as a palliative for the latent contradictions of industrialized society; the avant-garde thereby confronts its own history of participation in the reification of nature and human activity. But, as Vallejo's poetry reminds us, any attempt to transcribe this European metadiscourse on art into an Andean context must also account for important historical differences: unlike Europe, the modernization projects first undertaken in the second half of the nineteenth century in Latin America are at best only partially realized, and never come close to the tendential "seamlessness" of their European counterparts. In Latin America, these projects continue both to manifest and to reproduce the violent contradictions that modernity was expected to resolve. In this light, the European avant-garde project—which aims to demystify the lingering "aura" of the work of art, or the myth of a sovereign art world as yet uncontaminated by capital—is simply inconceivable in Latin America. For Vallejo, the experience of Andean modernity perhaps requires that we hear the term "epoch" (from the Greek *epokhē*) in its literal meaning, as naming a pause or suspension between times.

Trilce's consideration of the disjunctive character of Peruvian modernity is accompanied by a poetic questioning of "modernity" as a dominant theme in the Enlightenment tradition. The tragic topos that guides my discussion of Vallejo is considerably different from those of Borges and Rulfo. Vallejo's poetry is a lyrical reflection on what I term the fundamentally tragic character of modern thought. For Vallejo, this means a sustained reflection on what it means to think, write, and act in a time marked both by the absolute abandonment of the gods and by the echoes of an ancient world in ruins. At the same time, *Trilce*'s experimental form, which brings a considerable strain to bear upon the Spanish language, in fact shares more with indigenist literary projects than has often been acknowledged. Akin to the radical formulations of José Carlos Mariátegui and José María Arguedas, Vallejo's poetry links its consideration of ethnicity and subalternity to a reflection on language itself. By representing Andean society as a tragic disjunction between epochs, *Trilce* initiates a highly paradoxical form of mourning whose idiomatic conditions of possibility coincide precisely with the loss that poetry laments.

The fifth and final section, "Heterotopic Memory and the Narration of Disaster in Piglia," serves as a conclusion to this study. This chapter examines two novels by the Argentine writer Ricardo Piglia, published during and after the country's 1976 to 1983 military dictatorship. These works pose new difficulties for my interpretive scheme, and appear to signal a limit for tragedy's capacity to find meaning in catastrophe. While the idea of tragedy resonates throughout Piglia's writing, I suggest that in certain (aesthetic and ethical) respects, the idea of trauma serves to better define the stakes of Piglia's literary project. I distinguish between *Respiración artificial* (1980) as a novel of the dictatorship and *La ciudad ausente* (1992) as a novel of the postdictatorship. The earlier work portrays dictatorship as an experience of radical disorientation, but it nonetheless offers the hope of renewing collective memory through supplementation, by combining heterogeneous and partial histories. The novel places the event of dictatorship in a tragic frame: in order to reconstitute itself, historical memory must begin by reckoning with its own limits, with the impossibility of knowing the past in its entirety. One way in which the limit of collective memory makes itself known is through a referential aporia: in order to do justice to the experiences of dictatorship, collective memory must seek other historical points of comparison and contrast; yet the "experience" of disaster, as many survivor narratives indicate, is of something incomparable and in a certain sense "outside of" experiential time. On one hand, then, Piglia implies that it is other twentieth-century disasters such as the Holocaust (rather than the symbolic material of the Argentine tradition) that constitutes the proper frame of reference for recent experiences of dictatorship and terror in Argentina. At the same time, Piglia is one of the first Southern Cone writers to describe the circumstances of state terrorism as radically unprecedented, as an experience that both defies and destroys the epistemological markers or referential framework through which human experience is constituted. Piglia's literary treatment of dictatorship suggests that, paradoxically, the language of silence can at times be more "faithful" to the past than the language of speech.

In *La ciudad ausente*, the disruptive effects of dictatorship are extended during the postdictatorship, and the earlier novel's hermeneutic motifs are displaced by figures of repetition: translation and interminable mourning. In the 1992 novel, traumatic aftershocks from the dictatorship era are accompanied by a new array of problems posed by the transition from state economy to a transnational market economy. Transition is experienced as ideological crisis in which traditional political models have been suddenly rendered obsolete, and the only apparent alternative is the neoliberal plan first introduced by force under dictatorship. Surrounded by the collapse of personal and political horizons, Piglia's transitional novel confronts the prospect that literature, and particularly the aesthetic ideal embodied by tragedy, is unable to register and do justice to the magnitude of this transformation. The historical rupture brought about by the end of dictatorship and the advent of "postmodernity" in Argentina thus announces the culmination of an entire aesthetic tradition. In this time of interregnum, we could say, the old affective registers of fear and pity no longer provide sufficient impetus for coming to terms with societal catastrophe and terror. While Piglia's works continue to speak in the language of tradition, his writing also attests to the exhaustion of its fundamental promise. This seeming contradiction engenders what could be termed a heterotopic effect. Literature both mourns a loss it cannot repair while asserting the need to testify to experiences for which we have no adequate words.

1
The Idea of Tragedy: Form and Institution of Modernity

WITH THE ASCENT OF GERMAN IDEALISM IN JENA AT THE BEGINNING of the nineteenth century, philosophy manifests a renewed interest in Greek tragedy. In its turn to ancient tragic drama, speculative philosophy seeks a formal dynamic or a logic that it could claim as the fundamental mechanism of its own dialectical system. The search for a formal definition of tragedy by Hegel, Schelling, and Hölderlin marks a departure from the Aristotelean interpretation of tragedy according to the effects it produces in the spectator. Whereas Aristotle is generally understood as emphasizing the theatrical basis of tragedy, German Idealism is intent on reading tragedy as if it were first and foremost a written text. In the words of Peter Szondi, "since Aristotle there has been a poetics of tragedy . . . it is only since Schelling that there has been a philosophy of the tragic."[1] My interest in discussing this turn or return to tragedy hinges on what this reading says about philosophy itself. This chapter will examine some of the important moments in the relation between the metaphysical tradition and Greek tragedy, which relation I believe could provide a model for the history of interaction between philosophy and literature in general. Furthermore, I will indicate several instances in which the limit of this reflective transfer between philosophy and tragedy is made to appear. Such a limit is of primary concern in contemporary rereadings of German Idealism (particularly in psychoanalysis and deconstruction), but it already surfaces in Idealism's very attempt to reengender or repeat the greatness of classical culture in a modern environment. It is in Friedrich Hölderlin's attempts to "translate" Greek tragedy into a modern context that the limit—or what Hölderlin refers to as the "caesura"—of speculative thought is first made to resonate.

Hegel's references to Greek tragedy, most notably in the essay on "Natural Law," the *Phenomenology of Spirit*, and the *Aesthetic*, offer a formal definition of tragedy that has since proven highly influential—if not always acknowledged—for cultural production in Europe and the Americas. Not only does Hegel offer a new way of understanding the *pragma* and the mechanics of tragedy, he is also among the first to attempt to clarify the insights that tragedy offers for history. The affinity between speculative philosophy and Greek tragedy is partially explained by the fact that, for Hegel, Schelling, and Hölderlin, the inner unfolding of the tragic work exemplifies the movement of the dialectic itself, providing an illustration of Spirit's wont to split itself in twain and go against itself, and likewise giving shape to its desire to recover itself again.[2] Hegel views tragedy as comprising a series of "moments" that together form the gradual unfolding of a kind of reflected relation or "identity" between opposites. In the first instance, tragedy stages a violent encounter [*polemos*] between two conflicting forces or "worlds"—for instance, the modern perspective informed by the Enlightenment opposed to a "premodern" perspective—each of whose internal logic precisely negates or excludes the claims of the other. Tragedy begins by presenting the unreflected "moment" of the dialectic, wherein a particular perspective (let us say, the discourse of the Enlightenment) keeps to itself and refuses to recognize the ways in which it depends upon what it is not. The Enlightenment derives its identity and its moral authority from its promise to vanquish "superstition" and "barbarism." But it forgets that its truth is dependent on that which it negates, and is itself nothing outside of this relation; and likewise, it ignores the fact that this archaic other—"superstition" or "barbarism"—is in fact and in name nothing other than a projection of Enlightenment discourse itself. In setting out to tame or annihilate this "other," then, enlightened reason ends by unwittingly turning its hand against itself. At the same time, tragedy also promises a reconciliation of this unmediated encounter. In Hegel's terms, the tragic promise of reconciliation lies in the production of a third term that would incorporate fundamental aspects of both particulars: for instance, the democratic state. If a tragedy such as Aeschylus' *Oresteia* recalls and celebrates the birth of Athenian democracy, it is also possible—precisely on the basis of what the Jena school has helped to reveal about the relation between culture and the state apparatus—to understand modern appropriations of the tragic aesthetic as the *embodiment* of this promise of reconciliation. Tragedy would deliver via its performance and its pragma the neutral and unifying space that form the pedagogical ground of the modern state. If what is meant by "the state" is frequently restricted to the institutional mechanisms and spaces that act upon and mediate between discrete social spheres and actors, then the aesthetic function of tragedy would provide the *idea* of the state, a locus of identification through which the institutionalization of the modern subject or citizen would become not only possible but desirable.[3] Hegel's turn to tragedy seeks an exemplary and foundational form; tragedy's radiant image is charged with providing the symbolic basis for a transition from the "heroic times" of the old gods and their factional conflicts to the institution of what Hegel calls the "universal ethical forces" of the modern state. Tragedy exposes history as "absolute catastrophe," and in so doing it invites us to think history as event, as a rupture that radically transforms the terms and possibilities of history. The tragedy of history, then, describes a double movement: catastrophe, a complete (*kata*) destruction and overturning (*strophē*) of the old, is also an opening onto a new beginning.

In the exalted tone of Hegel's reading of tragedy, we should not lose sight of the fact that classical tragedy also gives rise to a tone of mourning that is likewise proper to the dialectic. In staging an epochal confrontation between *nomos* and *dikē*, or "organic" and "inorganic" law, tragedy strives to come to terms with a kind of hermeneutic blindness, a structure of misrecognition that haunts the founding of these orders. It is not that philosophy believes tragedy capable of correcting this theoretical errancy and the destruction that issues from history. Tragedy can only hope to acknowledge an originary gap in the history of knowledge (or, in Hegel's terms, between reason and being), a missed encounter that can only be *supposed* and *assumed* on the basis of its effects. The promise of reconciliation announced in Greek tragedy entails two discrete instances—one of production and the other of reflection—whose combined effects do not necessarily coincide with standard views of the speculative dialectic as total incorporation and mastery of difference. Tragedy acts on one hand to mark a profoundly paradoxical relation between the law and the archaic violence it would claim to have overcome, while at the same time working to heal this wound that reason inflicts upon itself.[4]

For Schelling, the project of identifying a formal essence of tragedy that could be appropriated by philosophy takes the form of a meditation on the paradoxical character of human freedom. In the following remarks I will be referring to the tenth of Schelling's "Letters on Dogmatism and Criticism." In tragedy, Schelling seeks to locate an expression of the rational identity between two modes of thought, which he terms "dogmatism" and "criticism," and in so doing to provide an aesthetic calculus of guilt and justice. Tragedy makes this unexpected identity manifest by using the concrete terms of the *pragma* or action to stage a confrontation between the abstract notions of freedom and necessity. In *Oedipus Rex*, which provides the basis for Schelling's analysis, the hero's defiance of divine law [*dikē*] has the surprising effect of unsettling and threatening to suspend any hope for justice in the community. The silent defiance of Oedipus underscores our suspicion that no rational explanation could possibly be found for judging Oedipus as guilty: according to Schelling, the divine determination of Oedipus' guilt should strike us mortals as a profound injustice. Schelling suggests that fate, interwoven with the hero's myriad attempts and ultimate failure to avoid the crime and downfall that have been prophesied for him, must have presented a profound contradiction for Greek thought. He offers that the weight of this antinomy could only have been made bearable—not to mention enjoyable—through the simultaneous presentation of a thought of freedom, an idea that would emerge from the scarcely discernible gap between guilt and necessity or fate. According to Schelling, the hero's defiance of divine judgment proves to be "excessive" in that he protests loudly— too loudly, in fact—against a judgment that is already recognized by all reasonable minds as unjust. This intransigent contention between the human and the divine casts doubt on the economic relation between defiance and punishment; it forces us to reexamine our initial assumption that Oedipus' defiance stems from and protests against the punishment itself. Schelling suggests that the true aim of the tragic hero's intransigence lies beyond any simple question of his guilt or innocence. The contempt that Oedipus shows in the face of divine judgment strangely forces open a space in which the binding necessity of objective fate—which in its unmediated form is unthinkable and horrifying to us—can become legible under a different, less blinding light. Once we accept that Oedipus cannot by any rational standard be held accountable for the crimes of patricide and incest, then we must henceforth understand *tragic* necessity—not the blind necessity of fate, but rather that of the hero's condemnation for a crime of which he could not have been aware—as the effect, remainder or *re*mark of a certain freedom, or what I will later term heteronomy. Fate returns in tragedy in the form of a freedom that becomes intelligible—retroactively—from "within" objective necessity while remaining irreducible to the terms of the latter; it is a freedom that we can only *suppose* on the basis of its effects. Divine judgment and punishment, then, are not to be interpreted as a measured response to the crimes of patricide and incest. Instead, divine judgment points back to hubris, to that excessive human defiance or intransigence in the face of the unknown. The attempt to elude the crime or fate foretold by the oracle is itself the true crime and the freely assumed cause for which the hero is cast out of the polis. Schelling's reading thus suggests a paradoxical relation between freedom and its elevated representation, in which tragic drama helps to set the meaning of what it would seem to mourn. Freedom, always in excess of objective necessity, is both honored [*ehrte*] and realized via the tragic representation: freedom, in other words, *is* only insofar as it is shown to have been lost, and only to the extent that its loss is freely assumed. The tragic presentation presupposes this freedom as something that is iterable (it can only be "honored" to the degree that it can be repeated); and yet, at the same time, we are left with the impression—and this might help to explain the inestimable cultural value accorded to tragedy as a mode of representation—that, in the absence of the eulogizing act which will have ensured its legibility, tragic freedom *is not*. The difference between what Hegel would call the positing (performative) and the external (constative) determinations of freedom is *aufgehoben* [canceled out and raised to a higher order] in an absolute freedom that emerges from the tragic image of fate or necessity.

Many of the concerns that define Hegel's and Schelling's project are also prominent in the theoretical and dramatic works of Friedrich Hölderlin. Hölderlin's interest in Oedipus and Empedocles engages two histories that could be said to embody the philosophical conception of self-consciousness itself: both its relentless interrogation of origin and its claim upon a kind of freedom or detachment that would allow it to contemplate its own end or limits. Hölderlin's theory of tragedy remains dialectical or "onto-theological" (the term is Heidegger's) both in its endeavor to define a formal theory or calculus of the genre, and likewise in its attempt to identify a specular relation between tragic form and tragic content (form as *aufhebung* of content, and consequently as production of the Idea). As several recent commentaries have indicated, however, Hölderlin's relation to classical tragedy is probably even more intimate and searching than those of Hegel and Schelling. Whatever interests he may have shared with Hegel and Schelling on the side of an appropriation of tragedy for philosophy, Hölderlin also seeks to renew in its radicality what these latter were primarily interested in appropriating for other purposes. And so Hölderlin's contribution to philosophical thinking about tragedy also causes the speculative project's edifice to begin to tremble: for Hölderlin, as we will see, tragedy signals and attends to a rupture within dialectics itself.

Hölderlin's interpretation of the tragic is rooted in his well-known or infamous efforts to "translate" Greek tragedy into a modern setting. This project reveals a peculiar notion of translation, in part because there repetition does not aim for likeness but rather yields dissymmetry. The translations of *Oedipus Rex* and *Oedipus at Colonus*, derided and dismissed by Hegel and Schelling as overly literal and somewhat mad renditions, in fact give cause for reexamining the central premise—i.e., that tragedy can be mastered by dialectical thinking in an operation that leaves no remainder—that brought Schelling and Hegel to the tragic in the first place. Hölderlin's contribution to speculative reflection on tragedy focuses on a dual problem of history and production: tragedy must be seen as a fundamentally Greek mode of art (it is a manifestation of what Hölderlin calls Greek "culture"), and a modern tragedy would thus be inconceivable except as a translation of ancient tragedy. However, any attempt to produce a modern tragedy must also confront the limits of traditional conceptions of translation, i.e. as transparency, faithfulness, or adequation to the original. As Hölderlin demonstrates, the proper model for translation is not a mirror that would pretend to reflect or to duplicate the original work in its unity. Rather, translation *imposes* itself on the receiving language (the violent metaphor is crucial) as it ushers the original into a new or foreign context. Translation exposes the receiving language (German) to what it is not (Greek expression, thought, etc.), to something it can perhaps never hope to grasp entirely. And thus, the relation that translation assumes to the original can never be that which the original bore to itself. Translation cannot and does not seek to reproduce the "content" or "meaning" that was already immanent in the original.

In order to see why translation marks both the possibility of (modern) tragedy and its limit or impossibility, we must turn to a thought of history that signals an important distinction between

Hölderlin and his Idealist peers. For Hölderlin, history is not primarily a progression or evolution of form and idea; instead, its structure resembles a chiasmus. In this light, the relation between moderns and ancients is irreducible to any idea of identity, reflection, symmetry or progress. The only hope for articulating a relation between these two epochs requires that we expose two aspects of each—the domains of culture and nature—to a kind of mutual inversion. In other words, that which is most proper to modern man—his "nature," which Hölderlin understands as a modern lyrical "sobriety" in the face of alienation from Nature and the divine—must be grasped as more closely resembling what had functioned for the ancients as "culture," or what Nietzsche in *The Birth of Tragedy* calls the Greeks' "healthy pessimism." And while the modern determination of "culture" ought then by all rights to coincide closely with Greek "nature," Hölderlin asserts that what was most proper to the Greeks, their nature, in fact remained a secret from the Greeks themselves. Greek "nature" is something that never took place as such. This dissymmetrical relation between the ancient and the modern has important implications for translation as an experience of historicity. According to Hölderlin, the modern determination of translation as mimesis—be it construed as contention with, emulation of or surpassing of the original—is in truth an avoidance of the impossibility of translation when it comes to an original truth that was never in fact articulated as such. For Hölderlin, this limit-relation forms the point of departure for what would be modern tragedy. It issues as the exigency of repeating what was *there* before, albeit in the mode of not (yet) *being*. It echoes an eternally silent word whose contours can only be glimpsed at its limit: in that turn away from the proper that was Greek art. The structure of repetition in Hölderlin's thinking marks an implicit but important difference with the Hegelian philosophy of history: modern poetry, in taking aim at what was unnamed or unrealized in Greek tragedy, is nonetheless something other than the evolution or perfection of the classical tradition. In passing over the gaps and silences of the original, translation both demarcates and re-marks the original at its limit. Translation is a testament to the "limitedness" of both original and copy, in the sense that there could be no translation outside of these lacunae and the essential blindness they impose.

Hölderlin assigns this limit-structure an "internal" and "formal" place within the tragic work, suggesting that the epochal rifts of which tragedy speaks are echoed by a formal rupture in the rhythmic pattern of tragedy's poetic verse. This formal turning point, an event following which things will never be the same again, is what Hölderlin calls the tragic *caesura*:

> There, in the rhythmic sequence of the representation, wherein *transport* presents itself, there becomes necessary *what in poetic meter is called caesura*, the pure word, the counter-rhythmic rupture; namely, in order to meet the onrushing charge of representations at its highest point in such a manner that very soon there does not appear the change of representation but the representation itself (*Sämtliche Werke* 5: 196; *Essays and Letters on Theory*, 102).

In Sophoclean tragedy, Hölderlin locates the caesura in the appearance of the blind seer Tiresias, and thereby clearly indicates that this formal break is to be associated with the *peripeteia* or irreversible symbolic transformation (from king to patricide, etc.) brought about by the tragic pragma. To a certain extent, Hölderlin's description shares a good deal with the Aristotelian interpretation of tragedy. As middle point in the tragic verse, the caesura formally divides the work and thus gives shape to a kind of narrative chronology that has a "beginning," a "middle" and an "end." The stichomythic exchange between antagonists (which Hölderlin formalizes as an "onrushing charge of representations") is mediated by the caesura in a way that highlights the tragic polemos, or the strife and conflict between warring particulars (for instance, the mutual accusations of betrayal and tyranny traded by Oedipus and Tiresias). However, in framing this back-and-forth exchange, the caesura also introduces what Hölderlin terms "the pure word," a remainder that perhaps cannot be recuperated by any dialectical thought of identity and difference. In representing antagonism between conflicting social codes or languages, and in approaching the point of maximum intensity of this conflict, tragedy produces something in excess of its own symbolic economy. As a result, tragedy—modern tragedy—also compels us to reexamine our conceptualization of the relation between art (or the work) and truth: for Hölderlin, the caesura enures that tragedy "can no longer resemble the beginning in what follows" (*Essays and Letters in Theory*, 108).

Along with translation and history, mourning provides a key topos for understanding the importance of tragedy for Hölderlin.

Indeed, mourning could probably be called the decisive or proper tone in modern reflection on tragedy in general. But this does not mean that a general consensus exists within modern philosophical concerning tragedy, nor does it necessarily imply that the meaning of "tone" itself has already been established. On the contrary, the ambiguous relation between tragedy and philosophy also reminds us that the object of "tone" is anything but a calculable sum, and that tone in fact has to do with an irreducible multiplicity of cadences or registers.[5] It would be a mistake, then, to assume that the motif of mourning receives its only possible meaning either with Schelling's notion of reason learning to bear its own internal contradictions, or similarly through René Girard's theorization of ritual sacrifice (or identification and expulsion) as the essence of Greek tragedy. Hölderlin, once again, provides one indication of the complexity at stake in thinking what is meant by the tonality of mourning: mourning, if it defines the relation between modernity and classical tragedy, marks both the proper cadence *and* the limit of Greek tragedy, signaling both its unrepeatability *and* the necessity of repeating—and hence losing or altering—its secret truth. For Hölderlin, the mood of mourning that helps to provide the fundamental attunement of modernity is evinced in lyrical poetry, which attests to the experience of being modern as a radical separation from being and divine truth. It is on this basis, of the necessity and impossibility of repeating tragedy, that I will make reference to a tragic form of thinking in chapter 4.

While German Idealism sees in tragedy a perfect manifestation of the mechanics of philosophy itself, in *The Birth of Tragedy* Nietzsche positions Greek tragedy as a mode of expression that is radically foreign to the modern (and metaphysical) concepts of the subject or the individual. With Hegel, Nietzsche reads ancient tragedy as a manifestation of the epochal strife between conflicting forces or tendencies, which Nietzsche associates with the mythical figures of Apollo and Dionysius. Apollo is "der Scheinende": the god of art, of form, of light or illumination, and also of illusion (*Schein* can refer to light or illusion). And thus he is also associated with the inner world of dreams and fantasy, but only to the extent that these latter exist in moderation and restraint. The Apollinian is also a regulating force for the creative drives, imposing form and intelligibility on that which emerges in the world. Dionysius, on the other hand, is the antithesis of the Apollinian *principium individuationis*: the Dionysian signals a breaking away from the individual, an overturning of social order and hierarchies, and a blending or confusion of what the metaphysical tradition regards as opposites (master and slave, man and nature, etc.). Its limitations notwithstanding, *The Birth of Tragedy* remains an influential reading for twentieth-century thinkers in that it constitutes one of the first (and most exuberant) departures from the standard set by German Idealism.[6] Nietzsche's view of Greek tragedy is of interest not only because it presents tragedy as incommensurable with the modern notions of individuality and the subject. Likewise, his reading is also one of the first (modern) examples of a philosophical engagement with the nonideational aspects of tragedy, such as music, tone, and emotion.

A number of twentieth-century thinkers have also turned to classical tragedy as a point of departure for engaging with the philosophical tradition. In the wake of the Heideggerian "closure of metaphysics," however, reflections on classical culture are marked by a paradoxical bind that does not allow thought either to continue in or to extract itself from the idea of a general system regulating the production of meaning. This paradox can be elucidated through two conflicting conditions or constraints which every philosophical project must confront: 1) every metaphysical theory or system is haunted by a kind of founding excess, to which the system is indebted but for which the resources of the system cannot account; 2) nevertheless, thinking does not have access to an easy exit from the constraints of metaphysics, since the self-proclaimed departure from metaphysics (or ideology) is itself one of the metaphysical (ideological) gestures par excellence.

Tragedy plays a decisive role in Heidegger's reading of the history of philosophy, and particularly for his attempt to free this history from teleology and historicism. In *An Introduction to Metaphysics*, the title of a series of lectures delivered in 1935, Heidegger turns to tragedy in an effort to think the historicity of truth, or the way that truth emerges through human practice (language, politics, technology, etc.). According to Heidegger, the speculative approach to tragedy should be included with other "onto-theological" attempts to enforce a certain predetermination of truth or being. In the Idealist tradition, this silent determination derives from a reinterpretation of the Platonic and Cartesian understandings of truth as adequation, but it is nonetheless a forgetting of what Heidegger calls the *question of being*, an obscuring of history as the site of reciprocal and unsettling claims issuing from human activity and language.

Like the Idealists of Jena, Heidegger bases his interpretation of Sophoclean tragedy on a formal determination of the genre. That is to say, he distances his analysis from questions about theatricality, catharsis and spectacle. Yet an important difference also emerges between Heidegger and Idealism: for Heidegger, Greek tragedy's presentation of the "historical being" of *Dasein* (Heidegger's term for human existence) is not oriented by a synthetic movement from particularity to universality. Tragedy, for Heidegger, has to do with an irreducible difference that informs human activity, a difference that could be said to reproduce itself—but never fully present itself—in and as history. What can be said of this difference that inscribes language, technology and politics from the beginning? Tragedy revolves around the idea that human activity bears and conceals multiple "faces" or takes place in multiple "worlds," and that every act is thus marked by a kind of latency: while we may well always understand ourselves as acting within a given context or "world" (for instance, a political activist may understand himself as acting within the sphere of civil society), what we do also has ramifications in other spheres or "worlds." And thus a given act—let us say, the famous example of Antigone's decision to disobey Creon's edict and bury her brother's corpse—may well bear entirely different meanings in discrete "worlds": for instance, it might appear as treason within political society and as a rightful act of mourning within the sphere of the family. Tragedy hinges on this ontological structure of overexposure to which every act is subject: as soon as we join the community of language and symbols, we are immediately separated from oneness and omniscience. We always act in multiple spheres, but by the same token we can never know the consequences that our decisions will take on in each and every world; tragedy is a name for the radical errancy to which every decision must submit itself.

This thought of the founding difference of pragma is evidenced in Heidegger's discussion of *Antigone*, and of the chorus' evocation of man as *to deinotaton*, which Heidegger translates as "the strangest" (*Antigone*, lines 332–75). The Sophoclean eulogy wrests the human figure away from its familiar surroundings while underscoring the passion and violence at work in all human activity. Tragedy thus gives an account of the inherently violent nature of passion, desire and activity: technē, through which human practice endeavors to bestow order upon the world, begins by tearing open and seizing the pure and undivided nature of being. In Heideggerian terminology, it "brings being to stand." In lieu of a conventional distinction between production and destruction, ordering and violence, tragedy posits the violence of ordering itself:

> It is this breaking out and breaking up, capturing and subjugating that opens up the essent [*Seiende*, Heidegger's term for "a being"] *as* sea, *as* earth, *as* animal. It happens only insofar as the powers of language, of understanding, of temperament, and of building are themselves mastered [*bewältigt*] in violence. The violence of poetic speech, of thinking projection, of building configuration, of the action that creates states is not a function of faculties that man has, but a taming and ordering of powers by virtue of which the essent opens up as such when man moves into it. This disclosure of the essent is the power that man must master in order to become himself amid the essent, i.e. in order to be historical (*Introduction to Metaphysics*, 157).

For Heidegger, the tragic presentation of human "passion for disclosure of being" (*Introduction to Metaphysics*, 107) does not show us the will of an intentional subject; instead, it sheds light on history as a reciprocal and violent transformation of the human and its world. A people must master the violent use of force (that is, both initiate or "bring [it] forth" *and* subjugate it) in order to realize itself as a people. But the source of this mastering, which seeks to "bring being forth" as a project, is not the subject as it has traditionally been conceived by the metaphysical tradition, i.e., as self-identical, rational, and intentional. If a people must engage and transform nature in order to realize itself as belonging to a world, this engagement must also expose itself to a kind of reciprocal violence: not just that of brute nature, but moreover the violence of history understood as event. Heidegger elsewhere describes this exchange of forces as "usage" [*Brauch*]: in the moment that one deploys language toward a given end, language likewise "uses" human speech in order to become what it is.[7] Tragic violence thus manifests itself via two antithetical movements. The first involves the human appropriation of nature and the accompanying use of force through technology, language and so on. The second moment manifests something like the "death of intention" at work in the Hegelian universal.[8] In the chorus's speech in *Antigone*, the polyvalent term *to deinataton* suggests a bifurcation of force, naming the human as both *pantaporos aporos* (Heidegger translates this as "everywhere journeying, inexperienced and without issue") and *hypsipolis apolis* ("rising high above his place"). These two phrases, ciphers of *to deinataton*, characterize human existence as exile from the familiar, and as having been cast into the radically estranging spheres of desire, language and history. These motifs of banishment, errancy and uncertainty have more than one implication, however: for one, they relate the old Heideggerian story of mistaking appearances for being and thus losing sight of appearing as such; but they likewise render a heroic account of the founding potential of human activity. The tragic act, in transcending the time, place and norms of its inscription, bears a certain opacity that inveighs against its becoming fully intelligible at any given moment. There is no single privileged moment in tragedy at which the entire truth will have made itself present; the emergence of truth coincides by necessity with the disappearance of the possibility of changing or avoiding the destiny it prescribes. For Heidegger it is the *unheimlich* ("unhomely" rather than "uncanny") that provides the interpretive key for the experience of historicity: human passion in its excessiveness is both exiled *from* being (or from truth as self-certainty) and, at the same time, exiled *in* being: "In his exile from home, the home is first disclosed as such" (167). For Heidegger, Greek tragedy provides one of the first sites for thinking history in the death of the metaphysical subject and the collapse of historicism. It provides a schema for history as event or *Ereignis*, as the double movement of disclosure and reciprocal appropriation that determines a relation between a people and world. Heidegger describes this tragic violence as the shattering of *Dasein* against being: in opposing technē to dikē, human activity both violently tears into the undifferentiated nature of being and, in the very course of producing history, is in turn exposed to the possibility of downfall or cataclysm.

This turning point constitutes the necessary, assumed risk of Dasein itself: "Violence against the preponderant power of being *must* shatter against being, if being rules in its essence, as *physis*, as emerging power" (*Introduction to Metaphysics*, 162). Just as human activity violently appropriates the undifferentiated and tames its force in producing a world, being in turn "uses" the human in order to take place *as* being. The motif of shattering does more than merely reinforce the dialectical character of violence in Heidegger's reading of tragedy: it points toward a limit beyond all limits, toward death as the unsignifiable limit of all signifying practice. Rather than representing death as a particular moment to come, this image of absolute fragmentation indicates that death, as the unsignified shadow of all symbolic work, is always already at work within the domain of praxis.

Among so-called "post-Heideggerian" thinkers, Jacques Derrida has contributed significantly to elaborating the ruptures and slippages located by Heidegger within the metaphysical project, while also calling attention to a "blindness" that continues to haunt this period in Heidegger's thinking. A key point for Derrida's rereading of the metaphysical tradition is found in the discussion of Hegel's treatment of *Antigone* in *Glas* (see the left-hand column, between the bottom of 141 and 189), and in particular concerning a pair of motifs addressed by Hegel: sexual difference—along with its Aufhebung in the brother-sister relation—and the tomb. The presence of these figures in Hegel's thought illustrate what Derrida terms an "ellipse" in the passage from (self)consciousness and reason to absolute Spirit. In the *Phenomenology*, Hegel uses *Antigone* to exemplify a number of related passages or transitions in the dialectic: from nature to culture, from singularity to universality, and from family and civil society to ethical sphere [*Sittlichkeit*]. According to a standardized reading of Hegel, each of these movements entails a remainder-less operation capable of accounting for the differences it engenders and reconciling the breach that is its birth. Derrida's notion of ellipse, a polycentric metaphor that promises to guide us through this uneven and violent passage that is the dialectic, also points to its other semantic possibility, an orthographic mark that holds the place of a lacuna or an elision. The ellipse is a dyadic center whose dual presence inaugurates the redoubling of unity, while threatening the One with a silence that belies all calculation.

Hegel places the family, in contradistinction to civil society, both in the privacy of the home and in close proximity to the tomb. It is woman, as representative of the private sphere, who tends to the sepulcher and safeguards the corpse against the forces of nature. She honors the dead by evoking singularity: mourning, as feminine activity par excellence, works not by reference to general concepts such as "citizen" but by reciting the proper name in its unicity. (Of course, it is Sophocles' *Antigone* who provides the model for Hegel's thinking here.) The grave, along with its feminine attendants, is thus the cradle of Spirit, the cultivation of the singular that has divested itself of its contingencies and accidents and is now raised above matter to the power of the universal. The tomb exemplifies the speculative operation, as a (re)turning point through which Spirit both breaks away from itself and returns to itself as other. Derrida suggests that it is this dyadic and undecidable point, at which Spirit both is and is not itself, that the dialectic seeks to recover and introject into its own mechanism. The dialectic would be a process of mastering its own limits and contingencies—and ultimately death itself—through contemplation: "What speculative dialectics means (to say) is that the crypt can still be incorporated into the system" (*Glas*, left column, 166).

The motif of the tomb in *Glas* is accompanied by a semantic ambiguity whose reverberations lend supplementary support to this reading. In the frequent recurrence of the reflexive verb *se tomber* ["to fall," but also echoing a tomb], *Glas* seeks to make audible the always receding echo of what does *not* return, and thereby to remind us that something somewhere must always be surrendered or lost in order for the speculative game to be won. Derrida suggests that a liminal cadence resonates in the reflexive *se tomber*: the *Klang* (sound, ringing, peal, tone) which in a number of Hegel's texts strikes a middle ground between oppositions of distinct epochal orders: between house and column, family and civil society and so on (see *Glas*, left column, 3). Klang, which designates both a primordial state of inarticulateness and a breach of silence that opens onto sonority, is strictly untranslatable. It remains on the other side of voice, lingering in the shadows of reason's silence. But in its reticence, Klang already provides the echo in Hegel of an encounter with reason's pinnacle, that metaphor of metaphor itself, the sun. This seeming ontological paradox should not be judged too hastily as a blind spot in the Hegelian system. This *it is both and neither* answers to a specific logical problem, and functions as the axis of the speculative dialectic: in order to avoid tautology or theologism, the origin of reason, of articulate speech and signification, must be rooted outside of language itself. Voice, in order to become "the voice of reason," must already have been, elsewhere, what it will later become as speech.

The real problem which the Klang inaugurates for Derrida is something taken up elsewhere under the heading of *tone*.[9] Tone presents an array of difficulties for ontology and its fundamental line of questioning ("*what is* x?"), constituting a limit for any attempt to definitively determine an inside and an outside of discourse. Tone is generally considered to be distinct from the content of speech; yet, with or against the content or signified, "saying"

1: THE IDEA OF TRAGEDY: FORM AND INSTITUTION OF MODERNITY   45

what is at times left unsaid, tone often indicates precisely what is at stake in a particular address or debate. It would be too hasty to define tone either as the "other" of reason or as a distinct category within reason. When we refer to tone and thus seek to describe a "way of saying" or an undercurrent in discourse that either reinforces or goes beyond or astray from "what is said," we necessarily engage in a theoretical fiction: we think in terms of unity (*a* tone, *her* tone) where there is in fact irreducible multiplicity. Tone, derived from the Greek *tonos*, means "chord." It implies a certain straining and reverberation (for instance, of a string or of the vocal cords), as well as an indistinct noise or "din" (the Latin *don* and the German *Ton*). In fact, the very thing or occurrence that we call "tone" destroys any possibility of self-identity. "Tone" describes a happening that is radically differential: no tone or chord receives its character from itself alone. Tone emerges both as difference—both within itself qua vibration and as a variation on all other possible tones—and as highly specific, in that every tone bears and helps to determine the character or resonance of a particular place and time. There is no tone that is not always already dated.

"Une mimesis ouvre la fiction du ton. C'est la tragédie du 'Viens' qui doit être répétable (a priori répété en lui-même) pour résonner. Rien ne garantit la bonne intonation, celle-ci reste à la disposition et sous la responsabilité de l'autre" ["A mimesis opens the fiction of tone. The tragedy of 'Come' is that it must be repeatable (a priori repeated in itself) in order to resonate. Nothing guarantees good intonation, which remains at the disposal and as the responsibility of the other"] (*Les fins de l'homme*, 480). Derrida, in the passage just cited, suggests that what he terms "the fiction of tone" receives its fundamentally tragic determination from a structure of iterability, from the fact that tone must always and already have submitted itself to a structure of repeatability in order to be heard as such and for the first time. In order to become audible as such, the singularity of tone—sine qua non of any good hearing—must expose itself to duplication, and hence the risk of falsification and alteration. This limit(ing) condition is not an accident that happens *to* tone so much as it is the pull and tension that tone imparts (to) itself. The uniqueness of the call, its singularity, necessitates the abandonment of all certainty of address, location and direction: that there is no guarantee of a good intonation or a just hearing indicates that one is never fully assured of having been the proper recipient of tone's solicitation. The risks of misdirection, errancy and misinterpretation all belong to the same structural limit. And yet, at the same time, the latency that informs this structure of emission and reception (determining it as fallen, as always already in ruins) also issues as the necessity of intervening at the site of this call. The specter haunting the call, that of the impossibility of capturing and repeating its original purity, is also what imparts to the call its urgency. The *Viens!* is a summons without content, a beckoning that "is" its own content as it cites the listener and bids him or her appear before it, prior to knowing either what is being asked of one or who it is that does the asking. The voice of reason or the voice of madness? The voice of justice or the voice of vengeance?

Derrida's account of the tragic character of the call also relies heavily on the discussion of family in Hegel. In the passage from nature to culture and from family to *Sittlichkeit*, every human interaction bears two "sides" which consciousness is structurally unable to grasp at once (see *Glas*, especially left column, 166–74). As Antigone's intervention in the affairs of Thebes shows, every human act can be interpreted both through the code of the state (as treason) and through the code of the family (as mourning). The brother-sister relation is indeed exemplary in this respect: the couple exemplifies both departure (the brother, who leaves the family and enters into the world of Sittlichkeit) and remaining (the sister, who stays behind and—at least according to Hegelian principle—reengenders family by becoming a wife and mother). For Hegel, the bifurcation of this exemplary family relation leads to an overcoming of natural sexual difference or "diversity," as the (man's) passage into Sittlichkeit opens up the reign of oppositional difference, of which man (formerly brother) and woman (formerly sister) both take part, separated only by degree. Derrida terms this passage from "diversity" to "opposition" a "speculative copulation" (*Glas*, 170; this image also brings to mind Hölderlin's description of tragedy as a "monstrous coupling of opposites"). Sittlichkeit, as the field into which natural difference is thrust in order to become determined or oppositional difference, is thus marked a priori by the possibility of catastrophe and tragedy: the structure of interaction and strife between competitors that informs Sittlichkeit also recreates the very split that this space was supposed to heal. There is a kind of double exposure at work in the entrance into the political, and the remark—which is also a kind of lag time—determines every act or interaction as having (yet) another side and a different law. Every transaction in the space and time of Sittlichkeit produces effects and potentially becomes legible in more than one register at the same time. The law of double exposure indicates that every decision is always already *overexposed*: one never knows what one does on both sides at once, and likewise one can never fully account for one's responsibilities by conforming to the codes and demands of one or the other order. The ethical character of Sittlichkeit thus discovers the risk of misrecognition, crime and tragedy as inscribed in its very origin. The necessarily "unconscious" nature of the crime, or the fact that one cannot be in two places and function under two mutually exclusive laws at once, does not rule out the responsibility that this tragic structure bestows upon its agent. And yet, strangely, the structural character of what Derrida terms the subject's "culpable" [*coupable*] character (implying both guilt and "cut-ability" or exposure to the limit in its two-sidedness) also *demands* that we act in the face of this (partial) ethical blindness. To attempt to recuse oneself from this ethical bind by renouncing or deferring decision is already a form of decision, and one thus only succeeds in turning one's back on the alterity of the relation itself. To deny that the decision is ours, or to answer its exigency with decisionism: both are equally guilty of ignoring the *irreversibility* of the event of contact with others. The alterity of the decision reveals that, from the moment there is a decision to be faced, one has already been indelibly exposed.

Classical tragedy likewise plays an important role in Philippe Lacoue-Labarthe's investigations of the role of mimesis in the philosophical tradition spanning from Plato to Heidegger. While tragedy is viewed by speculative philosophy as expressing the essence of philosophy's own logical mechanics, its appropriation also evinces a repeated slippage, a "repression" or an "exclusion," through which this tradition constitutes itself.[10] The speculative project, in its attempt to theorize a formal essence to tragedy, performs a negation of the Aristotelean "poetics" of tragedy and its understanding of tragedy according to its effects. As Lacoue-Labarthe demonstrates, everything that speculative dialectics would appear to have surpassed or elevated in delivering a theory of the tragic—that is, all that falls under the heading of theatricality, spectacle and the emotions—continues secretly to orient the speculative venture, *relieving* its contradictions (necessity and freedom, dogmatism and criticism, etc.) while operating under the flag of a different ontological order.[11] And while the identification of tragic form allows German Idealism to envision philosophy's role in the reconciliation of opposites, the "negation" that is implied in this presentation of a theory of the tragic extends beyond or back before Aristotle: what is in fact sought in the speculative dismissal of "poetics" and "catharsis" is a strange repetition of Plato, an ontological domestication of mimesis. In seizing tragedy and attempting to locate its own origins therein, speculative philosophy would like to isolate and bring under control a certain aspect of language or representation that, for the philosophical tradition beginning with Plato, has always threatened categorical thinking with its abyssal ruination.

Lacoue-Labarthe's rereading of the relation between philosophy and tragedy also contains important insights into the intervention of psychoanalysis in this history (see "The Scene is Primal"). While noting the theatrical analogue which, since Freud, has allowed us to think of tragedy as a "model" for psychoanalytic theory and practice, Lacoue-Labarthe is also careful to distinguish between a *transferral* of identificatory relations and libidinal deadlocks from one "scene" to another and an *essentialization* of these relations and of the mechanisms through which they are represented. Freud's contribution to critical commentary on tragedy, while constituting one of psychoanalysis' founding acts, also has the effect of unsettling the "economic system" that provides support to both the Aristotelean and the speculative theories of tragedy. One way in which psychoanalysis intervenes in this history can developed through Freud's transfer of tragic insight and recognition (Aristotle's *anagnorisis*) from the hero to the spectator.[12] This shifting of the tragic dynamic not only anticipates the possibility of "recognizing" one's own neurosis in the drama, it likewise prepares the way for Freud's far-reaching reinterpretation of the relation between aesthetics and violence, or of the (Nietzschean) question of how it is that we can derive pleasure from the spectacle of suffering, catastrophe, and death. Both the "moralizing" and "aestheticist" responses to this query (that we take satisfaction either in the restoration of order or in the limitlessness of aesthetic play) miss Freud's point entirely, and the thesis that tragedy provides us with a means of contemplating what is otherwise unpresentable—in a word, our own death—is only half of the story (the Schellingean half, I might add). Freud's account of the relation between suffering and pleasure is further complicated by what turns out to be a split within (the theory of) sexual pleasure itself, a division that supports the paradoxical duality of the drives. As Lacoue-Labarthe demonstrates, the aim of "forepleasure" [*Vorlust*] is to enable us to avoid unbearable libidinal contradictions by "blowing off steam" [*das Austoben*], and here the echos of Aristotelean "catharsis" are unmistakable. But the subject's buildup to this point of discharge also yields an unanticipated "surplus tension" [*Höherspannung*] that produces its own kind of pleasure. The economic model, in which representation serves to restore equilibrium through an accumulation and release of tension, is thus supplemented by a counter-movement in which a certain "surplus" in tension is sought—and found "pleasurable"—for its own sake.[13] This paradoxical interrelation between tension and pleasure also gives shape to the Freudian theory of the drives, which, insofar as they all take aim at death, paradoxically derive enjoyment from the deferral of their own end. "Theatrical pleasure," Lacoue-Labarthe tells us, "is thoroughly masochistic" (108).

And yet, moving from one reading of psychoanalysis to another, it would seem that psychoanalysis tells us that not all such tragic relations are reducible to the contradictory logic of masochism. Lacan's discussion of *Antigone* in the *Ethics of Psychoanalysis* seminar receives its orientation from an attempt to displace a long tradition of thinking about ethics and aesthetics.[14] In particular, Lacan takes issue with a conventional understanding of sublimation that characterizes all cultural production and artistic activity as the substitution of socially acceptable work for stigmatized or prohibited wishes. The reduction of sublimation to a regulatory mechanism pervades not only the philosophical and critical traditions following Aristotle's ethics, but likewise gives shape to a prevailing perception of Freud's thought. The "average reading" of sublimation against which Lacan moves is reflected in any number of representations of the good that are primarily invested in walling off the more unsettling aspects of desire and its limit, *jouissance*. Lacan, on the contrary, seeks to lay bare the bifurcating effects of desire's encounter with beauty in tragedy: the radiant figure of Antigone, he suggests, creates both a "reflection" and "refraction" of our desire as we seek to grasp her in her essence. Tragedy's staging of this encounter between beauty and desire or knowledge is unique insofar as this genre tends to present the hero in the aftermath of his or her greatness, on the threshold between life and death or "between two deaths."[15] In *Antigone*, the tragic presentation of the beautiful acts on one hand to arrest the advance of desire in its imaginary pursuit of an image of wholeness; the encounter with beauty is always startling and somewhat terrifying. At the same time, beauty lures desire on through its imaginary circuit and into a field of anamorphic dissolution and decadence; it impels desire toward what lies beyond the law of exchange and good order. Artistic production, then, cannot be reduced to an economic process of substitution, in which one (bad) object is exchanged for another (good or partial) object. In Lacan's somewhat enigmatic words, the event of sublimation "raises an object to the dignity of the Thing."[16]

Lacan's reading of *Antigone* moves against the philosophical tradition and, specifically, contra the notions of reconciliation and synthesis that lend support to speculative idealism. Against Hegel, Lacan argues that the clash between Creon and Antigone does not entail an encounter between opposing claims and ethoi, each justified in its own right and equally blind to the other. He suggests that symmetrical oppositions do not apply here, and that the passion of Antigone—the one and only psychoanalytic hero of the tragedy—produces a striking dissymmetry with the tyrannical intransigence of Creon.[17] While Creon seeks to win a unlimited application of the *nomos*, extending the law of the living and the state to rule over the dead, Antigone receives her direction from a different law entirely, one whose call belongs to the silent support that death affords to the symbol and to the world of the living. Consistent with Lacan's return to Freud, it is a certain notion of the death drive that Antigone evinces: not as a biologically determined instinct, but as repetition as it becomes pertinent to the "here and now" (*EP* 236), in its link to a familial history of which Antigone has recently come herself as the solitary bearer. The death drive should be understood in relation to the advent of language, or to a linguistic *event* that is prior to and irreducible to history understood as chronology of meaningful events (the death drive, in Lacan's reading, is perhaps not all that far from what Heidegger described as the double violence of "usage"). The familial history of the house of Labdacus, which encompasses both the infamy of Antigone's origin (Oedipus is both her father and her half-brother) and the recent catastrophe that has left her devoid of both parents *and* brothers, takes the form of a desolation that is at once singular and shared. The familial *Atē* names a mortal limit, a point at which she announces that she is already dead. Antigone's passionate defense of Polynices' corpse could be described as a radicalized form of restitution: she cares precisely for what the law of the state is unwilling or unable to recognize and assimilate; in a sense, she turns her attention to the founding exclusion that both gives rise to and disappears beneath the law. Yet her decision does not claim to recover some *thing*, some positive content that had been lost, nor does she claim to restore her brother to wholeness. Indeed, the aspect of her dead brother that Antigone honors is not anything that was ever *his* to begin with. Rather, it is to the signifier—or to *what he was called*—that she in turn feels compelled to respond. Antigone's insistence on honoring the uniqueness of her brother's existence *at this limit* (rather than capitulating to the state's demand that she turn away from it and allow it to be forgotten) is a tribute to language as what both joins and irreparably separates the two as speaking beings. Her attention to the corpse honors, in Lacan's words, "the ineffaceable character of what is":

> Antigone invokes no other right than that one . . . that emerges in the language of the ineffaceable character of what is—ineffaceable, that is, from the moment when the emergent signifier freezes it like a fixed object in spite of the flood of possible transformations. What is, is, and it is to this, to this surface, that the unshakeable, unyielding position of Antigone is fixed (*EP* 279).

The echo that hardens her stance reverberates as the irreversible event that is the human entrance into language. Antigone turns toward what is both *in* Polynices and phantasmatically *more than* "Polynices," more than all of the deeds, crimes, and accidents that accumulate around the name, itself a kind of scar. It is not to an "essence" in any tradition sense (form, soul, reason) that Antigone finds herself responsible. Instead, responsibility issues from the purity of a catastrophic turn, the rupture that the opening of language inaugurates for history; and from a present that at any point might have turned out differently, but which is also precisely the one she has (again, the resonances with the Heideggerian "passionate disclosure of being" are unmistakable here). It is to her brother's relation to language that Antigone responds, to a relation that marked him bodily both at birth and in death, while remaining necessarily beyond him. Lacan seeks to distinguish Antigone's radically uncompromising position from madness or suicidal renunciation. For Antigone, the true value and worth of life can only be discerned at that point where life has already been lost; or, to invert this seeming fatalistic formula, life must have already have been essentially lost—that is, it must have been *wagered* and *risked*—in order to be lived.

Here the question of tragic reconciliation arises again, only to hang in the balance indefinitely. Lacan's point about Antigone's unbending nature is seemingly inarguable: the law to which she responds cannot be recuperated within an economy of sacrifice and profit; it neither hides nor shies away from anything. Her emergence as the key figure in what Lacan is attempting to think as the ethical space of psychoanalysis reveals a complex and perhaps undecidable relation to itself as *example*. In what would constitute the most radical possibilities for Lacanian analysis, Antigone's act both is and is not exemplary. Her sacrificial gesture points to an "object" (the "small a" or negative remainder of the symbolization process) whose value is inexhaustible for analysis and which therefore calls for an interminable work of interpretation. In this sense, she reveals or embodies the difference according to which psychoanalysis both receives its heading and reaches its limit. It is her refusal of Creon's political norms, a risk that renounces any imagined reserve, which defines the stakes for Lacanian praxis. And yet at the same time this move declares its inimitability: the truth of Antigone's act (is that it) does not want to be followed. Strictly speaking, nothing should be able to withstand or follow *Antigone*.

2
Visages of the Other: On a Phantasmatic Recurrence in Borges' "El Sur"

IN HIS STUDY OF THE MYTHIC BASIS OF ARGENTINE NATION-BUILDING (*The Invention of Argentina*, 1991), Nicholas Shumway offers a standard and seemingly irrefutable assessment of the work of Jorge Luis Borges: in his rejection of nationalism and all other forms of popular struggle, Borges conceives of modernity as the tendential depoliticization of literature. That any number of Borges' own self-critical comments could be used to buttress this claim would seem to place him well within a tradition that derives its impetus from Plato's meditations on the organization of the polis. According to this line of thinking, history in its essence comprises a movement toward the completion or elimination of the political (of strife, conflict, and disorder), culminating in the realization of a state of permanent accord and stability. Such a teleology is the basis of Francis Fukuyama's celebration of the "end of history," which he understands as the inauguration of a postideological epoch in which politics is determined as the bureaucratic work of navigation and administration. Like history, however, the "end of history" does not just happen. The realization of this state of permanent accord would presuppose the emergence of a sphere of absolute neutrality within the social, a kind of ideological vacuum that has freed itself of all strife and conflict while remaining—at least in principle— accessible to anyone. Beginning sometime in the nineteenth century, literature has often been viewed as an ideal medium in which to realize such a space.[1] Such a utopian conception of artistic practice no doubt resonates strongly with Borges' own thinking, in view both of the tumultuous history of Argentine politics following the 1930 military coup d'etat and of Borges' deeply adversarial relation with the populist-authoritarian regime of Juan Perón. In the absence of any foreseeable end to ideological conflict in twentieth-century

Argentina, literature holds the utopian place of a postpolitical state (or so the argument goes).

This chapter examines a tension between politics and literary aesthetics in the Argentine tradition, and suggests that such a crossing of disciplinary registers comprises an important site for reflection in Borges' literary practice. The chapter begins with a brief discussion of two of the discourses competing for dominance during the first century of Argentine independence: Liberal identifications with European and Anglo-American Enlightenment traditions on the one hand, and nationalist attempts to define Argentine identity according to autochthonous (*criollo*) or Hispanist lines on the other. My initial discussion of the Argentine tradition is based on two well-known essays, Domingo Sarmiento's *Facundo* and Leopoldo Lugones' *El Payador*. This excursus is by no means an attempt to provide a comprehensive overview of those two authors, their thinking and their works, nor is it my intention to pit Sarmiento, an essay writer and a politician, against Lugones, who is in fact best known as a poet and writer of prose. Rather, my intent is to use these two essays to tease out two influential and conflicting ways of conceiving national identity: two attitudes, we could say, each of which have played influential roles in Argentine cultural production during the past two centuries.

Following the discussion of Sarmiento and Lugones, I then turn to Borges' short story "El Sur," focusing on certain aspects of his writing that exceed or mark the limits of the myriad attempts to organize the Argentine nation into "One," or a self-identical and self-sufficient totality. The story is a rewriting of the gaucho poem, whose rustic and heroic ethos Borges places in a decidedly modern context. At the same time, I will argue that this text borrows extensively from classical tragedy in its engagement with the Argentine tradition. The tragic motifs of blindness and fate, together with the close proximity of self-knowledge and death to one another, provide a literary context in which Borges juxtaposes questions of personal and national identity. Both Sarmiento and Lugones envision modernity as a time when the nation will have freed itself from its prior constraints (for Sarmiento, these limits are manifested as the barbarism or impropriety of all that resists modernization, whereas for Lugones the limits are represented by what has come to infect and contaminate national character through modernization), and thereby arrive at or return to a state of self-agreement or wholeness. For Borges, on the other hand, the tragic superimposition of two domains (the civilized and the barbaric, modernity and the premodern) yields neither an easy reconciliation of the conflict nor a resolution in favor of one or the other. On the contrary, Borges' text points to a secret truth about which both discourses on national identity would prefer to remain ignorant. This tragic juxtaposition is expressed as a dawning awareness of the catastrophic failure of modernity itself. The text does not just hint at a crisis in this or that feature of modernity (economic, political, aesthetic, etc.), but points to the imminent failure of the *chain of signifiers* that constitutes modernity as a hegemonic project in Argentina. It is regarding modernity's capacity to account for the whole—an accounting procedure that is at once cultural and political—that Borges' text expresses its gravest doubts. I will suggest that the allusions to and appropriations of tragedy in Borges' text open onto an ethical space, a moment of decision that is also an impasse: the story's protagonist finds himself both *without ground* (having reached the limit of both the liberal and the nationalist versions of how the modern nation-state ought to be) and at the same time *obligated* in a way that rules out any decisionist solution to the impasse. What I will call the tragic sense of Borges' text is not unlike that of Sophocles' *Antigone*: faced with the imminent collapse of his symbolic world, Borges' hero does not abandon his ground and retreat into a compensatory world that could better sustain the illusion of wholeness. Instead, the ethical (and tragic) character of the decision is that he chooses to assume this symbolic collapse as his own.

It is my belief that Shumway's assessment of the apolitical nature of Borgesian prose must be confronted with one of the crucial lessons provided by Borges' text (even and especially if this logic eludes Borges himself at times): that which announces itself as the end of ideology is nothing but an ideological fantasy.[2] Rather than assuming with Shumway that *the political* corresponds to a field that has been defined and consolidated beforehand (e.g., "organized politics" or "political society"), I will suggest that Borges' text evinces and reflects on the absence of a clear definition of what is political. Thus, his writing gives thought to a kind of *politicality* at work in the processes of inheritance, translation, and interpretation. What is meant here by politicality? In our time we have grown accustomed to the notion that every act of interpretation or judgment presupposes, whether one wishes to know it or not, a certain personal and social bias. There is no such thing as a neutral perspective: on the contrary, every perspective is compromised in advanced by a particular constellation of social codes, values and prejudices. It is in this vein that Borges' "El Sur" offers a literary critique of Argentine nationalism: it is a "particular" that attempts to pass itself off as "universal," and thereby to avoid confronting the more unsettling aspects of particularity or finitude. The stakes of this critique, then, involve more than showing how what nationalism takes to be an "authentic" or "true" national character is in fact part invention and part idealization. At the same time, Borges' text shows how nationalism's fictionalization also serves to mask or expel a more disturbing truth. Cosmopolitan artifice and the immigrant, which nationalism finger as contaminants of a certain national purity, are in fact stand-ins whose *marked* impropriety (to be found in accent, mannerisms, etc.) serves as a convenient screen that allows us to forget that we are all more or less "improper" and "homeless." I will discuss this at greater length below.

CIVILIZATION AND BARBARISM: LIBERALISM, NATIONALISM, AND THE DEBATE ON ARGENTINE MODERNITY

The title of Domingo Sarmiento's 1845 treatise on Argentine culture, *Facundo: Civilización y Barbarie*, has provided an important topos for a number of cultural interpretations of the Argentine nation, its origin and its destiny. The paradigm of "civilization and barbarism" comprises a foundational text not only for the Argentine tradition but throughout much of postindependence Latin America.[3] Sarmiento's text envisions a form of knowledge that would be both *of* and *by* the Argentine, while at the same time coinciding with the general framework of the Enlightenment tradition. One of the central concerns of *Facundo* is to deliver a perspective, or more specifically a form of self-reflexivity, that would in turn engender or establish the bearings for Argentine modernity.[4] The "barbarism" against which Sarmiento posits his notion of modernity stands for both the Spanish tradition (a marginal tradition within Europe) as well as various non-European practices and groups (for instance, Amerindian and popular creole traditions). As a thesis on Argentine modernity, *Facundo* posits a difference (the "civilized" vs. the "barbaric") that derives its determinant force and its inscription of value not from eternal truths but from the *structure of opposition* itself. Contrary to what Sarmiento himself might claim, the terms "civilization" and "barbarism" do not correspond to any preexisting meanings but instead name a geopolitical and socioeconomic field of contention. Taken by itself, either term is indeterminate: what is shared by all of those who happen to fall under the category of "barbarism" in Sarmiento's view—all of those Spaniards, Africans, Indians and *mestizos*; all gauchos and other analphabetics—is not any one, particular characteristic. Instead, it is on the basis of what one cannot cover up, disown or dissimulate—that is, according to a "lack" that Sarmiento would like to render indelibly self-evident and natural, a "lack" whose nature it is *to show too much*—that barbarism becomes visible as such. Likewise, "civilization" does not correspond to some possession, an immanence or a wholeness—or a lack of "lack," as Sarmiento would have it—but instead corresponds to one's capacity to conceal or pass off that which barbarism *cannot not* reveal. Civilization names the capacity to claim, as if it were an inheritance or a birthright, that with which one would pass oneself off as not "lacking," not barbaric.

The image of barbarism as an indelible mark or imprint—and hence something "natural" and unchangeable—is established in the first chapter of the *Facundo* through a series of telluric metaphors, which assign to barbarism a geographic origin in the Pampa or the uncultivated interior of the country. Sarmiento begins by describing the Pampa as an "immense extension," and it is to the colossal nature of this expanse that he first attributes the essence of barbarism as *mal* or "evil."[5] The ramifications of this moral determinism are multiple. On one hand, a kind of fatalism begins to accumulate around the figure of the barbaric. When all is said and done, Sarmiento's definition of barbarism might well be *that which could not have been otherwise*: it names the absence of will and reason, and thus the impossibility of self-transformation. And, by linking barbarism to Argentine nature while associating civilization with culture, Sarmiento attempts to naturalize the civilization/barbarism opposition. If a definitive link can be established between barbarism and brute, passive nature, then civilization will in turn belong to the dynamic force of Enlightenment reason. It will signify the capacity to negate or transform nature. The influence of a pseudo-Hegelian logic in Sarmiento's thesis is clear, but this also requires a caveat: civilization does not arrive from afar in a predetermined form so much as it *arises* from the locale through the active and self-controlled work of negation. The text thus endeavors to *install* (to make visible, to erect) the nation-building project by selling us on a motif of cultivation: Sarmiento presents socioeconomic modernization as having to pass through culture as the first furrowing of a previously unbroken field. In a similar way, Alberdi's motto—"gobernar es poblar" ["to govern is to populate"]—will convert this organic metaphor into an institutional practice, thus determining Argentine modernity as a colonization of the real by way of the transplant. The ideological basis for the immigration policies of the late nineteenth and early twentieth century are thus established in *Facundo* with the determination of barbarism as "lack" and civilization as negation of lack.[6]

For Sarmiento, the "civilization versus barbarism" opposition corresponds to the presence or absence of the logos, and stages a national conflict between *razón* [reason] and *sinrazón* [nonreason]. Sarmiento frames the "barbaric" other—for instance, the gaucho who is said to be little more than an extension of nature—as an opaque mystery, inaccessible to reason. This image of impenetrability is reinforced in the text's complaint that Argentina has lacked a "Tocqueville," an outside observer who would reflect and secure the nation's standing with respect to universal culture. (The Eurocentric longing in *Facundo* is not a desire to be more like Europeans: it expresses a desire to *appear*—and thus to be recognized as—"European.") Of course, it is Sarmiento himself who would fill this role of observer and mediator, recording and reporting knowledge of the other. This is at least one way of understanding the classical evocation of Facundo Quiroga's ghost ("sombra terrible") that inaugurates the introductory chapter. This Homeric gesture of summoning and eulogizing the hero's wrath also presents the other (Facundo) as being in possession of an endogenous knowledge or "secret" that shrinks away from reason: "Tú posees el secreto, ¡revélanoslo!" ["You possess the secret. Reveal it to us!"]. Of course, Sarmiento does not mean to portray the other as the rightful owner of this knowledge: rather, by citing the other and calling him out, Sarmiento suggests that it is he himself—the narrating subject—who will eventually come to occupy the position of the subject of knowledge, at that turning point indicated by the Hegelian "native realm of truth" [*das einheimische Reich der Wahrheit*].[7] Sarmiento's text situates itself at the center of a kind of hermeneutic circle, according to which self-consciousness ceaselessly surpasses itself in order to know itself in and as *other*. Civilized reason takes leave of the familiar and passes into the foreign precisely in order to have returned. In this schema, barbarism indicates both an absence of reason and an opacity within self-knowledge itself. It is a "knot" or enigma that resists the civilizing threat of the sword ("este nudo que no ha podido cortar la espada" ["this knot that the sword has been unable to cut"], 12). The origin of Argentine cultural production could thus be described as a crisis of the ontotheological subject, or of the Western, metaphysical determination of the subject as self-presence. At least implicit in this dramatic evocation of a national "secret" is the possibility that what the West has understood at least since Descartes as the necessary and sufficient conditions for knowledge and truth is no longer sustainable when it comes to Argentina.

The writing of *Facundo*, which Sarmiento began during his exile to Chile and completed after his journey to Europe and the United States, bears witness to a shift in Sarmiento's thinking about the nation-building project and its proper orientation or *idea*. Prior to his exile, Sarmiento had coincided with other liberals in envisioning the future nation-state as an extension of European (primarily French) history. The project of modernity was felt to begin with the task of securing a cultural inheritance from Paris (and this anxiety can no doubt still be heard in the lamentation in *Facundo* that Argentina has lacked a "Toqueville"). However, the trans-Atlantic voyage Sarmiento undertakes during his years in exile leads him to the conclusion that the United States in fact offers a more vibrant model for nation-building in the Americas. His admiration of North American capitalist entrepreneurship, which he views as a revitalization of a classical spirit grown stagnant in Europe, marks an important transformation in the Argentine conception of modernity. Following the writing of *Facundo*, Argentine liberalism should no longer be said to conceive of modernity exclusively on the basis of emulating European culture. At the same time, Sarmiento's thinking also turns to something resembling what we would today call transculturation, exemplified by what the author of the *Viajes por Europa, África y América* sees in the U.S. as a renewal of classical spirit through the transformation of matter or nature.[8]

Sarmiento's treatise attests to a fault line that runs through the Enlightenment conception of history as a progressive movement toward universal civilization. There is no logic that could begin with "barbarism," understood as lack or negativity, and arrive at "civilization" understood as truth or self-presence. An absolute and irreversible division separates the two. This is why the encroachment of the barbarism of the interior upon the civilized port city of

Buenos Aires, first with Facundo and later with Rosas, constitutes something like an unthinkable event for Argentine liberalism. But the text also invites another way of reading the surprising evocation of Facundo Quiroga as possessor of a state secret. While the arrival of Facundo in Buenos Aires signals the embarrassing and catastrophic inversion of the Eurocentric paradigm (only in Argentina does the interior colonize the metropolis, etc.), the barbaric caudillo is also fascinating because he accomplishes precisely what liberalism has been unable to realize on its own. Facundo's great and mysterious accomplishment is to have somehow organized and mobilized the impoverished, illiterate masses into a *people*. (Yes, but how? Why him? What did he have over them? These are the questions without answers that haunt Sarmiento's text from beginning to end.) "Facundo Quiroga *enlaza y eslabona* todos los elementos de desorden que hasta antes de su aparición estaban agitándose aisladamente en cada provincia; él hace de la guerra local la *guerra nacional argentina*, y presente triunfante, al fin de diez años de trabajos, de devastación y de combates, el resultado de que sólo supo aprovecharse el que lo asesinó" ["Facundo Quiroga *binds and links* all of the elements of disorder that had, until his appearance, been agitating in isolation in every province. It is he who turns the local war into a *national, Argentine war*, and presents in triumphant manner, following ten years of hard work, devastation and combat, what only his assassin would know how to take advantage of"] (5, my emphasis). Facundo, in whom we find condensed all of the defining traits of barbarism, is also the one and only figure capable of articulating a hegemonic coup in which all of the isolated, self-contained pockets and fiefdoms would become linked to a common axis (the chain-like verbs "enlazar" and "eslabonar" are signifiers of the hegemonic project itself, in contrast to that of domination). *Facundo* is the story of a theft, of a singular charisma or magnetism whose fruits Rosas purloins from Facundo, and which Sarmiento in turn proposes to steal once again.

Compulsion and domination are never far removed from Sarmiento's "civilized" discourse.[9] Nonetheless, the postulated end of the "civilizing" process should *in principle* bear closer resemblance to the formation of a consensus—even if this precisely means having annihilated beforehand all of forms of potential resistance to this suturing process (what is in fact sought is a hegemony dominated by the elite). We can further explore the tension between consensus and domination in *Facundo* by turning briefly to a tropological use of the written word in Sarmiento's text. The undeveloped Pampa, first likened to a desert or a void, is then transposed, via a figure of writing, into the image an empty page. The tropological juxtaposition of barbarism as blank surface to civilization as writing process allows Sarmiento to advance an entire army of judgments and clichés concerning barbarism: the barbaric other lacks writing, and is therefore also bereft of memory, history, law, educability, etc. But the commonplace distinction between lettered civilization and analphabetic barbarism in fact proves to be less absolute—and hence less stable—than one might expect. One passage in particular is worth citing at some length:

> Existe, pues, un fondo de poesía que nace de los accidentes naturales del país y de las costumbres excepcionales que engendra. La poesía, para despertarse, porque la poesía es, como el sentimiento religioso, una facultad del espíritu humano, necesita el espectáculo de lo bello, del poder terrible, de la inmensidad de la extensión, de lo vago, de lo incomprensible; porque sólo donde acaba lo palpable y vulgar, empiezan las mentiras de la imaginación, el mundo ideal. Ahora, yo pregunto: ¿que impresiones ha de dejar en el habitante de la República Argentina el simple acto de clavar los ojos en el horizonte, y ver . . . , no ver nada? Porque cuanto más hunde los ojos en aquel horizonte incierto, vaporoso, indefinido, más se aleja, más lo fascina, lo confunde y lo sume en la contemplación y la duda. Dónde termina aquel mundo que quiere en vano penetrar? ¡No se sabe! ¿Qué hay más allá de lo que ve? La soledad, el peligro, el salvaje, la muerte. He aquí la poesía.

> [A poetic depth is born of the country's natural accidents and the exceptional customs which the latter engender. Poetry, like religious sentiment, is a faculty of the human spirit. In order to awaken, it requires the spectacle of the beautiful, of terrible power, of immensity, of the vague or the incomprehensible; only where the palpable and the vulgar end do the lies of the imagination begin: the ideal world. Now I ask: What impressions are left on the inhabitant of the Argentine Republic by the simple act of fixing his eyes on the horizon so as to see . . . nothing? Because the more he sinks his eyes into that uncertain horizon, the more it retreats, and the more it fascinates and confounds him, stranding him in contemplation and self-doubt. Where does that world end that he seeks in vain to penetrate? He doesn't know! What lies beyond what he can see? Solitude, danger, savagery, and death. But here too we have poetry.]

Barbarism is here the site of a kind of poetic transference, in which negativity (barbarism as the utter lack of being, as that about which we can say nothing) somehow yields or reveals the sublime object of poetic reflection and production. Or, rather, as sublime this object does not reveal itself at all; as we have suggested apropos the figure of Facundo ("The Conqueror of Buenos Aires!"), the return of barbarism coincides with the catastrophe of presentation. For Sarmiento's poetics, barbarism is the momentary appearance of the fact of the unthinkable. Yet, according to the poetic logic of *Facundo*, this opaque, self-concealing secret must also precisely yield to and become the site of the new republic's self-presentation. The preponderance of telluric figures in this passage should not dissuade us from our suspicion that it is in fact the caudillo Facundo and not nature that constitutes the true object of poetic desire. It is the interrelation between the history of "Facundo"—of the proper name as much as the historical man—and the brief but tumultuous history of the Argentine postindependence that motivates Sarmiento's attempts to make barbarism give birth to an experience of the sublime, and hence to become (albeit retroactively and in purely tropological terms) the origin of national cultural production.

As we shall now see, this passage provides an important clue for understanding what can broadly be termed the literary-poetic dimension of nation-building. The nation-building project seeks to make the nation-state visible to all as the unquestioned truth of the social order. In order for the nation to triumph over its history of colonial dependency and local allegiances, force and constraint alone are not sufficient: the nation-state must convince as an idea. And thus one of the fundamental concerns of Sarmiento's project is to define and cultivate a *cultural* domain that would both unify and supercede the myriad isolated, local associations and allegiances of the past, while at the same time making this unity visible as an example to all. In addition to developing a new network of centralized institutions to take the place of the old colonial and feudal social, economic, and political structures, nation-building also presupposes an accompanying pedagogical project whose aim is to produce a new national subject or citizen. Sarmiento's most famous contribution in this regard is no doubt his conceptualization of an integrated educational system designed to implement a single national language with a standardized orthography. Along with this newly established linguistic community, the aim of national culture will be to bring the idea of the nation-state into view by providing a site for the interpellation of modern citizens: national culture both exemplifies the right models for conduct (not barbaric but civilized), and it teaches citizens to desire inclusion *via representation* (in contradistinction to the old systems of patronage, etc.) on the national political stage. The operative metaphor here is of culture as a mirror; but in this case the mirror not only reflects the sum of whatever parts are placed before it, but also adds to this aggregate of parts a sense of unity or wholeness.[10] The pedagogical basis of nation-building thus presupposes a fundamental connection between language and the administrative, institutional apparatus, or between culture and the state.[11] It is through the institution of the written word, a privileged form of cultural production, that Sarmiento initiates the pedagogical task of forming citizens. Similarly, it is via a certain aesthetic ideology of literature, Schillerian rather than Kantian in its origin, that liberalism seeks to secure the mechanism for producing new national subjects.[12] Literature, according to this view, introduces universal judgement (or a form of *sensus comunis*) and a neutral ground that has freed itself from the particular interests and conflicts of social space. In principle, literature enables each of us to overcome our mere particularity and, through the cultivation of judgment (or both reason and universal values), to emerge as the ethical subjects of a community. The literary aesthetic exemplifies the identificatory model or *idea* of the state, presenting itself as a force capable of synthesizing the conflicting particulars of the social sphere. (This helps to explain why, despite everything else, poiēsis must always make room for a thought of barbarism at the origin of the speculative operation in Sarmiento's text.) The end of this process, the well-adapted modern citizen, is the one who will have come to see him or herself in the state: that is, as one will have learned how to desire his or her own political representation. Literature itself, then, would seem to constitute Sarmiento's reply to the mysterious question of Facundo Quiroga and his secret: it is through universal culture and writing that liberalism will seek to repeat Quiroga's hegemonic procedure, only this time by converting the illiterate masses into literate citizens.

Readers of Sarmiento have frequently noted the difficulty of assigning *Facundo* to any one specific genre of writing. The text displays characteristics of a number of fictional and nonfictional modes, including epic poetry (see the Homeric evocations of Facundo and of the civil war between Unitarians and Federalists), the pseudoscientific or naturalist travelogue (Sarmiento as European explorer reporting from the exotic interior), the essay, the political tract, and so on. What is more, this difficulty with classifying *Fa-*

cundo within any traditional taxonomy of literature is augmented by an ongoing struggle in the text between what we could term the political and literary dimensions of Sarmiento's writing. On one hand, as I have been saying, the object of the text's "literariness" (its myths and fabrications, but also its profound dependence on a performative tropology, or rhetorical devices that actually produce the reality effects they claim to describe) is no doubt a political end: the institution of a centralized state through the forging of a certain national consensus. In this sense, writing represents one step in a process which eventually, were it fully realizable, would do away with the necessity of fiction. At the same time, however, it is precisely from *the impossibility of politics*—at least at the moment that Sarmiento writes, having gone into exile in Chile—that the literary character of the text issues in its exigency. It is, for instance, only at the moment that Sarmiento has been estranged from the polis and passes into exile that he truly becomes a writer. Ricardo Piglia, one of Sarmiento's most incisive critics, has commented in several media on this relation between writing and politics. The main target of Piglia's reading is the famous prelude to *Facundo* entitled "Advertencia del autor" [Author's Remark].[13] In this brief note Sarmiento complains of the persecution he experienced at the hands of Rosas' *mazorca* or secret police, and of the symbolic revenge he carried out at the moment of his departure into exile: he tells us that he paused momentarily at the baths of Zonda along the Argentine-Chilean border, and on the stone walls there he inscribed in charcoal the words "On ne tue point les idées" ["One does not kill ideas"]. Sarmiento notes with satisfaction that Rosas was forced to bring in outsiders to decipher the oracular French text. The chasm between civilization and barbarism is staged anecdotally with the revelation of one's ability or inability to negotiate in an imported, universal language. Or so it would seem. But, as Piglia notes, Sarmiento in fact misquotes *and* misattributes the source of the aphorism: he names Fortoul as its source, whereas the closest approximation of this quote to have been identified is found in an essay by Diderot. To make matters even more confusing, the "translation" Sarmiento offers to his noninitiated readers is in fact an imprecise paraphrase of the French text he claims to cite by memory: "On ne tue pas les idées" becomes "A los hombres se les desgüella; a las ideas, no" ["One can behead men, but not ideas"]. The crucial point, both revealed and concealed by this game of cultural one-upmanship, is a moment at which translation fails; and let us not forget that the war of citation initiated by Sarmiento as he exits the national stage is part and parcel of the nation-building project itself, insofar as the construction of Argentine modernity will proceed by way of infusion, graft, and transferral of cultural capital. Translation misses the mark not, as Eurocentrism would have it, because the Latin American copy falls short of the truth embodied by the original. Rather, the failure of translation stems from a radical negativity or errancy already at work in the original work or culture. As Borges will suggest, the work of citation and repetition is scandalous because it strips away the *semblance* of permanent truth or fixed meaning that attaches itself to the original. Citation sets in motion a corrosive force that is both the limit and the possibility of (new) meaning. I will return to this point later in this chapter.

By the first decades of the twentieth century, opposition to modernization had begun to crystalize in the form of a nationalist discourse. Under the influence of the poet laureate Leopoldo Lugones, Argentine nationalism articulates its opposition to modernization by developing a counternarrative of a return to origins, to a supposed purity that had been lost through immigration and imports. In disparaging immigrants and urban cosmopolitanism, nationalism posits an autochthonous Argentine "essence" or *argentinidad* presumed to have been diluted and contaminated by modernization and immigration. In his essays, Lugones sees literature as a medium capable of bringing this national essence back into view at a time marked by increasing uncertainty as to what exactly constitutes a true Argentine.[14] David Rock's phrase "futurism of the past" (*Authoritarian Argentina*, 1) is one possible definition of what is at stake in the nationalist conception of history. Nineteenth-century liberalism, its internal debates and differences notwithstanding, was more or less unanimous in its view of history as progression toward a certain form of universalism. By contrast, Argentine nationalism seeks to define, recover and perfect a certain particularity: an archaic, premodern spirit or *patria* whose purity and unicity must be preserved from degradation. The "lost object" of nationalism, or the truth in whose recovery the nation will find itself as a whole (that is, as not lacking), is a "good" shared equally by all members of the national community, but which remains inaccessible and unintelligible to outsiders. It is thus also fundamentally unnameable. For Lugones, the cultural birthright of the true Argentina is not the French Revolution and the age of Reason, but rather ancient Greece and medieval Spain (that is to say *a certain Greece,* given that much of the Enlightenment tradition also defines itself as a continuation of the classical). The difference between Eurocentrism and nationalism can be glimpsed in distinct views of history: while liberalism thinks of history as an eternal progression toward truth, as a movement toward universal accord with the Idea of reason, nationalism envisions history as a perpetual falling outside of and away from truth and being.

In a series of lectures later published under the title *El payador* (1916), Lugones points to the vestiges of an authentic, autochthonous tradition in what had previously been regarded as an inferior literary genre, the "gauchesque" poem. The modern exemplar of this tradition, according to Lugones, is Miguel Hernández's epic poem *Martín Fierro* (1872), which Lugones reads as a monument to the heroic self-realization of the Argentine *pueblo*:

> Monumento, ya se lo erigió el poeta en esa perpetuidad de la fama con que el verso del otro dio parangón al metal. Más el pueblo le debe todavía aquella prenda de su gratitud. Martín Fierro necesita su bronce. Este será la carne heroica en la cual hemos de encerrar su espíritu para que así rehabite entre nosotros una materia, al fin, análoga. Porque, efectivamente, él mismo habíasela formado. De tierra pampeana y de sol nuestro, de trabajo y de dolor que nos pertenecen, estaba construido aquel antecesor. Como en la aleación donde se combinan la rojura y la palidez de los sendos metales, el furor de la llama original ennoblecía su raza

> [The poet has already erected a monument to Marín Fierro, fusing his verse into the perpetual fame of metal. But the people still owe him that token of their gratitude. Martín Fierro needs his bronce. This will be the heroic flesh in which we must entomb his spirit so that it might finally form an analogous ground among us. In essence, he himself has given shape to this substance. That ancestor was formed from the soil of the Pampa and from our own sun, from the labor and travails that are ours. Just as with the alloy that combines the red and pale hues of metals, the fury of that original flame ennobled his race.] ("El linaje de Hércules," *El Payador*, 337).

Through his reinterpretation of the Argentine tradition, Lugones presents literature (or "poetry" in the broad sense of the term) as the ideal mirror of an archaic national spirit, in much the same way that the West has often affirmed the greatness of Greek culture by way of what are taken to be its highest forms of production, epic and tragic poetry. Gauchesque poetry is revered, among other reasons, for its supposed proximity to what nationalism referred to as the "free, spontaneous poetry of the gauchos," and which Lugones here conveys through the fervent and perhaps infernal tone of "el furor de la llama original." As a modern poetic mode, the gauchesque is presumed to reproduce faithfully a form of expression, thought and feeling proper to an earlier time. The gauchesque precisely reflects national expression in its pure and unmediated form, i.e., before it had been domesticated and contaminated by foreign, apocryphal influences and interests. Lugones' project thus departs from a convention understanding of literature as (mere) reflection or imitation, and it affirms an intimate correlation between literature and the unmediated mediator (Nature or the divine). By the same logic, literature does not merely call back and reinstate a way of being or a truth that has since fallen on hard times. It does this, but never simply by providing a reflection of its object: instead, literature's task is to *produce* this truth by becoming its monument (the reference to "bronze" in the passage cited above underscores both the monumental function of poetry and the idea that poetry enjoys a privileged relation to the classical age). This is also to say—although Lugones would surely not put it this way—that literature must bring truth forth *as if* it were the way things have always (truly) been. The complete absence of socioeconomic or class distinctions in Lugones' interpretation of national culture can be interpreted as a strategic silence within a counterhegemonic project that seeks to do away with all difference as such. Lugones' project, unlike José Martí's "Nuestra América," is not governed by an antiimperialist intention. Rather, the idealization of the gauchesque genre in *El Payador* is an attempt to rid the nation of all finitude, contingency, and difference. It calls upon literature to become a representation of the nation as One, as an extension without limits that has freed itself from any necessary contact with others.

It is, of course, in deliberate contrast to Sarmiento that Lugones chooses the gaucho as emblem of national spirit, an avatar of self-realizing autonomy. Lugones' gaucho is the one who negates nature in order to realize it as a total work: the sovereign nation-state. In the process, the sociopolitical conflict accompanying the "integration" of the gaucho into the national economy and the state is idealized—and hence negated—by Lugones as a form of sacrifice for the patria.[15] The telluric references to soil and metals in the "Linaje de Hércules" passage cited above reinforces the preeminence of the autochthonous, an index of native knowledge and permanence, over the littoral, associated with the imported, the artificial, and the contingent. The nationalist critique of immigration portrays the port city as a metonym of all things improper, a part of the outside within the inside. Akin to Scalabrini Ortiz's critique of the British-built railway system—"all tracks lead to Buenos Aires . . . and none from Buenos Aires"—Lugones describes modernization as an ongoing depletion of provincial plenitude and authenticity at the hands of the port city. This equivalency between infrastructure and imperialism echoes the fantasy of an enjoyment that has been stolen by "the other": if the nation is "lacking" (that is, if it experiences its finite being as a lack), this must be because it was once whole and only subsequently (and hence contingently) came to be dispossessed of this immanence. The "theft" of this national good sets the stage for the nationalist representation of history as a fall from truth; and, by the same token, literature would offer itself as a recuperative measure able to bring truth back into view.

In a certain sense, however, Lugones' inversion is never far from the Sarmentine original it seeks to displace. Lugones too defines the gauchesque form according to its telluric origin, the order of permanence and (for Lugones) truth. As Spirit ("la llama original"), national culture complements nature and brings it to stand: culture is the completion and perfection of what nature is unable to realize on its own. And thus, according to the nationalist narrative, literature must take the place of what has been transformed or displaced by modernization—that is, it must compensate for the near-elimination of that way of life portrayed in the gaucho narrative—in order for truth to become visible again. "[P]ara que así rehabite entre nosotros": what Lugones is in fact suggesting is that the recovery and reinstitutionalization of truth must follow a logic of repetition: truth emerges from ritual and *habitus*, which render what is otherwise a contingent, meaningless action into something natural, authentic, and true.

The exemplary value of the gaucho text resides not in its content but in its mode of presentation, or in poetic language as such. And thus, according to Lugones, poetry exemplifies the highest truth of the nation as patria: "De esta manera, la poesía que transforma un idioma en obra de arte, lo impone con ello entre los organismos vivos de la misma naturaleza; y como el idioma es el rasgo superior de la raza, como constituye la patria en cuanto ésta es fenómeno espiritual, resulta que para todo país digno de la civilización no existe negocio más importante que la poesía" ["In this way, poetry, which transforms a language into a work of art, also imposes it on the living organisms of a like nature. As language is the superior trait of our race, and as it constitutes the patria as a spiritual phenomenon, it so happens that, for any nation worthy of the name civilization, there is no business more important than poetry"] (*El Payador* 44). Once again, the literary mirror assumes a productive role in the scene it is, according to the classical tradition, supposed to reproduce. Poetry, as the highest expression of a people, does not merely imitate, reflect or echo the living spirit of a people. As language, poetry *is* the emerging spiritual self-affirmation of a people in its exemplary form.[16]

Before proceeding any further, a brief digression can help to define the stakes—and perhaps mark the limit—of Borges' engagement with the Argentine tradition. In *El género gauchesco*, Josefina Ludmer describes gauchesque poetry as a genre marked by conflicting codes, aims and possibilities. The motif organizing Ludmer's study is a double movement that she calls "la Ida" [the Departure] and "la Vuelta" [the Return]. The gauchesque is both the rise to written language of voices that have never before been seen in print, and it is the descent of civilizing writing to the level of vox populi. The possibilities it puts into play include both the restitution and the domestication of "the gaucho," understood as standing for the subaltern excess of the Argentine nation-building project. For Ludmer, the gauchesque is constituted as a genre not through successive emulations of a master schema or an original, but rather through an ongoing process marked by strife, misrecognition, transformation, and war. This literary form attests to how the gaucho was used—and often used up—by the state, first in the War of Independence, then in the ensuing decades of factional battles, and later still in the "Conquest of the Desert" or the state's orchestrated extermination of Argentina's indigenous populations. But the construction of the gauchesque genre is also the appropriation of popular oral traditions by a cultivated literary idiom. The gauchesque involves institutional uses of popular discourse to exemplify the desirability of "civilized" life over the "barbaric" existence of the gaucho (for instance, the transformation of the "lawless" *valientes gauchos* [valiant gauchos] into the "heroic," law abiding *gaucho patriota* [patriotic gaucho], or in the celebrated passage from war to productivity, from *luchar* [fighting] to *trabajar* [working]). The genre does not reflect a unitary idea that would constitute the identity of the many, but rather an ongoing process of negotiation and resignification. In agreement with Borges, Ludmer sees the nineteenth-century Argentine literary tradition as part of a widespread effort to construct an image of national unity, unanimity and necessity. At certain moments, however, gauchesque poetry also marks a limit for this attempt to represent unity, consensus and necessity; poetry bears witness to the fact that national hegemony is accompanied by exclusion and forgetting, the traces of which hegemony is always attempting to sweep away. However, in referring to Borges' own contribution to the Argentine tradition, Ludmer points to what we might term an excess that escapes Borges' reading. She notes that the gauchesque genre is characterized by a special attention to oral address or "canto": "*Todo está en el canto* dice de entrada el cantor, y esto debe ser tomado literalmente . . . el hacer (cantar), coincide totalmente con lo que se hace (canto) y con lo que se es (cantor)" [*"It's all in the singing*, says the *cantor* upon entering, and this should be heard literally . . . the act of making something (singing) coincides precisely with what one makes (one sings) and with what one is (*cantor*)"] (*El género gauchesco*, 158–59). The meaning of the poetic act qua production (cantar: singing, reciting, or praising) is always more or less than its content or message. What is spoken (the content) cannot be separated from *the fact that one is speaking* (the formal act); and likewise, what one is (identity or essence) cannot be separated from what one does at the moment (existence) as a speaking being. The poetic act, then, does not reflect a preexisting idea or eidos. Rather, the truth of the act is to be found in the fact that the gaucho speaks as he does—which is to say, among other things, in a way that marks a difference from the administrative, technoscientific and literary discourses of the state. The gauchesque does not necessarily *define* this difference in the sense of assigning it a concept (in that case it would quickly become indistinguishable from the statist project of categorization and surveillance); but it does insist upon the irreducible dignity of this popular idiom. On the other hand, according to Ludmer, Borges' twentieth-century rewriting of the gauchesque (see, for instance, "El Fin," "Biografía de Tadeo Isidoro Cruz" and "El Sur") tends to idealize and hence efface the material traces of the oral register by rendering them in a stylized poetic diction (of course, this is not to suggest that the gauchesque itself is anything but a stylized, literary representation).[17] According to Ludmer, however, Borges takes this literary operation one step further when he transfers the immanence of spoken address—whose truth is to be found in the fact of speaking here and now—to the transcendent realm of a highly literary language. Among the consequences of the Borgesian tropological appropriation of popular speech is that literature asserts itself once again as the privileged interpreter or mouthpiece of "the other." The literary appropriation of subaltern discourse is a prosopopeic operation that pretends to leave behind no remainder. Ludmer's astute reading can assist preemptively in avoiding an unintended idealization of Borges' relation to the Argentine tradition.

This is not, however, to suggest that Borges' writing is left without a conceivable reply to Ludmer's critique. One possible response would be to acknowledge the critique—yes indeed, Borges is guilty of vampirizing the subaltern and appropriating its discourse in a thoroughly literary way—while also asserting that the recipient of this appropriation (literature) is itself subjected to a radical loss of ground. The literary appropriation of the oral in Borges does not leave literature intact; it can no longer pretend to be "literature," a neutral ground that has nothing to do with ideology.

Borges and Nationalism: Repetition as Parody or Tragedy?

Critics frequently distinguish between what might be termed the "early Borges" and the "later Borges." The latter period, in which the majority of Borges' better-known works are written, is generally agreed to commence with the 1939 publication in the journal *Sur* of "Pierre Menard, autor del *Quijote*." It is at this point that Borges begins to consider himself a writer of *ficciones*, of short stories and parables, whereas prior to 1939 his published work consisted primarily of poetry (three volumes) and essays (seven collections).[18] Although a thorough critical examination of this turn to writing "fictions" remains to be done, it is easy to discern a shift in tone and address between the "early" and "later" texts. As Beatriz Sarlo has shown in her important study of the topical resonance of Buenos Aires in the work of Borges (*Jorge Luis Borges: A Writer on the Edge*), one of the principal concerns of the "early" work is to describe the contradictory process of modernization in the port city, together with the writer's awareness that an entire way of life is receding from view. The "early" Borges views writing as a potential meeting ground for the conflicting forces shaping Argentina from abroad and from within. In contradistinction to the "universal" themes in which the later *ficciones* move, the texts from this period share with the gauchesque and nationalist traditions an array of poetic figures that could be partially (yet not entirely) subsumed under the heading of local color. A significant number of these poems and essays are explorations of the heroic ethos of the gaucho poem. Borges' apotheosis of a certain past and its life-world resonates with Lugones' attempt to delineate a stable ground in juxtaposition to the climate of frenetic change in early twentieth-century Buenos Aires, albeit with a crucial difference: where Lugones seeks in the past an uncontaminated essence, Borges reminds us that an inheritance is necessarily transformed by the one who receives and recognizes it. Sarlo names the guiding topos of this period in Borges' writing as *las orillas*, the suburban or intermediate zone where the urban and the pastoral, and the cosmopolitan and the autochthonous, encounter one another on uncertain ground. Rather than a simple conglomeration of differences, this space functions in Borges' lexicon as a third term: a strategic invention marking the limit of each opposing element, while also embodying the possibility of exchange between the two. The logic of las orillas is thus fundamentally democratic: neither cosmopolitanism nor autochthony can legitimately claim to represent *all* of Argentina.

The shift between the "early" and the "late" Borges marks a movement from a writing engaged with local concerns to a form of writing whose scope is sweeping and at times atopical. This transformation leaves in its wake a tension that can be glimpsed in some of Borges' efforts, beginning in the early 1960s, to revise or even conceal the existence of a number of the earlier works. While one might speculate at length regarding possible motives behind this revisionism, a discussion of this turn is not feasible here.[19] Instead, the line of inquiry I would like to pursue concerns the possibility that the importance of this literary turn for Borges' thinking has been somewhat overstated, and that what criticism finds in the "later" texts under the sign of the universal precisely *is* the concern of the "early" Borges. I would suggest that what falls under the heading of the particular, the array of Argentine or *porteño* problems that form the critical focus of the poetry and essays of the 1920s, in fact recur—albeit by way of an unmistakable displacement that is itself part and parcel of what is at stake here—in the presumed universalist orientation of the later "fictions." But if it can be said that the central concern of Borges' writing never departs from the real issues articulated in those early texts, it must also be remembered that the sociopolitical climate in Argentine undergoes a number of catastrophic transformations and crises during this same period. Borges' understanding of the relation between the nation and "the West" is exposed to a profound crisis during the decade of the 1930s, following which it is perhaps no longer possible to imagine a creative synthesis between historical epochs, and between literature and nation-building.

In an early essay entitled "El tamaño de mi esperanza" (1926), we find Borges lamenting the retreat of tradition in the face of modernization. A sense of this withdrawal is palpable in his poetic accounts of Buenos Aires, a cosmopolitan port city arising suddenly in the midst of late nineteenth-century waves of immigration and industrial modernization, and which thus also functions as a reminder of the invisible retreat of local tradition. However, the "Tamaño" essay also advocates in a strange way the need to *create* the tradition one would presume to have been placed at risk during modernization. As the young Borges proclaims dramatically, "No se ha engendrado en estas tierras ni un místico ni un metafísico, ¡ni un sentido de la vida! . . . No hay leyendas en esta tierra y ni un solo fantasma camina por nuestras calles. Ese es nuestro baldón." ["These lands have not engendered a single mystic or a single metaphysician—not even a sense of life! . . . There are no legends in these lands, and nary a ghost haunts our streets. This is our disgrace"]. The rhetorical gesture punctuating this passage, in which Borges inserts the figure of a ghost, is worth pausing over. What exactly would it mean to lack a ghost? And, supposing that we read this dirge as a kind of manifesto, a call to arms, what would it look like to engender one? This tropological phantasm produces a kind of trembling within the logical structure of the plaintive: as a sign upon which Borges hangs his portrait-like assessment of the state of Argentine literature, the specter (or the absence thereof) is an indicator of a cultural lack, an insufficient share of heritage. It provides a figure for the disparity that exists between the Argentine tradition and others (and we might credibly presume that, in combining phantasms with the hallowed ground of tradition Borges is thinking of Greek epic and tragic poetry, as well as Shakesperean tragedy). The phantasm—if there were one—would constitute the seal of tradition. But the problem evinced by this rhetoric figuration tends to multiply beyond any good measure: Can a ghost actually be "present"? And could it for that matter be "absent"? What, again, would it mean to lack a phantasm when, in the tradition to which we have recourse, such a figure is the index par excellence of a score that remains unsettled, a time that is out of joint, haunted by a reminder that is no longer present and not yet absent? Perhaps this figure, strangely positioned as it is, should be heard to attest to something resonating beyond the homogenizing forces of modernity. Perhaps it evokes, in the face of relentless commodification, the need to produce a disruption within the cultural text that is the Argentine tradition. The phantasm, which Borges quite literally seeks to summon into existence, would attest to a lacuna within the mechanics and the systematicity of modernization; it would hold the place of a something nameless that remains unsettled in the ostensibly seamless face of modernity. For Borges, tradition will from this point forward bear an enigmatic association with what would seem to be its antithesis: alteration and displacement, difference and loss. This moment in Borges' thought, which attends to a certain outstanding balance in the Argentine tradition, in fact functions as a cipher for a number of the later *ficciones* [fictions] as well. While the thematic content of Borges' texts reveals marked shifts at certain points, the suspicion that something in the Argentine remains out of joint will never be far from the central concerns of Borges' writing.

The short story "El Sur" (1953) can be read as a parody of criollo nationalism. On one hand, this treatment is consistent with Borges' efforts, beginning in the mid-1930s, to dissociate himself from various mythopoetic representations of national identity. At the same time, however, the text is marked by concerns that do not entirely fit into the critical paradigm of a writer who has successfully effaced the topos of Argentine particularity from his work. While the text is a brilliant critique of nationalist ideology, it also points to a deeper failure in the modernization project itself, an inability to efface and forget the traces of the nation's "barbaric" past. And thus a critique of liberalism's own history of disavowal is at least implicit here. The story alludes to a past that is felt as a shared inheritance, or what Borges elsewhere terms a "collective dream." But the past is also akin to an illegible mark or a scar, something that can neither be revived, outstripped nor made meaningful. At certain points, the structure of the text resembles that of classical tragedy. At its most fundamental level, the tragic dimension of Borges's text explores a connection between death and self-knowledge, giving shape to a fundamental paradox: death and finitude mark the limit of self-consciousness, but at the same time determine the conditions in which relations between self and world are born.

What I calling the tragic index in "El Sur" is in fact overdetermined by multiple and potentially conflicting registers. On one hand, the echoes of tragedy assist in bringing the gauchesque, which Lugones had described as a timeless form, to a close (see *Jorge Luis Borges: A Writer on the Edge*). By presenting the protagonist's death as a kind of tragedy (we come to suspect in the end that Dahlmann is in truth fighting his own shadow), Borges effectively "kills" the gauchesque tradition: that is, his text destroys the idea of tradition as emulation of and adequation to a prior truth, and advances instead a notion of tradition as rewriting and reinterpretation. At the same time, the formal resonances with tragedy in Borges' text (e.g., the references to blindness and destiny, the fatal peripeteia, etc.) call for new ways of naming or coming to terms with the catastrophic events of the recent past. Through a series of references to "destiny," the text attempts to establish an important symbolic link between the past and the present. Like tragedy, "El Sur" could be read as an effort to make meaning of an event that otherwise exceeds our understanding: the assignation of "destiny" is an attempt to symbolize (as a form of necessity) what is otherwise purely contingent or even unthinkable. For Borges, however, destiny does not secure a predetermined direction or foregone conclusion; it is neither a fatalism nor a voluntarism. Destiny is both "blind to a fault" and "ruthless" [*despiadado*: ruthless, cruel, inhuman, or even impious]. I will suggest that these "negative" inflections name the conditions in which we make decisions and act as structured by a kind of errancy or radical finitude. Decision is marked beforehand by blindness, separation, and scission, and yet the recurrence to "destiny" suggests that it also has to do with a certain trace of transcendence. In pausing over this term, I do not mean to suggest that destiny becomes the theme of "El Sur," as if the text were a treatise or an essay. "El Sur" is not *about* destiny. Rather, the question of destiny informs the plot or *pragma* of the text, which in turn offers a thought of what could be called the *literariness* of its topos.[20] My reading of this short story focuses on two moments. In the first instance, the protagonist reenacts nationalism's quest romance, while the second moment produces what was only latent in this tradition: the truth of the subject as a *lost cause*.

The story told in "El Sur" is set in 1939, several decades after the culmination of modernization projects in Argentina. The protagonist, Juan Dahlmann, is a *porteño* bureaucrat who, in the midst of modernity and its attendant ills (proliferating technology, urban anonymity, immigration along with changing social codes, etc.), imagines that his existence in Buenos Aires is lacking something. Dahlmann feels that his true identity resides in the Pampa of the south, which he invests with the mythic value of a place still untainted by the metropolis and its frenetic technological metastasis. By way of this simple sketch, Borges illustrates the unavowed logic of the nationalist project: 1) for Dahlmann, modernity equals alienation, an experience that equates finitude with falsity; what has been lost through modernization is not just the true national character but precisely the difference between the One (truth) and the many (the copy); 2) Dahlmann "represses" the truth of this experience of finitude by generating a counter-notion: that finitude and history could be overcome through the return to a primordial order or One-ness; and 3) therefore Dahlmann sustains a belief in this Other as a timeless reserve, and which guarantees his own identity as an essence removed from the continency of history. We can follow Borges' parody of nationalism in multiple directions. To begin with, the text offers a warning concerning not only what could be described as the inauthenticity of "authenticity," but moreover of a danger that lies in the attempt to actualize such a nexus of imaginary identifications by converting them into a political program. At the same time, parody also underscores the literary basis of such identifications: literariness, for Borges, is both the beginning and the limit of identity. Literature provides the (non)ground of Borges' attempt to think identity and meaning. Literary language illustrates an enigmatic link between the national imaginary and the constitution of borders. I will follow this bifurcation of narrative by indicating key points in the unfolding of this literary dimension of the text, after which I underscore some of the critical and political implications of this reading. Finally, it should be possible to address the relation between the literary and political dimensions of the text.

Dahlmann is a product of what the text terms the discord between discrete lineages and bloodlines. The account of Dahlmann's ancestry, a mixture of Germanic and Spanish blood, closely mirrors Borges' own genealogical identifications, and likewise helps to generate a theory of the Argentine tradition as informed by a nexus of influences and genealogies. The nation, for Borges, is not a simple unity but the subject of an originary encounter or crossing—which is also to say, an intermingling or mutual contamination. Dahlmann, however, identifies with only one of these traditions. More precisely, he identifies with the "Romantic death" of his creole grandfather, Francisco Flores (who was killed during the Conquest of the Desert), rather than the Evangelical life of his paternal grandfather, Johannes Dahlmann.[21] At the heart of this identification is the fantasy of being able to choose one's own death. Dahlmann's desire is invested in exchanging an impersonal, anonymous death for a romanticized, memorable death: "en la discordia de sus dos linajes, Juan Dahlmann (tal vez a impulsos de la sangre germánica) eligió el de ese antepasado romántico, o de muerte romántica" ["amidst the discord of his two lineages, Juan Dahlmann (perhaps it was an impulse of his Germanic blood) cast his lot with his Romantic ancestor, he of the Romantic death"] (195). This portrait is no doubt an allusion to the "arms and letters" debate discussed in chapter 37 of Cervantes's *Don Quixote*. However, in the context of the Argentine tradition, Borges' ironic and mocking reference to the role of "Germanic blood" also points to a blind spot in the discourse of Argentine nationalism: this catachrestic figure calls attention to the mutual contamination and disruption of lineages, or what the text terms "discordia." The silent role played by "Germanic blood" in Dahlmann's identification points to an encounter or exposure which, Borges suggests, in fact precedes the determination of different identities. In other words, what I am calling the crossing or encounter—or the "discord"—is not so much a meeting ground for preestablished identities: rather, it is the secret origin of identity itself. This play and tension between stocks and types destabilizes nationalism's projection of an *argentinidad* based on purity of blood, race, and spirit. At the same time, the tropological substitution enacted by Borges' text is in fact endemic to nationalist discourse itself: while the nationalist project hinges on the belief that the Argentine tradition is properly Hispanic and anticosmopolitan, it nonetheless derives its rhetorical apparatus from, precisely, German and French texts (on European influences in Argentine nationalism, see David Rock's *Authoritarian Argentina*).

Borges thus invites us to reexamine what we understand by identity itself. Dahlmann's voluntaristic belief in the possibility of "choosing" an identity—or choosing a death—is contaminated from the beginning by the uncertainty it strives to rule out. His choice produces not certainty but increased confusion between identities. However, above and beyond the distinction between Hispanic and Germanic lineages, the text invites us to consider identity as limit of the national subject. Behind the illusion of choosing between opposing identities, Borges proposes that *our identity in fact chooses us*. This is a tragic thought which turns all consideration of identity away from the illusion of autonomy and choice, and toward a question of *heteronomy*. My point is not simply that Dahlmann's destiny—and hence his identity and all possible permutations thereof—is shaped by mysterious forces beyond his reach or command. Rather, the thought of heteronomy (literally, being named or receiving one's law from outside) means that self-knowledge is not an approximation toward an unchanging truth; rather, it points to an ethical relation, or to an encounter with alterity. Dahlmann must *come to see himself* (he must see his own hand, his own doing) where he once saw only the foreign, the other.

An ancestral ranch owned by the Flores family, located to the south of Buenos Aires, provides another crucial element in developing the connection between the protagonist's personal history and the debates over national history. Dahlmann maintains this country house as a birthright, but he does not occupy it. In fact, the enjoyment he derives from it stems not from an experience of the place at all, but rather from the abstract idea of it. For Dahlmann, Buenos Aires is a space of frenetic transformation and anonymity, of proliferating foreign tongues and the increasing ubiquity of modern technology. In contrast to all of this artifice and duplicity, the ranch promises a return to the Same or the One, a reserve of permanence and stability. The imaginary relation Dahlmann sustains to the ranch is akin to nationalism's discussion of *argentinidad*: a national essence that is always kept offstage, in reserve, protected from everyday existence and thus immune from the catastrophic changes of history. In contesting liberal representations of national interest, nationalism conflates modernization (a particular design for change) with history understood as transformation in general or as such. And thus nationalism becomes the attempt to conceive and recover a time prior to history.

Despite the protagonist's endeavor to preserve essence from existence, he one day falls prey to catastrophe. Climbing a dark staircase while immersed in a book (he is reading the *1001 Nights*), Dahlmann is oblivious to a door jutting out over the stairwell. In brushing against the door, he receives a cut on his forehead. However, it is not until he reaches his destination at the top of the stairs and is "struck" once again, this time by the horrified look of a woman who opens the door to him, that Dahlmann begins to register the fact that he has been cut—and I will also suggest, *marked*. This scene of chance and misfortune stages an encounter with the unknown, with the other. What Dahlmann "sees" in the exchange of looks with this anonymous woman is the fact that he does not see all, even and especially when it comes to himself. He sees *that he is seen* from a locus he cannot step into, and this fact of being seen "from beyond" exposes him to a part of himself that he can neither grasp as his own nor renounce as completely foreign, other. This encounter with the other is in fact a *missed* encounter in which two gazes cross but do not meet. He can see that he cannot see what she sees, and the protagonist is all the same obligated in a profound way to this chiasmatic limit. The passage marks an important point in Borges' engagement with the philosophical tradition, and particularly with Hegel's account of self-knowledge. For Hegel, my identity is affirmed when another reflects something of myself back to me. (For example, consider Shakespeare's *The Tempest*: Prospero is only a master to the degree that he can convey his learning to another, and then induce the other to reproduce this knowledge through speech. In teaching Caliban to speak, Prospero does not merely display his command of nature, he in fact constitutes his own being qua master.) Borges, on the other hand, here invites us to consider that the reflexive exchange between self and other or subject and object also has the potential to unsettle the formation of absolute subjects.[22]

The following day, Dahlmann awakes with a fever. His condition progressively worsens, until he is transported to a clinic [*sanatorio*], where he is subjected to a grueling treatment to save his life. We are told that Dahlmann, who suffers from septicemia, will eventually recover his *sanitas*. In the motifs of blood and blood poisoning, together with the etymology of the word sanatorio [*sanitas*: health, sanity, purity], it is also possible to hear a long-standing tradition of likening the nation to a body.[23] This corporeal metaphor in turn conveys the idea that any kind of disturbance within the regular functioning of the nation-state is in fact a form of sickness, and that the nation, like any other body, will naturally generate "antibodies" to fight off and expel the "disease."

We are told that Dahlmann decides to complete his convalescence at his ancestral ranch in the South, and that he begins the journey by train. While seated on the train, he engages half-heartedly in reading the *1001 Nights* (the same book that had precipitated his catastrophe), until he finally puts the book down and turns his eyes to the window. Reflecting on the journey from the modern, littoral setting of the metropolis into the archaic space of the South, the protagonist tells himself that he is moving from mere literature to life, from artifice to authenticity. But in fact, Dahlmann's interpretation serves to return to nationalism its own message—its critique of modernity as artifice—in inverted form.[24]

> A los lados del tren, la ciudad se desgarraba en suburbios; esta visión y luego la de jardines y quintas demoraron el principio de la lectura. La verdad es que Dahlmann leyó poco; la montaña de piedra imán y el genio que ha jurado matar a su bienhechor eran, quién lo niega, maravillosas, pero no mucho más que la mañana y que el hecho de ser. La felicidad lo distraía de Shahrazad y de sus milagros superfluos; Dahlmann cerraba el libro y se dejaba simplemente vivir (199).

> [Along both sides of the train, the city broke up into suburbs. This sight, soon followed by the view of gardens and country villas, kept Dahlmann from his reading. The truth was, he read very little; the magnetic mountain and the genie who had sworn to kill his benefactor were—who would deny it?—marvelous, but no more so than the morning and the brute fact of being. These joys distracted Dahlmann from Scheherezade and his superfluous miracles; he closed the book and allowed himself simply to live.]

This remarkable passage comprises an allegory of ideology. That is, it demonstrates the ideological nature of the escape from ideology. The back-and-forth movement between literature and nature, or fiction and the real, culminates in a gesture that would seem to signal a renunciation of artifice (cosmopolitan life, imported literature) and a restoration of the realm of permanent truth. Here nature represents a space of secure, autochthonous knowledge, uncontaminated by the foreign knowledge and confusion that reigns in the littoral polis.[25] This, at least, is the story Dahlmann tells himself. However, the act of closing the book on artifice also turns out to constitute the literary gesture par excellence. It will have been necessary to go through literature in order to emerge from contingency: the renunciation of cosmopolitan falsity is an act that Dahlmann could carry out only by reaffirming a profoundly literary and nostalgic knowledge of the South.

Let us momentarily suspend this discussion of the story in order to call attention to a repetition and displacement at work in the text. This pattern concerns the aisthesis of the protagonist, whom we repeatedly encounter in a state of "distraction": in his desire to truly *be* he is never quite *there*. In retrospect, this repeated dislocation will have provided one of the first indications that the journey to the South is perhaps nothing more than a story the protagonist tells himself while in the clinic. But the traditional complicity between reader and omniscient narrator is also shattered in the process: it is as if what began as an account of the blind spot in nationalist ideology ran aground and were transformed into an allegory of the impossibility of fully accounting for ideology. An earlier allusion to "destiny" allows us, in light of these later developments, to situate this tropological state of detachment or "distraction" between two separate spheres of inquiry: between the aesthetic and the ethical. Immediately preceding Dahlmann's accident in the stairwell, the narrative issues an oracular warning: "Ciego a culpas, el destino puede ser despiadado con las mínimas distracciones" ["Blind to a fault, destiny can be ruthless in the face of the slightest distraction"] (198). What does it mean for the text to speak of the essential "blindness" of destiny? For the time being, we are only able to see how this errancy introduces another literary motif into the Borgesian text: as an aesthetic moment, "distraction" marks a threshold for consciousness; it signals the opening of a relation—or an "exposure"—that is in fact the origin of any ontological distinction between "self" and "other." The origin of the subject as "distraction" (in contrast to the idea of a subject who becomes distracted) bears witness to—albeit precisely as the failure to completely register—a limit-relation, a relation that has not yet been formatted by the cognitive processes as a possible aesthetic experience. As we have seen, Dahlmann's relation to the South takes root in his fetishization of a topos that he knows only through his familiarity with gauchesque literature. I will return to this discussion of "destiny" and "distraction" below, where I suggest that these references help to shape a tragic conception of national history.

Dahlmann's arrival at his ancestral home is deferred by an encounter that can be read either as a realization or an interruption of the imaginary return that we have been tracing. In the story's final scene, we find a textual knot that will require some time to unravel.

Nearing the end of his journey, Dahlmann stops at an *almacén,* a country store and inn which is also a standard meeting place in the gauchesque narrative. His attention first settles on an ancient gaucho lying on the floor, whom the text describes as having been "reducido y pulido como las aguas a una piedra o las generaciones de los hombres a una sentencia" ["reduced and polished as water does to a stone, or as generations of men do to a sentence"] (201). While absorbed in dining, Dahlmann finds himself harassed by a group of *campesinos,* who strike the protagonist as anachronistically resembling gauchos from a prior era. His attempts to ignore and then to escape from their insults are short-circuited: before Dahlmann can take leave, the owner intervenes apologetically and—inexplicably—addresses Dahlmann (whom he does not know) by the patronymic. What had until this moment taken the form of a purely anonymous form of hostility, directed against the metropolitan outsider, is suddenly and retroactively transformed into an assault upon the proper name, on Dahlmann's very being. And although the protagonist is unarmed, one of the *peones* proposes a duel by knife. Then, the completely unexpected occurs: the old, wizened gaucho, whom Dahlmann sees as a "cipher of the South," inexplicably tosses a dagger at his feet. The protagonist takes this gesture to be a sign of his destiny, and tells himself that he has no choice but to accept: "Desde un rincón, el viejo gaucho extático, en el que Dahlmann vio una cifra del Sur (del Sur que era suyo), le tiró una daga desnuda que vino a caer a sus pies. Era como si el Sur hubiera resuelto que Dahlmann aceptara el duelo" ["From one corner the old, ecstatic gaucho, in whom Dahlmann saw a cipher of the South (his South), threw him a naked dagger which landed at his feet. It was as if the South had resolved that Dahlmann accept the duel"] (203). The knife, which the text tells us he "perhaps" would not know how to use ("que acaso no sabrá manejar," 204), provides a metonym for the gauchesque ethos, for the ethical substance on the basis of which Lugones had sought to identify an Argentine essence.

The narrative anticipates but does not incorporate the events of the duel itself. Instead, it concludes with Dahlmann and the other exiting onto the plain. Something important appears to be missing, however, from this imminent confrontation between Dahlmann and the other: it appears to lack precisely the element of uncertainty that distinguishes the duel as a social practice. The efficacy of the duel as a mediating function is maintained only insofar as the outcome—and hence the possibility of doing justice rather than mere vengeance—has not been determined in advance, in favor of one party or the other. The duel contains the promise of justice only to the degree that it leaves open a space, however minute, of indeterminacy. Dahlmann, however, bears no relation to the outcome as such. Or rather, his relation to the end is one of disinterest. The protagonist's attention is directed exclusively to the origin, to the call through which he believes himself to have been summoned, and for which the end—there is little doubt that it will be his death—will have been a reaffirmation or a countersignature. The absence of suspense notwithstanding, a fundamental ambiguity inheres in the decision that bears Dahlmann across the threshold. It is possible to read Dahlmann's grasping of the knife, the gesture whereby he seems to assent to his own death, as the final, catastrophic literalization of the fantasy that has oriented the narrative from the outset. Dahlmann's identity would thus be constituted (or recovered) insofar as he is at last able to extract himself from anonymity and situate himself as the true addressee of an appeal from the Other, the locus of meaning and truth in the world. This reciprocal recognition of and by the Other would compensate for the anonymous and meaningless death that awaited Dahlmann in the clinic. In this light, the decision transforms what was previously the illegibility of the limit into a Work. It deploys a logic that Althusser would term the "interpellation" of the national subject: the subject's identity is presumably secured when the subject identifies and responds to a call ("hey you!"). Through this maneuver, the subject inserts him or herself into a network of meaning: the law recognizes me; there is a place for me there. Interpellation, however, is perhaps just another name for disavowal: what is refused in this identification is the "groundless" basis of the decision (to fight or not to fight: no one and nothing can provide an a priori basis upon which this decision could be resolved *for me*, in advance and as a universally recognizable principle). The form that Dahlmann's acceptance takes serves to deflect responsibility for the decision onto the Other; he effectively chooses to see himself as the instrument of a higher power. I will suggest, however, that things are perhaps not quite so simple as this scenario would imply. This first reading must in turn be confronted with a register of errancy from which it cannot entirely remove itself.

First, however, another brief digression is in order. It can be seen how the protagonist's aestheticization of death could lay the groundwork for reading this text as a tragedy, in precisely the Hegelian terms outlined in the previous chapter. Dahlmann, by converting his own death into an aesthetic work in the service of the nation—i.e., as a sacrifice for the greater glory of the South—would allow the text to reconcile an event that otherwise exceeds the understanding. This analysis could be extended to incorporate what Schelling attempts to think as tragedy's presentation of a rational identity between freedom and necessity: the tone or mood established by Dahlmann's decision entails a resymbolization of contingency or finitude as necessity. In concrete terms, such a formal analysis of the tragic dimension of Borges' text could be linked to the historical context of Argentine modernity. For one, we could read this story as an allegory of the violent encounters between discourses and traditions vying for supremacy during the nation-building and modernization processes in Argentina. Or we can read it as pointing to an uncanny link between the rational, systematizing tendency of Enlightenment thought and the authoritarian and at times fascist discourse of Argentine nationalism. Or—another possibility—we could read the text as pointing to a connection between the utopian character of Argentine political projects and the dystopian irruptions that haunt national history from its outset. Taking any or all of these historical and metahistorical scenarios, Borges' text could be read as issuing a warning to any attempt to seize the transcendental postulates of a particular line of thinking and to bring these regulating principles into the world.[26]

I suggested earlier that a question of literature or literariness is central to Borges' text and its reflection on historicity or destiny. How does literature help us to reexamine the nexus of identity, sovereignty and responsibility—in short, those terms according to which the Western tradition has always conceived of the subject? And how does the thought of tragedy help us to follow Borges in his attempt to reposition the age-old question of the subject? I would argue that "El Sur" offers a thought of the subject as an ethical problem: not in the sense of a problem to be submitted to a formal system of ethical inquiry, but as posing a problem *for* this very philosophical tradition of thinking. I have suggested that Borges' text refrains from replacing ambiguity with transparent meaning. Indeed, the textual process of unveiling and decoding the fantasy-structure of nationalism affirms nothing other than *the failure of narrative itself*. By remaining in close proximity to the language of the text, we see that any attempt to resolve its hermeneutic knot(s) in favor of a particular position (interpretive or ideological) misses a more fundamental point. Whatever we can say about the text will be based on its prior demonstration of the impossibility of providing a total and adequate account of the event. We can begin to see how this is the case by turning once again to the decision for the duel, and by attending to the very letter of the text's concluding statement. In the final passage of the text, we find the protagonist resolutely embracing a future that has been determined as ineluctable. And in the context of the sanitized, calculated, and overproduced world of modernity, this resoluteness might even be termed a tragic defiance. The suggestion that Dahlmann "might not" know how to handle the weapon he grasps [*que acaso no sabrá manejar*] is of course yet another reminder of the literary basis of his knowledge of the South. But the crucial point in the final passage hinges on the irreducibility of this *acaso*. It is a placeholder which, in one sense, utters the protagonist's death sentence, while, in another sense, is all that remains *between* Dahlmann and his death.

Several critics have commented on this "acaso" clause.[27] These commentaries have tended to assign a literal basis to this "perhaps," regarding it as a residue of ambiguity that would continue to complicate the fable's conclusion. It would be easy to find a place for this final "acaso" within the terms already laid out, i.e., as a refusal of narrative closure. This clause could lend support to the suspicion that, rather than providing the semblance of a hermeneutic totality, the text reveals how narrative in fact reproduces the very uncertainty it seeks to resolve. Insofar as these interpretations insist on the irreducible presence of literary ambiguity, they are also deeply suspicious of the idea that the text can be interpreted from a single, dominant temporality, a unified time that we could designate as the text's "reality." All of this would present little or no problem for Borges criticism.

Commentators have also noted, along with Borges himself, that the text allows for two mutually exclusive readings.[28] One way to interpret the text is what we might call the naïve reading, which proceeds from beginning to end as if the narrative were a more or less faithful account of the protagonist's life. Another possible interpretation, and probably the most accepted reading of "El Sur," is that the second half of the story, beginning with the train passage, is a fiction or an artifice that serves to mask a more disturbing truth. According to this reading, Dahlmann in fact never leaves the clinic, and the journey to the South is only imagined by him as he lies dying from septicemia or suffering from a psychic collapse. A number of clues in the final scene lend support to this reading, including the unexplained fact that the owner of the *almacén* knows Dahlmann by name, and a marked similitude between the gaucho's knife (which could also be likened to a pen) and the doctor's needle. The protagonist's affinity for *The 1001 Nights* would thus allow us to see him as a modern version of Scheherazad, and the text itself (but beginning and ending where?) as an effect of his attempt to ward off death. More to the point, the act of writing or narrating participates in the search for a substitute death that was the basis of the protagonist's nationalism, his original identification with Francisco Flores. Literature would provide a compensatory world for we moderns, returning to us the aura of a traditional, heroic and meaningful death at a historical juncture where this authenticity has been irreversibly lost. This interpretation would seem to suggest that the ostensible "omniscient narrator" has himself been duped: it compels us to recognize that while the second half of the story is told *as if* it were grounded in an objective point of view, the third person narrative perspective has in fact been compromised or taken over by the protagonist's imagination—or by his ghost. Let us note that this hypothetical reading has (perhaps unintended) consequences for our understanding of literature and literary interpretation. By retrospectively throwing the traditional omniscient point of view into doubt, the reader thereby reinstalls *him or herself* in the position of the one supposed to know. In doing so, one necessarily loses sight of the way in which Borges' text repeatedly undermines the certainty of self-knowledge. In a sense, the nonnaïve reader is here compelled to repeat the errancy of Juan Dahlmann on the staircase—who is himself, of course, a reader. Caught up in this vicious circle, "El Sur" could be described as a story about the partial but ineluctable failure of reading. It tells the story of reading's inability to account for all loose ends, or of reading's tendency to produce unforeseen connections and developments in the wake of the knots it unravels. And thus the story also reminds us of the need for more reading.

While critical attention to irreducible ambiguity in the text offers an important insight into Borges' conception of literature, it cannot avoid missing an equally fundamental point here. Despite everything we have learned from reading Borges, I am suggesting that the conclusion must be read against the grain, so to speak, as an effort to think *absolute certainty as such*. It is as if the only means of conveying the ineluctable character of the limit that emerges here were by way of yet another negation, or via a partial negation that would repeat the protagonist's own refusal of finitude. Apropos of what is often called the "unreliability" of literary narrative (though with Borges it is perhaps more to the point to state that the issue of reliability is simply not a literary one), the hermeneutic problem arising here concerns the relation between contingency and meaning, or the possibility or impossibility of giving shape to reality as necessity. The interpretive problem introduced and left open in the conclusion does not concern the text's "reality" or lack thereof: it is not a question of whether or not Dahlmann "really" dies. Rather, the problem announced through this "perhaps" is a literary problem: that of signification itself, of how to give shape to or symbolize an encounter with that which eludes or falls out of symbolization, or with what Lacan calls the real. In other words, Borges' text confronts the problem of how to give form to a thought of necessity in the midst of a sustained narrative labor of drawing out the contingent ground of every representational or ideological construct.

In his "Autobiographical Essay," while describing an early interest in the figures and idiom of *las orillas* and with literary representations of "local color," Borges confesses to a fascination with the idea of a destiny such as Dahlmann's. He describes his interest as revolving around "the motiveless, or disinterested, duel—of courage for its own sake" ("Autobiographical Essay," 231–32). In this final clarification, Borges would like to distance himself from nationalist memorializations of the gaucho ethos, and of the duel as a heroic act that is "interested," or "pathological" in the Kantian sense. The ethical weight that nationalism assigns to the act masks a particular desire operating under the sign of the unconditioned universal. And one can imagine any number of variations on this cloaking: for instance, the duel eulogized nostalgically as unmediated and transparent human act, free from modern artifice. By locating the decisive or captivating aspect of the duel in its disinterested character, Borges might of course be attempting to substitute an aesthetic value for the political implications of this practice. At the same time, Borges's rewriting of the myth of argentinidad could also be explained as a kind of absolute or unmediated attraction, an interest in disinterest. In other words, perhaps the attraction that this scene holds for Borges consists in its proximity to the "zero degree"—or object-cause—of desire. What if motivelessness, far from describing the absence of animation and passion, in fact describes a subject who confronts the world while having nothing left to lose? Contrary to a frequent misconception, it is not that Borges holds the philosopheme of the subject to be a mere pseudo-problem. Rather, it is a matter of pursuing the subject at that point where it goes beyond the economy of the same. At this point, as Borges' comments suggest, the subject can only be thought as a *lost cause*.[29]

It was suggested in the previous chapter that modern philosophy, by assigning an exemplary value to classical tragedy, anticipates a conduit from tragic aesthetics to an ethical dimension. Philosophy takes the tragic sublime to be a route to the good. Or, in slightly different terms, it views the affective energy put into play by tragedy as a merely contingent step, one that will subsequently be voided or raised [*aufgehoben*] to the higher power of reason. Lacan, on the other hand, reads Greek tragedy as attesting to a limit that cannot be administered by the economy of sublimation. For Lacan, the possibility of an ethical relation begins precisely where our secure access to the good begins to waver. Greek tragedy stages this moment as the catastrophic collapse of the hero's world. But rather than leading to a nihilistic celebration of destruction and loss, tragedy requires that we also attempt to see this shattering of a world of meaning as a kind of "beginning." The crucial distinction between Lacan and the onto-theological tradition on this point is that the dimension opened up by tragedy in Lacan's reading *does not lead anywhere*. The limit named in Sophocles' *Antigone* as *Atē* does not provide a step toward the dialectical resolution of collapse and regeneration, withdrawal and emergence. On the contrary, it is the unassimilated *remainder* that is left over when and where reconciliation leaves off or fails. In this sense, the opening staged by tragedy is both an absolute (unmediated, irreducible to both that which precedes it and that which is still to come) and a fragment (unable to be completed or transformed into a whole). The ethical relation to which tragedy points cannot be judged by the degree to which one's actions do or do not correspond to preestablished codes of conduct. Nor, for that matter, is it a question of measuring a particular decision on the basis of its outcome. Rather, the ethical dimension is opened up only at the limit of these laws, through a relation that discovers the other in his or her alterity.

We can at this time revisit several of the interpretive problems that arose in my initial reading of "El Sur," difficulties we should now be able to confront under a different light. I noted that critical commentaries have typically emphasized that the text's conclusion supports two mutually exclusive interpretations: either the second half of the story takes place on the same level of reality as the first half, or it in fact comprises a fiction within a fiction, a disavowal of the culmination of the first half. It should now be possible to make clear the limit of this either/or paradigm. Critical attention to narrative ambiguity is a function of a particular understanding of literature, and presupposes a natural teleological design, of which a reversion into "ambiguity" is one possible derivation. In pointing out the ambiguity of the conclusion, criticism tends to lose sight of another possibility: that this interpretive impasse is in fact a condition of the text's legibility. Indeed, we can see in Borges' text how the slippage between "denotative" and "connotative" registers, and between descriptive and performative uses of language, creates an opening in which meaning can take place. Ambiguity is thus not the end of reading but rather the beginning: the attempt to "signify" ambiguity by turning it into the message or meaning cannot help but miss the very thing to which it calls attention. This opening is akin to the singular dimension that Lacan, in reference to Antigone's relation to the corpse of Polynices, characterizes as *between two deaths*. Thus the textual redoubling of "death"—which is only confusedly termed an "ambiguity" in what is supposed to be an otherwise univocal narrative—aspires to nothing other than a consideration of this impossible space between two deaths.

What does it mean to speak of a space "between two deaths" in conjunction with Borges' text? We can situate this phrase within the discussion of ambiguity by returning to the "first" of two deaths, the moment in which the question of Dahlmann's mortality first comes to the fore. From there, we can begin to see Borges' text as a literary consideration of a profound interrelation between existence and death. This "first death," which can be located in the staircase scene, should be understood as limit-experience. This scene anticipates the voiding and cancellation of Dahlmann's *being* (his subjectivity construed as wholeness) and the "death" of the subject qua symbolic entity. At the same time, let us note the profound ambivalence with which the text approaches this region. It will be helpful to pause and attempt to hear the conflicting imperatives that put Borges's text in motion.

The Borgesian critique of nationalism hinges on the appeal of a "disinterest" whose secret truth is an "experience" of the limit—of the opening that gives rise to and vanishes before every possible experience. But while attention to this liminal moment is crucial to understanding how the text relates to the Argentine tradition—it perhaps constitute Borges' most original attempt to engage a Latin American topos—one would be equally justified in arguing that the text maintains a sympathetic relation to Dahlmann and his voluntaristic identifications. The concluding scene also participates, by way of its own substitutions and displacements, in the elaborate concealment of a truth that nevertheless speaks from behind the textual mask. Through this simultaneous approach toward and retreat from the limit, writing seeks to resolve the impasse that is Dahlmann, to expel the petrified remainder of the ancestral *domus* and release itself from the hold of imminent catastrophe. Writing approaches this mortal limit with both fascination and horror. As with many of Borges' ficciones, the text at times tends toward a literary nihilism, reveling in the dissipation of meaning it has helped to bring about. At the same time, the act of writing—which finds its allegorical index in the knife—seeks to establish a barrier that would separate and protect it from the devastating effects of symbolic collapse. These two tendencies coincide with a pair of conflicting imperatives found in many of the ficciones: for one, writing is a labor that brings us to the very edge of what Lacan calls "the real" in its unmediated state; yet, at the same time, writing also seeks to preserve itself from this domain and its debilitating effects.[30] Writing is marked by anxiety and yearning for a world that borders on being lost for all time. At the same time, writing endeavors to concretize this loss and bring it to term; it seeks to register loss or absence and thereby to delimit its scope. The *sense* of Borges' writing—its indication or direction, but also its mood—could be described paradoxically as an approach through withdrawal, and as safeguarding through proximity. By definition, the real (just like "the South") is never available to experience immediately. However, in the process of mediation through which writing seek to lay hold of it (either to draw it nearer or to ward off its disastrous return), the real ceases to be what it "is"—that is, beyond or at the limits of signification. The only possible relation that writing can assume to the real is that of representing both its *impossibility* and its *indictment*, its having been lost or foreclosed twice over. Wittgenstein cautions, "that of which we cannot speak we must remain silent." Borges' text is a ceaseless deliberation over this impossibility/prohibition, while also seeking to break away from any form of nostalgic reflection that would remain prisoner of the real in its absence. Borgesian writing thus undergoes a fissure and a bifurcation: its return to the site of the real also initiates a mourning of loss and an attempt to purge itself of an archaic, petrified remainder. It is via the repetition of these apparently conflicting mandates that a new world is anticipated in Borges' oeuvre. The process of mourning, in distinction from nostalgic remembrance or monumentalization, affixes a limit to the dream of recovery. Literary mourning points to a paradox: writing seeks to allow the real to take (its) place so as to prevent it from happening.

How does this vacillation, between writing's "melancholic" fascination with the real qua remainder and its attempt to expel the real through repetition, relate to what has been termed the region between two deaths? This question also returns us to the connection between Borges and tragedy. The problem of the protagonist's relation or nonrelation to his own mortality has been implicit in every facet of this discussion. This singular relation is repeatedly disturbed by the specter of its own impossibility: death, as the ultimate limit of the self-conscious subject, resists all specular efforts to recognize it as such. "My death" is both uniquely mine and it is that which "I" can never experience insofar as it constitutes the blind spot and division of every "I." As absolute master, death is that from which nothing returns. But that which shrinks from recognition is also what returns over and again in the form of a specter. Thus, according to the double imperative that informs and constrains Borges' text, it is necessary that death be given a place within the symbolic life of the community. The "second death" is a way of naming this necessity. Death must be circumscribed—if not by traditional terms such as recognition, then by recourse to a different order of inscription—*in order for it to take place.*

Borges' text concerns itself with the relation that the human, from the moment of its birth into language, assumes toward death. In a scene immediately prior to the protagonist's journey to the South, we find an allusion to a radical separation between human experience and that of other beings. This gap is described as an incommensurable relation between temporality and infinitude—and thus the gap also separates the human *from itself*. Dahlmann, while awaiting the train that will convey him to his destiny in the South, enters a café that he had frequented during an earlier time in his life. He is drawn inside by the recollection of a certain cat, which he remembers as both "enormous" and a "disdainful divinity." The mnemonic image that attracts Dahlmann contains the promise of unmediated contact with existence. But the pure presence he had imagined awaiting him in the café vanishes in the shattering of a mirror: "pensó . . . que aquel contacto era ilusorio y que estaban como separados por un cristal, porque el hombre vive en el tiempo, en la sucesión, y el mágico animal, en la actualidad, en la eternidad del instante" ["he thought . . . that such contact was illusory, and that he and the cat were separated by a pane of glass, because man lives in the world of temporality and succession, whereas that magical animal lives in the world of actuality, in the eternity of an instant"] (198–99). As is the case with "Funes el memorioso," this scene is a consideration of *anamnesis* as structured around originary loss. The structure of memory—of the archaic memory of pure presence, unmediated by artifice—is shaped a priori by the loss of singularity and the forgetting of difference. In his attempt to grasp the sublime in its absolute self-identity, the protagonist is in fact exposed to alterity. The cat reveals to Dahlmann that "the Same" is in fact another name for death. The very fact that Dahlmann *remembers* this avatar of pure presence already signals its irrevocable loss.

This negative moment prepares the way for the final scene in the *almacén* and allows the later scene to assign to human existence its "ek-static" character. It is the narrative time between the initial catastrophic accident in the stairwell and these later moments that gives shape to the thesis of "two deaths." As has already been suggested, this "in-between time" is also the opening of an ethical space, the protagonist's confrontation with the zero-degree of desire, or the real. The hypothesis of "two deaths" affirms that, in addition to the biological death that humans undergo along with all other beings, the human has also to do with a second, symbolic "death." This symbolic death, which typically follows and remarks on the biological death (for instance, in a burial and funeral rites), signifies by cutting, by marking the difference between the living and the dead. This symbolic, supplementary death is not just a metaphor for the "true" biological death. Rather, the symbolic death constitutes a radical separation from immanence, and it is on the basis of this cut that humans have access to language and metaphor. However, the mark itself is irreducible to substitution. Strangely, the second death is *prior to* biological death in the sense that it prepares one for it as possibility: no creature that has not been submitted to this in-between space can have any experience of the possibility of his or her own death. It will have be necessary to have suffered the mark of a second, symbolic death in order to assume a relation toward the reality of death itself.

In discussing the concluding scene in the *almacén*, I have argued that the protagonist's identification with his "destiny" was based on a kind of misrecognition—of a mortality or "errancy" that is his, albeit in a radically improper form. Dahlmann's attribution of responsibility for the decision to a higher authority ("the South") seemed to entail a retroactive effacement of the real groundlessness of decision. However, things are somewhat more complicated than this critique of ideology would imply. For one, the protagonist's act could also be seen to undermine the nationalist attempt to monumentalize the destruction of the gaucho as a heroic sacrifice. The decision by which Dahlmann prepares to risk everything reveals a disjunction between conflicting "senses." The act inscribes itself within multiple and antagonistic historical epochs: it becomes legible simultaneously within the nineteenth-century debate between "civilization and barbarism," and within a twentieth-century sphere in which modernization has already canceled one of the terms of the decision.[31] But the simultaneity of these disjunctive epochal registers, in which one represents the precise negation of the other, does not merely impose a gratuitous irony, since it is also in the later time that the collective memory and meaning of the former time will be produced: the "heroic" ethos is precisely a product of postheroic times. The act is thus an attempt to come to terms with the absolute (nonnegatable) negativity of its horizon. It finds itself responsible to a call that issues from catastrophe, and is in fact a testimony to this responsibility. Such a indebtedness cannot be accounted for by a critique of the concept of ground.

An index of this "responsibility" can be found in the earlier incident on the staircase. The relation that establishes the stakes of this obligatedness is not a relation in the usual sense, i.e., a relation of identity and difference, of a self to another. It is inscribed as a liminal space of contact, strictly prior to the reflexive exchange of subject and object. In the encounter on the staircase, death and finitude are not remarked on at all. In fact, this encounter between Dahlmann and the other can only appear under the sign of a missed encounter. The significance of this staircase scene is indicated by a reference to the other's face. It is in the gaze and the expression of the woman who opens the door to him that the protagonist is struck by the fact that, simply put, he cannot see. He sees *that he is seen* from a place he does not see himself. This locus of in-visibility opens onto a dimension of his being that is neither proper nor to be renounced. This "fact" no doubt fails to become one for the protagonist himself: it is not to be negated or sublimated, but can only be repeated. The encounter with the other is a missed encounter in that two gazes cross but do not meet. Dahlmann can see that he cannot see what the other sees, but he is all the same obligated in a profound way to this limit.

The spectacular scene on the staircase recalls us to some of the exemplary episodes in the *Phenomenology of Spirit*, through which Hegel gives body to the dialectical structure of self-consciousness. But while Borges provides a sketch of self-consciousness seeking out the other in order to find or reaffirm itself, his text also traces the limit of this self-identification-via-negation. The face, which localizes and corporealizes this encounter with the other, gives shape to the origin of self-consciousness as surprise, as a being taken unawares.[32] The face is perhaps an index of self-consciousness, which can only approach its own features and its own limits by way of the other—and via this latter's nonrelation to his or her own death. Through the flashing of repetition in this scene, we find condensed an entire thesis regarding the traumatic kernel of self-consciousness. At the same time, the other's visage reflects and puts into play a broader, less determinate condition: it provides a figure for self-consciousness as a structure of openness and exposure. As the locus from which the subject looks onto and engages the world, the face must initially *expose itself*, beyond what it can know, to the irreducibly other, the alter. Relationality names a radically finite existence that is "exposed" to others even prior to the distinction between inside and outside, self and other.[33] But the spatial metaphor of "exposure," which can help to deconstruct rigid ideas about "purity" or "inside" and "outside," is unable to account fully for what is at stake here in Borges' text. After all, relations do not just happen: as exchanges, as demarcations of the past and introductions of a possible future, they must also be assumed.

Another key element in this consideration is the "gaucho extático" of the final scene, who presents a further difficulty for interpretation. As I noted earlier, the archaic gaucho is described as a cipher worn smooth by use and repetition. The phrase used by Borges' text—"los muchos años lo habían reducido y pulido como las aguas o una piedra o las generaciones de los hombres a una sentencia"—has to be read more than once, while paying attention to the terms of repetition, generation (in two senses), historicity and the dual function of speech act (performative/poietic and constative/ juridical: *sentencia* is an aphorism and a juridical decision or judgment in addition to the colloquial meaning of "sentence"). This gaucho, which the text names as a key to the South, embodies an irruption of the real, an "ahistorical" kernel that recurs throughout the history of the gauchesque genre. At this point in the story, the presence of this archaic gaze is the only element distinguishing the narrative from a "realistic" narrative, and it thus serves as a reminder of the always-partial nature of any particular interpretation. Its uneasy presence in the text suggests both a parody and a renewal of the gauchesque tradition. Through this metonymical figure, Borges' engagement of the gauchesque offers itself as but one reading among others: a brilliant reading perhaps, but not the reading to end all readings. As a cipher, the gaucho is an auto-inscription in the text of literary language as *potens*. But this gesture of literature referring to itself is also what could be termed an alter-inscription: an inscription of "the other of literature." I have already suggested one way in which this phrase "the other of literature" might be heard (see the preceding discussion of Ludmer's critique of Borges). A broader consideration of Borges' oeuvre, however—and I am thinking in particular of "Pierre Menard"—would also enable us to relate this phrase to a material facet of literary language, or to what Borges elsewhere describes as the peculiar latency that language presents for history. Strictly illegible or incomprehensible in thematic terms, the gaucho is an internal distortion or gap that gives the narrative its cohesion. Borges' text tells the story of meaning constituted by way of repetition and supplementation. The anachronistic gaucho holds the place of an absence that can neither be filled nor signified. This figure stands in for and holds the place of the "lack" of that essential signifier that would close the circuit of the gauchesque in particular, and of Argentine *historias* [histories or stories] in general. And of course, one could say that the nonpresence of this transcendental signified is no lack at all, since what was never present to begin with cannot subsequently become a "lack." The erosion of meaning within modernity is momentarily brought to a halt around this figure, and the text is able to function *as if* it were the account of a completed circuit. The void of which this figure is a shadowy fill-in is neither secondary nor exogenous to the signifying system that is the gauchesque tradition. Rather, as an endogenous limit, it calls attention to the signifier (the South, the nation or *la patria*—or all of these at one time or another) in its inability to *signify itself*. The signifier must always summon yet another signifier in the infinite appeal to the unity of what is not yet one.

"En el suelo, apoyando en el mostrador, se acurrucaba, inmóvil como una cosa, un hombre muy viejo. Los muchos años lo habían reducido y pulido como las aguas a una piedra o las generaciones de los hombres a una sentencia. Era oscuro, chico y reseco, y estaba como fuera del tiempo, en una eternidad" ["On the floor, leaning against the bar, squatted an ancient man, immobile as a thing. The many years had reduced and polished him as water does a stone, or as the generations of men do a sentence. He was small dark, and shriveled up, and seemed to be eternal, as if he were outside of time itself"] (201–2). This portrait, which initially gives appearance to nothing more than a decrepit and loathsome figure, provides the ledger in which we can read what the narrative will soon nominate "a cipher of the South." It is via a back-and-forth movement, between a portrait of decrepitude and the conceptual index of the cipher or key, that the South appears as an object of the protagonist's desire: as that which can only be ascertained as hieroglyph or as empty set. We are told parenthetically that this gaucho pertains to *Dahlmann's* South ("del Sur que era suyo"). We might hear in this repetition a warning that the protagonist's relation to this motif has undergone a certain shift in the course of his journey, and that the material difference at the heart of the traumatic encounter on the staircase, the excess and opacity, as what always remains to be deciphered in the look of the other, reappears here as a possible opening toward the other. Could the disparity between the two enunciations of *el Sur*—between *el Sur* and *el Sur que era suyo*—allude to the possibility of this opening? In other words, might the phrase *el Sur que era suyo*, rather than describing a property or a subjective impression, instead name a primordial debt of the subject, a temporality and an obligatedness into which the subject is thrust prior to knowing to whom or to what the decision is owed, but which must be assumed nonetheless? This thought of an incommensurable debt could render a different inflection of the classical motif of destiny, thereby turning toward the past in effort to signify its difference anew and at the same time acting to delimit tradition as "permanence." This notion of destiny no longer envisions history or inheritance as the ground of self-identity. Rather, it underlines a need to act that remains both irreducible to calculation and irremediably caught up in the violence of existence; it addresses an exigency which issues precisely *within* and not despite the opacity of tradition (this is the thought of a profound errancy in Borges' reflection on inheritance). This imperative is a sort of call to arms, but it is also a summons to language which, in placing a limit upon what is possible, gives shape to possibility—that is, the possibility of engaging the other. As Jacques Derrida writes in relation to another thinker of the human face as site of radical relationality, "Speech is doubtless the first defeat of violence, but paradoxically, violence did not exist before the possibility of speech. The philosopher (man) *must* speak and write within this war of light, a war in which he always already knows himself to be engaged; a war which he knows is inescapable, except by denying discourse, that is, by risking the worst violence" ("Violence and Metaphysics" 117). The act of decision, introducing itself as a signifier into the world it delimits, gives itself over to a labor of death. At the same time, insofar as it gives place to the limit, it is also the advent of life.

3
Exígele lo nuestro: Transition and Restitution in Rulfo's *Pedro Páramo*

> *Une mimesis ouvre la fiction du ton. C'est la tragédie du "Viens" qui doit être répétable (a priori répété en lui-même) pour résonner. Rien ne garantit la bonne intonation, celle-ci reste à la disposition et sous la responsabilité de l'autre.*
>
> [A mimesis opens the fiction of tone. The tragedy of "Come" is that it must be repeatable (a priori repeated in itself) in order to resonate. Nothing guarantees good intonation, which remains at the disposal and as the responsibility of the other.]
> —Jacques Derrida, *Les Fins de l'homme*

ALTHOUGH HIS PUBLISHED LITERARY WORKS CONSIST OF LITTLE more than a collection of short stories (*El llano en llamas*, 1953) and a novella (*Pedro Páramo*, 1955), the Mexican writer Juan Rulfo is generally recognized as one of the major figures in twentieth-century Latin American letters and an important influence for the "Boom" novelists of the 1960s and 70s. Carlos Fuentes finds in Rulfo's work "not only the highest expression achieved so far in the Mexican novel . . . [but also] a thread that leads us into the new Latin American novel, and to its relation with the so-called international crisis of the novel."[1] One of Rulfo's major contributions to Latin American literature is to have helped bring to a close the naturalist aesthetic that dominated during the first decades of the twentieth century. Rulfo's juxtaposition of "popular" and "literary" idioms is often regarded as having the prepared the way for a subsequent generation of Latin American writers, including Fuentes and Gabriel García Márquez, whose highly sophisticated and self-consciously literary works definitively establish Latin America as a producer—and no longer just a consumer—of universal culture. I will argue, however, that Rulfo's work also calls into question traditional views about literature and its role in the historical development of a people or culture. If the Western tradition generally thinks of culture as a collective good, an archive of shared knowledge, memories and values, then literature in turn is thought to preserve, display and disseminate these cultural goods. In this tradition, modern literature is frequently held to exemplify and disseminate the idea of the modern state.[2] But if we attempt to place Rulfo's oeuvre within a genealogy of Latin American cultural production, with a view to understanding how his writing contributes to the emergence of an autonomous national or regional tradition, we find that what Fuentes regards as the threshold also announces the impossibility of tradition. At the very moment that Latin American literature establishes an authentic expression of its own particular truth—and thus, by extension, assumes an active position in the global cultural market that is no longer relegated to consuming and producing bad copies of European works—at this very moment, the autonomous poetic act exposes a crisis situation in which the possibility of literature, or of its capacity to represent truth or essence, is profoundly shaken.

The notion of "modernity" will play a key role in my discussion of Rulfo's work, in the dual context of literary history and societal transition. My use of the term "modernity" is intended to be descriptive and not normative; nonetheless, my own usage cannot entirely avoid the teleological and Eurocentric connotations that frequently accompany this term. I do, however, hope to show how Rulfo's work helps to mark the limit of these ideological narratives. Moreover, in alluding to a tension between (socioeconomic) *modernization* and (aesthetic) *modernism* in Mexico, I do not mean to imply that such a thing as a fully self-identical modernity ever truly arrives here or elsewhere. My use of the term has two related intentions: first, to identify related but contrasting representations of history in center and periphery; and second, to examine the real effects that are produced by the appearance of these symbolic differences in twentieth-century Mexican cultural production. In speaking of modernity, I am attempting to provide a sketch of how literature relates to shared artistic, cultural and political aspirations to contemporaneity, autonomy and the possibility of a new beginning, sentiments which could be heard in the expression "we moderns."

I begin by discussing Rulfo's work in the context of societal transition. My primary concern is not with transition as a thematic concern, but rather with the way that Rulfo's text intervenes in the debates over national culture and identity following the 1910 to 1920 revolution. A number of critics have previously noted Rulfo's tendency to borrow from the classical aesthetic tradition in writing of Mexican modernity.[3] The consequences of this "repetition" or "citation" of classical culture and its tropes are nearly the opposite from what one might expect. The echoes of the classical tradition in *Pedro Páramo* do not provide a bridge between the unprecedented singularity of a certain event—for instance, the Mexican Revolution as spontaneous popular uprising—and a world of order and meaning. On the contrary, in the context of peripheral modernity, these classical symbols attest to their inability—and this is perhaps to say the inability of "literature" in general—to heal the wounds and mend the rifts of history. This "failure" is not merely a negative moment in which literary modernity breaks away from the orbit of literary history. If we follow the logic of Rulfo's narrative, the failure must itself be made part of a history: that is, its story must be told.

My use of tragedy as an interpretive framework for reading *Pedro Páramo* helps to shed light on several related points concerning literary aesthetics and national culture. In arguing for a correspondence between Rulfo's novella and classical tragedy, I suggest that the story of Juan Preciado's journey to Comala and his search for a father he has never known mirrors the structuring dynamics of certain Greek tragedies. As with tragedy, the action is propelled forward by an ongoing interrogation of origins that has both ethical and political implications: Where do I come from? What was there before me? What do others want of me? To whom or to what am I responsible? Likewise, in the hero's attempt to uncover the secret truth of personal, familial and communal histories, the desire for a *proper* (filial, patriarchal, and sanctified) history of how the present order came into being must be reconciled with an obscene crime at the origin of the law. In other words, the order of law must be reconciled with what the law itself makes unthinkable or unknowable. Like classical tragedy, Rulfo's novella is a story of strife between two orders or "worlds"—in Rulfo's case, the domains of tradition and modernity, or colonialism and the nation-state—whose temporalities and codes are at first glance irreconcilable with one another. Tragedy evinces an umbilical connection between these otherwise incommensurable worlds. My interest in investigating such a link between Rulfo's novella and tragedy extends beyond these various thematic resonances, however, and includes a consideration of the formal relation between literature and the organization of social spaces such as the modern nation-state. In this respect, my use of tragedy is modal rather than thematically based. However, the echoes of classical forms and themes in Rulfo's work give shape to a literary project that is decidedly *modern* in its conception and tone. In the first chapter I suggested that, since the Greeks, tragedy has historically been regarded as a foundational work par excellence: tragedy represents an event that otherwise exceeds our personal and collective understanding, in a way that makes the event meaningful to a community. Rulfo's writing shares a good deal with this understanding of tragic poetics. One could argue that *Pedro Páramo* is an attempt to render meaningful the violent origins of modern Mexico, not by mirroring the state's monolithic account of national tradition, but instead through a juxtaposition of conflicting histories of domination and perseverance. The novella could thus be seen as an attempt to break the impasse of a suspended modernity in Mexico by enacting a passage from myth to history.[4] Through literary aesthetics, the work would aim at a restitution of the dissymmetries that attend nation-building and modernization processes. It would offer itself as a public "memory" of the violence and forgetting that accompany these historical processes, a memory that at the same time interrupts the asphyxiating cycle of vengeance and internecine warfare and allows the nation to move on. If Rulfo's writing can be described as an attempt to produce (a) history there where there was once only myth, this literary project could also be understood as juxtaposing the postrevolutionary state with what the state by definition represses or cannot recognize: the subaltern and its silent history of domination, exclusion and perseverance. In other words, it is a matter of exposing the statist myth of a "full society" (or a social space that has been cleansed of all contradictions and exclusions) to its secret truth: the subaltern qua originary exclusion.

One of the most persistent views in Rulfo criticism has been that the author stands at the crossroads between "traditional" and "modern" literary traditions. Fuentes, who situates Rulfo at a key point in his genealogy of modern Latin American letters, alludes in the same breath to a crisis or rupture in tradition and to the promise of an absolutely new beginning. This paradoxical juxtaposition of crisis and origin affords one way of understanding what is at stake in the term "modernity": Rulfo's oeuvre, while reproducing some of the most recognizable traits of the regionalist and naturalist traditions, also presents a new form of expression that shatters the realist-naturalist framework of his predecessors.[5] For Fuentes, Rulfo's writing performs a formal synthesis of naturalist and vanguard literary aesthetics, while at the same time merging an autochthonous, regional style with the universal forms of allegory and tragedy.[6] Octavio Paz similarly describes Rulfo's impact on the Mexican tradition in terms of poetic vision: while virtually every Mexican writer in this century has produced a commentary on national identity and revolution, Rulfo is the first to have provided what Paz nominates as an "image," a poetic vision that would provide impetus to the question of what it means to be Mexican and modern.

We can further elucidate the complex question of modernity in Rulfo by contrasting *Pedro Páramo* with the cultural commentary found in Paz's *The Labyrinth of Solitude* (1950). Paz's essay takes as its point of departure an allegorical reflection on the Mexican Revolution, which Paz introduces as a quintessentially modern event. He compares the postrevolutionary nation-state, which has undergone a catastrophic transition from oligarchy to bourgeois democracy, to an adolescent facing a rite of passage into adulthood. This time of transition and uncertainty is also an ethical moment in which the nation confronts the twofold question, "What are we, and how can we fulfill our obligations to ourselves as we are?" (Paz, *Labyrinth of Solitude*, 9). A new dimension opens through this interrogation: it illuminates a new network of relations, of affiliations and responsibilities that could not have been anticipated before, and which at once pass through, bypass and exceed the geopolitical boundaries that constitute Mexico as one nation-state among many. The question situates both nation and modernity within the future structure of a promise: "nation" and "modernity" become synonymous in Paz's thought with a certain autonomy-to-come that would be secured in the synthesis of cultural expression with a gradual overcoming of the historical experience of debt and dependency, inequality, and tyranny. Paz's question is grounded in a notion of modernity as new beginning. But at the same time he acknowledges that the revolution has in many ways failed to live up to this promise of renewal and second origin, and that modern Mexico remains caught up in a fundamental contradiction. "We have an exuberant modernism with a deficient modernization," is one of the central themes of *The Labyrinth of Solitude*. Modernity, understood as an affirmation of political and aesthetic autonomy, or as the culmination of a people's project of self-realization through literature, remains only partially imprinted in the case of Mexico. Whence the central irony of Paz's text: the flourishing of "modernism," of a newly emergent field of cultural production that has put an end to Mexico's historical dependency upon imported (French) cultural, exists in stark contrast to the chronic shortcomings of socioeconomic modernization and the failure of postrevolutionary reform measures.[7]

This diagnosis of an incomplete modernity masks another Pazian supposition, one that would place Paz well within the conflict he attempts to describe: the notion of a partial, bad modernity, one that is underway but not yet accomplished, is governed by the unstated premise that artistic production can somehow compensate for, rectify or redeem the disaster of modernization in Mexico. I will term this view "compensatory modernism."[8] The question orienting Paz's inquiry is subject to an originary division, which we might today describe as a tension between performative and constative potentialities of the enunciation of "we moderns." Paz's question presupposes an essential distinction between "high" and "popular" culture, where the former becomes synonymous with an autonomous domain governed by a pair of freedoms: the (aesthetic) freedom of formal innovation, and the (sociopolitical) freedom from external constraints and determinations. Culture, in Paz's view, represents a standing reserve of humanism, in opposition to the homogenizing and dehumanizing forces of socioeconomic modernization, or what is today termed "globalization." By positioning modernism as a compensation for (a lack of) modernization, Pazian culturalism veils its interest in recreating the dissymmetrical conditions in which it emerges.

It is, on the other hand, precisely this idea that art can compensate for the catastrophes of history that Rulfo's writing challenges. *Pedro Páramo*, published five years after Paz's *Labyrinth of Solitude*, similarly offers an allegorical account of the Mexican revolution. And, as we will see, Rulfian allegory likewise underscores the contradictory nature of Mexican modernity. But whereas Paz conceives of modernity as the end (conclusion or telos) of a process in which Mexico has yet to fully realize itself, Rulfo's writing presents modernity as an *antinomy*, as an irreconcilable difference both between modernization and modernist poetics, and between images of cosmopolitan modernity and subalternity. For Rulfo, literary modernism cannot be explained as something occurring despite or in place of a problematic modernization process; paradoxically, literary modernism must be seen to occur alongside or as another facet of this problem. What Paz presented as the aesthetic overcoming of a historical contradiction is shown, in Rulfo, to constitute the two faces of an impasse. In discussing what this antinomy means for literature, I will suggest that its recognition in Rulfo necessitates a far-reaching reexamination of the place and possibilities that remain available to literature.[9]

Rulfo's novella begins by staging a scene strikingly reminiscent of the Pazian analogy of nascent nation and adolescent. We first encounter Juan Preciado through a first-person recollection of his journey to Comala, the town in which he was conceived but from which his mother was exiled prior to his birth. This return to what is tantamount to a primal scene, stages questions about memory, filiation, and identity. The narrator has promised his dying mother that he will seek out the father he has never met, and, in the words of her final injunction, *exígele lo nuestro*, or demand from him what is "ours." This pretext invites us to read the novella as an allegorical treatment of the nation as it seeks to free itself from the vestiges of the colonial epoch and its structures of feudalism, corruption, tyranny, and ownership of the land by the few—all of which are embodied by the figure of Pedro Páramo.[10] However, allegory also forces us to reexamine the progressivist conception of modernity, as we gradually unravel an uncanny homology between the narrator's father, a *cacique*, and the postrevolutionary state. The narrator's speculative return to origins places the issue of birthright, of culture and identity, within a tragic framework: the son's passage into adulthood, in which he seeks a way between the antagonistic and mutually annihilating demands of maternal and paternal lineages, will give rise to an aporia at the heart of personal and national identity. This return prepares something akin to the discovery that confronts Oedipus in his attempt to master the Delphic oracle: the hermeneutic will to mastery strives to include *itself* within its own field of vision by inserting itself retroactively at the scene of its conception. The will to knowledge is forced to confront the limit of its project, which might be termed "fate," "desire" or "errancy," but which in any case cannot be placed definitively within or outside of the speculative mechanism of reason. As we shall see shortly, the impetus for Juan Preciado's search—or what his mother terms "lo nuestro"—is not proper and familiar, but nor can it be termed "improper" in the sense of something that could be dismissed or disowned. The exigency that marks the mother's words is seemingly beyond naming. The hermeneutic process, embodied by the son's search for a father he never knew, must reconcile itself with an errant destiny that both is and is not its own, and through which the designation of "one's own" suffers a cut that both delivers it to its fundamental possibilities while remaining out of reach of knowledge.

Before entering into a detailed discussion of the novella, a brief digression will help to situate the protagonist's return as a commentary on national culture in postrevolutionary Mexico. While Paz's analysis looks to the future as the time in which the nation will realize itself as One, a number of postrevolutionary reflections on national identity have turned an eye toward the past, viewing the 1910 to 1920 revolution as a grand synthesis of discrete historical epochs, or as a suturing of the myriad and discrete "fragments" that comprise the history of the nation. To be sure, the revolution was widely perceived as a just and necessary remedy to the structural inequalities perpetrated under the oligarchical society of Porfirio Díaz (1876–1911). For one, the revolution stakes its legitimacy on the claim that it realizes what independence failed to accomplish: a definitive break with the structure of colonialism, which in many Latin American countries extends well beyond the historical period of Spanish rule. At the same time, the postrevolutionary state presents itself as a unifying force for national history: as the newly-appointed guardian of the nation's archaic past and its millennial traditions, the state would reconcile postbourgeois society with a distant past that would otherwise risk falling into oblivion.

In his analyses of Mexican popular culture, Néstor García Canclini has mapped the dyadic procedure by which the state depends on cultural production as a stabilizing support structure. The increased interest in indigenous and pre-Columbian traditions and iconography following the revolution—a tendency strongly promoted by statist institutions—is far from a simple, disinterested hearkening back to an earlier time. This renewed interest in the past in fact constitutes an *invention of tradition* that operates in the interests of the state.[11] The state's claim to have recovered and preserved the past in its meaning or value serves as a pretext for this (re)production process: behind the image of a restored national tradition unfolds a second space, a space that will in turn be occupied by the state—which henceforth proclaims its legitimacy as curator, protector, and guarantor of this inheritance. The state's role is that of a fabulist, projecting a field of legibility in which the failures and limitations of the present moment can be passed off as merely temporary and epiphenomenal, a necessary collective sacrifice in the process of realizing what the historian Héctor Águilar Camín terms "the true Mexico . . . the one that had not yet appeared and was to be conquered in the future" (Águilar Camín and Meyer, *In the Shadow of the Mexican Revolution*, 159).

As the curator of tradition, the state simultaneously justifies and effaces its presence. It legitimates its own existence as well as the dissymmetries it permits and propagates on the dual basis of a past to be recovered and a future to be realized. At the same time, it masks the fact that it only represents certain particular interests by passing itself off as universal law of necessity. A crucial sleight of hand relegates social negativity—that is, the moments of loss, violence, uncertainty and contingency that are part of any national history—to a merely temporary, accidental existence, or to a condition that the nation, thanks to the uplifting power of the state, will some day surpass. Through its orchestration of cultural production, the state posits the *being* of the nation as off-stage, as a reserve—and thus as removed from the transitory nature of history.[12] Cultural production following the revolution was, whether knowingly or not, frequently complicit in these rituals of legitimation. One could examine any number of examples of such complicity between culture and the state: for instance, with the rise of Muralism in the 1920s, which often claimed to realize a harmonious unification of the pre-Columbian symbolic world with revolutionary and modernizing projects; or, similarly, in the essay tradition founded by Samuel Ramos, José Vasconcelos, Alfonso Reyes, and Paz, which envisioned and celebrated a timeless national character or *mexicanidad* ["Mexicanness"]; and, likewise, with the literary tradition known as *la novela de la revolución* [the Novel of the Revolution], which frequently memorialized the revolution in the form of heroic fables.

The epic accounts of the revolution popularized by Mariano Azuela and others are especially significant for my discussion of how Rulfo engages the questions of national culture and modernity. Antonio Castro Leal, in his two volume anthology of the literature of the revolution (*La novela de la revolución mexicana*), describes this genre as undertaking a transformation of the very concept of *el pueblo* or "the people." According to Castro Leal, the novela de la revolución comprises a kind of collective memory, documenting the "deeds and excesses" of the pueblo, recording both the important transitions—from subjugation to liberty, from the illegality of the *Porfiriato* to the Constitutional government of 1917—while also registering the shortcomings of the revolutionary project: the military defeats of Zapata and Villa, the state's dissipation of radicalized peasant demands, and the cycle of violence, personalism, and vengeance that perpetuates conflict between rival *caudillos*. The epic sentiment found in many postrevolutionary narratives, in which the nation is frequently conceived as a "Whole" or "Work" (albeit frequently one "in progress," or in the process of self-recovery), is complemented by a literary form of mourning. For the novela de la revolución tradition, national autonomy is won at the cost of a wound inflicted upon history. In the well-known example of Azuela's *Los de abajo*, the spontaneous fervor which gave rise to revolution—seemingly *ex nihilo*—makes its return in the destructive form of factional rivalry; and the figure of the liberator recurs, metamorphosed, in that the tyrant, the caudillo or cacique. The tragic confrontation described by the novela de la revolución is of Mexico with itself, opposing revolutionary and democratizing force to the return of reactionary force, and the modernizing aspirations of a new generation to the indelible remainders of a previous epoch, returning over and again in fantasmatic fashion during the proceeding decades. The novela de la revolución thus situates itself at the border of an ontological rift that threatens to engulf the entire emancipatory project: the discourse of liberation and social justice must come to see tyranny and repression as (chronologically and logically) contemporary possibilities, as belonging to this discourse's own time and place, or as possibilities attending the same historical process. The literary representation of national tragedy thereby echoes the civilization/barbarism dyad that governed much of nineteenth-century Latin American thinking. The formal homology between revolutionary/reactionary and civilization/barbarism constitutes a kind of ideological "escape hatch" for the representation of the revolution as tragic: the barbaric impulse that comprises one facet of Mexican history need only be tamed, overcome or converted through a greater exertion of national effort, through enhanced cultivation and pedagogical focus, and so on.[13]

The Exigency of *lo nuestro*: Deconstruction, Restitution and the Limits of the Proper

I will begin by examining the first two "fragments" of *Pedro Páramo*, which provide a point of departure for the text's engagement with postrevolutionary national culture. The first pages of the novella establish the pretext mentioned above: the protagonist promises his dying mother that he will journey to Comala in search of his father, and that he will vindicate his mother's own memories of Comala as a place of abundance. However, these first pages also prepare us for the novella's exposition of "national culture" and the discourse of mexicanidad as an ideological veil, a screen that permits us to avoid looking at the contradictions and uncertainty at the origin of national identity.[14] In contrast to literary apotheoses of the revolution, in Rulfo's writing this event looms as a historical rupture. While the protagonist's "return" to an origin in which he has never yet set foot is clearly set in the postrevolutionary era, and much of the town's history is inscribed in the events leading from the Porfiriato to the modern state, the revolution itself is scarcely mentioned (the sole exceptions are two passages recalling Pedro Páramo's encounter with counterrevolutionary *Cristero* soldiers). It is my contention that this "silence" with respect to the revolution should be interpreted as a strategic move on Rulfo's part, as if the insight he were seeking could only become available by assuming an oblique angle to the topic in question, or by viewing the event awry.

For Rulfo, the revolution is unable to provide any guarantee about the future, or to ensure a safe and proper passage into a new state of being. As absolute suspension and scission, revolution can only play itself out by inaugurating a time of transition, which is both an experience of nascent emergence (*nātiō*, the Latin root of "nation," means both a people and a birth) and a moment of destitution, of being orphaned and thrown into the unknown. In my view, the narrative strategy of Rulfo's novella thus invites us to interpret the figure of the tyrant, the caudillo or cacique, as a transitional and liminal figure—and as a kind of prosthesis covering up a traumatic wound. Let us recall the first pages of Paz's *The Labyrinth of Solitude* for their paradigmatic sketch of postrevolutionary discourse on national identity. Paz reminds us that the act of narration, which must account for both the origin and the present in which one speaks, is fundamental to the self-presentation of any national subject. In other words, the problem of national identity in Mexico is irreducibly linked to language and representation. The postrevolutionary discourse on national identity, in its attempt to secure a sense of national unity (we Mexicans are united insofar as we can tell ourselves who we truly are), produces a redoubling of the Mexican into a reflecting subject and a reflected object. With Rulfo, this reflection will introduce a series of interwoven and unsettling questions about the nation-building process, and consequently about the status of identity itself. We have already glimpsed how the staging of identity gives shape to a question of justice, expressed as the maternal demand for restitution. As we will now see, this demand in fact articulates the time and space of togetherness and solidarity ("lo nuestro") as at once excessive and limited, or as "out of joint." Moreover, the *lapsus* that afflicts "lo nuestro" is the errancy of community and shared meaning, and thus cannot be grasped and categorized once and for all by any particular reading.

The demand is simultaneously proscriptive and prescriptive, conveying on one hand an exigency that must not be relinquished while retaining on the other a fundamental opacity: "No vayas a pedirle nada. Exígele lo nuestro. Lo que estuvo obligado a darme y nunca me dio. . . . El olvido en que nos tuvo, mi hijo, cóbraselo caro" ["Don't go asking him for anything. Demand what is ours. What he was obliged to give me and never did. . . . Make him pay, my son, for the way he forgot us"]. These dying words constitute a threshold and a cipher for the text. The juxtaposition between injunction (exact from him what is ours) and prohibition (do not plead; do not demean us any further and thereby elevate him all the more) gives some indication of the degree to which the restitutive demand suffers from an excess and a split. The tonality of this charge points at once toward the necessary and the impossible, or perhaps in the direction of something exigent yet incapable of being fully articulated.

Of course, we should hear this demand as resonating within the tradition of popular struggle in Mexico over the land and its usage and ownership. In this light, "lo nuestro" designates not a possession but rather an *ought*, an injustice that remains to be redressed. We should recall that, in Mexico, the history of nation-building and modernization is also that of repeated appropriations of land by the elite. The ethical or political force of the mother's injunction, then, pertains to the signifier and not the signified: the possessive phrase "lo nuestro" aims beyond the usurpation or reappropriation of a good, a property or a right. What is most exigent here is not just a symbolic restitution—of a name, a title or a particular good—but instead an intervention *in the symbolic itself*. If we are to take popular, collective struggle as one likely index for this passage, the enunciation of a collective ("lo nuestro") would be found to have immediately redoubled as a question about the very principles of ownership and right—and thus to suspend any suspicion that this demand simply calls for the return of the same.

I will return to the issue of restitution shortly. First, an additional point needs to be made concerning this pronouncement of lo nuestro. This phrase sustains a palpable tension between urgency and ambiguity, the insistent and the indefinite. The semantic indeterminacy of the pronoun lo nuestro suggests that this phrase calls for something other than an exchange or a return. We might wonder whether this demand does not mark a limit in the pursuit of justice, insofar as the thought of redress also brings forth the possibility of the impossibility of representation, the seeming futility—and, moreover, the impropriety—of attempting to provide this "ours" with a determinate content. In other words, what has been lost in this history of expropriation and domination may well include the possibility of describing or accounting for the loss itself: the loss is beyond measure, or it is the very loss of measure itself. The text will maintain a prolonged silence over the specificity of lo nuestro, and this reticence produces a form of hermeneutic unease: is its meaning singular and therefor incapable of being translated into the general terms of exchange value or distributive justice? Or does silence here portend a more originary experience of emptiness and alienation, to which the demand itself might belong? Does this speech, which issues from a site of destitution, invite us to pose philosophical questions about community, identity and the limits of restitution? Or does it stand at the very limit of the philosophical mode of questioning? Perhaps the radical demand resonating in the maternal injunction is that we are to read its letter ("exact from him what is ours") *not* as a metaphor for something ephemeral, abstract or beyond language. What if, on the contrary, it insists on being read absolutely literally, in the sense of finding (out) what is ours?

The first half of the novella is structured by a tragic dynamic which links identity to crime. The narrator's pursuit of the father he has never met is literally a staging of a primal scene. But the narrator's "return" to Comala does not lead to the recovery of an originary, more truthful state of being: rather, the restitutive endeavor he undertakes seeks to *produce* a set of circumstances which have never before existed. Juan Preciado is akin to the nation itself as it emerges from revolution and promises itself to its modernity, to a time in which a lasting accord would finally be reached between the present and its violent, fragmented history. Rulfo's novella thus stages a parable of postrevolutionary modernization: it tells of the return to and recovery of a shadowy time prior to the birth of the nation. In Rulfo's text, however, the profit to be gained from this specular return is displaced by the knowledge it yields: the Juan Preciado who arises to tell his story is not the "same" as the one who set out in search of his father. This is what Rulfo demonstrates in rewriting the history of the revolution as allegory of caciquismo. The tragic endeavor by which national culture seeks retroactively to incorporate its own scene of conception is mirrored by a second movement, likewise tragic, which displaces the grounding principle of the first. The initial return on Juan Preciado's search for the recognition of his father arrives when he learns that the father is already dead. The filial quest began with an unspoken paternal identification whose projection served as its explicit telos: in effect, the narrator must already have identified with the (name of the) Father in order to identify with (the notion of identifying with) this particular father. But the history of Pedro Páramo—he is or was a cacique who, we gather from the words of the narrator's first guide, has in fact fathered a majority of the town—indicates that this desired identification is in fact impossible. The quest for paternal recognition, based on the narrator's own identification with the paternal law of filiation, would also be obligated to identify with an obscene crime at the origin of the law.

This second tragic dynamic, which marks the limit of the "recognition" paradigm, is sustained up until the narrator's death at the midway point in the novella, at which point the textual production of knowledge is discovered to have undergone a second important shift in its mode of presentation. At the midpoint, the text's enunciative position places the interrogation of identity in an allegorical locus.[15] Throughout the first half of the narrative, we encounter a series of reversals in which the narrator meets various residents of the village, only to eventually discover that each is in fact a ghost. This repeated conflation of the dead with the living culminates in the discovery (it is his as well as ours) that the narrator too is already dead. The narrator's postmortem testimony that inaugurates the second half of the novella at once repeats and displaces the tragic theme of filial origins. It reports a confrontation with the limits of knowledge, and with the sublime (and perhaps obscene) existence of what cannot be made present, of what cannot be elucidated under the light of being and the patronymic logos.

Despite Rulfo's declared preference for an economy of simplicity, *Pedro Páramo* is one of the most difficult texts in the Latin American canon. Many of the interpretive problems arising in a first reading can be attributed to the fragmentary character of the narrative. Crucial shifts in time, place, and narrative voice often take place unannounced and must be pieced together after the fact. At the same time, the textual production of images remains shrouded in darkness: along with Juan Preciado, we encounter Comala through a profoundly opaque lens. Does this world flee from our gaze, refusing to reveal to us its true nature? Or does the refusal of our interpretive vision precisely constitute the truth of Comala? In view of both the extreme poverty of the Rulfian landscape and the myriad hermeneutic problems that confront us in approaching this text, reading could itself be described as undergoing an experience of blindness. The opacity of Rulfo's images, together with the hollowing out of the visible field, testify jointly to a tragic connection between theoretical sight and blindness, between self-reflection and the limits of knowledge. The foreclosure of the image's plenitude and the repeated short-circuiting of interpretation leaves the reader in a state of uneasy premonition. In groping his or her way through Comala, the reader is repeatedly made to experience the proximity of the unknowable or the unpresentable. The reduction of the visible in *Pedro Páramo* reiterates the interpretive problem posed in the opening passage: the palpable uncertainty as to "what is ours" opens onto a form of responsibility that precedes any possible knowledge of exactly "to whom" or "to what" one is obligated. Responsibility names an opening which in turn demands a reply; but it only *becomes* this opening through the return or the folding back that is the initiation of the reply.

The "blindness" that accompanies the narrator's return signals an aporia in the hermeneutic search for self-knowledge, illustrated in his impossible testimony that brings the first half of the novella to a close: "Sí, Dorotea. Me mataron los murmullos" ["Yes, Dorotea. The murmurs killed me"]. This elliptical affirmation is spoken from Juan Preciado's grave, which he shares with Dorotea, one of his guides in Comala. The prevailing sense of obscurity is here revealed to have a basis in the scene of narration itself. Juan Preciado's words are the hinge upon which operates a *peripeteia*: following this affirmation, in which the narrator for the first time names Dorotea as the true addressee, the reader is compelled to return to the beginning of the *relato*, to the first words spoken by the narrator as he sought to justify himself: "Vine a Comala porque . . ." ["I came to Comala because . . ."]. In the thirty-some passages leading up to the words "me mataron los murmullos," literary convention has allowed us to presume that the narrator's relato is naturally directed to "us." These six postmortem words, however, reveal retroactively that all along it has been Dorotea—and not we the readers—who represented the true addressee. This untimely displacement of the reader calls attention to the function of *misrecognition*, a groundless act of appropriation and self-insertion, on the basis of which it was possible to begin reading in the first place. This hermeneutic rupture is akin to what was earlier described in Hölderlin's reflection on the tragic caesura: a decisive break in the rhythm of poetic verse coinciding with an irreversible shift in the hermeneutic direction of the narrative.[16] The erroneous appropriation, however, can only be recognized after the fact and on the basis of what it has produced or yielded in the way of understanding—and so, like the tragic peripeteia, the error is irreversible and belongs to an underlying structure of errancy. Misunderstanding cannot be separated from the textual mechanism that produces legibility. In order to "understand" it will have been necessary to misunderstand, to appropriate as "our own" a message addressed to another or to the Other—which is to say no one in particular, to the dead or the dead-letter office. The act of sending, dispatching, or addressing thus reveals a political consequence: the radical "impropriety" at the origin of communication, address, and understanding—"impropriety" before any possibility of the proper—underscores the anarchic basis of agency. Reception constitutes a groundless act, a decision that *must* be undertaken (to refuse to read would likewise constitute a decision of reading) prior to the certainty of destination.

Let us now return once more to the maternal demand. The phrase "exígele lo nuestro" forms a threshold for the text's consideration of the question of modernity. By establishing an analogue between the narrator's journey to Comala and postrevoluntionary reflection on national identity, Rulfo's text initiates a labor of deconstruction, which would both engage and mark a limit for the various treatises on mexicanidad. The fantasy of an archaic paradise which the mother conveys to the narrator will at a certain point prove to be nothing other than a phantasm covering over a site of alienation and disillusionment. Rulfo's text repeats or echoes the myth of lost plenitude; but in so doing it reveals the complicity of this national mythologeme with the self-affirmation project of the modern state.

The movement between two tragic threads in Rulfo thus initiates the deconstruction of the state's claim upon tradition, and in this manner the text sets its sights on a mystery—the story of a crime—at the origin of the law.

At the same time, the suggestion that Rulfo's text points to or invites a "deconstruction" of state reason must itself be subjected to scrutiny. While the labor of re-marking and demystification provides much of the critical thrust for Rulfo's project, interpretation must also find *itself* implicated in the very movement of delimitation it attempts to map (and I in turn include my own reading in this gesture of bracketing). If the nexus of tragedy and allegory enables us to trace the limits of various culturalist appropriations of mexicanidad, reading must not remain deaf to the lesson it imparts: that *no* discourse, including deconstruction, can provide a total and conclusive account of its own origin without at the same time displacing or regenerating the very limit for which it attempts to account. A reading of the novella as critique of systematic authority—be it the system of state power or that of positivist will to knowledge—must also reckon with a demand for justice whose emergence cannot be fully and satisfactorily accounted for by the format of a critique. This call leaves open the possibility of solidarity ("lo nuestro" could refer to any or all who have suffered under caciquismo) that operates under the banner of the proper name. The maternal injunction, I have argued, gives a name to something foreign or irreducible to the genus of systematic organization. It is thus, strictly speaking, undeconstructable. The exigency of the demand indicates a redoubling of the demand itself: this appointment calls for a restitution which, if we take the act of narration seriously, cannot be separated from the act of speaking or rendering an account of oneself. That is to say, the demand would hold the other—Pedro Páramo—accountable by calling upon him to make an account. Or, similarly, we could say that the mother's demand is that there be another demand, that the son *demand* (both in the sense of insisting and asking) of the father. A tension thus arises, at the threshold, between a pair of discourses that I now name deconstruction and restitution.

Between two possible readings of Rulfo, each of which could be described as inevitable and irrefutable in its own right, a limit emerges. The exigency I have been discussing is named and transferred, from mother to son, from text to its possible reading, and each by way of something that cannot readily be brought into the framework of representation or demonstration. The transfer makes each of these discourses—and this is perhaps ultimately to say, reading itself—possible, only to reemerge as the *impossibility* of each discourse, or of reading itself. Let me be clear: this is the impossibility of deconstruction itself, its inability to come fully to terms with its own scene of production, and thus to have had the last word over, for instance, the politics of identity and restitution. Deconstruction finds itself in a position of incommensurable indebtedness with regard to this spoken limit: reading remains responsible to this liminal passage, which it can neither outstrip and move beyond nor account for in each of its possibilities. And thus it finds itself repeating the very gesture it set out to re-mark.

Deconstruction seizes an injunction such as this pronouncement over lo nuestro, and in working it over demonstrates the paradoxical structure and undecidable kernel that haunts the discourse of restitution. Deconstruction points to an impasse or an aporia, a limit that both is and is not proper to this language: the "we" that has been evoked as the subject of this exacting demand is not yet a *we*, it is not the being-in-communion-with-itself that is imagined by nationalism or identity politics. But in underscoring the textuality and performative character of this injunction, deconstruction itself has already become caught up in the very demand upon which it would seek to comment. The deconstructive reading owes itself to this limit, which it passes over repeatedly without getting any closer to relinquishing or resolving it.

The mother's demand cannot conceal its "groundlessness" because its object is not now and never has been of the order of "the proper" (such as, for example, a demonstrable property right). But, then again, the mother's speech also reveals that the decision called for *cannot not* be grounded: its recipient is held responsible and is summoned to action prior to the time of representation, prior to the self-certain knowledge of to whom or to what one is responsible in the address. A response or decision in the face of this demand necessarily enters into irreducible uncertainty, without which it would be a purely formulaic and mechanistic application of rules (and hence no decision at all). And yet, in a different but related sense, the decision must always have been decided beforehand—claimed and incised—in order to become what it is: a decision. There can be no decision, no initiation of a search, that has not already found or been encountered by that which it seeks.

The mother's dying words name memory, justice and restitution as the possible terms and conditions of her demand. To recall the mother—and, as we see from the recurrent interpolations of maternal desire and nostalgia in Juan Preciado's narrative, his journey to Comala, despite all pretenses to the contrary, never ceases to do precisely that: this narrative is also a monumental gesture constructed to a nexus of archaic unity and originary loss—to recall the mother is to confront the impossible weight of this restitutive injunction. How to demand of the father one-knows-not-what (only that it is "ours"), and in a language of accounting that is precisely that of the–dead–Father? The tropological threads have become thoroughly entangled here. If the pretext of return, which would amount to remembrance or recovery of the maternal or communal "thing," must proceed by way of this impossible demand, does not this charge also call on the son to break the maternal bond and expose the primordial "thing" to the travail of naming, to what is *ours*—though not in the form of a property? If the narrator is to live up to his mother's dying words, he must also take leave of the mother, put her in the ground or "kill" her once again, in order to then pass into the world of the Name—a world which, as we already know, pertains to the dead Father. Is the demand therefore like what Hegel would call the movement of spirit? Does it point to a paternal and speculative birthright whose logic mandates that it must be assumed or supposed on the basis of a "rational faith," over against the empirical evidence of maternal origin? What exactly is being said in this demand? "*Demand* from him what is ours"? "Demand from him what is *ours*"? "Demand from him, *what is ours*?!"?

The Temporalities of Epochal Transition: Transculturation and Modernity

Relatively little has been said in Rulfo criticism about the possible ramifications of the author's much-discussed stylistic innovations for Latin Americanist thought. I will suggest that Rulfo's formal experimentation links literary aesthetics to a consideration of both history and historical rupture in the periphery. The nostalgic-depressive tone that dominates *Pedro Páramo* gives shape to a reflection on peripheral modernity as a suspension between times.[17] Such a resonance between tonal and thematic registers would appear to offer a new way of looking at the relation between literature, cultural modernity and socioeconomic modernization. Rulfian aesthetics initiates a kind of antipoetics in which literary language gradually disrupts or dissolves the bond that Paz envisions between aesthetics and the forces of sociopolitical assimilation and development. Instead of idealizing or monumentalizing these historical processes, literature assumes the dual task of dispelling the aura of inevitability surrounding any particular ideological formation, while seeking to render visible the violence and contingency of all social organization. In this section, I will examine the relation between Rulfo's writing—insofar as it is generally viewed as a stylized modernist poetics—and the work of delimiting the universal claims made, for instance, by the modern state.

Let us begin by noting one of the central tenets of literary modernism: the modernist affirmation of literature's formal autonomy is based on the assumption that literature, as it emerges from its economic dependency on the aristocracy, inaugurates a new democratic space: a space in which it is possible, at least in principle, to say anything. A similar hope for a "literary" democracy helps to shape the horizon of postrevolutionary intellectual circles in Mexico: not only does the transition from oligarchy to bourgeois society herald new possibilities for literary innovation, but this emancipation of literature is itself one of the sine qua nons of democracy for postrevolutionary Mexican intellectuals.[18] But Rulfo's text invites us to reconsider the relation between freedom, speech, and democracy that is at the basis of the historical emergence of modernism. The questions of literary autonomy and democracy must be submitted to two competing tendencies in Rulfo's writing: regionalism and cosmopolitanism. We will see how the emergence of these questions is further elucidated by reference to Ángel Rama's theory of transculturation. At the same time, Rulfo's treatment of the problems of societal transition and cultural translation in the periphery will lead me to critically reexamine Rama's thesis—or at least the standard readings it has received over the past two decades. Paraphrasing Shoshanna Felman, we could say that Rulfo's text and Rama's thesis will be seen to *implicate* one another.[19]

In helping to reveal a certain dissymmetry between socioeconomic processes (modernization) and literary aesthetics (modernism) in Mexico, Rulfo's text poses unsettling questions about the event of societal transition. Rather than offering a literary treatise on modernity, Rulfo's literary treatments of the transition period in both *Pedro Páramo* and *El llano en llamas* reflect on modernity as a problem of representation: that is, they suggest that modernity as event might not be presentable as such.[20] I will thus refer to "transition" as a theoretical index rather than as an empirically verifiable occurrence. As a theoretical notion, "transition" names both the emergence of a new order and the erasures carried out through nation-building and modernization processes. It can be understood in the historical context of class-based, ethnic, communal and regional alliances, divisions, and antagonisms—all of which inform and are in turn affected by the emergence and naming of a new democratic and "revolutionary" order. I have already suggested that Rulfo's writing sheds light on an uneasy juxtaposition between, on the one hand, an increasing tendency toward aesthetic innovation in Mexico and elsewhere in Latin America, and the chronic problems of inequity, corruption, and tyranny on the other hand—problems that are at best glossed over and in many cases intensified in the implementation of modernization programs throughout the region. This dissymmetry compels us to look beyond progressive or sequential models for describing how transition takes place and is (or is not) registered through cultural production. If transition becomes visible as a literary topos in Rulfo—and this remains a question: *if* the event as event can be submitted to representation—it would take the form of a sedimentation of discrete cultural and epistemological forms and attitudes that are not necessarily compatible or reconcilable with one another. Paradoxically, Rulfo's writing traces transition in Mexico as a lapsus: as a suspension of time or as a "temporality" of suspension. The key notion of suspension does not simply mean that Mexico requires a different model of history to be opposed to the Eurocentric paradigm of linear progression—indeed, to pose this as a difference between "progression" and "suspension" is already to buy into Eurocentrism's reigning logic of opposition. Rather, the difference I am attempting to indicate with the term "suspension" is a kind of tension—possibly nondialectical in nature—between epochs (the Greek epokhē precisely signals a suspension). Thus, the event of transition, on which hinges the very possibility of a future, is also a kind of epochal syncope that gives notice of the impending, disastrous collapse of a world. Within this knot of conflicting possibilities and danger, transition marks both an originary coalescence of forces and an equally primordial dissemination of effects. A close reading of Rulfo's text will discover that any interpretive strategy grounded in historicism, any attempt to reduce history to a mere sequence of occurrences—for example, the progression leading from colonialism, the War of

Independence, the liberal reforms of 1857, through the *Porfiriato* and culminating in the revolution of 1910 to 1920—will find itself haunted by what has repeatedly failed to take shape or been foreclosed in this history. Thus, while Paz's national hero emerges from the revolution with an eye toward the future, Rulfo's national subject enters into modernity with a different disposition: by turning back toward the past, toward a difference that remains to be thought in all inheritance.

In his book *Transculteración narrativa en América Latina*, Ángel Rama offers a new model for interpreting the history of Latin American cultural production. His theory of transculturation, borrowed from the Cuban ethnographer Fernando Ortiz, is an attempt to free Latin Americanist critical thinking from its historical Eurocentric biases. Most importantly, Rama seeks to implement Ortiz's thinking about cultural transition in colonial contexts, a theory based on the premise that colonial encounters involve something other than a simple "acculturation" of subservient groups to the traditions of the dominant group. Rama discusses a number of cases in which Latin American writers such as Rulfo, Arguedas, and Asturias borrow from the Western tradition in order to describe and respond to the specificity of local circumstances. In particular, transculturation seeks to explain how what are generally regarded as subaltern, indigenous, or non-Western perspectives are integrated into cultural production processes whose essential determination is a Western model: the modern nation-state. While indicating that the one-way street described by acculturation theory is in fact more complicated and less unidirectional than it might appear, Rama's thesis also reconsiders a number of key concepts—including agency, repetition and change—in cultural anthropology's account of historical encounter between cultures. In the place of the bad (passive and peripheral) copies of good (active and central) originals envisioned by acculturation theory, Rama seeks to show how secondary and peripheral production yields memories and forms of knowledge that are irreducible to classical models of truth (such as the Platonic distinction between copies and original). In reading Rama, we can emphasize one of two different points or "moments," with considerably different consequences. First, the theory of transculturation can be shown to describe how certain authors or literary works function as "mediators" during the transition from colonialism to the modern nation-state. Literary negotiations between different ethnic perspectives and cultural forms (for instance, the narration of an Andean "tragedy") aim to facilitate transition from colonial conditions and attitudes to the postulated unity of the modern nation. In the second reading, however, Rama's thesis also reveals a potentially more radical dimension, through which transculturation would unsettle the illusory equation between tradition and permanent truth, and thereby disrupt the imaginary field through which the modern nation-state secures its authoritative role as ideal unity of all social differences. This alternative reading, taking advantage of the affinity between "transculturation" and Walter Benjamin's theory of "translation," would note that in reproducing certain aspects of the Western tradition in a context that is not yet fully "Westernized," the peripheral writer in fact alters the meaning of what is appropriated. At the same time, he or she reveals that the monumental "original," the cultural canon itself, is in truth already dead: the original has always already been separated from immanence or self-presence and thus remains essentially lacking, in need of supplementation or translation.[21] In this respect, transculturation bring a critical force to bear both on the history of Eurocentric thinking and on the representation of the nation-state as the necessary and sufficient ground for modern Latin Americanist thinking.

Transculturation seeks to register the event of transition as such, as a passage whose truth is indissociable from the finitude and contingency that lays bare a particular culture at its margins. What is at issue in literary transculturation is not a journey from one more or less stable ground to another, but rather a poetic or literary marking of a fissure: a rift or tear which, seen from a different angle, is also an opening. But transition is not easily subsumed as an object of representation: to give a concise or readily recognizable (that is to say: repeatable) account of transition would be to precisely efface its most important and unsettling features. In Rama's theory, the "work" of transculturation is thus an inherently problematic concept. The transcultural text records the processes of arbitration and suturing through which a particular, contingent sociopolitical paradigm lays claim to the universal stature of a common ground or state. At the same time, transculturation bears witness to the dissolution of this illusory universality. Pulled in both directions and unable to commit itself to either, the transculturating text evinces an enigmatic relation between representation and dissolution or death. While it borrows certain paradigms from metropolitan canons in order to consolidate and institutionalize newly emerging peripheral experiences, it also discovers that this strategic "grafting" can never fully live up to its symbolic mandate. The troubling truth uncovered by transculturation is not that these paradigms, while more or less adequate in their original metropolitan contexts, tend to misrepresent peripheral experiences. Rather, it is that paradigmatic representation *as such*—that is, the very possibility of a truth that could be emulated, applied, or transmitted—is marked in advance by errancy. There can be no tradition, no transmission or translation, prior to the risk that the truth it exemplifies will have been lost; no tradition without the attending possibility of its impossibility.

In a short section of his book, entitled "Regiones maceradas aisladamente" ["Isolated, mortified regions"] (*Transculturación narrativa*, 94–116), Rama presents Rulfo as an example of how the transcultural writer intervenes in the processes of cultural transition and modernization. According to Rama, Rulfo's oeuvre is an attempt to mediate, translate, or render in a poetic manner the encounter between conflicting forces in modern Mexico—a clash which, on historical evidence, threatens the irrevocable annihilation of one or both of these worlds.[22] Rulfo's contribution to the theory of transculturation is to have displaced the literary reflection on "transition" from the usual paradigm of identity and difference, and to make transition appear in the context of language and translation. The topos of transition in *Pedro Páramo* hinges on a series of differences that seem to multiply as we read. One such difference emerges in the contrast between the work's highly stylized, metropolitan style of writing and its projection or simulation of the popular speech of rural Jalisco. The stylized presence of a *voz popular* [popular voice] in Rulfo's writing is an attempt to destabilize the binary division of culture into "high" and "popular" realms. Furthermore, each of these terms—the cosmopolitan as well as the popular—is itself subjected to a certain division or splitting: for instance, between various institutional conceptions of writing (literary, anthropological, bureaucratic) and their respective rationales (aesthetic, scientific, surveillance, etc.), and between the popular traditions of different regions of Mexico (in contrast to much of the country, the popular traditions of Jalisco are not indigenous but predominantly creole).[23] Rama's discussion of Rulfo's intervention in the postrevolutionary debates over national culture also underscores a linguistic turn within Rama's own theory. The reference to Rulfo causes the theory of transculturation to appear increasingly less like a process of integration and adaptation between already established, stable identities, and more as a discursive act, as the praxis of a poiēsis.

Rulfo's contribution to transculturation deals a fatal blow to the culturalist idea of "the original," which comes into view in Rulfo—most notably in the recurrent allusions to the classical tropes of tragedy and allegory—only to have its tropological power suspended or shown to be hollow. The literary citations of numerous canonical tropes in *Pedro Páramo* has the opposite effect of what might be expected: this strategy of borrowing, rather than painting a full, rich portrait of Jalisco in its regional specificity, in fact calls attention to a rupture within the mimetic economy of the transplant. The abundance of classical tropes and metaliterary references in *Pedro Páramo* does not help to map and secure a previously uncharted region, as it seemed to do for the Spanish *Conquistadores*. Rather, the "literary" dimension Rulfo's text evinces the collapse of the distinction between the proper and the improper, the original and the copy. Rulfo's writing takes aim at a point in the original that is already secretly compromised by a kind of impropriety or death. It is no doubt possible to read the ongoing dissolution of subjectivity in Rulfo as a form of pure negation that would ultimately leave nothing intact. My concern, however, is to examine the possibility that the figures of desubjectivization and death are not merely emblems of what Maurice Blanchot would call a high-class nihilism. They should not be confused with the reduction of Latin America to a postmodern cliché that blindly celebrates the subversion of the Western tradition. Instead, I am interested in what happens to the questions of agency and subjectivity when the modern conceptualization of "the subject"—of which the Juan Preciado of the novella's first pages is an exemplary instance—finds itself overtaken by an "experience" of death or finitude. What needs to be worked out here is the question of whether the literary experience of finitude can in some sense—politically, epistemologically, or otherwise—point us toward a different possibility, a new way of relating to and/or thinking about "the other" (or simply, others).

It is by now a commonplace to point out that dominant discourses, in using European paradigms to understand experiences taking place on the periphery, misrepresent the non-European, assigning to "the other" a certain excess or lack (the exotic, the barbaric, etc.) that the European perspective also intuits *in itself* but would prefer to disown. But Rama's theory of transculturation should not be confused with a construction of new, autochthonous paradigms on the basis of which the non-European "other" would finally become visible or present as such.[24] As a mutual implication of European and non-European perspectives, of center and periphery, transculturation involves itself in both the construction and the dissolution of meaning. Its form displays characteristics of both production and translation: the transcultural work would insert itself into the fray as a kind of "third term" between the diametrically opposed center and periphery. In addition to forging a link between opposing positions or perspectives, transculturation addresses a form of *contortion* which, in Rama's words, "asume los desgarramientos y problemas de la colisión cultural" ["assumes the rending problems associated with cultural collision"] (*Transculturación narrativa*, 116). This statement forces us to reconsider the classical view of literature as secondary "reflection" of a reality that precedes it. What would the "assumption" to which Rama refers look like? Transcultural writing attempts to render visible or audible the dissymmetries and fissures that underlie the transfer of languages, models, ideas, resources, and goods from center and periphery. That is, it would bring out into the open those conditions and experiences that the dominant colonial and postcolonial discourses (Eurocentric or nationalist) prefer to keep offstage. The key term *desgarramientos*, derived from the transitive verb *desgarrar* [to rend, tear or rip up], suggests that the object of transculturation has to do with an abrasive and violent historical process, in which one or both traditions risks destruction. But desgarrar can also mean "to cough up," and thus denotes a reflexive, "corporeal" violence which the work assumes and inflicts upon itself. Transcultural literature does not just "describe" the true violence of transition and thereby demystify the "civilizing" pretenses of colonialism and imperialism; it likewise subjects the aesthetic—along with its claim to an ideal state of neutrality above and beyond the strife between particular interests—to a kind of internal distortion. In this sense, the text is both the subject *and* the object of transculturative violence, both the "word" and the "body" of its expression. As "body," the text would become a "symptom" of the historical processes of (post)colonialism. It would signal the return of something disgusting and sickening in the process of cultural assimilation, a nongustable or indigestible remainder within acculturation's digestive economy.[25] Transculturation attests to a long history of violence, of which literature—including the transcultural work itself—is itself a product. But the violence and turmoil in which transculturation finds itself has more than one side. The rending movement of transition is also the opening up of new spaces and possibilities, in which new contact and flows between cultures become possible. Transcultural writing does not aim to naturalize this violence or render it enjoyable through aestheticization. The repetition or reenactment of violence at the textual level seeks to unmask the contradictions or unsymbolized conflicts that attend colonial and neocolonial societies. Or rather, this reflexive movement reveals how what we generally refer to as "social contradictions" are in fact not contradictions at all: the fact that certain dissymmetries are idealized or remain unmarked is a necessary condition for any representation of social unity.[26]

To see what this strange resonance between social antagonism and textual violence might look like, let us now examine the literary indexing of local and regional experience in *Pedro Páramo*. Although Rulfo's novella ostensibly reflects the popular speech patterns of Rulfo's native Jalisco, it does so in a highly stylized and literary manner. Rulfo explains the prominence of "voz popular" in his writing as an attempt to expose cultivated literary language to the oral traditions of the region. Critics have often taken the author's remarks as distinguishing between a "false" (universal literature) and a "true" (local speech) mimesis. In so doing, criticism either overstates the potentiality of these juxtapositions of the lettered and the popular, the written and the oral, or it misses the more radical point of Rulfo's juxtaposition of these discursive modes. A close examination will reveal that Rulfo conceives of literature not as the "mirror" of a particular social reality, but rather as a poiēsis, a production stemming from an encounter with the signifier. It is simply not the case that Rulfo replaces a false (literary) language with a true (lived) language; the manifestations of "voz popular" at certain points in the novella are every bit as literary (fictive, fabricated) as the recognizably "expressionistic" prose.

A fault line of sustained fabrication underlies the Rulfian text. This rift has too often been ignored or downplayed in critical appraisals of Rulfo's relation to regionalism. In an often cited interview with Joseph Sommers, Rulfo describes his prose as an attempt to convey "the language of the people" for what it is: a spoken rather than written expression.[27] The author claims to transcribe an economy and rhythm of speech that presided in this rural area at the time of the revolution, and which reflected social practices dating back to the time of the conquest, when the region was populated by

Spaniards and its indigenous populations displaced or exterminated—but decidedly not assimilated, Rulfo tells us. Many critics have interpreted such authorial statements as proof that this speech reflects a certain popular "spirit," including a concise and transparent thought process as well as a laconic and perhaps melancholic disposition. What is more, these spoken vestiges of archaic life would represent a negation of the dissimulating effects of mimesis (or, in Rulfo's terms, the falsity of "academic" diction) and a return to a time prior to change and artifice, prior to time itself. But the traces of the "popular" in Rulfo's writing are overdetermined by potentially conflicting memories and significations. The popular is *not the elite* (the cultured, the lettered, the cosmopolitan, or the oligarchic); and at the same time—and by virtue of what it is not, on the evidence of its difference vis-à-vis other regional idioms or dialects—it constitutes the sole remaining memory trace corresponding to catastrophic encounter and erasure, and to the nearly invisible and inaudible violence of its origin.

In another interview (this one with Reina Roffé), Rulfo characterizes this "language of the people" in somewhat surprising terms: as a reservedness and even a miserliness that extends beyond speech and affects the entirety of the social and economic practices of the community. "La gente es hermética. Tal vez por desconfianza no sólo con el que va, con el que llega, sino entre ellos. No quieren hablar de sus cosas, de lo que hacen. Uno no sabe a que se dedican. Hay pueblos que se dedican exclusivamente al agio. La gente allí no habla de nada" ["The people are hermetic. They're not only suspicious of outsiders, but even of each other. They don't talk about things. One never knows what they do for a living. There are entire towns that devote themselves to usury. The people there won't talk to anyone"] (Ruffé, *Autobiografía armada*, 43). We find an echo of this peculiar economy of speech in Rulfo's description of his own literary endeavors. While characterizing this regional dialect as the object that gives shape to his writing, he also confesses that the literary process of transcription or translation always somehow misses its mark: "Lo que yo no quería era hablar como un libro escrito. Quería no hablar como se escribe, sino escribir como se habla. . . . Llegar al tratamiento que me he asignado. No es una cuestión de palabras. Siempre sobran, en realidad. Sobran un qué o un cuándo, está un dé o un más de más, o algo así" ["I didn't want to sound like a written book. The strategy I adopted was not to speak as one writes, but to write as one speaks. It's not just a question of words: there's always some left over, an extra *what* or a *when*, an *of* or an *and* too many, or something like that"] (Autobiografía armada, 55). *Llegar al tratamiento que me he asignado*: this promise that links assignation and arrival, is it not the fundamental circuit and impossible task of writing? The designated arrival at the point where one has already assigned and signified oneself in advance: this conduit determines the enunciative force of naming or writing as a work of temporalization, giving rise to what will have been the meaning of a given inscription. To name a thing is to assign it an unspecified value; it is to hollow out a space within the totality of a language, a site in which the thing will have found its meaning. The meaning Rulfo assigns to this particular spoken idiom is thus strictly differential: it is based not on an eternal meaning or an unchanging trait (e.g., one that has been in place since the conquest), but rather on a relation to other contemporary signs and assignations. The limit of this transcription of "voice" into writing is not the fact that its duplication might lead to misrepresentation; or fail to give adequate treatment to this or that trait. Rather, the limit of writing's capacity to transcribe this reticent and parsimonious speech is to be found in an *over*-production occurring within reproduction. It coincides with the momentary appearance of representation itself, a surplus or remainder within graphic supplementation.

While the function of the popular in Rulfo is easily conflated, at least at first glance, with the naturalism of earlier generations of Mexican writers, this confusion must both be recognized as inevitable and be renounced at the same time. In my reading, I hope to elaborate on the possible ramifications that this discrepancy holds for the theory of transculturation by remaining at the level where Rama initiates his reflections on cultural mediation. I will argue that Rulfo's writing is concerned with cultural transition as a problem of language, and that the text indicates this problem via a twofold consideration of translation and agency. By arguing for the importance that language brings to bear on these questions, I mean to suggest that transition names an *event*, an occurrence that radically transforms the way in which social space is imagined, configured and signified. As the "origin" of a certain signifying regime, the event's own signification is thus inherently problematic. Transition, then, names an instance of erasure and (re)inscription that only becomes visible after the fact and on the basis of its effects. In Rulfo's case, this time of visibility is the aftermath of revolution, and its cadence the tone of mourning as the text contemplates the modern nation as site of irreparable loss and forgetting.[28]

In order to elaborate how Rulfo's treatment of transition is not reducible to a nihilism, I now briefly to Alberto Moreiras' essay "Trasculturación y pérdida del sentido." Moreiras proposes an interpretation of the negativity or emptiness that characterizes the Rulfian landscape as a transcultural signifier of what he terms "pure loss," an absence that we must somehow learn to reconcile with subjective or cultural agency (again, it is not a matter of privileging "loss" over "subjectivity," but rather of thinking the umbilical relation between these two registers). It seems to me that this reading of Rulfian "deterritorialization" can and must be extended toward an equally primordial site: that of language itself. While the question of land and property/propriety are essential for any inquiry into the relation between culture and the state in modern Mexico, Rulfo's own attempts to think cultural transition begin by taking up the function of narrative and address. The ethical and political concerns named by deterritorialization are posed, for Rulfo, in the potentiality of (spoken) praxis, of the speech act, and by the glimmering offer passed between speech and action. In *Pedro Páramo*, the dynamic potential of speech marks a key moment in the consideration of Mexican identity in the wake of the revolution. It is through language, and within the space opened up by speech itself, that we come into relation with a share of ourselves, outside of ourselves. What is brought to the fore through the emergence of orality as a literary topos is both *Mexico itself* (as a geopolitical and cultural entity that takes shape both with and in juxtaposition to the Western tradition) and *the other of Mexico* (or the subaltern topos that is both engendered as detritus and endangered within the modern process of nation-building). Speech, we might say, marks the difference of "Mexico" from itself.

The classical tropology of return or descent, which prepares us for an allegorical treatment of national history, is at once reiterated and severely strained in the first pages of Rulfo's novella by the narrator's exchange with the mule-driver Abundio (*Pedro Páramo*, 2). The conversation between Juan Preciado and his first guide illustrates an encounter between conflicting social codes, while evincing what could be characterized as a clash between cultures in the transition from oligarchic to bourgeois society. This scene stages a meeting between two regimes of signification: between the modern space of urban, cosmopolitan, and industrializing Mexico City (figured by the *apretado* ["stuck up"] Juan Preciado) and the archaic topos of rural, semifeudal, agrarian life represented by the (*pelado* or "shorn") mule driver.[29] This conversation, which inaugurates the narrator into a world from which he has been exiled prior to his birth, also serves to cast doubt on the possibility of translation or arbitration between conflicting systems. This meeting gives rise to and highlights a series of symbolic differences, which it then seeks to bring into agreement. The diachronic character of the exchange has the effect, at once humorous and disturbing, of a burlesque. Juan Preciado begins his account by citing Abundio's overly formal speech, which is itself already a form of recitation:

—¿Y a qué va usted a Comala, si se puede saber?—oí que me preguntaban.
—Voy a ver a mi padre—contesté.
—¡Ah!—dijo él.
Y volvimos a silencio.

. . . .

—Bonita fiesta le va a armar—volví a oír la voz del que iba allí a mi lado—. Se pondrá contento de ver a alguien después de tantos años que nadie viene por aquí.
   Luego añadió:
—Sea usted quien sea, se alegrará de verlo.

. . . .

—¿Y qué trazas tiene su padre, si se puede saber?
—No lo conozco—le dije—. Sólo sé que se llama Pedro Páramo.

["And why are you going to Comala, if I may ask?," I head him asking me.
"I'm going to see my father," I answered.
"Oh!", he said.
We fell silent again.

. . . .

"You're going to get quite a welcome." Again I heard the voice of the one walking beside me. "They're going to be happy to see a new face after so many years."
   Later he added:
"Whoever you are, they'll be happy to see you."

. . . .

"And what does your father look like, if I may ask?"
"I don't know him," I said. "All I know is that his name is Pedro Páramo."]

This exchange is overdetermined by a sedimentation of meanings that threaten to render its "true" meaning unintelligible.[30] To begin with, the deferential speech of Abundio, replete with *señor* and *si se puede saber*, easily metamorphoses into a mockery of formal conventions; his formal address scarcely conceals his caustic, Harlequinesque wit. The proliferation of convention in this address to a stranger has the effect of transforming decorum—the initial supposition of a social and semantic equivalency—into an absurd cliché. But the parodic effects of Abundio's discourse also call into question the possibility of reading and understanding in the context of transition: in juxtaposition to his nonsensical repetition of *si se puede saber* (literally, "if one might know"), the narrator's reply (*no lo conozco*: "I don't know him") allows knowledge itself to appear as a problem. Knowledge both multiplies and divides as *saber* and *conocer*.[31] I have named this tension as an encounter between antithetical social "types," the *apretado* [literally, "uptight"] and the *pelado* [literally, "shorn"], and between cosmopolitan elements and a nexus of rural, provincial interests that appear to resist being incorporated into modernity. At least for the discourse of modernization, however, this antagonism must not be allowed to appear as such: the pelado or urbanized peasant would serve as a reminder of the socioeconomic dissymmetries perpetuated or intensified during the late nineteenth and early twentieth centuries. This antagonism is further underscored through the subsequent appearance of a series of semantic disjunctions or non sequiturs. These narrative disjunctions create, for both narrator and reader, a disturbing experience of disorientation. It would be a mistake to attribute the strangeness of this exchange entirely to the buffoonery or malevolence of the mule driver. Above and beyond the question of local character, this exchange illustrates transition as the emergence and partial failure of the signifier. At a decisive moment in the encounter, the narrator identifies himself as Pedro Páramo's legitimate son. This claim is staked in opposition to Abundio's assertion of a universally shared bastardy, to which Juan Preciado immediately issues a radical refusal: *no me acuerdo* [although "I don't remember" is clearly what Juan Preciado intends to say, *un acuerdo* is also an agreement between two or more parties]. Via a performative process linking identity and social difference to recollection, forgetting and agreement, the narrator both authenticates his own object of genealogical desire—which begins with and returns to the affirmation of a paternal birthright awaiting realization and recognition—while at the same time dismissing or refusing to hear the common claim of solidarity proffered through Abundio's self-deprecating tale:

> A:—El caso es que nuestras madres nos malparieron en un petate aunque éramos hijos de Pedro Páramo. Y lo más chistoso es que él nos llevó a bautizar. Con usted debe haber pasado lo mismo, ¿no?
> J:—No me acuerdo.
> A:—¡Váyase mucho al carajo!
> J:—¿Qué dice usted?
> A:—Que ya estamos llegando, señor.[32]

["We're all sons of Pedro Páramo, but it so happens that our mothers brought us into the world on straw mats. And the funniest part about it is that he's the one who brought us to our baptisms. That's how it was with you, right?"]
"I don't remember."
"Go to hell!"
"What did you say?"
"I said, we're coming into town, sir."[33]

Abundio's anecdote about the shared and improper, bastard origin is a parodic condensation of the discourse of mexicanidad, often celebrated in the phrase "¡Somos todos hijos de la Chingada!" ["We're all sons and daughters of *la Chingada*!": see, for instance, Paz's discussion of the national myth in *Laberintos*). Caught between "literal" and "figurative" levels of meaning, Abundio's anecdote extends the offer of a leveled-out social field. That is, it attempts to rule out the possibility of the exception, the legitimate heir, and hence to circumvent the vicious cycle of filial rivalry and factionalism by declaring, "we're all sons of Pedro Páramo all right—*but*...." What is more, this anecdote of universal impropriety introduces a self-critical element into the signifying economy of allegory. Abundio's speech forces the *figurative* reference and the allegorical index to be taken *literally*, as he claims to "remember" a rite of initiation, the recollection of which is strictly impossible. His speech violates the allegorical prohibition on direct representation, and thus ruins the unspoken correspondence. His address transfers a previously shared allusion to origin into a direct reference. It attempts to share too much, we might say, and thus the anticipation of a sacred or tragic revelation dissolves into a crass parody. What had until now proceeded as a presentation-through-deferral suddenly breaches the gap that constitutes allegory and, coming too close to its object, produces in the place of this illusion a disconcerting and nauseating distortion.

Figures of Transition: Revolution and the Return of Caciquismo

As Juan Preciado's return to Comala takes place after both the revolution and the counterrevolution led by Catholic priests (the "Cristero" rebellion), the narrative could be described as the search for a decisive image for the Mexican Revolution and its claim upon modernity. But one of the formal lessons imparted in the first half of the work is that a return is never simply a return, that it is always both more and less. And so Juan Preciado's journey also attest to an unthought remainder that haunts the national memory of revolution and the hopes associated with the political, economic, and aesthetic project of modernity. This "haunting" effect constitutes a key object of literary reflection for Rulfo's text, as what has been left out, left over and elided during modernization. But, as we shall see shortly, these spectral remainders also have an affect on the formal composition of the work, disrupting and complicating the referential and signifying structures of the narrative. *Pedro Páramo* delivers something resembling an allegory of revolution, reflecting how the event of institutionalization (of the state, the Partido Revolucionario Institucional, etc.) also serves to mask or remove from view the social dissymmetries which threaten to destabilize the bourgeois-nationalist project.[34] At one level, the state's interest in displaying images of a unified national tradition reveals a complicity with the cacique's counterrevolutionary project: the state seeks to sublimate social reality, to cancel out and raise to a higher value the internal differences—concerning ethnicity, idiom, class, sex, and so on—that mark the nation prior to any work of unification and communion. By way of this suturing operation, the nation would attain its unity in modernity. Likewise, in the cacique's outright denial of borders ("No habrá lienzos. La tierra no tiene divisiones" ["There will be no property lines. The land has no division."]) there resonates the modern state's attempt to be All. This desire for totality coincides with an endless disavowal of limits, an attempt to efface any trace of real difference that would dis-tract from the representation of the nation as a homogeneous body without divisions.

While revolution may well emerge out of a series of demands for radical reform or transformation of the oligarchic system, it also constitutes a kind of anarchy, a momentary suspension of all order. Despite the later claims of various political and intellectual circles to have represented the true authorship of the revolution, the driving force behind the collective uprisings of 1910 and 1911 is not a preconceived vision of what the new nation should look like.[35] The manifestoes speaking in the name of a collective agency against the *Porfiriato* tend to emphasize the systematic injustices of the Díaz regime rather than detailing a plan for a new national politics. The event manifests a stark discontinuity between, on one hand, the social and political dynamics whereby discrete instances of collective opposition take shape independently from one another and, apparently, to the complete surprise of the political establishment; and, on the other hand, the politics of direction, orchestration and naming, through which these multiple "sparks" are channeled into the institutional setting of what will later become known as the PRM/PRI Party.[36] The revolution comprises both the historical context of Rulfo's writing and a metahistorical object, insofar as literary reflection is doubled and divided between history and historicity, or between history understood as a sequence of events and as the opening or rupture by virtue of which history can happen in the first place.

This is perhaps why the themes of revolution and modernization only appear at the margins of Rulfo's writing. The short stories in particular contain obvious critiques of the postrevolutionary political programs and their disastrous social consequences. But the critical component of Rulfo's work is confronted by a considerable obstacle: there is seemingly no such thing as a direct representation of history in Rulfo's writing. On the contrary, literary reflection can only pursue its object by way of the effects and the distortions that the latter generates. Although many of the memories that comprise the second half of *Pedro Páramo* are drawn explicitly from the 1920s, we are never at the epicenter of revolutionary upheaval. Instead, we find ourselves in the periphery, assimilating the historical unfolding of the event through rumors and secondhand accounts. Thus we must look for other figures or topoi through which to elaborate the question of transition in Rulfo's text.

One such figure is the cacique, who strictly speaking belongs to a prerevolutionary time. The permanence of the Rulfian cacique (the name "Pedro" resonates as "piedra" or stone) invites us to reflect on the intractability of certain social configurations in the periphery, and perhaps remarks as well on the return of caciquismo (or "neo-caciquismo") following the revolution. But, at the same time, I will suggest that the phenomenon of caciquismo functions as a kind of prism, illuminating by way of diffraction and distortion. This allegorical device sheds new light on certain historical formations—such as the modern state—from an oblique angle, revealing commonalities that these institutions would prefer not to acknowledge. Before turning to an examination of caciquismo as an index of transition in Rulfo, I will clarify briefly the context in which this phenomenon is inscribed.

As has already been noted, debate over land tenure and ownership forms a fundamental axis in Mexican history. In the colonial period, and likewise following the wars of independence and with the emerging issues of national sovereignty and unity, *la tierra* marks an intersection for conflicting understandings of ownership, possession, culture, and use: for instance, between European and indigenous conceptions of property and cultivation; and between capitalist and premodern modes of production. Moreover, la tierra is overdetermined in each of these systems, comprising a nexus of multiple and potentially conflicting significations.[37] On one hand, land presents an indisputably concrete element for political struggle, and it is part and parcel of the world that humans set out to transform. At the same time, land—as home, territory, and soil— operates as an index of transcendence in national and prenational Mexican history, designating a communal or national good or right. As a register of transcendence, the land is not a reservoir of permanent meaning but the condensation of a *surplus of meaning*: the significance of la tierra is always more than the sum of its calculative appropriations and valuations.

To the degree that it embodies a certain social surplus, the land allows some of the "decoding" and "deterritorialization" effects of capitalist development to become visible. One of the effects of the incursion of capital into rural Mexican society is the displacement of previous systems and practices of land tenure, many of which were based on indigenous forms of communal ownership that had been protected by the Spanish crown in order to facilitate the integration of indigenous groups into the colonial system. With the liberal constitutional reform of 1857, an early effort to modernize the national agrarian economy, the state sought to stigmatize such collective structures as remainders from a barbaric past. Collective and corporate entitlements belonging to communities and the church were invalidated and replaced by a system of individual, private ownership.[38] In the wake of this structural transformation, the bond that formerly sustained agrarian communities in a relatively cohesive fashion rapidly disintegrated, culminating in a series of mass exoduses from rural Mexico, first during the latter years of the *Porfiriato* and then again during the violence of the revolution. The disastrous effects of reform are repeated, *mutatis mutandi*, in the postrevolutionary *reparto* program.[39] Viewed by the state as another step toward a fully modernized agrarian system based on private ownership—as well as a placative gesture toward the radicalized peasantry of the southern districts—redistribution in fact only served to reinforce the structure of caciquismo that had been momentarily dislodged by the emancipatory demands of 1910.

This history of contention over land usage reveals the contradictions, incomplete erasures and partial reinscriptions that attend the emergence of the modern nation-state in Mexico. For the national consolidation projects of the nineteenth and early twentieth centuries, the land embodies both what must be accomplished *and* what must be surpassed in the teleology of national self-realization.[40] As a sign, la tierra simultaneously functions as a universal (for instance, a proper and common domain—soil, patria, etc.—that must be consolidated, staked out, and domesticated) and as a limit for national expansion. This sign puts in play an array of boundaries and borders without which the nation cannot be one—that is, one nation among many—yet with which the nation is continually confronted with the fact that it has limits. Moreover, it is reminded that every limit, before it can become a limit, is necessarily *shared*. The radical "im-property" of borders constitutes a threat that no spatial metaphor can fully grasp: indeed, the improper nature of borders is threatening precisely because it disrupts or exceeds all efforts to pin down the limit. If the land is converted into an ideal point of reference for national projects in Mexico during the nineteenth and twentieth centuries, it likewise comprises a field of inscription for differences not easily assimilated into the institutional life of the nation-state. In order for the nation-state to realize itself as a totality or a unity of differences, the state must not only address the problem of borders as sites of international relations. It must also attend to, organize, and regulate the nation's internal boundaries, the divisions and vestigial marks (such as signs of ethnic and regional differences: accent, mannerism, complexion, etc.) that both stubbornly persist and become visible in new ways during new incursions of capital into the periphery in the second half of the nineteenth and early twentieth centuries. The function of "land" within national discourse is thus akin to that of "culture," which provides an abstraction or idealization of social practices. While culture offers a supplement that would make up for what we are lacking individually or as a group, no cultural system can be or say everything—and we encounter this limit every time we move from one culture to another. The "sense" of a particular culture remains forever in need of an "other" over and against which to define and refine its difference as identity. Logically speaking, the outsider is thus "inside" the inside: the "other" is postulated and presupposed as what will have been excluded, ruled out or forgotten.

The transition to capitalist modes of production in agrarian sectors of Mexico is neither instantaneous nor total, and the hegemonic success of modernization demands that there be a semblance of inclusion and choice. As García Canclini's notion of the "invention of tradition" indicates, modernization repackages the past in consumable form, as a self-consistent tradition that would provide a comforting alternative to modern experiences of fragmentation and alienation. As has already been suggested, the contact between metropolis and periphery generates a temporality bordering on suspension between epochs: between a modernity that has visibly not yet arrived or taken hold and the vestiges of a past that at various points remains firmly entrenched.[41] But this epochal suspension cannot be adequately represented as either a "mixture" or a "hybrid," nor is it necessarily cause for celebration: the flowery tropology of "hybridity" is an insufficient bandage for the suffering incurred under such conditions. This suspension is itself an invisible source of production, generating new social, political, and aesthetic forms. In her study of agrarian societies in the Puebla region of Mexico, Luisa Paré (see Bartra, *Caciquismo y poder político en el México rural*) notes that the encounters between capitalist and noncapitalist modes of production in rural areas require the presence of a mediator, a "third term" through which the conflicting demands of discrete systems can pass. One such figure is the cacique: at once a reservoir of tradition and at the forefront of capital's incursions into rural sectors, the cacique facilitates modernization and enjoys its benefits. The cacique's estate organizes local production and distribution, and likewise initiates economic contact with other regions. At the same time, the phenomenon of caciquismo is deeply invested in an economy of traditionalism (the term "cacique" is derived from *kassiquan*, a Carib term meaning "to keep house"). Caciquismo renews or pretends to restore the traditional values of family, filiation, and personalism, promising to counter the threat of an indifferent and depersonalizing modernization process. Akin to the sovereign in medieval Europe, the cacique could be said to possess two "bodies." But whereas the prince negotiates between the transcendent or divine and the material or secular realms, the cacique facilitates relations between the worlds of capital and tradition, metropolis and periphery, in such a way that these domains are prevented from collapsing in on one another. Thus the cacique presents transcultural analyses with a fundamental irreducibility: this figure does not have an analogue in modernized societies through which it could be "translated" (on this point, see Ernesto Laclau, *Tres ensayos sobre América Latina*) This is to say that the cacique is a *figure of translation itself*. What the standard cultural referents for cacique—tyrant, political boss, etc.—fail to transcribe and register is the overdetermination of this figure, through whom lawlessness, tyranny and boundless enjoyment must somehow be related to the institution of law. The law, in other words, will have been inscribed across a radical social division, which it will henceforth claim to have sutured. The cacique, as something like the "reverse side" of the proper legal system, its shadowy, unacknowledged other, negotiates this impossible transition by standing in and lending support at the site of this cultural divide. The associations of cacique with tyranny are therefore complicated by the thought of an anarchic or groundless act of substitution: as despotic overseer, the cacique stands at the site of a rift that divides the region from itself. The informal, unauthorized or self-authorizing force of caciquismo seeks to close and mend the incommensurable wound suffered repeatedly in modern, peripheral society. Caciquismo presents binary, either/or morality with an indigestible limits: as for good or evil, he is both and neither.

    We encounter the history of caciquismo in Rulfo's novella in a fragmented and anecdotal fashion, amidst the passages in which Pedro Páramo is seen constructing an empire. These scenes shed light on power as both a matter of relationality and as a limit. Following the death of his father, Pedro Páramo converts the family's bankrupt estate into a fiefdom by effectively expropriating the land holdings of others in the community. The cacique's arrangement of his own marriage to Dolores, the narrator's mother, provides the first indication of this project of empire-building.[42] The crucial point in this literary presentation of accumulation and monopolization—of women, land and goods—lies in the specific nature of its violence, which depends less on physical violence (although there is that too) and more upon a relentless work of *reinscription*. Caciquismo is a project of domination and expropriation that operates by transforming the social and discursive field in which it will become legible. It presupposes a form of "primitive accumulation," a subreption or theft that covers over not only its own traces but also the more originary impropriety at the origin of the law itself. The cacique's expropriation of rights, titles, and goods masks an aporia at the origin of the proper. The domain of law and legality is informed by a moment that cannot properly appear within the field of legibility it shapes—it can only appear as a "stain" or an excess. In other words, the proper presupposes an (always invisible) act of subtraction that does away with its own improper traces.

The "illegibility" that the origin assumes when regarded from the perspective of the order that it constitutes does not amount to a moral condemnation. Literally speaking, the origin cannot be read (interpreted, understood) in terms of the contract or context it inaugurates. The visible emergence of Pedro Páramo's empire is organized around just such an eclipse of the origin, which cannot be reintroduced into the system it inaugurates except at the cost of a blinding distortion and total collapse of the field itself. Do we not encounter here a logic similar to that of Sophocles' *Oedipus Rex*, in the form of a hermeneutic drive that, in seeking to identify an ancient impropriety and cast its author out of the polis, discovers—much to its horror—its own traces at the scene of unthinkable crime? *Legein*, usually translated as "to speak" or "to gather," also names a field a visibility, of legality and legibility [*legere*] whose emergence, as Rulfo shows, remains incommensurable with the cause it would seem to safeguard. And thus caciquismo, an "illegitimate" social and political form, presents an uncanny reflection of "legitimate" forms of political organization such as the modern state. In the strange temporality of the event, the law first emerges as a particular crime that has managed to surpass itself, to pass itself off as a universal. The difference between the law and crime is itself the crime.

This paradox evinces what Hegel would term the absolute identity between law and crime. In order to further elaborate what this connection means for the context in which Rulfo is writing, we must first take a closer look at some passages that have just been summarized somewhat schematically. In Rulfo's novella it is the cacique's right-hand man, Fulgor Sedano, who best illustrates the machine-like logic of caciquismo. The reemergence of the despotic figure of the cacique could be traced to the time when Pedro Páramo attempts to vindicate his father's death. Indeed, caciquismo both initiates and conceals an attempt to rid itself of all limits by precisely ingesting or incorporating what is foreign to it. Rulfo's identification of caciquismo with the disavowal of limits is supported by the passages portraying the immediate aftermath of the death of the cacique's father. We are told that his father was killed inadvertently during a quarrel at a wedding. While the actual killer is never identified, the son bides his time and eventually enacts his revenge by methodically eliminating *all* of the guests. However, the terrifying image of his father's death continues to resonate long after the occurrence:

> Nunca quiso revivir ese recuerdo porque le traía otros, como si rompiera un costal repleto y luego quisiera contener el grano. La muerte de su padre que arrastró otras muertes y en cada una de ellas estaba siempre la imagen de la cara despedazada; roto un ojo, mirando vengativo el otro. Y otro y otro más, hasta que la había borrado del recuerdo cuando ya no hubo nadie que se la recordara (40).
>
> [He refused to relive that memory because it brought others with it, as if a swollen feed bag had burst and he were trying to keep the kernels from spilling out. His father's death dragged other deaths along with it, and within each of them there was the image of that shattered face; one eye ruptured, the other staring vengefully. It brought another memory, and another, and that death was not erased from memory until there was at last no longer anyone left to remember it.]

These "other deaths," the deaths through which the cacique hopes to pay off a disproportionate paternal debt, cannot ward off the memories of the dead father: indeed, his image is even more terrifying in death than in life. Moreover, the payback is unable to dispel the son's knowledge that the Father—not the biological father, but the father in relation to his symbolic mandate—is always already dead. It is ultimately self-knowledge that must be avoided at all costs here: the son must prevent the father from discovering that the restitution of his murder is impossible. But it is precisely this unthinkable and catastrophic knowledge of his own death that is already engraved in the father's shattered visage. This half-blinded, half-vengeful gaze is traumatic precisely because it is unable to hide the fact that *it knows* (or that it sees: *ça-voir*?), that it has uncovered the work of death within or beneath its own logic. The monumental scope of the project of caciquismo amounts to an attempt to cover over a singular and unreplaceable death with a mountain of secondary deaths. It is at once an attempt to forget and an effort to restore the memory of the father to the dignity of non-knowledge. But the postulated end of this project produces anything but a delimitation or banishment of death: rather, it ends in an overflowing and boundless death, a death without end, which is at the same time the annihilation of all memory. And thus one might say that what truly afflicts the cacique is not death per se but precisely his inability to die.

I have suggested that a similar logic underlies the very different contexts in which the modern state and caciquismo operate. If the state regulates the nation's interior and its divisions through an immense bureaucratic network that includes processes of documentation, archiving and displaying the signs of difference on a national stage (for instance, a museum), then caciquismo projects a similar image of totality through the work of expropriation. We will see momentarily how these two operations, which at first glance appear to be diametrically opposed, in fact share a common thread. When Fulgor Sedano tries to warn the cacique of a neighbor's refusal to be cowed by his program of expropriation, the cacique's response is to deny the very existence of limits:

> [Fulgor Sedano]: Cuestión de límites. Él ya mandó cercar y ahora pide que nos echemos el lienzo que falta para hacer la división.
> [Pedro Páramo]: Eso déjalo para después. No te preocupen los lienzos. No habrá lienzos. La tierra no tiene divisiones (20).[43]

> ["It's a matter of limits. He already put up his fences, and now he's asking us to put up the last part in order to establish the property line." "Leave that for later. Don't worry about the fences. There will be no fences. The land has divisions."]

The denial of divisions or limits is the particular's attempt to pass itself off as the universal. The cacique's project would be the negation of negation itself; it would recover from history the ground of an original and proper wholeness. In a similar manner, the state assumes the role of sovereign guardian of a nation that has only been unified through the emergence of the state itself. The postrevolutionary state assigns itself the ironic title "Partido Revolucionario Institucional" [Institutional Revolutionary Party], which makes a claim upon the catastrophic movement of revolution itself. The state would take ownership not only of the name ("revolution"), but also of the act of naming as such. In this seemingly contradictory assignation there resonates an anxiety about the truth of revolution. The state's appropriation of the revolution is an attempt to institutionalize what is in fact an unprecedented and unrepeatable break: revolution, as a suspension of history, progress, law, and rationality, renders the momentary infinite while irreparably shaking our preconceived, comforting belief in rational agency, in a connection between calculation, action, and a good end.

Two passages warrant a close examination in further considering Rulfo's treatment of the political as a double question of erasure and reinscription. These two passages trace a process through which what begins as a groundless, illegitimate moment is retroactively transformed into the only conceivable basis of legality and propriety. Together, they mark the obscene origin of the law. In the first of two scenes (*Pedro Párano*, fragment 19), the cacique's lieutenant files a writ against Torribio Aldrete, charging the latter with "ususfuto".[44] This passage provides a sketch of the force of caciquismo, which for Rulfo consists in maintaining the semblance of a reserve, the show of sovereign potestas in restraint. Sedano completes the charges against Aldrete, who responds by alluding somewhat enigmatically to the ominous force behind Sedano, all the while attempting to drive a wedge between tyrant and lieutenant:

> "Fulgor Sedano, hombre de 54 años, soltero, de oficio administrador, apto para entablar y seguir pleitos, por poder y por mi propio derecho, reclamo y alego lo siguiente . . ."
> Eso había dicho cuando levantó el acta contra actos de Toribio Aldrete. Y terminó: "Que conste mi acusación por usufruto".
> —A usted ni quien le quite lo hombre, don Fulgor. Sé que usted las puede. Y no por el poder que tiene atrás, sino por usted mismo.
> . . . .
> —Con ese papel nos vamos a limpiar usted y yo, don Fulgor, porque no va a servir para otra cosa. Y eso usted lo sabe. Ahora ya sé de qué se

trata y me da risa. Dizque "usufruto". Vergüenza debía darle a su patrón ser tan ignorante (19).

["I, Fulgor Sedano, fifty-four years of age, bachelor, administrator by profession and skilled in filing and prosecuting law, by the power invested in me and by my own authority, do claim and allege the following..."

That was what he had written when he filed the complaint against deeds committed by Toribio Aldrete. And he had ended: "The charge is usufruct."

"There's no one can call you less than a man, don Fulgor. I know you can hold your own. And not because of the power behind you, but on your own account."

. . . .

"We'll wipe our asses with this paper, you and I, don Fulgor, because that's all it's good for. You know that. Now I know what it's all about, it makes me laugh. You say 'usufruct' and it makes me laugh. Your boss should be ashamed if he's really that dumb."]

Sedano's address, which begins with an affirmation of the accuser's symbolic status vis-à-vis the law, directs itself to an impersonal, abstract addressee (the law itself), culminating in the deployment of a performative: "let my accusation of usufruct be known." Aldrete's ingratiating reply appears to confirm Sedano's rhetorical power, but his speech likewise aims to deflect the other's resolve, and in so doing to diminish the colossal power of the cacique.[45] By pretending to acknowledge Sedano for who he is, and not for whom or what he represents, Aldrete hopes to forge a crack in this alliance. His message should be heard as stating the inverse of what it declares: while he seems to raise Sedano out of his mere particularity and accord him more than a subservient function ("you're something in your own right, not just because you represent him"), Aldrete seeks in fact to reduce the colossal figure of the cacique to the level of a mere particular. And thus his words might have been: "Pedro Páramo . . . he scares me even less than you do."

The exchange ends disastrously for Aldrete, and his death provides a cipher for understanding what transpires in the following fragments.[46] The cacique's strategic maneuver hinges on a subreption within the conceptual determination of ownership and property. As the following passage will further clarify, the maneuver enacted by the cacique is countersigned by a kind of misrecognition, on the part of those who stand to lose the most, of the essentially contingent or symbolic nature of ownership. Like the nation-state, the domain of property is nothing without mutually recognized borders. But boundaries also constitute a necessary risk for ownership: they are sites at which the proper, the known, or the within-bounds, remains inextricably exposed to invasion, theft, or displacement. There can be no proper, no lo nuestro, prior to its possible loss or expropriation. The threat represented by the other and by the outside is perhaps only a secondary manifestation of a more radical risk: the domain of the proper risks being undone by precisely the marks and boundary walls that inform it and make it what it is. For, while property has no being without recognizable and repeatable boundaries, these inscriptions are themselves entirely bereft of being: they are contingent, without essence, and hence subject to misinterpretation. The being of the proper in its necessity depends upon the impropriety and contingency of the material mark.

The maneuvering of the cacique's lieutenant illustrates that the effects of caciquismo can best be gauged in the absence of the cacique himself. That is because the cacique is he who shows that he does not show all. As a figure of enjoyment-without-bounds, the cacique's power derives from his capacity *not to appear*, to maintain a part of himself in reserve. This calculus of being, of being as withdrawal and withholding, shows another side when it becomes clear in the chronology of the narrative that the counterrevolutionary drive of caciquismo has effectively consolidated the postrevolutionary social sphere. We encounter the traces of this reinscription in an exchange between two neighbors in Comala (28). The outcome of this conversation between a peasant named Galileo and his neighboring brother-in-law is itself unremarkable. The brother-in-law, another Rulfian usurer, first reminds Galileo of a long-standing debt. Galileo in turn disputes a rumor that he has sold his land to the cacique. The nearly stichomythic sequentiality of the exchange reveals, retroactively, a radical reinscription of social space. This peripeteia is difficult to locate exactly, and it not only bears on the peasant Galileo's fortunes, but casts a new light on the fate of the revolution itself. The narrative echoes a radical transformation of the social, in the sense that the event of reinscription does away with all traces of its having taken place. In the wake of the event, it is as if things had always already been—and always will be—as they are now. The trace of this reinscription is purely negative: it inheres only in the shadow of doubt lingering over the misplaced or fatal certainty upheld by Galileo, who conflates the contingency of the sign (property lines) with an essence or a propriety. As Paul de Man remarks in his reading of Rousseau's *Social Contract*, "There is nothing legitimate about property, but the rhetoric of property confers the illusion of legitimacy" (*Allegories of Reading*, 262).

> Neighbor: No te exijo. Ya sabes que he sido consecuente contigo. Pero la tierra no es tuya. Te has puesto a trabajar en terreno ajeno. ¿De dónde vas a conseguir para pagarme?
> Galileo: ¿Y quién dice que la tierra no es mía?
> N: Se afirma que se la has vendido a Pedro Páramo.
> G: Yo ni me he acercado a ese señor. La tierra sigue siendo mía.
> N: Eso dices tú. Pero por ahí dicen que todo es de él.
> G: Que me lo vengan a decir a mí.
> N: Mira, Galileo, yo a ti, aquí en confianza, te aprecio. . . . Pero a mí no me vas a negar que vendiste las tierras.
> G: Te digo que a nadie se las he vendido.
> N: Pues son de Pedro Páramo. Seguramente él asi lo ha dispuesto. ¿No te ha venido a ver don Fulgor?
> G: No.
> N: Seguramente mañana lo verás venir. Y si no mañana, cualquier otro día.
> G: Pues me mata o se muere; pero no se saldrá con la suya.

> [Neighbor: I'm not rushing you. You know I've always been patient with you. But the land isn't yours. You're working someone else's land. How do you plan to pay me back?
> Galileo: Who says it's not mine?
> N: I hear you sold it to Pedro Páramo.
> G: I've never even seen that man. The land is still mine.
> N: That's what you say. But over there they're saying it's all his.
> G: Let them come here and say it to my face.
> N: Look, Galileo, just between you and me, I like you. . . . But don't go telling me you didn't sell the land.
> G: I'm telling you I haven't sold it to anyone.
> N: Well, it belongs to Pedro Páramo. He's got it all layed out. Hasn't don Fulgor been by to see you?
> G: No.
> N: Well then, surely you'll see him tomorrow. And if not tomorrow, some day soon.
> G: He'll get his way over my dead body.]

The pathos of Galileo's stance—he would play the defiant hero to the cacique's relentless, tyrannical drive—is belied by a suspicion, which grows incrementally throughout the passage, that he in fact plays the fool. Indeed, one wonders exactly what mandate this Galileo fulfills: what relation does he take to the name, "his" name, which comes up in the context of another Copernican revolution, a revolution that is increasingly difficult to distinguish from counterrevolutionary ebb? Galileo's disbelieving rejection of hearsay, his unshakable belief in the ideal status of propriety, are the signs of a—nearly blind—faith in the rationality of the proper, and of a refusal to be duped by the fraudulent tactics of misrepresentation employed by the tyrant. But Galileo's rational belief also masks a refusal of the contingency of all symbolic assignments. Behind the recognizable marks of property lines—which might at any moment be imposed, effaced and redrawn—this rational faith presupposes a permanent truth of which these contingent marks would be mere reflections. It is precisely by situating himself on this side of the fence that Galileo in fact errs. In refusing to be duped and defrauded, he must have recourse to an essential definition (despite all appearances, contrary to what "they" say, it is in fact my land) for what is in fact a strictly symbolic (contingent and shared) determination. Galileo seeks a heroic ground upon which to reject the constitutive (rather than secondary) role of representation, of marking and recognition, in the demarcation of the proper. This ominous exchange traces a sequence in which interpretation (the community's or the reader's) finds itself on both sides of a societal breach, while having necessarily missed the juncture that divides the field. The determination and delineation of the proper is anonymous and has always already transpired: it arrives as having already been decided *por ahí* by an anonymous "they." What is repeatedly passed over (crossed *and* missed) in this exchange of iterability and recognition is the event itself, the instant at which things both happened as they did but also could have turned out differently. We have begun to see that the fault line of caciquismo articulates or makes possible a certain question of justice, which in the passage just cited arises precisely as we become aware of the retreat and the impossibility of repairing the damage of modernization: the true violence of caciquismo resides not in a subjective assertion of will, but rather in the mechanics through which this inscription becomes visible and irreversible. Moreover, a certain violence inheres in our collective inability to hear the appeal of the other in the wake of this event of erasure and rewriting of boundaries. The appeal can only be heard as an always receding and impossible echo, of a singular and unrepeatable call that has already been missed.

The Desolation of Speech in Rulfo:
Language, Testimony, and Death

In the previous chapter I argued that societal transition is a central concern in *Pedro Páramo*. I would now like to clarify my earlier claim that "transition" cannot be reduced to a thematic concern in Rulfo's writing. This is in part because the problem of transition is posed as a question of language: that is, of speech, representation, and absence. This also means that "representation" must not be taken for granted: the event that inaugurates transition, which is also the instant following which things can never go back to being the way they were, remains irreducible to the terms or temporality of either the "before" or the "after." How, then, can the event—or some trace thereof—impart itself freely onto the circuitry of personal or collective memory? How to speak of the event *as* event without losing sight of it as something unprecedented and irreducible to the progressive temporality of representation? How can we think the event in its disjunctive simultaneity—as both rupture and new beginning—without also imposing an order of intelligibility that the event itself strictly "precedes" or "exceeds"? ("The event itself": even these words run the risk of imposing a self-consistent identity where there is in fact none.) These questions inform Rulfo's literary treatment of transition, and I will pursue them in this section by turning again to the notion of tragedy. However, in discussing the second half of the novella, I will suggest that Rulfo's writing also exhausts the tragic paradigm or pushes it to its limit.

Up until now, the discussion of tragedy in this chapter has been organized by the schema of conflicting epochs, and by the idea that literature can bring about a kind of reconciliation between different perspectives, epochal attunements or discourses (e.g., colonial and postcolonial, dominant and subaltern, etc.). However, it is in confronting the question of an "other knowledge" that Rulfo's writing makes its most important break with traditional literary aesthetics. In so doing, the work offers a distinctly modern interpretation of the tragic dynamic. While reconciliation of social antagonism and the restitution of loss jointly describe one tendency or possibility in Rulfo's literary project, the nature of these experiences also requires us to reexamine the notions of "restitution" and "reconciliation." The possibility of a "restitution" of the subaltern would seem to hinge on literature's capacity to represent or create a forum for those modes of expression and knowledge that bear witness to long histories of domination and perseverance. These perspectives call for restitution insofar as they have been "excluded" or "marginalized" by the dominant regime of signification—that is, by the myriad scientific, medical, academic, and juridical discourses through which the postrevolutionary state identifies its own emergence with the unification of the nation. But in undertaking such a restitutive project, literature must confront the problem of how to give "voice" to such perspectives while at the same time avoiding the danger of reproducing yet another seamless history of the Same. The problem could be expressed thus: how to render "present" or "audible" that which the hegemonic order tends to efface—not just *this* or *that* order but *any* hegemonic configuration? In other words, the dilemma facing literary restitution is intensified by the suspicion that hegemonic politics in general—and this is also to say *representation as such*—cannot easily be separated from the reproduction of subalternity. It would seem that a literary restitution of the subaltern, were it successful, both would remove the condition of negativity or invisibility that afflicts the subaltern and it would initiate a new (counter-) hegemonic process, which would in turn begin to reproduce the condition of subalternity. Can literature break with this vicious circle of restitution and violence without resigning itself to nihilism? With Rulfo, this problem invites a new—and distinctly modern—way of thinking about tragedy, one that is perhaps akin to Hölderlin's idea of modern tragedy as a mode in which beginning and end no longer "rhyme."

Rulfo was known to remark that the true protagonist of *Pedro Páramo* is not any particular character but the pueblo itself. One might also wonder whether, following Juan Preciado's death, language does not itself emerge as a decisive voice in this historia. At the midway point in the novella, following his impossible testimony, the narrator has been transformed into a witness to the dead and their "infraworldly" speech. This reversal from narrator to witness suggests a kind of poetic transfer between literary and testimonial documents: we first encounter Comala through the perspective of cultural modernity (Juan Preciado's postlapsarian, specular return to his natal village), but this modern viewpoint is gradually exposed to the traces and remainders of what modernization has failed to assimilate or transform. Through the emergence of the "others" of modernity, yet another voice becomes audible: not the articulated expression of a plurality of individuals, but a murmuring that constitutes an asynchronous multiplicity of voices. This key difference between "voice" as articulateness and "voice" as murmur invites a distinction between the ideality of signifying language and language as "materiality."[47]

Multiplicity is not plurality. The question of "voice" in Rulfo's work introduces an excess into the narrative's signifying economy, a remainder that cannot be definitively situated "inside" or "outside" of the textual apparatus. Such an indeterminacy occurs, for instance, in the text's sole reference to "los indios," who descend from Apango to the valley of Comala to sell their goods (48). As doubly subaltern, the indios constitute an irreducible opacity or stain in the signifying economy of the text. Their presence at the periphery of the creole peasant community, which takes the form of silent waiting as well as laughter and jokes that are "audible" but not intelligible within the narrative (we are simply told that they laugh, joke and wait silently), is not at all the abject presence that Western thought often assigns to its "others." But neither do the indios simply represent one perspective—or one "other"—among many. The singular reference to los indios introduces a limit for the concept of perspective itself, an ethical barrier beyond which narrative cognition cannot and must not pass.[48] If we compare Rulfo's treatment of the question of non-Western consciousness to the way in which the "Boom" novel frequently approaches this matrix of ethnicity, subalternity, and alterity, we see that the "Boom" envisions itself as a synthetic force capable of assimilating such previously excluded or marginal perspectives into the symbolic constellation of Latin American modernity. Through such aesthetic practices as magical realism, modern literature would bring "the other" into the realm of representation while at same time constituting itself as *the* symbolic space in which the intelligibility of the other's voice can finally be ensured. I would like to propose an anachronistic reading of Rulfo in relation to later generations of Latin Americanist texts: his writing effectively destroys any such recuperative or compensatory ground for literature. Rulfo's novella poses the event of societal transition as a literary problem. This is not to say that the different facets of transition, including cultural, linguistic, sociological, economic, and political concerns, can in the final instance be subsumed under or explained by a single, privileged category such as literature. To produce a literary treatment of transition and its attendant conflicts, exclusions and dissymmetries is to alter irreparably the literary medium itself. As soon as it comes into contact with the event of transition, literature no longer says the same. It no longer means what it once meant, and it likewise ceases to speak *of the same*: of the eidos or the permanent self-identity of a truth that resides behind the contingent world of appearances. The unsettling appearance of los indios in Rulfo's text opens up a new array of questions in the ongoing literary interrogation of lo nuestro: Should these indigenous "others" be assigned a place within the collective interest named by "lo nuestro," insofar as they too can be considered to have suffered the injustices and indignities perpetuated by the colonial and postcolonial state? Or is the naming of "lo nuestro," as an index of collective and popular but also Hispanist or mestizo interest, in fact based on the silent annihilation or expulsion of other social and political forms? It is the tragedy of "lo nuestro" that it must seek to open itself to the possibility of radical difference, affirming an encounter for which no common ground can be presupposed, *and* that to name this difference—as a difference of "culture," "perspective," or whatever else—is already to have incorporated the difference into the register of the Same.

A number of commentaries have noted that the narrative discourse of *Pedro Páramo* enacts a departure from traditional notions of temporality.[49] As we will see, these disruptions of narrative temporality also play an important role in literary reflection on textuality itself, or the "produced" quality of literary discourse. Rulfo's well-known characterization of his literary locales as places where time has "come to a stop" finds an echo in the myriad repetitions, omissions, and unmarked juxtapositions of disparate times. But the question of time does not simply revert from one mythologeme to another—from, say, the progressivist temporality of modernization to the motif of an arrested or circular time outside of history. Neither progress nor stasis can fully account for the narrative construction of temporality in Rulfo's text. Rather, narration is marked by a rupture whose echoes reverberate within the texture of narrative time. By way of a dyadic tension between disjunction and repetition, we come to see modernity as haunted by a past that is no longer "present" but not yet "absent" (not yet buried or decisively placed in the past). In *Pedro Páramo* the past is not experienced as plenitude or as memory but as an unintegrated spectral remainder. Thus the postulated temporality of the narrator's "return" to Comala—which ought to confirm a sequential, progressive ordering of past and present—is displaced by the awareness that this return is both belated and, in a certain sense, too early.

The combination of temporal arrest and stammering repetition in Rulfian narrative gives notice of a lapsus within the temporal and historical or spiritual progression of the nation. The ontotheological conception of history as the progressive work of a subject is flattened out. The oblique perspective on the revolution offered by Rulfo's writing bespeaks both disillusionment and fascination: within the juxtaposition of conflicting tones and temporalities, Rulfo's text mourns the passing of an event that, strictly speaking, never arrived. Despite what Juan Preciado's first words would have us believe, *Pedro Páramo* does not in fact enact the narrating subject's return to a scene prior to his birth—or before history—in the way that national culture would like, i.e., by claiming to recover or redeem a lost, archaic purity. Instead, the text marks the *limit* of this primal fantasy: for Rulfo, the origin is always already dead, and its death is what makes it—or what will have made it—an origin.

Rulfo's narrative is characterized by a series of distortions of traditional tropological constructions. These "errant" tropes serve to underscore some of the problems of temporality and cultural identity I have been discussing. In one of Juan Preciado's first descriptions of Comala, the repeated striking of a church bell marks the passing of the hours. Yet we are told that this periodic tolling in fact signals a suspension of temporality, as if time had "shriveled up" (8). Comala is likewise described as a place where time has "regressed" (33) and is "varying" or "differing" (39). In following the narrator in his descent to Comala, we move from a time "populated" by occurrences to a pure and quivering temporality. The indices of contraction, arrest, and wavering, together with the text's abstraction of time, are complemented by a pair of extraordinary descriptions of the night sky and heavenly bodies (and that *tiempo* can mean "time" or "weather" reinforces an association between temporality and the divine). This celestial, tropological irruption situates the problem of temporality within a question of signification and its limits. The scenes in question immediately follow the death of Miguel Páramo, the feared and hated son of the cacique. In the first, a group of villagers observe a cluster of shooting stars: "Había estrellas fugaces. Caían como si el cielo estuviera lloviznando lumbre" ["There were shooting stars. They fell as if the sky were raining light."] (17). Resorting to a kind of gallows humor, the peasants speculate that this celestial disturbance is the sign of a colossal miscarriage of justice: the cacique's son has escaped the damnation that was his due and been welcomed into heaven.[50] The second scene, in which Padre Rentería recalls the same meteorological phenomenon, evokes Walter Benjamin's description of the shooting star as allegorical object par excellence. The tropological movement of these celestial bodies contains two tendencies not easily reconciled with one another. First, this movement gives shape to a surface of inscription upon which it becomes visible as signification: the night sky, when is it is "written" on, becomes a metaphor for the blank—or infinitely full—page. At the same time, however, there is a turning within or against the ideal signifying process that serves as the background of this scene. This second, countersignifying turn stems from the suspicion that these celestial signs portend a disastrous injustice. Each movement or tendency catches the other by surprise. The shooting stars display a disjunctive simultaneity, sustaining a tension between distinct eschatological possibilities. Padre Rentería's description of the night sky is nearly identical to that of the villagers: "Había estrellas fugaces. Las luces en Comala se apagaron. / Entonces el cielo se adueñó de la noche" (18). The tropological errancy of the meteors—they are literally "fugitive" or "errant" stars—produces an inversion of the classical schema of signification established by St. Augustine.[51] For Augustine, a finger pointed toward the stars establishes a certain sense or direction in the here and now; it gives an indication that is visible to and repeatable by all, and through which the inaccessible—the divine eidos—can be brought into view. In this passage, on the other hand, the dimming of Comala's earthly lights does not afford an ideal vantage point for reflection upon the divine. Rather, it gives way to a catachrestic, abyssal turn within the figurative economy of poetic language: here the *sky* takes over the *night*, rather than the poetic rendering of dusk as the time when night overtakes the sky. This scene of tropological multiplication and excess cannot readily be explained by reference to metaphor. It remarks on the end of the colonial-theological epoch in Mexico, announcing the collapse of that age's redemptive, providential promise. At the same time, however, it tells of—or demonstrates—the impossibility of signifying this historical rupture. The exhaustion of that epoch also suspends the systematic aesthetic and epistemological resources by which its demise could have been measured.

The "murmuring" that ceaselessly haunts Rulfo's work has been a topic of considerable critical debate. What has yet to emerge from such discussion, however, is a sustained inquiry into the meaning of the narrator's impossible testimony. Attempts to account for the meaning of this "death"—not to mention the fact that the narrator continues to "speak" beyond and of it—by attributing it to the influence of certain international literary movements (expressionism, surrealism, magical realism, etc.) precisely miss the disturbing question this scene opens onto: what would it mean *to die into language*?[52] Or, for that matter, what would it mean to testify to one's own death? This affirmation raises an array of difficult questions. For instance, the fact that the narrator appears to account for his own death: is this impossible act merely a continuation of the primal-scene fantasy that inaugurates the first half of the novella (the metaphysical dream of being there at the beginning or the end, here expressed in terms of an absolute knowledge that extends—qua voice—beyond one's own death), or does the knowledge attested to here in fact shatter that speculative surface? The "murmurs" indicate that signification has turned back on itself and ceases to refer outside of itself, i.e., to an ideal or transcendental signified. For the moment, let us merely note that a troubling connection between death, language and self-consciousness has been broached here. As we reach the conclusion of the novella, this uneasy relation will be seen to have governed the denouement of the entire work, leading up to the enigmatic scene in which the cacique confronts and verbally "recognizes" his own death.

As mentioned earlier, a number of critics have interpreted the myriad formal allusions and citations of classical mythology in *Pedro Páramo* as evidence that the author sought to integrate Mexican literature into a universal Western tradition. However, we are now in a position to see how Rulfo's text in fact distorts and undermines the myth of "tradition" as reserve and transmission of universal values. The effect of this distortion is akin to what in the visual arts is know as *anamorphosis.* Anamorphosis highlights a point in a visual representation that, when viewed from a right angle, is apparently nothing more than an amorphous blob or stain surrounded by integrated form and meaning. At an oblique angle, however, and as the rest of the scene begins to lose its proper perspective, the stain suddenly emerges in its intelligibility.[53] This formal superimposition yields a juxtaposition of two incommensurable registers of intelligibility, each of which spells the dissolution or unintelligibility of the other. The relation between these registers is a nonrelation insofar as the perspective that organizes one order of intelligibility necessarily excludes the other in advance. This juxtaposition points to the very emergence of visibility as an originary distortion or exclusion (just as a camera lens must "exclude" in order to frame a view). In so doing, it shows the price that must be payed for there to be a representation: the picture produces its own *internal exclusion*, an unacknowledged "reverse side" whose elision is the basis of the picture's ideational self-consistency.

A similar formal and structural disjunction appears in Rulfo's writing under the auspices of literary identification with a timeless and universal truth. For argument's sake, let us call this the idea of conveying the sacred truths of the Western, Judeo-Christian tradition through cultural translation. This synthetic hypothesis runs up against a limit in the textual juxtaposition of the revolution with caciquismo. The sacrificial gesture that gives birth to the spirit of the modern nation, the collective and systematic "murder" of the primordial figure of the cacique (one of the well-known rallying cries of the revolution is "¡Muerte a los caciques!" ["Death to the caciques!"]), is seen to lapse back into the very despotic structure it claims to have abolished. The founding moment of modernity, in which the emergence of the modern state announces the end of all that is primordial and barbaric, turns out to be the repetition of a primordial murder. The end will have been a return: not of "the same" but rather of the elided difference—what is improper or unthinkable—that is the reverse side of the same. Anachronistically juxtaposed to the modern state, the cacique presents an opaque, nearly invisible figure within the cultural field delineated by the revolution. From a certain angle, though, the tyrannical force of caciquismo is seen to constitute the unacknowledged or disavowed truth of the revolution: the founding of order or the law is always already marked by a certain abyssal "lawlessness."

A grammatical trait in Rulfo's writing can assist us in further sketching out this pattern of formal disfiguration and tropological rupture. At least one critic has identified a proliferation of the conditional subjunctive mood in *El llano en llamas* and *Pedro Páramo*, often in the form of a hypothetical comparison between animate and inanimate orders. This pattern both affirms and denies equivalence in the formula: "X era como si" + conditional subjunctive + Y, or "X was as if it were Y."[54] Although the ubiquity of this grammatical construct in Rulfo's works makes it infeasible to provide a complete account of its circumstances and effects, it should be sufficient to indicate that the grammatical (ordering or signifying) function of the "as if" structure is consistently strained by the nature of the combinatory relations themselves. One might expect this tropology of paradigmatic substitution to provide a richer description and an added dimension to the Rulfian topography, much as for Aristotle metaphor works to reveal previously unsuspected connections between things. But the proliferation of these juxtapositions in Rulfo in fact produces a tremendous strain on formal-ideational cohesion in the narrative. For instance, a face—the most "human" surface of all—becomes stretched leather or a transparent, bloodless surface; voice becomes *hebras humanas* [human fiber, thread or hair]; and so on. The "as if" structure frequently yields a somatic or corporeal "language" of gestures, murmurs and raspy voices, but also has the effect of intensifying the depressive poverty of the Rulfian landscape. In each case, the second term does not secure but threatens the radical desubjectivization of the first term. This grammatical and tropological "anamorphosis" carries out a semiotic transposition of signification and affect, in which the indication or emergence of tone, mood, emotion or "inner life" presents a limit for the ideal relation between signifier and meaning. The naming of substitution as promise ("it was as if") turns out to short-circuit metaphor's dialectic of difference and signification, introducing within this virtual affirmation a negativity or opacity that cannot subsequently be converted into meaning.

One of the most dramatic instances of this anamorphic distortion occurs immediately prior to the narrator's death, when he sees or imagines a woman "decomposing" before his very eyes. "El calor me hizo despertar al filo de la medianoche. Y el sudor. El cuerpo de aquella mujer hecho de tierra, envuelto en costras de tierra, *se desbarataba como si estuviera derritiéndose* en un charco de lodo. Yo me sentía nadar entre el sudor que chorreaba de ella y me faltó el aire que se necesita para respirar" ["The heat awakened me close to midnight. And the sweat. That woman's body, made of earth, encrustred in earth, went to pieces as if it were melting into a pool of mud. I felt myself swimming in the sweat that poured off her body, and it was so hot I couldn't even breathe] (36, my emphasis).[55] This passage is an extreme manifestation of a phantasmatic tendency that began when the narrator first arrived in Comala: the first person he meets in town suddenly disappears "como si no existiera" ["as if she did not exist"] (3), and in nearly every subsequent encounter, the other ultimately proves to have been a ghost.[56] The dissonance that marks the later passage allows us to locate and develop another related question in relation to Rulfian speech: beginning with Juan Preciado's impossible testimony of his own "death," the second half of Rulfo's text unfolds by posing a question of memory and testimony in relation to death. The description of corporeal and somatic dissolution just cited is striking for the manner in which it brings together a certain corporeal intimacy (Juan Preciado has just taken part in a sexual encounter with the woman) and a dissolution that cannot be separated from the vicissitudes of the language in which it is described. It is as if the anamorphic turn in literature were being played out to the letter of the law. Up until this point, the narrative has displayed what we could call a "phallic" structure, whose sequences are organized around a series of scopic metaphors. As if it were a camera, the narrative calls attention to the line of approach it takes to its object and thereby simulates an asymptotic "zooming in" on truth itself. The passage cited above marks a limit for narrative teleology, a point at which "being" retreats and vanishes before our eyes. The proximity between anamorphosis and affect is underscored by a term that resists translation: in the reflexive *desbaratarse* ("to fall apart," "to go to pieces"), which Juan Preciado uses to describe a shattered intimacy with the other, we can also hear one of the intransitive forms of *desbaratar*: "to speak nonsense" as opposed to the voice of reason. The body of the other performs a double and paradoxical function in organizing the presentation of catastrophic dissolution. With the allegorical presentation of a kind of *horror vacui*, the somatic body has been evacuated of its transcendence, its spirit or soul. Hollowed out or deprived of its transcendent ground, the body appears to collapse under the weight of its own nothingness. At the same time, however, the body—or the corpse—begins to perform a second function that is antithetical to the first, negated possibility: as its capacity to function as a sign is exhausted, what remains or emerges is the insistence of the body in its materiality. This somatic-corporeal dissolution "speaks" its own "language" precisely as its being exhausts itself. Literal and figurative meanings here become intertwined and confused as the decomposition of the other opens onto a tortured expression.

What then becomes of the relation between speech and dissolution in the second half of *Pedro Páramo*, where the privileged perspective no longer belongs to one individual but has been given over to a multiplicity of fragmentary memories, belonging both to the perpetrators and to the victims of tyranny? The second half of the work marks a significant turn within and against the tradition of the modern novel and its historical link to the modern conception of the "subject" or "individual." I am thinking of the relatively recent emergence of *testimonio* writing as a distinctively Latin American phenomenon, and of the possibility that Rulfo's text might have something important to say on the question of testimony.[57] Latin Americanist testimonial ethos is indebted to the famous gesture enacted by Pablo Neruda in his 1945 epic poem, *Las Alturas de Macchu Picchu*. In canto 12, the poet invokes the spirit of an unknown Andean slave through prosopopeia, a tropological gesture of figuration or masking carried forth in the unmarked difference between the multiple uses of *por* (meaning either "through" or "for," and thus seeking to affirm a solidarity linking instrumentality and transcendence): "Sube a nacer conmigo, hermano / . . . Yo vengo a hablar por vuestra boca muerta / . . . Hablad por mis palabras y mi sangre" ["Rise to be born with me, brother / . . . I come to speak for your dead mouth / . . . Speak through my words and my blood"]. What the poet is proposing with these words lays bare the exorbitant weight of testimony: whether it entails lending one's voice *to* the other or speaking *for* the other, prosopopeic speech would render an account of an event that left behind no witnesses. The ethical dimension of Neruda's gesture is established through a promise of restitution, a redress of voice and truth through the gift of "figure." The restitutive tropology is carried between two moments. The first marks the site of loss, affirming a prior deprivation suffered by the other. But here the poetic affirmation is in fact double, as the poet asserts both the *fact* of loss and its ostensible meaning: what has been lost is or was an essence. In the second moment, meanwhile, the poet pledges his own voice in exchange for the postulated loss. Prosopopeic restitution seeks to define and repair an injustice by "giving voice to" or "speaking for" an other who is absent or silenced, or, more precisely, who is (already) *represented* as being thus. In claiming to give or return voice to the voiceless, the poetics of prosopopeia thereby reintroduces the first principle of mimesis: it is a representation that brings the truth into view (Plato). Prosopopeic restitution thus belongs essentially to the ontotheological tradition.

It may be difficult to separate Rulfo's writing from the restitutive project just described. However, in staging the transfer of speech from the master to those who have suffered most from modernization in Mexico, Rulfo's text is not satisfied with using literary discourse to enact or approximate a reform or redistribution of "voice." The strategy pursued by Rulfo's work is more radical: the text in fact ruins the distinction between good and bad mimesis. The pattern of tropological rupture discussed above acts to unsettle modern, Enlightenment conceptions of what it means to bear witness and to testify—notions that Neruda's poetics, whether willingly or otherwise, tends to reaffirm. Rulfo's treatment of symbol and metaphor constitutes an assault on the privileged status of the ideologeme of the self-present or self-representing subject, according to which traditional conceptions of witnessing are formed (that is, of a *reliable* witness: one who was present at the event in question, in full possession of his or her faculties, who can be held accountable for what she or he says, etc.). If prosopopeia does in fact constitute the unquestioned ground of Latin American testimonio and its restitutive intentions, *Pedro Páramo* introduces a literary element that is both irreducible to and indissociable from the testimonio mode. The consideration of testimony has its point of departure in the topos of *dis*figuration. The fragmentary accounts in the second half of Rulfo's novella introduce a dimension of poetic speech that turns precisely away from the Platonic discourse of truth. But what is this "other side" of testimony, this point where language can no longer be regarded as epiphenomenal but begins to attain the status of an *object*? What happens if we read this transformation in the light of what has been called for as the vindication of lo nuestro? The emergence of language itself as a key topos in the restitutive project would require a new round of deciphering: along with Juan Preciado, we as readers are engaged in a search for what is "ours," for that to which we are indebted or obligated prior to any capacity to account for ourselves as "responsible" subjects or citizens.

As I have been indicating, following Juan Preciado's death the more or less unitary narrative perspective gives way to the multiple, fragmentary, and at times unidentifiable interpolations of the pueblo's dead, many of whom had suffered individually and collectively under the tyrannical rule of Pedro Páramo. Along with the narrator, we thus find ourselves on the "other side" of the primal scene of individual and national origins. We have entered into a kind of "afterlife" that has been rendered void of the immanence and communion associated with the Christian conception of eternity. It is easy to see how this sudden and unexpected reversal might be read as a literary restitution, in which the work returns voice to those who have at some point been silenced. Or, as in Greek tragedy, we might expect this "peripetea" to lead us to a kind of reconciliation between past and present, assigning a sense of meaning ("destiny," "necessity," etc.) to a past that until now has languished in obscurity and oblivion. However, it is at this point that Rulfo's narrative enacts a radically antirepresentational, antimimetic move, leaving undecided—and perhaps undecidable—how the text stands with respect to mimesis and restitution. Instead of presenting mimesis as a redress of exclusion and domination, as a "gift" taken from the master and returned to the dominated, Rulfo's text emphasizes a facet of voice that cannot be mastered by the master. This literary treatment of testimony cannot be equated with substitution in the interest of truth, or with an exchange of one speaker for another that leaves the ground of exchange intact. The emergence of a multiplicity of narrative or testimonial voices and perspectives profoundly alters the determination of subjectivity in the second half of the novella. This multiplicity unleashes a destructive sequence whose effects the work itself cannot evade: the murmuring of this chorus turns away from the *eidos* and thereby destabilizes the possibility of distinguishing between good and bad copies, or between false copies and the true original.

A clarification needs to be made concerning the vicissitudes of "testimony" in the novella, and particularly as this mode traces a movement from the disjunctive sequences of the first half of the narrative to the melancholic tone that organizes the second part. Many of these mnemonic fragments refer to the cacique's childhood beloved, Susana San Juan. The complexity that her figure presents for the text cannot be adequately addressed in this study.[58] But it is important to note at least the specific limit her mnemonic fragments bring to the hegemonic processes of caciquismo, and to point out the crucial role her discourse plays in the production and vicissitudes of (tragic) textual knowledge. It is ultimately Susana San Juan who, in her radiant and mortal appearance, will provide the cipher over and against which caciquismo must be interpreted. Melancholic discourse is a primary concern in Rulfo's novella, and would present considerable problems for any project claiming to give or restore voice to the other. In Rulfo's writing, the identity of the melancholic cannot easily be extracted from experiences of violence and oppression, as if these latter were merely accidental circumstances affecting an already established identity. Rather than imagining the discourse of Susana San Juan as reflecting a "different perspective" that departs from the dominant national and local discourses, perhaps her speech—somewhat akin to the presence of los indios—should be taken to mark the limit of perspective itself as a theoretical construct.

We have followed a recurrent tension between the tropological poles of figuration and disfiguration, first in the somewhat stylized performance of the "desbaratarse" passage, and then again as the question of testimony emerges in the second half of the novella. This double movement receives what is likely its most brilliant expression in the text's final passage, in which the cacique has just been attacked and mortally wounded by the mule driver, Abundio. Let us here recall the argument that Rulfian aesthetics present serious problems for the culturalist determination of modernity. We have seen how Rulfo's text transforms the Pazian pseudoopposition between "exuberant modernism" and "deficient modernization" to reveal a paradoxical and repressed identity between the two. For Rulfo, the distinctive force of literary aesthetics cannot be separated from—and neither can it compensate for—the deficiencies and dissymmetries of the latter. Modernity is *both* indissociable from *and* irreducible to the articulation of societal rupture. There can be no sense of literary modernity or contemporaneity that does not also recall the exclusions, erasures, and fissures attending the construction of the modern nation. At the same time, if literature, as a work of symbolic production or naming, hopes to relate to these gaps and silences, it must refrain from speaking *for* or in *the place of* what has been silenced or lost.

In this concluding passage, we encounter a recognition akin to what Aristotle describes as *anagnorisis*. The cacique's dying gaze, lifted skyward, is confronted by the image of Susana San Juan, who has recently preceded him in death. The beloved's radiant splendor is localized around the region of the lips and mouth, as topoi of affect and arrested—and yet we must now add, *arresting*—expression:

> Había una luna grande en medio del mundo. Se me perdían los ojos mirándote. Los rayos de la luna filtrándose sobre tu cara. No me cansaba de ver esa aparición que eras tú. Suave, restregada de luna; tu boca abullonada, humecida, irisada de estrellas; tu cuerpo transparentándose en el agua de la noche.

> [A giant moon hovered over the world. I was dazzled by the sight of you. The rays of moonlight flowing over your face. I never tired of

watching you, that apparition that you were. Soft, polished by the moonlight, your embullioned mouth was moist and iridescent among the stars; your body becoming transparent in the night dew.]⁵⁹ (70)

In this figure we find the tragic coincidence of revelation and apocalypse: here literary language would reveal what presentation itself destroys. While we could read this passage as an exaltation that restores to the subaltern something that had previously been lost or stolen, I believe that this poetic figure has to do with a kind of dignity that is not reducible to the terms of an individual or collective essence or property. This figure belongs to the sublime, and does not return the other to a previous state of wholeness or self-identity. On the contrary, it poses the limit of presentation as a constitutive moment for identity, community or, yes, love. The sublime is imprinted here by a literary device: the "boca embullonada."⁶⁰ It would seem that this epiphanic relation to the other—or, more precisely, to the other's death—is determined as a temporality of reading. This memory is also a retracing of the mark, a repetition of what only now is seen to have marked the other for death before her time. Sublimation, in this case, is not the *re*presentation of anything the other might once have held, only to lose later. As a placeholder, the *bullón* constitutes an image par excellence, in the sense described by Walter Benjamin's "dialectical image": "an image is that in which the past and the now flash into a constellation. In other words: image is dialectic at a standstill." ["Konvolut N": N 2a, 3]). The bullón marks and guards the testimonial secret, the perhaps divine mystery of pueblo memory, which caciquismo is unable to appropriate and consume. But it does so by guarding *itself* at the same time, by keeping itself secret and refusing to confirm the existence of the secret. This concealment guards a heterotopic place, unlocatable within representation, but it also marks a tragic conception of finite relation. Finitude, mortality, and transcendence are glimpsed only by way of the absolute alterity of the other: that is, via this other's impossible experience of her own alterity or death, a site of exposure in which the cacique has suddenly become doubly visible as both perpetrator and witness. It is not the case that Pedro Páramo has found, by turning to the other, what he himself lacked or desired. On the contrary, it is repetition and missed encounter—that is, through a kind of reading, the reiteration of a mark that is itself already a cite—that he gains awareness of the limits of mastery, as what precisely does not return or reflect sameness. This, anyway, is one possible reading of the conclusion.⁶¹

The sublime not only bespeaks the imminent death of Pedro Páramo. It also coincides with another instance of impossible testimony issuing from the cacique: "'Ésta es mi muerte,' dijo" ["'This is my death', he said"]. Of course, this enunciation resonates with Juan Preciado's earlier revelation of his own death to Dorotea. However, the distance separating these two speech acts also allows an interpretive difference to emerge: what has become apparent between these moments is the logical structure of caciquismo as an attempt to appropriate or annihilate all limits—and thereby to abolish death itself. As we see from the relation between cacique and pueblo, however, the relentless negation of limits engaged by the cacique is itself another kind of death. The endeavor to outstrip or shed finitude produces nothing other than a death without end. This recognition thus yields a somewhat different thematization of the death of the (symbolic) Father: if we follow the cacique from the traumatic event of his father's death up to the death of Susana San Juan (in the wake of the village's untimely celebration, he effectively condemns the pueblo to death), we see that caciquismo take shape as an institutionalization of death. The final, mortal enunciation thus offers itself as enigma: it will be necessary to die in order to have lived. The cacique's affirmation is at once a form of recognition ("*this* is my death") and a performative statement ("this *is* my death") that helps to shape or bring about the very reality it seems to describe. While the cacique's words aim to render visible and recognizable something that is already underway, in a strange way the enunciative act also prepares the way for death and allows it to take place. It does not describe a reality that would occur indifferently, with it or without it, so much as it produces and delimits the space of this happening. It is at this point, then, that the maternal demand with which this reading began also offers itself to be heard in a different register. Lo nuestro, which is spoken from out of the oblivion of forgetting, resonates here as the property of a plural we—only this is a we which is not (yet) *one*, and whose dimensions and parameters cannot be fixed or decided once and for all. The structure of community and relationality attains its crucial dimension from the double movement of enunciation, which, as an incision delimiting the plenitude and permanence of the One, thereby opens itself to the incalculable possibility of shared, future meaning.

4
The Catastrophe of Modernity: Vallejo's *Trilce* between Indigenism and the Avant-Garde

> As a man, I can sympathize with and work for the Revolution. As an artist, however, I do not control—and nor does anyone else for that matter—the political possibilities that may conceal themselves in my poems.
> —César Vallejo (Angel Flores, *Aproximaciones*)

THIS CHAPTER IDENTIFIES A TRAGIC ATTUNEMENT IN THE WORK OF the Peruvian poet César Vallejo. Focusing on a handful of the poems published in the volume *Trilce* (1922), I argue that tragic tone provides an important point of departure for a lyrical reflection on Peruvian modernity. The tragic sense that informs *Trilce* has a good deal in common with Hölderlin's attempt to incorporate the idea of tragedy into the lyrical form. This common ground is not a shared identity or destiny, as would be the case if Vallejo were merely "imitating" Hölderlin or simply picking up where the latter left off. Instead, it amounts to a similar way of juxtaposing literary history and literary modernity—such that the two are understood as both inseparable *and* incommensurable with one another. Let us recall that, for Hölderlin, modern tragedy is essentially a "translation" that sets out to realize what was only latent in the classical form: its unthought truth. Modernity thus both repeats and deconstructs the idea of tragedy as a foundational cultural text. For Vallejo, meanwhile, tragic tone gives shape to a poetic reflection on the vicissitudes of tradition in a "peripheral" region that is neither fully part of, nor fully separable from, what is often referred to as "the West." Demarcating and defining what is meant by the tragic in Vallejo presents a considerable challenge. As I am using it in this chapter, the term points both to a certain way of thinking and to an affective register (a tragic tone) that together help to define the specific—albeit by no means homogeneous—"mood" of *Trilce* as a modern and Latin Americanist text. As with Hölderlin, tragic tone for Vallejo is a decidedly modern inflection of classical form, ideation, and spirit: the tragic intonation of Vallejo's lyric poetry is not based on a mimetic intention, such as an attempt to emulate or surpass a classical master. It is far from certain, then, that what I am calling the tragic tone of Vallejo's poetry could be adequately explained in terms of the age-old quarrel between the moderns and the ancients. At the same time—and perhaps unlike Hölderlin—the poetry of *Trilce* is also marked by an endeavor to reconfigure the role that literature has traditionally played vis-à-vis the nation-state: i.e., in organizing consensus for particular nation-building projects, and in promoting the formation of citizens who identify their lot with the state. If it is admittedly difficult to imagine tragedy as something wholly other than a foundational text, the tragic tone in Vallejo's poetry nonetheless marks a limit for literature as an interpellative force. For Hölderlin, modern tragedy repeats the past in a way that would symbolize what occurred there without ever actually *taking place*. For Vallejo, meanwhile, modern tragedy points to the *impossibility* of tradition in a sociocultural and geopolitical context marked both by violent conflict between competing traditions and by the dominant tradition's desire to uproot and annihilate all others.

The tragic topos can help to shed light on this structure of historical dissymmetry and antagonism in Vallejo's work in more than one way. First, we will see how a certain affective dimension or tragic tone—which I will present in the context of poetic mourning—responds to experiences of radical loss and destitution that accompany the institutionalization of the modern nation-state in Peru. Not only does tragic tone lament the fragmentation of other traditions and social forms through colonialism and nation-building; moreover, tragedy points to and mourns an originary loss that haunts any event of institutionalization as such. In this regard, tragedy is not merely a vehicle for personal or collective mourning: it is also a thought of the *impossibility* of mourning, or of the aporetic incompatibility between mourning's commencement and its end or closure. In the second section of this chapter, I will incorporate my discussion of tragedy with another critical tendency in Vallejo criticism, which reads *Trilce* in the context of the European and Latin

American avant-garde traditions. In this way I do not mean to suggest that the aesthetic and political concerns that Vallejo may have shared with other "vanguard" poets and artists of the late nineteenth and early twentieth century are by themselves capable of accounting for all that is at stake in *Trilce*. If we are not careful, the "avant-garde" reading risks eliding many of the important differences that distinguish Vallejo from his European and Latin American peers. However, it is my belief that this interpretive frame helps to illuminate a crucial aspect of the tragic mood of Vallejo's poetry. I find the tension between "tradition" and "rupture" that characterizes the avant garde extremely useful for framing questions about Vallejo's own position vis-à-vis the question of tradition and modernity in Latin America. For instance: Is there a Latin American tradition? And if so, what relation does it assume to the general idea of tradition, or "the Western tradition" as it is first defined by European modernity? Is Latin America part of this general tradition? Or is it antagonistic toward it? Or—another possibility—does Vallejo's Latin Americanist poetics reject both of these choices and deliberately assume what we could call a "supplementary" role? Finally, in moving from the second to the third section, I will argue that the tragic mood of *Trilce* also gives rise to a reflection on the ethicopolitical, and specifically to what I have termed the groundless ground of decision. In contrast to the first two sections, where "mourning" and the "avant-garde" help to clarify a specific aspect of tragedy, in the third section the interpretive frame is a messianic tone found in some of Vallejo's poems. The messianic index in *Trilce* gives rise to a recurrent tension between the theological and the political. While a number of previous studies have shown how Vallejo undermines or "deconstructs" Catholicism by deriving profane images from sacred contexts, I will argue that the uneasy relation between theology and radical politics in *Trilce* seeks to mobilize what is in fact for Vallejo the undeconstructable kernel of Catholicism: the question of faith as it pertains to the unpresentable, or to what presentation itself destroys. Theology and politics are incommensurable for Vallejo in the sense that his poetry is neither a theology of revolution nor a revolutionary theology. However, these two domains do share a certain border, which is also a limit for both. I name this limit as a question of faith, which is always already both a form of conviction and a leap into action—and thus, as Kierkegaard put it, also a kind of madness.

Although this tripartite structure admittedly complicates my attempt to define and tease out a tragic tone in Vallejo's poetry, I believe that the resulting tensions between different aesthetic, social and political codes and contexts can in fact be quite productive. It is my belief that the "sense" of a particular code (say, the aesthetic project of the avant-garde) only truly emerges at the limit of such a project, which entails both the differences that separate it from other codes (for instance, the discourse of messianism in Latin America) and the concerns it may share with these latter. Before turning to an analysis of *Trilce*, I will first pause to clarify what is at stake in my references to Peruvian modernity. In so doing, I will indicate both what this particular modernity shares with the notion of modernity in Europe, and how it differs from the latter. My points of reference will include two well-known theorists of Peruvian modernity, José Carlos Mariátegui and Antonio Cornejo Polar.

The Duality of National Culture: on Hegemony and Heterogeneity in Postcolonial Peru

In his 1989 book *La formación de la tradición peruana*, Antonio Cornejo Polar characterizes the history of national cultural production in Peru as an ongoing conflict between two opposing tendencies, which he terms "centripetal" and "centrifugal." These movements and their conflicting torsion correspond to what Cornejo terms the "heterogeneity" of Peruvian society, or the societal disjunctions that ensue from repeated clashes between European and non-European social forms. Heterogeneity is not just a name for the differences between creole and indigenous sectors and their respective practices, perspectives and so on; in the context of the modern nation-state, it suggests that these differences have only ever been allowed to appear under the sign of the Same. That is, the appearance of difference coincides with its disappearance under the ontotheological and postcolonial regime of truth, which can only conceive of difference as a variation on identity, or as a deviation from the self-identity of the true, the One, the original.

Cornejo traces the history of national cultural production over more than a century, paying particular attention to the status of the indigenous in the postindependence tradition. In the early decades of the nineteenth century, the lettered creole elite envisioned culture—and specifically literature—as an ideal means of consolidating and disseminating a certain image of the nation and national identity. Literature was viewed as an ideal medium for promoting the idea of a white, Spanish-speaking, land-owning national subject; a subject in the same mold of those who, a generation earlier, had liberated the nation from its colonizing oppressor.[1] During the second half of the nineteenth century, however, a series of economic, political and military crises—including the military defeat and invasion of Peru at the hands of the Chilean army—began to expose the fault lines in the creole national imaginary. In view of the elite's failure to establish its own image as *the* model for national unification, new cultural icons were needed that would appeal to, exemplify and solidify a collective sense of national belonging.[2] Surprisingly, at least for creole elite, it was the indigenous populations of the Sierra—among the least "integrated" of all—who offered the most dynamic resistance to imperialism and military conquest during the first half-century of independence (although, of course, this cultural and political resistance had been occurring for approximately three hundred years). This resiliency would lead to the increased visibility of "the Indian" in post-1870s national cultural production—although the appreciation in cultural capital did not necessarily correspond to any significant improvement in the living conditions of indigenous peoples in Peru.[3] As was the case elsewhere in Latin America, such a transformation of the national imaginary, from a patently fictive homogeneity to what was ostensibly a more realistic representation of Peruvian society in its diversity or *mestizaje*, coincides with a transition from one political form to another: from the state as instrument of domination (colonialism) to the state as hegemonic suturing of social differences (modernity). In describing this latter state as "postcolonial," however, I do not mean to imply that the social, political, and economic features of colonial rule have been completely transformed following independence. Postcoloniality does not come "after" colonialism in the sense of having resolved colonialism's historical contradictions: on the contrary, in certain respects postcolonialism is precisely an extension of these antagonisms beyond the historical period known as colonialism.

Cornejo Polar maintains that the "centrifugal" culturalist drive for assimilation and unity is only half the story. With certain writers, indigenism provides a symbolic index for imagining resistance to domination; it points toward a radical exterior of modernity: radical indigenism gestures to a site that is irreducible to the sphere of modernization administered by the creole elite, a topos corresponding to the exclusions and effacements that are constitutive of Peruvian modernity (and by this latter term I understand more than just a historical period: modernity is the projected self-representation of a people or nation in its contemporaneity). To be sure, the indigenist vindication of a "matriz andina" [Andean womb] presents a competing account of both national origin and modernity, and thus potentially resembles the creole nation-building discourse even as it seeks to distinguish itself from the latter. But the competitive intent only goes so far in clarifying what is at stake in radical indigenism. What Cornejo calls the "centrifugal" force of indigenism is also a literary drive to destruction bent on exposing creole hegemony to its own disavowed and fatal truth. Indigenism is thus only insufficiently understood as providing an alternative site for the interpellation of national subjects. It may be that its most radical intervention is to be found in an attempt to shatter the illusory mirror of national unity that takes shape under the sign of *mestizaje*.

Cornejo's theory of a "centrifugal" literary force provides a basis for rethinking the relation between literature and modernity in Latin America. Whereas Ángel Rama's theory of transculturation—to take one particularly influential account of cultural modernity in Latin America—is usually understood as a normative account of literature's participation in the tendential incorporation of indigenous sectors into the national imaginary, heterogeneity calls our attention to a subaltern, "extimate" remainder that is both *within* the nation-state—or engendered by the dominant modes of production and likewise subject to the repressive apparatuses of the state—and *excluded* from the nation-state, in the sense of not enjoying the privileges and responsibilities of the national subject or citizen. Radical indigenism enacts a tropological "return" to a certain archaic Andean past, but this step back also prepares for the possibility of a leap that would break with the ideologeme of modernity as such.[4] Of course, such a rupture would necessarily affect "culture" in its modern determination as well. And so, whereas it would seem that the best that Rama's theory of transculturation could offer is a more democratic or egalitarian form of incorporation into the modern nation-state (albeit one that maintains intact the dominant relation between literary cultural production and the state), radical indigenism sets its sights on the limits of the culturalist project of assimilation, reminding us that every hegemonic suturing of society, no matter how democratic, also produces an extimate, subaltern remainder.

One could trace the idea of heterogeneity to the work of another Peruvian thinker writing in the early decades of the twentieth century, where it provides the central focus of José Carlos Mariátegui's *Siete ensayos de interpretación de la realidad peruana* (1928). For Mariátegui, the problem of Peruvian modernity cannot be explained using models developed to understand the transition from feudalism to industrial capitalism in Western Europe. Latin American modernity—or perhaps we should say, modernit*ies*—are only misunderstood when viewed as a partial, arrested, protracted, or delayed version of what has already transpired in Europe and North America. Although both European and Latin American modernities silently presuppose the same history of colonialism and international exchange, they do so from perspectives that are radically incommensurate with one another. For Western Europe, the epoch of modernity could not have unfolded as it did in the "center" without the simultaneous existence of a "periphery." To speak of "modernity" in the European context is necessarily to presuppose a certain geopolitico-ethnocultural supplement: a premodern, savage or barbaric "other" in relation to which modernity could establish itself as an economic, political, and cultural force—and as the only reasonable option available. It is a poor copy that allows the truth of the original to be seen: no modernity without the bad example of barbarism to illustrate all that modernity is not; and no modernity without the good example of the native convert to underscore what modernity promises. By contrast, Latin American modernity would appear to be devoid of any such geopolitical, economic, and cultural supplement. There is no "other Latin America" over against which Latin American modernity might establish its unquestionable right—unless of course this logic of the supplement were to be fulfilled by a particular sector *within* Latin America itself: that is, by what we today would term the subaltern.

As we have already seen, heterogeneity does not amount to "difference" in the way that one identity differs from another. For Mariátegui, Peruvian modernity is not a reflection of European modernity, but neither can it be understood apart from the structural dissymmetries that are the legacy of colonialism, imperialism, and the unfolding of European modernity. Peruvian modernity is neither "like" nor "unlike" European modernity. It can neither be matched up with nor fully separated from the latter. If linear and comparative models of progression, evolution and development all fail to do justice to heterogeneity, perhaps it would be more precise to say that the event of Peruvian modernity resembles a suspension between epochs (the Greek root epokhē denotes both a fixed point in time and a stoppage). In socioeconomic terms, Peruvian modernity does not describe a progression, however slow or partial, from one mode of production to another; it is instead characterized by a stratification of various modes and their conflicting logics and temporalities. Mariátegui argues that the true impact of colonialism cannot be measured in any single historical moment (such as the destruction of the Incan state or *Twantinsuyu*), but rather must be gauged according to a recurrent failure to integrate indigenous sectors into the colonial and postcolonial economies. The initial catastrophic effects stemming from the destruction of the Incan society are thus repeated in the inability or refusal of the Spanish colonial apparatus to construct a new social system in its place. And thus the real violence of (neo)colonialism consists in the ways in which indigenous, non-Spanish speaking sectors are left world poor.[5]

As a reflection on Latin American modernity, *Trilce* manifests at the level of poetic language something analogous to the epochal dissymmetry described by Cornejo Polar and Mariátegui. On one hand, the poetry of *Trilce* belongs to the order of world production: as a poiēsis or production, it repeatedly invokes the divine relation between word and creation. At the same time, the language of the work unleashes a corrosive, nihilistic force that eats away at the substance and solidity of being. Vallejo's poetic language reveals the elisions and forgetting that silently accompany any particular determination and presentation of truth; and thus it causes the house of Being to tremble. This double movement of production and annihilation is no doubt consistent with a modern poetic tendency in Europe and the Americas. Beginning with Hölderlin, lyric poetry issues as a belated announcement of the withdrawal of the gods. As moderns, our time is precisely defined by a dawning awareness of the void that opens up in the gods' retreat. The dawn of modernity is marked by a loss beyond measure, or a loss of precisely that measure—the transcendent—that, in an earlier time, would have been offered as compensation for our worldly travails. The modern lyric mourns this absolute loss as a void that can neither be filled up nor left behind and forgotten. At the same time, the lyric seeks to hold this place open in anticipation of the arrival of a new world of gods. Lyricism's mourning of the godhead establishes a reflected relation between poetry, the divine and loss; and it is in this sense that the relation can be understood as tragic.

To see how "tragedy" provides a model for modern thought, let us consider the lyric in the context of the speculative tradition that runs from Descartes to Hegel, or in juxtaposition to what Martin Heidegger calls the ontotheological tradition. Beginning with Descartes, philosophy is assigned the task of repairing or bridging the abyssal gap between thought and being, or between representation and truth. As we saw in the first chapter, however, Hölderlin's theory of the modern lyric suggests that reason must learn to see its own hand in the loss it mourns. In bearing witness to withdrawal and loss, poetry also expresses the awareness that reason itself is implicated in the liminal catastrophe of our time, the radical separation of thought from being: reason is itself part and parcel of the wound inflicted upon being. Modern lyricism takes shape as a confrontation with its own inaugural state of crisis, with the possibility that its language and its truth in fact participate in the separation it mourns. The lyrical moment is an approach toward the abyssal origin of modern thought, and an attempt to withstand the deafening silence that this gap threatens to impose. Lyrical poetry provides a last echo of the departing gods, thereby keeping the departure itself from falling into oblivion.

Critics have frequently viewed Vallejo's early poetry, including *Los heraldos negros* (1918) and *Trilce*, as manifesting two conflicting tendencies or orientations. Whereas the *Heraldos* poems are informed by the local icons and idiolects of the Andean Sierra—in distinction from cosmopolitan Lima—*Trilce*, according to this widely held view, is characterized by formalist experimentation that resonates with the European avant-garde of the early twentieth century.[6] Among contemporary critics, Jean Franco has perhaps been most influential in advancing an avant-garde reading of Vallejo's Peruvian poetry.[7] The avant-garde readings tend to focus on Vallejo's use of poetry to reflect critically on at least two facets of modernity: in particular, the role played by art and culture in the formation and transformation of social relations in modernity; and, in general, the status of knowledge and representation—and their possible relation to violence and domination—in a posttheological world. It seems to me that the periodization underlying such a reading only makes sense if one is attempting to identify a mode of poetic reflection that is at once "timely" with regard to a certain history of linking cultural production to state formation in Latin America, and to a certain degree "universalist" in nature—for instance, in the sense of attempting to mark the limits of the nation-state as the sine qua non of politics. Such a reading need not demonstrate that Vallejo was in fact familiar with any particular avant-garde texts or poetic theories during his years in Peru. Criticism's identification of an avant-garde tendency in *Trilce* would point to a shared historical juncture linking cultural production and critical thinking in Europe and the Americas in the early twentieth century.

Vallejo's oeuvre, and *Trilce* in particular, could also be said to speak from within a certain *untimeliness*, a sense of disjuncture from which it draws much of its insight and critical force (as well as many of the difficulties it presents for interpretation). If we were to compile a register of the various indices of disjunction in *Trilce*, we would likely find that the majority are based on images of temporal rupture or linguistic heterogeneity. And it is here, I will argue, that *Trilce* shares an important point of emphasis with some of the radical elements of Peruvian indigenism, including Mariátegui, Luis Valcárcel, and José María Arguedas. My proposal to read *Trilce* alongside the literature of indigenism may seem a peculiar strategy, especially when Vallejo's earlier poetry, published in *Los heraldos negros*, offers a greater abundance of indigenous imagery and idiolects. However, I am less concerned with thematic resonances (or lack thereof) between Vallejo and the indigenists, and more interested in identifying the seed of a common discursive strategy or poetics. While I am not proposing to compare the lyrical poetics of *Trilce* and the literature of indigenism (which has its aesthetic roots in realism), both are literary attempts to expose what I have called the unthought excess or remainder that haunts national cultural production (and *Trilce* more so, I would argue, than *Los heraldos negros*). Perhaps the aim of *Trilce* could be described as an intensification of the *literary* dimension of this reflection on national culture and its other. By this I mean that Vallejo's poetry sheds light on the ways that cultural production in general, instead of merely reflecting essential truths about a nation or people, in fact contributes to producing these essences. That is, *Trilce* is concerned with—and seeks to reveal—the self-concealing fictions at work in every determination of truth or essence. In the context of national culture, these fictions frequently depend on language to act as a "mirror" that reflects the difference between the improper and the proper, and thus between the false and the truth (for instance, those who speak with or without a certain accent, in deviation from or in agreement with established grammatical, syntactical, and lexical norms, and so on). The "experimental" language of *Trilce*, which includes distortions operating at both the semantic and the semiotic levels, is thus anything but a gratuitous play with words and appearances. On the contrary, what Vallejo does with—and to—the Spanish language in *Trilce* must be examined in the context of an aporia: *Trilce* is a poetic attempt to symbolize and mourn the violence of colonialism and its aftermath; but in order to mourn what has been proscribed or extirpated from the domain of postcolonial modernity, this poetry must paradoxically assume the form of a language whose presence in the Andes precisely marks the catastrophe that poetry laments.

And so, if a sympathetic relation can be identified between *Trilce* and what Paul Mann calls the European avant-garde's "tradition of rupture," we must also take note of an important distinction between the avant-garde project and Vallejo's Peruvian texts. This difference is of an epochal order, and it concerns the background—or the historicity—that informs each of these projects: on one hand, the more or less uniform emergence of modern industrial capitalism in Western Europe, and, on the other hand, the heterogeneous social conditions in Peru, in which both modern/capitalist and premodern/feudal modes are present in varying degrees. In light of the epochal "between-ness" or suspension, there is nothing in Latin America that would resemble what could be described in Europe as the constitution of social identity corresponding to each socioeconomic mode (the subjects of the sovereign, the citizens of the nation, the modern individual consumer, etc.). In view of this epochal dissymmetry, to attribute an avant-garde schema to Vallejo's writing, or to describe it as an attempt to produce a rupture within a tendentially seamless image of unity and contemporaneity, would be nonsensical. It would be to ignore the difference between, on the one hand, the (arguably) cohesive and (secretly) symbiotic relation between socioeconomic modernization and cultural modernism in Europe, and on the other hand, a conflictive and fragmented opposition between these same elements in Peru and much of Latin America. In pointing to this historical distinction, I do not mean to say that the avant-garde reading of *Trilce* is wrong or should be discarded. On the contrary, my point is that the text demands multiple and conflictive readings, and that it will perhaps resist *any* attempt to situate it definitively within a given epistemological frame. The lesson it imparts to us as readers includes the awareness that no single reading can provide the final word as to the shared and mutual implication of text and context. I will address each of these possible readings separately, beginning with what I have called the poetics of mourning.

Before we turn to a reading of Vallejo's poetry, a word of caution is in order concerning one of the central interpretive problems posed by *Trilce* in particular. Vallejo criticism has repeatedly noted that these poems are largely comprised of "fragments"—partial images, neologisms, and catachrestic tropes—which, taken together, do not add up to a whole. What has received less critical attention, however, is the odd temporality of poetic discourse, which likewise presents considerable difficulties for readers attempting to identify an overarching theme or signified in any particular poem.[8] The hermeneutic work of deciphering and unraveling, whose wont is to assign some thematic teleology or other to the text (so that whatever meaning emerges at a given point in the text is presumed to have been latent or emergent from the beginning), misses a more fundamental point in *Trilce*, which concerns a poetic reflection on—or "performance" of—the limits of signification. Hermeneutics, which operates under the assumption that A anticipates or clears a path for B—always under a teleological blueprint—succumbs to the illusion of a metapoetic perspective from which the totality would finally become visible in its true (read: unified) meaning. In standing above the poem, hermeneutics risks blinding itself to the emergence of *sense*, or to the fact that the opening of poetic language in one direction or another is often accompanied by linguistic elements that are irreducible to the signifying economy, such as stammering, fragmentation, indecision, and silence. In disregarding these latter "negative" conditions as merely contingent obstacles to its own work of decipherment, hermeneutics ignores the possibility that these material (or nonideal) remnants of the signifying process are in fact part and parcel of the emergence of sense.

The Maternal Share of Mourning

A number of the poems in *Trilce* are shaped by the motif of mourning, which could be described as one of the predominant tonalities—if not *the* proper tone—of the work. This topos could easily comprise a book-length study unto itself, and I am unable to describe and address here all of the questions and problems that arise in reading Vallejo's poetry as a work of mourning. What I hope to accomplish is to indicate how mourning provides one point of departure for Vallejo's confrontation with—and radicalization of—Latin Americanist poetics. What is more, this discussion will help to situate the question of tragedy in Vallejo's poetry, not only for the simple reason that the two have always been connected (mourning likewise constitutes the proper tone of Greek tragedy), but because the manner in which Vallejo's poetry obliges us to rethink what we understand by "mourning" will also have an important bearing on what I am terming the tragic attunement of *Trilce*. The analysis of mourning in this chapter will hinge primarily on a reading of a single poem, XXIII ("Tahona estuosa de aquellos mis bizcochos" [Ardent bakery of my biscuits of yore]), written in elegiac style, in which the poet laments the death of his mother. Nevertheless, we should not be too hasty in concluding that the topos of mourning pertains exclusively either to the individual and personal as opposed to the communal and social, or to the interior and psychological as opposed to the corporeal and material. In fact, we will see that the topos of mourning in *Trilce* precisely destabilizes established divisions between, for example, theories of the subject (psychoanalysis, psychology) and theories of the social (sociology, Marxism, history).

What is more, the poetic discourse on mourning in *Trilce* is not necessarily the exclusive property of a human subject: it would also be possible to identify a similar motif at work in the representation of strife between nature and culture. For instance, the first lines in poem I ("Quién hace tánta bulla, y ni deja / testar las islas que van quedando" [Who is making such a racket, and does not even allow / testament from islands that keep remaining]) establish a motif of silence for nature, its speech or "testament" having been interrupted or drowned out by a more forceful projection. And thus at the threshold of the text we encounter a paradox: in modernity it is nature that mourns or *would mourn*, could it only speak. Nature mourns silently, and this silence is both the mark and the re-mark of its mourning. That silence is the mark of loss means that nature mourns what it can no longer express or represent: the transcendence that was its creative principle, and which in other times served as a bridge between the secular and divine worlds. Nature mourns the withdrawal of the gods from our horizon, which absence gives free reign to technē in its drive for total domination of the planet. That silence is the *re*-mark of mourning, on the other hand, means that silence *is* the singular language in which nature mourns or would mourn, if it could only speak. In contrast to the *bulla* [racket, bustle, haste or confusion] of technicity, silence would bespeak nature's bereavement, if we only had the proper ears with which to hear it.

My discussion of mourning takes as its point of departure the Freudian notions of introjection and expulsion, two aims which at first glance appear to be at cross-purposes.[9] According to Freud, one of mourning's possible responses to loss is "introjection," through which mourning seeks to recuperate the libidinal investment that previously had been assigned to the departed. The mourner attempts to recall—to remember but also to reinvest or put into circulation again—the unique value that the beloved held for him or her. Moreover, mourning is a struggle with what is both *singular* and *absolute* in the loss of the beloved: that aspect that is beyond measure, and which corresponds to a place that cannot be readily filled or substituted. In contrast to the economy of introjection, mourning also attempts to expel and bury the decaying remains that would hinder its work of retrieval and reinvestment. The sepulcher, a key topos for mourning, is a mnemonic symbol that holds the place of the departed in the world; but it is also a barrier or weight that guards against the disastrous return of the dead to the world of the living. The dual necessity of "introjection" and "expulsion" comprises a bind that mourning cannot easily elude. The logic of mourning indicates that interment in the crypt, through which one stands to lose the other once again, in fact represents the only chance for a proper remembrance. It is the sepulcher that, acting like a symbol, decisively *places* and *names* the departed as no longer of this world. To name the singular is to affix a limit and even to inflict a kind of death upon it: the name is a stand-in that causes the other to become absent, marking him or her in advance as mortal and potentially absent (after all, there would be no need for names if everything and everyone in our world were always present). But naming also enables the other to re-enter the world through language, and thus renders memory as a shared or interconnected bond. In a paradoxical way, the work of mourning realizes or actualizes the loss with which it seeks to come to terms: the advent of the signifier, the sepulcher or the name, *is* the absolute loss beyond measure, the measureless measure and the point of no return for which mourning seeks to account. The work of mourning reflects a decision in favor of loss *and* memory, as opposed to a disavowal of death that would maintain the other alive by incorporating and guarding the remains—and would in fact entail a form of death without end.

The aporia dictates that the condition of possibility for mourning is also the condition of mourning's impossibility. A completely successful mourning, one that achieved complete closure with the past and securely entombed it so as to get on with the present, would in fact be nothing more than a renunciation of mourning's travail. The rhetoric of closure is the symptom of a mourning that refuses to struggle with what precisely cannot be substituted in relation to others. By the same token, however, a mourning that resisted naming and obstinately refused to delimit, forget and surrender the departed to the earth, preferring instead to internalize and preserve the still-living image of the other, would fail to do justice to the vitality of remembrance, the spirit of life that mourning is charged with redirecting (this is one way of understanding the accusative tone of poem LXXV, with its "Estáis muertos, no habiendo vivido jamás" [You all are dead, never even having lived]: one cannot die if one has never truly lived). This fundamental impasse between introjection and expulsion, remembrance and forgetting, resonates throughout *Trilce*, and to a large extent defines the extreme demands of the work's poetic expression.

The topos of mourning in *Trilce* is frequently accompanied by images that speak of untimeliness and disjointure. Mourning finds its proper tone in the sense that, in one way or another, things are "out of joint." It thus takes shape as a belated confrontation with the *real*, passing over an event whose moment has already come and gone, but whose traces continue to haunt the present. To mourn is to grapple with an event that has already occurred without ever taking place.[10] If we consider mourning in the context of the problem of modernity discussed above, perhaps "disjunctive simultaneity" would provide a more precise metaphor for Peruvian modernity than "simultaneity" and "fullness." Poem XXXIII ("Si lloviera esta noche, retiraríame" [If it were to rain tonight, I would withdraw]), a consideration of solitude, self-reflection, and poetic insight, advances several such images in the context of mourning. In the second stanza, the poet describes his reflective solitude in terms of a missed encounter between two disparate times: "traza de haber tenido / por las narices / a dos badajos inacordes de tiempo / en una misma campana" [trace of having held / by the nose / two discordant clappers of time / in a single bell].[11] This image of disjunctive simultaneity provides an impetus for Vallejo's poetic critique of the ontotheological concept of the subject. Whereas the modern philosophical tradition, beginning with Descartes, views self-consciousness or self-presence as the unquestioned ground of the subject, Vallejo here proposes that poetic introspection—which in many circumstances constitutes an exemplary trope of self-consciousness—is in fact a confrontation with a certain *impossibility* (or, in psychoanalytic terminology, the traumatic kernel) at the heart of the subject.[12] As an attempt to construct a registry of both loss and renewal, mourning must begin by losing and mourning *itself* as the universal mode of reflection proper to an absolute subject. It is not difficult to see how this thought of the disjunctive ground or cause of the subject could likewise be linked to a modern conception of tragedy: we need only recall Schelling's interpretation of Greek tragedy as presenting the profound contradiction between freedom and necessity, which we—along with the tragic hero—must come to see as occupying the "same" place at the origin of the subject.

Eduardo Neale-Silva tells us that many of the *Trilce* poems were composed shortly after the death of the poet's mother in 1918, and it would not be difficult to see the work as a response to this singular, unsubstitutable loss. As an interpretive lens, however, the idea of mourning can also help to situate Vallejo's poetry in relation to social and historical questions specific to Peruvian or Andean society, at a time in Vallejo's career when cosmopolitan and internationalist influences were clearly strong. I thus propose what may at first glance appear to be a counterintuitive reading: I will treat mourning as a kind of social analogue, in which the singular and familial relation between mother and child establishes a tenuous resonance with questions of community and subalternity in Peru. Of course, literary analogies between the maternal and the indigenous community are nothing new: suffice it to recall what Peruvian indigenism terms the nation's "Andean womb." Add to this the fact both of Vallejo's grandmothers were of Chimú origin (a tribe in northern coastal Peru, first colonized by the Incas in the fifteenth century) rather than Spanish ethnicity, and it should be clear that the references to the maternal in Vallejo's poetry do not necessarily point exclusively to the biological mother. In mourning, the singular is obliged to open itself, albeit aporetically, to the universal spheres of exchange, substitution and metaphor.

In several of the poems, such as XXVIII ("He almorzado solo ahora, y no he tenido" [I have eaten alone now, and have not had]) and XXIII, the work of mourning also finds an analogue in the act of eating (a topos very close to the maternal for Vallejo). At the same time, the aporia of mourning is marked in these poems by the impossibility of eating (well) following the death of the mother. The impasse that is symptomatically represented by the impossibility of eating has the potential to complicate what we understand by "introjection." Rather than imagining mourning according to an economic metaphor, as a process of recuperation and reinvestment of libidinal energy that progresses toward a predetermined end without leaving any remainder or surplus, Vallejo's poetry suggests that mourning must begin by confronting the limits of the economic model of libidinal reinvestment (and it matters little whether we understand the aim of the economic model as "closure" or simply as the regulation of the libidinal system, its intake and its expenditures). Mourning must paradoxically begin where substitution and exchange fail. In the first two lines of XXVIII, the impossibility of substitution is itself revealed as one of the principle effects of loss: what has been displaced goes beyond the absence of the biological mother, and points to the symbolic mandate that would situate the subject (or the poet) in relation to others. This "call" is rendered metaphorically as a series of commands that a mother might give to a child at the dinner table: "He almorzado solo ahora, y no he tenido / madre, ni súplica, ni sírvete, ni agua. . . ." [I have eaten alone now, and have not had / mother, nor *ask first*, nor *serve yourself*, nor *water*. . . .]. And so, at first glance, the death of the mother is experienced as the oblivion of all address: it is not only the absence of that other who recognizes and responds to the child's needs, but also the withdrawal of the Other—the guarantor of meaning itself—through which any and all demands must a priori be directed. The stakes of mourning—as well as the specter of its impossibility—are thus defined as both personal, familial, and communal. What mourning must remember and recuperate through introjection is the originary and unique invitation that identifies and constitutes the subject as a member of the family or community. The subject is quite literally *called* into being: it is a subject only because it embraces the fact that it has been named, invoked, and made responsible before others. This echoing of the invitation ("súplicate, sírvete") affords another way of understanding the analogy between eating or orality and mourning: the motif of ingestion suggests a kind of inverted repetition of the commencement of speech, of the subject's entrance into language.[13] We thus find condensed in the affective registers of "mouth" and "voice" both the possibility and the impossibility of mourning. On one hand, Vallejo's poetry presents speech as a condition of possibility for mourning qua symbolization or articulation, both in the sense of verbalization and in the sense of joining or making a joint (the Latin root *artus* means joint). But words alone are not enough to mourn the loss of the beloved: it is also a matter of finding just the right pitch, intonation, and rhythm. As we will see, however, the poetic subject's relation to speech is always marked in advance by absence. The onset of speech itself bears witness to what must be mourned: the loss of that archaic, unbounded maternal plenitude that was once enjoyed by the infant.

The aforementioned link between mourning and ingestion is illustrated in a striking manner in the elegiac poem XXIII, and the remainder of this section will be a reading of this poem. The poet addresses the dead mother, lamenting both her absence as well as the abject conditions in which he and his fellow orphans have been left. While the elegy constitutes a well-established form of poetic remembrance, the formal development of the poem calls into question traditional conceptions of mourning: i.e., as a teleology of the Ego and its reconstruction, or as a process by which the Ego is first split by a traumatic wound and finally, through bereavement, manages to regain its former wholeness. The first stanza, which comprises a single nominal phrase, advances an image of the maternal order (or the mother along with the infant) as that of well-being and plenitude. In fact, this plenitude is not unlike the wholeness presupposed by the teleological model of mourning. We find the mother—who is not actually named until the final word of the stanza—linked to a kind of alimentary production and distribution: her first appearance is as a "Tahona estuosa," an ardent/glowing bakery. This metaphorical link between the maternal and production/alimentation will in subsequent stanzas yield at least several distinct implications, which together constitute something like the horizons of a world for the child: first the maternal "bakery" will be associated with physical and spiritual sustenance (warmth and food; the Eucharist), and then to time itself, which the poem presents as the condition of possibility for hope as well as memory and mourning. Prior to these associations, however, we encounter a poetic memory of the maternal as a pretemporal, quasi-utopian order of undifferentiated wholeness, or "pura yema infantil innumerable" [pure infantile innumerable yolk]. The grammatical structure of this short phrase, a clustering of nouns and adjectives devoid of punctuation, lends support to the image of an expanse without limits or divisions. The basis of this poetic memory, we might suspect, is akin to what Serge Leclaire calls "his majesty the infant": the prelinguistic child who has not yet begun to conceive of his or her own body as a whole that is distinct from other bodies, and who thus makes no distinction between the self and its limits, or between self and other.[14]

It is not until the second stanza that we hear of the mother's death, in a strange phrase which, while commenting on her absence, inexplicably inverts the subject-object relation between mourners and the deceased: "Oh tus cuatro gorgas, asombrosamente / mal plañidas, madre: tus mendigos" [Oh, your four gorges, so / badly lamented, mother: your beggars]. Grammatically speaking, it is the orphaned children—and not the mother—who are mourned poorly. The catastrophic consequences of her death are underscored by the pathetic self-portrait, in which orphanhood and indigence encroach on the child's tenuous and teetering relation to language: "y yo arrastrando todavía / una trenza por cada letra del abecedario" [and I still dragging / a braid for every letter of the primer].[15] This strange image of a child clinging (doggedly? precariously?) to language points out a connection between the death of the mother and a rupture in the symbolic world of the survivors. Earlier in this section, it was suggested that all mourning paradoxically recalls and laments, among other things, the loss that is the advent of language itself: mourning recalls the sacrifice of the "pura lema infantil" that is exacted of every speaking subject as the price of access to the world of shared meaning. To enter into a speaking relation with the world is necessarily to assume as our own certain limits that in fact precede us; and while the specificity of the limit (e.g., the proscription of incest) may well be contingent, the *fact* that there are limits is not: to speak is first and always to be unable to say everything. In Vallejo's poem, however, we encounter what is nearly the inverse of that proposition concerning the loss of primordial plenitude. The phrase "asombrosamente / mal plañidas" would seem to imply that, in the wake of the mother's death and in the void her departure leaves behind, it is precisely this secondary and compensatory time of language from which the children are alienated, unable to find themselves within the symbolic network of community or society. The quasi-originary loss of immediacy and plenitude—to be distinguished, logically and perhaps even chronologically, from the death of the biological mother—has not been substituted by a new foundation of symbolic relations and equivalencies. In ontological terms, the children are caught *between* the infantile fantasy of wholeness and the assumption of language; they belong to neither world. This image of orphanhood has unmistakable sociopolitical implications. As Alain Sicard has suggested, "orfandad" is synonymous with what Vallejo will later term "mis mendigos."[16] These linguistic and cultural orphans are decidedly not the masses (who, as masses, are always already interpellated: by populism, fascism, socialism, or what have you), but rather what Gramsci terms the subaltern: the unassimilated social and human "detritus" that is produced through modernization but precisely *not* incorporated into any hegemonic sociopolitical configuration. In addition, the proximity of "tus mendigos" (a class-based term) to the analphabetic child suggests that an ethnic question is at stake as well. In the context of postcolonial Peru, the image of a child dragging a spelling primer points to the contradictions that inhere to Spanish as the official, written language, the language of the state, in a nation with a substantial Quechua-speaking population. The mother's death thus allegorizes the condition of subalternity as that of being caught between two cultures, languages and epochs.

The third stanza is an idealized recollection of the mother as purveyor of the good, as the agent who distributed the archaic, unary stuff: "En la sala de arriba nos repartías / de mañana, de tarde, de dual estiba, / aquellas ricas hostias de tiempo. . . ." [In the room upstairs you meted out to us / morning, afternoon, from dual stowage, / those succulent hosts of time. . . .] The verb "repartir" [to apportion, to share out, to divide up, but also to cut or to break open] introduces a key development in this passage. The maternal function in organizing the shared space of family or community is a formal procedure of sharing out and delimiting the undivided expanse of infancy ("pura lema infantil"). By necessity, a just measuring and distribution of the good also breaks up the primordial image of a totality without limits or divisions. Again, it is my position that the distinction between family or the maternal order and community is not the sole concern here: the biological mother can also be seen as a stand-in for the organizing principle of social space in general. For Vallejo's poetry, in other words, the mother is—among other things—one of the names for the state. The metaphoric presentation of the breast(s) as "stowage" opens the door, in the following line, for a transition from feeding to communion or

4: THE CATASTROPHE OF MODERNITY

the establishment of (religious) community: the mother's milk is now rendered "aquellas ricas hostias de tiempo." The maternal thus becomes the sublation of the body in and as spirit. The mother represents the vanquishing of the physical and its limits—want, hunger, deprivation, and solitude—and the initiation of love and communuality. And thus a circuit of remembrance would appear to have been completed, having taken us from the time of archaic plenitude and limitlessness to that of loss and alienation, and finally to the birth of community as the mediation of the individual and its limits.

But the key motif of the third stanza, "repartir" as the maternal gesture par excellence, would also seem to echo a kind of division or difference inherent to the act of giving. In this light, the maternal metaphor *implies* the state as ordering principle, but it is not exhausted in this reference. What is more, this thought of the "difference" that inheres in the maternal gesture will shed new light on the treatment of mourning in *Trilce*. In "repartir" we can also hear the reflexive verb "partirse" [literally, "to divide oneself"], sometimes used as a figurative evocation of sorrow (e.g., "se me parte el alma" [roughly, "it breaks my heart"]). The maternal gift can only become what it is by imparting itself beyond itself, by giving what it *is not* or *has not*: time itself. But what does it mean, to give what one does not have? And what is it to give *time*, which nobody truly possesses?[17] One possible response to these questions is that the maternal gift—if there were one, if it were not to fall into oblivion prior to its arrival—would not consist in a tangible good that could be measured, exchanged, or returned. The gift lies beyond all power of (ap)propriation and all authorization, including that of the mother herself. The giver's intention can never provide the sufficient ground for determining what is (the meaning of) a gift: such calculative measures precisely destroy the gift by turning it into an object of exchange, something given *in order to have received in return* (even if the return is only measured in terms of recognition and gratitude). The maternal gift would seem to point to time and to the future as limits of all calculation: not a given, predetermined future or future-present—as in "I want you to be this or that, to do this or that"—but rather the future as pure possibility, as the chance that someday things might turn out otherwise than they are today. The gift is thus marked by its own a priori deferral or impossibility: the only gift worth giving is that which cannot be given. What if, in mourning, the subject finds itself indebted to the gift or to the event of giving, an act marked by something radically in excess of every intention, stated wish and command, something that eludes the economy of recognition that governs giving and receiving? What if mourning finds itself responsible or indebted to that which it precisely could not return to the other, since it was never hers to begin with?

In the final lines of the third stanza we are reminded of the aforementioned crisis brought on by the death of the mother. These lines bring us back to the destitution of the present through a striking divergence in tone between the third line—which recalls the promise of community and transcendence in the "ricas hostias de tiempo"—and the fourth line, which renders a powerful description of the present as hollowed out "cáscaras de relojes," empty husks of time devoid of any futurity. Here time as transcendental ground has been exhausted or has suffered a rupture. The fourth stanza further elaborates on this allegorical motif of "hollowed out" time. The language of this stanza warrants close attention, as it would appear to be proposing an important connection between mourning, poetry and the limits of both discourses. The poet begins by addressing the mother anew, while referring twice the present as moment of poetic enunciation: "Madre, y ahora! Ahora . . ." [Mother, and now! Now . . .]. The redoubling of "ahora" marks and re-marks the poetic present as no longer One, as having suffered a split. The need to repeat this affirmation (one "now" is never sufficient) yields a fragmentary address that borders on a kind of stammering. From here the address assumes the form of an unmarked question, about which there is much to say: ". . . en cuál alvéolo / quedaría, en qué retoño capilar, / cierta migaja que hoy se me ata el cuello / y no quiere pasar" [. . . in what alveole / does it remain, in what capillary shoot, / a certain crumb which today binds my throat / and does not want to pass through].[18] The deferral in specifying the grammatical subject (it is the "cierta migaja") for two full lines has the effect of extending the question and its force—"en cuál . . . quedaría," or roughly "in what . . . does *it* remain—while dispelling whatever notions the reader might harbor that some particular answer could close the gap this questioning opens up.[19] This prolonged question produces a kind of allegorical *Ubi sunt?*, an abyssal interrogation whose echoes exceed any determinate subject or specificity, while intensifying the prevailing tone of disillusionment and abandonment.

What is the meaning of the poet's appeal to or interrogation of the mother concerning this "cierta migaja"? The inquiry specifically asks about a "certain" remainder—it is precisely nameless—that has become lodged in one of the body's regulatory systems: either in the lungs (the alveoli, or the air sacs that exchange oxygen between the lungs and the blood), in the cardiovascular system (a *retoño* is the new sprout or shoot of a plant; in colloquial usage it can also refer to a young son), or in the throat. As an unaccounted-for leftover, this "cierta migaja" troubles these systems of circulation and exchange, these conduits between inside and outside, between *somos* and *pneuma*. In the context of the previous stanzas, this "certain crumb" clearly refers back to the communion host and the motifs of physical and spiritual sustenance. Now, in place of the Eucharist as the transcendent basis of communion, poetic reflection attempts to track down and grasp an unnamed or unnameable excess, a negative or material remainder that disturbs what is the governing rationale of every economic system: to regulate the whole and ensure its smooth (re)productive functioning.

But it would seem that poetry too finds itself affected and implicated by this troublesome remnant. Voice and breath, as possible metaphors for poetic activity or expression—and as conduits between inside and outside, between dead letter and living spirit—also stumble over this nameless remainder that is both inside and (of the) outside. This crumb of the real that sticks in the throat marks a limit for the pseudo-Romantic aesthetic ideology that dominated Latin American poetics for much of the nineteenth and early twentieth century. The uncategorizable and indigestible kernel signals an interruption of the aesthetic topology of gustation, pleasure, and digestion that has provided the foundation for one modern view of poetic production. Perhaps what is at issue here is finally a thought of the material limit of (spiritual, libidinal, aesthetic, or capitalist) economy as such. The poem is not simply a "critique" of any one of these systems. Rather, it is an attempt to shed light on what we could call the internal limit of these systems, or of systematicity as such: the point where the mechanism or passage—e.g., the cathexis, signification, or internalization, all of which imply raising the inanimate or the wasteful to the level of living production—trembles and begins to fail. This thought of an internal remainder is precisely the singular place from which the work of mourning must begin for Vallejo. Mourning receives its exigency from the echoes of the other's dying breath, and from the possibility that something there, silent and invisible, remains unaccounted for by traditional forms of remembrance. The need for mourning, which would cleanse the subject of this petrified remainder, cannot be separated from the impossibility of mourning: not only does this material remnant haunt any economic model of bereavement and closure, but in a certain sense it is precisely that singularity or alterity with which mourning must—and cannot—come to terms. It is the unrecognizable excess of all recognition.

In the fourth and fifth stanzas, the poet turns from this direct address of the mother to a consideration of the tomb and her remains. Her bones, now reduced to mere powder, are likened to the flour used to make biscuits in the first stanza; what is missing, however, is the "glue" that would hold the communal substance together. "[T]us puros huesos estarán harina /" [Your pure bones must be flour by now], the poet speculates, "que no habrá en qué amasar" [which has nowhere in which to become dough]: the verb *amasar* [to knead or mix] also contains an echo of the absent *masas* or the failure of interpellation represented by the mother's death. The fourth stanza's allusion to (arrested) poetic voice gives way in the fifth stanza to a juxtaposition of the dead and the living: the dead mother's eternal silence provides a kind of negative testimony to the surviving structure of domination: "Tal la tierra oirá en tu silenciar, / cómo nos van cobrando todos." [And so the earth will hear in your silencing, / how they keep charging us for everything]. In fact it is the mother's silenc*ing*—a strange juxtaposition of the passive and the active, of victim and agent—that conveys the (perhaps unspeakable) story of domination and expropriation.

Poetic reflection on the aporias of mourning sheds light on an important distinction between Vallejo's poetry and the theory of literature presupposed by Ángel Rama's notion of transculturation. It is not my intention to create a rigid opposition between two different poetic systems or theories of cultural production. In fact, I believe that what I am saying about Vallejo also holds to a large extent for the majority of the writers dealt with by Rama: transculturation and aporetic mourning presuppose one another and cannot exist without each other. I do mean to suggest, though, that Vallejo's poetics leads us in a direction that Rama might not be willing to follow. As we recall from the earlier chapter on Rulfo, transculturation is a literary attempt to come to terms with what Rama calls "los desgarramientos y problemas de la colisión cultural" [the rending problems of cultural collision]. In cases where national culture has tended to ignore or marginalize noncreole cultural traditions, transculturation attempts to disrupt or modify the postcolonial national imaginary, and thereby to alter the nation's official history of social, ethnic, and racial relations. All of the writers discussed by Rama are concerned with exposing the myth of a more or less complete "assimilation" of indigenous and noncreole sectors under the sign of the modern nation-state, a myth that is in fact a thin disguise for the structures of domination that have led to the near-total destruction of indigenous practices and traditions, including language, religion, and sociopolitical forms. However, the work of demystification is only part of what is at stake in the theory of transculturation: for Rama, literature is also charged with realizing a better, more just and democratic interpellation of the subaltern as national subjects. It would carry out a symbolic incorporation or naming of experiences and traditions that have heretofore been foreclosed from participating in national culture and politics. Transculturation would thus offer itself as a negation and dissolution of the condition of subalternity, first by exposing the history of false assimilations of the indigenous, and then by producing the symbolic and imaginary basis for a true or truer inscription of the indigenous as national subject or citizen.

Perhaps Vallejo's poetry, with its persistent attention to the figures of the mother and the orphan, could be said to attempt something similar with regard to patriarchal, creole-dominated national culture.[20] To a certain extent, the maternal figure in *Trilce* could well be understood as an alternative locus of identification and interpellation, in a context where the Father is always already complicit with the dominant discourse. But, for Vallejo, poetic mourning must also confront what precisely exceeds the restitutive and recuperative powers of literature. Mourning must attend to those points or moments in which the economic apparatuses of recognition, exchange, and sublimation all fail. And so, for Vallejo, it is both mourning *and* the impossibility of mourning: there cannot be one without the other. There is no proper language in which to mourn the destruction of language and community; and there is no adequate language in which to reveal what presentation itself destroys. And yet, as Vallejo understood, language—the language of poetry—always already says what it does not mean to say, saying both more than and otherwise than what the economy of signification would have it say.

TRILCE AND THE AVANT-GARDE:
SHATTERING THE "DUPLICITY" OF HARMONY

Jean Franco's *César Vallejo: The Dialectics of Poetry and Silence*, published in 1976, remains one of the most influential cultural studies-based interpretations of Vallejo's oeuvre, and a groundbreaking study of the "avant-garde" tendencies in Vallejo's early poetry. According to Franco, the importance of *Trilce* as a Latin Americanist text lies in its attempt to break with the pseudo-Romantic aesthetic ideology that dominated in Latin America during much of the nineteenth century and into the first decades of the twentieth century. The "rupture" that writers such as Vallejo seek to hasten would not only mean a change in poetic theory, style, and so on; it would also signal a radical transformation of the way that literature is understood as a social and historical force in modernity. The foreclosure of Romantic aesthetic ideology would mark the exhaustion of literature's role in organizing the construction and modernization of the Latin American nation-state. One of Franco's important contributions in this regard is to have demonstrated a connection between, on the one hand, this epochal determination of literature that takes the modern nation-state as its unquestioned ground, and, on the other hand, the philosophical tradition that—ever since Plato—conceives of truth as *presence* (or as the original: timeless, complete and self-knowing) and nontruth as *lack* (or as what is merely a copy: temporal and irrational or unconscious). Franco's discussion of the philosophical stakes of Vallejo's project opens up a new way of thinking about modern Latin Americanist poetics and its relation to cultural translation. In this section I will first clarify briefly what I understand to be at stake in the question of an avant-garde poetics in *Trilce*. Then, I will turn to a poem that illustrates at least some of the concerns raised under the heading of the avant-garde in Latin America.

Peter Bürger and others have shown that, as a self-described rupture within the modern tradition, the avant-garde entails both a reinterpretation of prevailing artistic norms and an intervention in political uses of the aesthetic.[21] As a critical phase of modern cultural production, the avant-garde exposes a historical complicity between high art and the forces of domination and alienation in modern society. What holds for art in general in Bürger's analysis is perhaps especially true of literature: beginning with Romanticism, literature is often viewed as both a sanctuary and a moral beacon within an increasingly hostile and disenchanted world. Modernity, according to this same view, is characterized by a number of negative side effects associated with industrialization and modernization, including the decline of traditional values amidst commercialization and commodification, the fragmentation of human experience through increasing specialization in education and the workplace, and the destruction of traditional social bonds (community and family) together with the market's tendency to define modern subjects as individual consumers. Literature, by contrast, offers a refuge and a last bastion of the humanist tradition, uncontaminated by the corrosive effects of modernization. Literature is a space of timeless and universal values. It promises a world of beauty and sublimity in exchange for the increasing homogenization and sterility of modern urban life; and, as aesthetic experience, it teaches us to pass judgment, and thus enables us to constitute ourselves as aesthetic subjects able to overcome our mere individuality and particularity through the universal language of literature. If this describes in a nutshell the aesthetic ideology that defines the role of literature as a compensatory modernism, then the avant-garde on the other hand attempts to expose the secret identity that underlies this opposition between modernization and modernism. There are at least two facets that need to be mentioned here. At the empirical level, it is not difficult to see how literature and high art are in fact already contaminated by the very forces they claim to oppose. The role of art markets—including museums, galleries, and best-seller lists—in shaping aesthetic tendencies and tastes should be enough to dispel the illusion that art and literature remain essentially untouched by capital. But there is also a theoretical level at which the high art of modernism could be said to constitute the secret reverse side of modernization. Insofar as art and literature present themselves or—why not?—market themselves as antidotes to the noxious side effects of modernization, they in fact—wittingly or otherwise—offer a space of resistance that modernity needs in order to thrive. In the absence of any (semblance of) alternative to or temporary escape from the ill effects of modernization, modernity would no doubt be judged to have exceeded its social mandate of democratizing and enhancing socioeconomic production. In order to secure its position, modernity must make itself into a self-negating work of negation: modernity must be the project of modernization, which undertakes the radical transformation of nature and all social relations, together with the projection of an outside, a reserve of timeless and universal values sheltered from the transitory and caustic effects of modernization. It is precisely this double register of negation and the negation of negation that the avant-garde seeks to expose as constituting two sides of the same coin.

In Franco's view, the relation that Vallejo's poetry assumes to the Latin American literary and artistic tradition is—at least as far as the preceding point goes—analogous to that of the avant-garde in Europe. Vallejo takes aim at the ideologemes that dominate Latin American poetic discourse at the turn of the century with the emergence of modernismo. Through such privileged figures as "image" (Darío) and "rhythm" (Valdelomar), literature idealizes its ability to suture the wounds inflicted by modernization, and thereby masks the role played by the aesthetic in reproducing the dominant socioeconomic conditions of production. In offering the aesthetic as a form of compensation for the violent contradictions imposed by modernization, literature in fact lends its support to the general project of modernity: it establishes aesthetic modernity as the ideological neutralization of the traumatic societal wounds reopened by dissymmetrical modernization in the periphery.[22]

Trilce XXXVI ("Pugnamos ensartarnos por un ojo de aguja" [We strive to thread ourselves through the eye of a needle]) will provide fertile ground for examining Vallejo as a poet of the avant-garde. As a critical rereading of the Western tradition, the poem takes as its point of departure the trope of ekphrasis, or the poetic representation of painting and sculpture. One of the focal points of the poem is the ancient Greek statue known as the Venus de Milo. As we will see, this statue, together with the name it bears, cannot avoid becoming entangled in a certain *textuality* inherent to the poem, the complexity of which can only be partially unraveled here.

Perhaps the most obvious textual index is to be found in the Venus de Milo's modern fame as an exemplar of classical beauty, or as a harmoniously proportioned whole. What is more, the notions of harmony and the beautiful that are exemplified by the statue provide much of the ideological support structure for compensatory modernism in Latin America (more on this in a moment). As its name indicates, the Venus is a bridge between the aesthetic ideals of grace and beauty on the one hand, and love on the other. It is an exemplary manifestation of the eternal and the undying, and of the sublime as a boundary for conceptual thinking. The statue's ekphrastic presence in the poem is a manifestation of what can only be conveyed at the limits of the economy of the sign—communicated, for instance, through a look or a gesture.

Of course, the Venus de Milo also plays an important role in modern Latin American poetry, figuring prominently in what is perhaps the high point of modernismo, Rubén Darío's "Yo persigo una forma" [I seek a form] (1900). For Darío, the Venus de Milo is the avatar of a culturalism that promises to transfer the knowledge, recognition and cultural capital of the Western tradition (and principally of nineteenth-century French culture) to Latin America, while asserting Latin America's equal right to engage with the tradition as a form of universal patrimony. When the poet of "Yo persigo una forma" refers to the "abrazo imposible de la Venus de Milo" [impossible embrace of the Venus de Milo], he is gesturing toward the ineffable secret of nature, the enigma that ordinary language seeks and fails to convey, and which can only be approached through the higher language of poetic discourse. I will suggest that, in alluding to the same statue, Vallejo's poem takes aim at something different and perhaps more radical in its design (though this is not to say that the Latin Americanist project in Darío's poetry is not also important). The use of ekphrasis in Vallejo's poem is a form of citation, or a citation of prior citations. The naming of the Venus, an object that at face value has nothing to do with Latin America, cannot avoid configuring this poem as an intervention in the Latin Americanist tradition, while also no doubt providing an index of Vallejo's attempts to distinguish himself from Darío. Vallejo's poem does not simply lay claim to the signs and touchstones of what I am calling "the Western tradition" for a Latin American context. On the contrary, Vallejo is concerned with the manner in which "tradition" or "*the* tradition" is established and reproduced through usage and citation; and likewise, his poetry is a consideration of what is forgotten or repressed in this traditio, this delivery or transmission of truth, value, and permanence. For Vallejo, the Venus is not a reserve of eternal truth or value, a vessel whose appropriation could confer legitimacy on the Latin American tradition. Instead, the statue is like a signifier, and its history the originary spacing or the breach that makes room for meaning. One of the principle goals of my reading, then, is to show how Vallejo's poem explores and exploits the limits of the culturalist determination of truth as a representation that conforms itself in adequate fashion to the original.

The statue's association with the ideal notwithstanding, the poem also underscores its object quality or "thinginess." In the poem's reference to the Venus, we can glimpse the material traces of a certain provenance, a history of travails and losses the statue has suffered; this history includes both the statue's "discovery" and expropriation in the early nineteenth century, and its subsequent display as an exemplar of the proper and of tradition qua permanence.[23] Vallejo's poem invites us to consider the statue as a kind of text, one that bears the signs of its own history in the form of marks and scars. But as marks and scars, these indices also remind us that the history that encompasses them cannot be learned, recuperated or recited in its totality. Take the famous arms, or what remains of them: the apparent fact that the Venus's arms were at some point broken off—one just above the elbow, the other completely sheared off at the shoulder—would seem to reinforce the culturalist idea of perfection that envelops it. These phantom appendages uphold what Walter Benjamin would call the statue's "aura." The Venus is like a ruin whose fragments tell the tale of a mysterious and irremediable loss. And yet, for we moderns, its fragmentary state seems only to strengthen our convictions regarding the unfathomable genius and plenitude of the ancients.

Earlier I mentioned that the poetry of *Trilce* is especially resistant to the totalizing and teleological tendencies of hermeneutics. Vallejo's poetry often appears to invite a particular line of literary exegesis, only to undermine the reader by abandoning that course and embarking on a tangential path. We are reminded in poem XXXVI of these hermeneutic limits through the use of ekphrasis, which strongly suggests that the "language" of sculpture may provide a better analogy for poetic discourse than the signifying economy of metaphor or the temporality of narrative. Even prior to the appearance of the Venus de Milo, the poem raises just this point in the first stanza with a catachrestic distortion of the Judeo-Christian promise of redemption: "Pugnamos ensartarnos por un ojo de aguja." This trope both reiterates and destabilizes the promise of eschatological redemption contained in the axiom, "It is easier for a camel to pass through the eye of a needle, than for a rich man to enter into the kingdom of God." Whereas the latter dictum implicitly exchanges suffering on earth for eternal salvation, Vallejo's paraphrastic citation casts doubt on the general possibility of transcendence or redemption: "pugnamos" fails to establish any eschatological distinction between the privileged few and the many; what is more, it seems to retract the Christian promise to redeem impoverishment on earth through eternal salvation. At a metatextual level, the tropological distortion also evokes the interpretive problem I alluded to at the beginning of the chapter: *pugnar* and *ensartar* invite us to envision the reader's struggle to "thread the needle" and account for all loose ends in the interpretation of the text. And, as we will see, this particular poem displays a remarkable tendency to foil its own exegesis: time and again it introduces a particular motif or thread—such as that of redemption—only to pull the rug out from under the reader who seeks to develop and follow the thread to its conclusion. The reader, it would seem, is left with a number of "dead ends" devoid of any master thread that could unite them and suture their differences.

The eschatological motif introduced in the first line will metamorphose, in the following lines of the first stanza, into an allusion to sex and sexual difference. The cumulative effect—if we can still speak like this—is that no single reading and no combination of readings can claim to deliver the truth of the poem in its entirety. Poetic *sense* cannot be separated from those points where referentiality begins to multiply and break down. Vallejo's poem is *allegorical* in the precise sense of exposing the mechanics and the internal limits of signification, underscoring the manner in which meaning is institutionalized through the forgetting of contingency and errancy.[24] No hermeneutic chronology or teleology could account for or calculate the vertiginous uncertainty that reading is liable to undergo at any given moment. The emergence of poetic sense (as opposed to meaning) cannot be neatly separated from its withdrawal (or the slippage or dissipation of meaning).[25] Here we can also take note of an important distinction between Vallejo's poetry and the poetics of the avant-garde. Even if the European avant-garde provides a useful framework for examining the aesthetic and political dimensions of *Trilce*—and I believe that it does—there is nevertheless an important ideological distinction to be made on this point: Vallejo's poetry does not present itself as the work of a *vanguard*, as a poetry that has risen above the particularity of its own social conditions and thereby come to occupy the position of absolute knowledge vis-à-vis the social totality.

Franco has shown how the first stanza of XXXVI sets the stage for Vallejo's critique of Platonism, which begins by seeking to destabilize the Platonic-Christian discourse on love as perfection of the individual or as communion.[26] The community of lovers, which for the philosophical tradition represents a shared, spiritual sublation of the individual and its limits, is here exposed to its unthought reverse side: the possibility that the institutionalization of sexual difference under the sign of gender does not overcome the limits of the particular, but rather amounts to a forgetting of *difference as such*. Identity and gender are masks that help to neutralize the real (antagonism, trauma, enjoyment) by rendering it as a momentary obstacle to be overcome. In this way, Vallejo's poetry effectively transfers social antagonism to another register—the aesthetic—in order to produce a kind of theoretico-poetic revelation, a momentary unveiling of the state mechanism itself. Let us begin reading the first stanza in order to see how the problem of sexual difference emerges as a key concern for Vallejo's writing.

I have already addressed the eschatological and hermeneutic motifs—and the attending problems—raised in the first stanza. The short second line, "enfrentados a las ganadas" [face to face, hell-bent on winning] elaborates on the previously unspecified "we" of the first line, which is now to be seen as a potentially conflictive face-to-face meeting. In the third line, the phrase "Amoniácase casi el cuarto ángulo del círculo" [The fourth angle of the circle almost becomes armonía] introduces at least two distinct interpretive possibilities. For one, it alludes to the harmonious reconciliation of strife that I have already termed ideological: the neologism *amoniácase* looks and sounds like *armonía* or harmony; and this association will be reiterated, albeit negatively, in the third stanza's exhortation to refuse the "seguridad dupla de la Armonía" [duplicitous security of Harmony]. Let me seek to clarify exactly what I understand by aesthetic ideology here. In the context of Vallejo's poem, I am not describing the aestheticist evocation of harmony as ideological in the traditional Marxian sense of lending support to "false consciousness," i.e., because it helps us to ignore or even desire our own exploitation and alienation, or because it passes these conditions off as enjoyable experiences for the reader. The recourse to harmony that Vallejo's poem cites is ideological insofar as it symbolically transforms a traumatic and necessary limit (in this case, sexual difference) into a contingent obstacle to be overcome.[27] The tropological function of "harmony" presupposes that the sexual relation as it stands today, together with its antagonisms, is simply "lacking" something the addition of which would restore it to its proper fullness (e.g., if we could only communicate rationally with respect for differences, there would no longer be any strife, domination, etc.). "Harmony" is a fetish sustaining the fiction that the limits or failure of relation (that is, the fact that the sexual relation does not produce a One, a unity or wholeness) are simply a malady from which the relation will one day recover.

Vallejo's peculiar neologistic orthography also has the effect of destabilizing the culturalist ideologeme of *armonía*: the root *amonia-* also looks and sounds like the pungent *amoníaco* [ammonia]. The notion of *armonía* in fact represents one of the central targets in Vallejo's grappling with the dominant aesthetic ideology in Latin America: as a metaliterary trope of literature itself, "harmony" helps to position literature as a secondary ground that could compensate for the catastrophic effects of peripheral modernization. For Vallejo, harmony is a false form of security that covers over the reality of social antagonism. To what, then, would the "fourth angle"—or squaring—of the circle refer? What does this impossible figure of speech, this trope of impossibility itself, open onto or open up? I will return to these questions momentarily.

The following lines (lines 4–6) turn from eschatology and geometry to sex and sexual difference, and thereby shed new light on the face-to-face encounter: "¡Hembra se continúa el macho, a raíz / de probables senos, y precisamente / a raíz de cuanto no florece!" [Female continues male, on the basis / of probable breasts, and precisely / on the basis of how much does not blossom!]. In my view, this postulation of a certain logical continuity or family resemblance between the sexes is in fact an axiomatic truth that, akin to the aestheticist notion of harmony, the poem both cites and seeks to expose as an ideological fiction. The naming of biological sex ("hembra" and "macho") obliges us to go back and reread the first three lines, which now can be seen to have set the stage for a conflictive sexual encounter together with a (failed) attempt to neutralize the antagonistic difference. The postulate would seem to be suggesting that man and woman, together with their differences, are to be thought under the same concept on the basis of their postulated likeness or kinship. The conceptual link or copula that affirms this analogy, the reflexive *se continua*, could be read either as a transitive or an intransitive verb: either "woman continues man" by supporting him and filling in where he falls short, or "woman is continued as man" in the sense that phallocentric, ontotheological thinking has only ever managed to think woman as a poor reflection of man, as lacking what man is presumed to possess.[28] Of course, the expression of likeness between the two sexes also presupposes a *third term*: a universal standard that grounds each term, and according to which each would be measured in kind. The differences—and there can be no resemblance without difference—must be gathered together and raised to the order of the Same. What is lost in the process is—perhaps—the face-to-face itself, which, like any encounter worthy of the name, is necessarily irreducible to any calculative measure. The possibility that Vallejo is concerned with a poetic vindication of the former term ("hembra"), and hence open to a kind of feminism, cannot be ignored here. Vallejo marks the limits of the patriarchal order by exposing the specular operation—as well as the political project—that lies concealed in every assignation of "natural" character or essence. If woman has only ever been thought under the terms of man (the logos), as innately lacking what the latter rightfully possesses, then man can only assume or be assigned this possession in a proper way (i.e., as something essential that has been acquired neither by accident nor by force) when there is some *other* who can be made to appear lacking. No Being without the attending and supplementary fiction of "lack." However, we should not be too hasty in assuming that the poet performs the (prototypically patriarchal) gesture of restoring the traditionally marginalized position to its true and proper position. "Woman [continues]/[is continued as] male . . . on the basis of probable breasts, and precisely on the basis of what does not flourish!": is this not to say that the duality of gender (take your pick: either masculine or feminine!) is always already a monology? Gender itself is "la seguridad *dupla* [double or duplicitous] de la Armonía": the choice between the two is no choice at all, but only a reiteration of the Same. The tyranny of the either/or lies in the fact that the couple—both of them together and each one separately—is always secretly determined by the patriarchal logic of the One. As soon as sexual difference, "enfrentados a las ganadas," is determined as either opposition or complementation, nothing else matters. Whatever dualism we opt for and however egalitarian or restitutive we make it out to be—whether man and woman are thought together as *polis* and *oikos*, mind and body, reason and emotions, culture and nature, active and passive, productive and receptive, and so on ad infinitum—the couple or the coupling has already been administered and calculated in advance by a way of thinking that locates *being* or *fullness* in the one and its antithesis, *non-being* or *lack*, in the other ("a raíz de cuanto no florece!"). There can be no opposition that is not silently predetermined by this third term: the thought of being as presence or wholeness.[29] This cautionary note would apply to all well-intentioned attempts to oppose the discourse of patriarchy by constructing alternative subject positions. If we seek restitution for the marginalized and dominated by inverting the hierarchy (e.g., "in a world run by women there would be no wars, no tyranny, no corruption, etc."), we only condemn ourselves more profoundly to ontotheological thinking.

Previously I paused over the strange phrase, "Amoniácase casi el cuarto ángulo del círculo." We can now see how this catachrestic figure silently opens in a number of directions at once. For one, it anticipates what is strictly unsignifiable in the sexual relation. If, as I have already suggested, the philosophical tradition has always tended to view the sexual relation in ideal terms—as a sublimation of the corporeal by the spiritual, and of unproductive drives and desires by the reproductive function—then Vallejo's poem would appear to be concerned with the limits of this sublimatory economy (and, as we saw in the last section, the limit is not necessarily what exceeds the economy per se, but is also the point at which the economy stumbles momentarily). At the same time, the trope of impossibility that governs Vallejo's poem would seem to invite a new way of thinking about poetics and literary aesthetics in a Latin Americanist context. Prior to Vallejo, cultural production in Latin America has frequently been conceived in what I have called compensatory terms: the task of culture is to make up for or suture the myriad rifts and wounds left behind by nation-building and modernization processes. For the poet of *Trilce*, however, it is precisely the ideological dimension of "harmony"—an exemplary instance of compensatory literary aesthetics—that must be exposed.

The first stanza of XXXVI offers an insight into what I earlier termed the tragic attunement of modern thinking. I suggested that the tragic character of modern thought first issues from philosophy's self-appointed task of healing the rift between thinking and being. What reason discovers in its pursuit of reconciliation, however—and this *however* initiates the tragic "peripeteia" or reversal—is that reason is itself of the abyss. Thinking, according to this tragic necessity, must discover the traces of its own hand in the wound inflicted upon being, insofar as it authors the silent predetermination of being as presence, fullness or permanence. I am proposing here a distinction between two different thoughts of exclusion, which could be termed a posteriori and a priori exclusion. The former consists of those particular and determinate exlcusions that define a given regime of signification: for instance, the organization of the Spanish colonial regime is based on a relentless identification and elimination of all indigenous social and theological practices. The latter form of exclusion, meanwhile, refers to the fact that identity itself (or the identity of each and every particular) presupposes a founding exclusion, one that is subsequently rendered invisible by the regime to which it gives rise. In the previous example, something like an a priori exclusion can be located in the distinction between the colonial state on the one hand, and the myriad practices and affective attachments the state seeks to identify and annihilate under the so-called *extirpación de ideologías* [extirpation of ideologies]. The very recourse to "ideology" sets this invisible and irreversible process in motion: through this delineation, certain practices are identified as mere particulars ("ideologies") and thus essentially false or fallen, while one particular is able to pass itself off as universal and thus essentially true. Whenever and wherever it takes place, thinking is necessarily accompanied by originary exclusion. Thinking is akin to "framing": it is simultaneously an inclusion and an exclusion, on the basis of which a whole (or a perspective) comes into view. But the emergence of a dominant perspective also tends to efface the traces of its own particularity, or the fact that, at one point, things might have turned out differently. The tragic attunement of modern thought thus leads us to the following conclusion: it is not the case that thought has at some point become separated or alienated from being and must now find its way back to authenticity. The rift that amputates thinking from being *is itself part of reason*; it is the originary cut, violence or framing in which all thinking, however reasonable, takes place. In Vallejo's poetry, this tragic tone emerges as the short-circuiting of reason in its drive for totalization or closure. Reason, in its attempt to grasp its other (in this case, sexual difference) *as other*—and not as a mere shadow of reason's own machinations—stumbles over an "almost" [*casi*] or an "almost almost" ["*amoniácase casi*"] that is like a wrench thrown into reason's machine. Why does this tragic "short circuit" afford a distinctively modern conception of tragedy? Because the dawning awareness of a self-inflicted wound that forms the tragic knot here also applies to the medium—or the poetic work—itself. For Vallejo, poetry itself is not above the law of radical finitude that defines the modern experience. The tragic sense in *Trilce* is thus not unlike Hölderlin's notion of "translating" tragedy into a modern literary and theoretical framework. What, then, if *Trilce* were the extreme logical outcome of what Hölderlin termed the tragic caesura, or the decidedly modern sentiment that in tragedy the "end" and the "beginning" no longer rhyme or resemble one another? Lyric poetry for Vallejo would thus be something like the tragedy of tragedy itself. The speculative maxim, "a raíz de cuanto no florece!," would not signal the self-enclosure of a dialectical process that had accounted for all remainders; rather, it would point to the beyond of all presentation, or to the unpresentable *fact* of presentation (*that there is sense* is what can never flourish as sense or become present as such). For Vallejo, the tragic dimension of lyric poetry would aim to be the revelation of what presentation itself destroys.

The second stanza addresses the Venus de Milo hesitantly, almost blindly, as if the poet found himself entirely in the dark: "¿Por ahí estás, Venus de Milo?" [Are you over that way, Venus de Milo?]. The ensuing poetic reflection on the statue both echoes the previous stanza's consideration of sexual difference and invites a Latin Americanist rethinking of the questions of cultural translation and transculturation. The poet alludes to the statue by way of its famous missing arm: "Tú manqueas apenas pululando" [You lack hardly pullulating].[30] The phrase introduces an important irony: as was suggested earlier, according to the culturalist tradition the statue's concrete "lack" coincides with—and is canceled by—what is generally presumed to be its ontological "fullness," its radiant embodiment of the cultural *eidos* or spirit of the West. At the same time, we can hear in "manquear" an echo of the previous stanza's treatment of sexual difference; and I will suggest that the poet is in fact using this register—of being and nonbeing determined according to sexual difference as "presence" versus "lack"—in order to open the concept of tradition to question. Of course, Vallejo's poem is not suggesting that the statue, as a supposed embodiment of Woman, is truly lacking anything: certainly not a penis, and not even the phallus (in both cases, one cannot lack what one never had). On the contrary, the poem unveils the fiction of lack as a pretext that allows for the silent determination of truth as potentia, as self-presence and fullness. The ideologeme of "lack" allows phallogocentric discourse to take what is in fact a general and necessary limit (the fact that we are all "exposed" and limited in an existential and ontological sense: in our relation to language, to others and ultimately to death) and to pass it off as a contingent, particular shortcoming (a "feminine" weakness, etc.). This, anyway, is one way to read the assignation of lack in the poem: it is an ironic trope that undermines its own ideological edifice. But could we not also say that the statue in fact *is* and *always was* lacking, and the "accidental" losses it has suffered are mere symptoms of a more profound finitude or errancy? While the residence of a statue such as the Venus de Milo in the Louvre might convey the impression that we have to do with an exemplary presentation of a culture at its self-conscious pinnacle, in fact the Venus was never necessarily the transparent work of an (individual or collective) creator, one who had either grasped its inner truth or installed this truth with his or her own hand. It only attains this self-reflexive greatness in the museum. The statue, we could speculate, did not reflect to the Greeks the truth of their own genius or originariness; it did not send back to them what it now shows to us. If it spoke at all, it would—as is always the case with truth—have spoken to them of something far stranger and more disconcerting. In the ambiguous assignation of "lack," the poet also suggests that loss, absence and fragmentation are in fact contemporaneous with the erection of the statue as an exemplar of "the tradition," as a shining example of truth, plenitude or wholeness. This passage, then, is an attempt to think a kind of loss or fragmentation that precedes the idea of the whole. This radical finitude would potentially open onto new ways of thinking about artistic creation and reception, writing and reading, and so on: there can be no tradition, no handing down or cultural inheritance, without the possibility that what is to be transferred and preserved will have been transformed or lost in the process. And, by the same token, there can be no subject—no one who says "I"— prior to the loss of fullness and enjoyment that the poem characterizes as the subject's alienation in existence or language.

The tropology of "fullness" and "lack" in this poem can be examined fruitfully in comparison with Lacan's discussion of the traumatic character of sexual difference, and of how the dyad of the phallus and "lack" serve to veil a more disturbing truth about the subject. For Lacan, the phallus is an imaginary object whose existence can be deduced from the proliferation of inadequate copies in the world. The idea of the phallus arises to fill a gap stemming from what the subject was obliged to sacrifice in order to become part of the social order: as a condition of becoming speaking subjects, we must all renounce direct access to meaning, plenitude and being.[31] The pact through which the subject comes into existence as one who says "I" entails a founding division of the world into that which is permitted (that which the subject can use, enjoy and speak of) and that which is proscribed and unspeakable. The phallus is not a penis, although the conflation of the two (through which we phenomenalize what is in fact imaginary) is part and parcel of its fetishistic logic. Whereas the presence or absence of penis is a contingent and biological fact, the phallus—and the "lack" thereof—are of an essential and ontological order, coinciding with being and nonbeing, original and copy, *eidos* and *phainesthai*, and so on. Nor is the phallus a Platonic idea that has no real corollary in the world: rather, it is a function of the fantasy that somewhere there exists a speaking being who has not yet renounced access to primordial wholeness. The phallus is a mythical object whose inordinate value enables us to ignore a more disturbing truth that lies concealed behind it. If what goes by the name "lack"—by which I now mean both our errors, losses and limitations, but also those points where we open up to others—could be attributed to a contingent circumstance that could someday be rectified (the fictive loss or deprivation of the phallus), then there would be no need to consider the possibility that our limits constitute an "essential" aspect of our identity. The phallus, symbol of a master who knows no limits, is a veil that obscures the shadow of the *absolute* master: death itself. Our belief in the phallus is what allows us to act as if our finitude were something imposed on us from outside: as if it were not really "ours," as if it were a disease from which we would some day recover.

This brief discussion of the reciprocal fictions of lack and wholeness can aid us in examining Vallejo's reflection on modernity as a translation or transferral of the classical tradition. For Vallejo, writing at the margins of the Western tradition, the idea of modernity as translation (of an older truth or prior origin) poses at least two problems. It belies the fact that in much of Latin America, and in Peru in particular, there can be no such thing as *a* tradition, understood as unified and self-comprehending totality. It would be necessary to speak both of *multiple traditions* (the European, the creole, and various indigenous traditions) and of the *impossibility of tradition*. This second category, the "impossibility of tradition" can itself be divided into two subsets. For one, Latin America occupies a marginal position that is neither inside nor outside "the West" as it has been defined by European modernity. Historically speaking, Latin American cultural production has only been (mis)recognized as a producer of bad copies of European or classical originals. Second, with the imposition of the Spanish colonial order, all practices and traditions not recognized as European and Catholic are fragmented and proscribed. And thus, in many cases, to speak of "the tradition" in the context of Peru is also to avoid speaking of what the implementation of tradition destroys, excludes or rules out. Vallejo's engagement with the general notion of "the Western tradition," as made evident by the figure of the Venus de Milo in poem XXXVI, thus also has a bearing on the specific question of Peruvian modernity: the transferral and reinterpretation of the classical tradition that forms the basis of European modernity does not necessarily function in the same way when it comes to Peru. This is not to say that transference and reinterpretation do not happen in Latin America, but that the traditional concept of translation that forms the basis of many views on European modernity cannot hope to account for the social conflict and antagonism that accompany the transition to modernity in many parts of Latin America. However, this caveat concerning the dangers of attempting to apply European models to Latin American contexts does not mean that the latter does not provide a fruitful site for thinking about modernity. On the contrary, Vallejo's poetry shows us that the always-partial nature of cultural translation in the periphery can indeed shed new light on the cultural texts that we moderns presume to inherit as our own. In this way, *Trilce* opens up a general critique of cultural modernity, insofar as the deployment of this concept—like that of the phallus—potentially blinds us to the real, the essential groundlessness of modernity.

As was noted in the first chapter, where I discussed the return to ancient tragedy in modern Europe, there is a specular relation at work in modernity's return to cultural origins. The project of cultural modernity operates via a series of projections, in which the postulation of an absolute value or truth in the original (in the art and literature of ancient Greece, for instance) cannot be fully separated from the desire of those latecomers who seek to recover and appropriate this truth. We never *simply and merely return* without adding something of ourselves to the scene of excavation and recuperation. Repetition, in the form of citation, reenactment, reinterpretation, imitation, emulation or even rivalry, tends to confer an absolute value on the time and place of origin. For modernity, it is as if "the Greeks" were their own self-generating and self-knowing origin. The Greeks imitated nobody. At the same time—and this is the other side of the specular return, a kind of cultural interest rate—the transcultural provenance established through repetition conveys a certain worth upon the one who repeats, appropriates or expropriates something associated with this absolute origin. In fact, however, it is we moderns who invent the classical tradition by repeating it: that is, we author the idea of the origin as a cohesive, self-conscious totality that remains available somewhere offstage for us to restore, renew or appropriate. In Vallejo's poem, the specular relation at play in the culturalist recourse to "tradition" is illustrated not only in the subtle discussion of "lack" and all it implies about originary "fullness," but likewise in the name itself: the Venus de Milo is an ancient Greek statue, but its name is a Roman translation (Venus for Aphrodite) chosen by the statue's French curators after its arrival at the Louvre in 1821. Indeed, something in the act of naming cannot help but alter that which it names, and this problematic—the impossibility of a purely constative or descriptive act of naming—also holds for the self-naming event that is the origin: as soon as the Greeks themselves uttered the words "we Greeks," they were no longer the same.

Darío's "Yo persigo una forma" eulogizes the Venus as an exemplar of culture qua substance, as the ground and underlying permanence for the social. Vallejo, meanwhile, appears to reproduce Darío's gesture in the second and third lines of the second stanza, presenting the Venus as "pululando / entrañada en los brazos plenarios / de la existencia." But the quasi-organic metaphor [*pululando*: sprouting, swarming, or proliferating] that has the statue figuratively buried deep in the "plenary arms of existence" is undermined, at the semiotic level, by the peculiar spacing of words between lines. Beginning with the fifth and sixth lines, and continuing the same sentence begun on the second line, we discover that this fecund existence is in fact "esta existencia que todaviiza / perenne imperfección" [this existence which still-izes / perennial imperfection].[32] The Venus's medium is existence qua imperfection, loss, errancy, mistranslation and forgetting. This "imperfect" existence is not a Platonic existence that deviates from the true order of things. It is an inversion of the ontotheological axiom, "essence precedes existence," and it marks the eidos as always already dead (a dead letter: there is no original prior to the copy—that which, as Plato suspected, reflects the death that is always already at work in the original). It would appear that Vallejo is not only engaged in a critique of Eurocentrism here—having dispelled the notion that the Venus de Milo could constitute a culturalist blueprint for Latin

American modernity—but that he is also *reading* Darío in the strong sense of realizing what was only implicit in the original. What was for Darío a self-conscious borrowing or appropriation of the Western tradition opens, with Vallejo, to a possibility that Darío himself may have been unwilling to consider. The fact that the poet of *Trilce* addresses the Venus from a locus that is "in the dark," so to speak: is this not to suggest that the passage named in translation and transculturation is always an experience of groundlessness or groundless ground? And that culturalism, whether it is of the metropolis or the periphery, is nothing other than an attempt to cover over the abyss that opens in every act of citation, translation, or communication? I will return to these questions by way of conclusion.

First, however, I will briefly discuss the final two stanzas of XXXVI, paying close attention to an ethical and political question—the problem of the decision, which is to say both the groundlessness and the always excessive ground of every decision—that opens here, and which will constitute an important feature of the final section of this chapter. The third stanza begins with a proscription that echoes the earlier trope of "squaring the circle": "Rehusad, y vosotros, a posar las plantas / en la seguridad dupla de la Armonía. / Rehusad la simetría a buen seguro" [Refuse, all of you, to set foot / in the duplicitous security of Harmony. / Refuse all symmetry with the almost certainty]. Up until this point, our discussion has provided ample basis for reading "la Armonía" and "la simetría" as references to tradition understood as the compensatory culturalist ground of modernity. In this respect, the address is similar in tone and style to a passage found in poem XIX ("Quemaremos todas las naves! / Quemaremos la última esencia!" [Let us burn all the bridges! Let us burn the ultimate essence!]): both are addressed to an unspecified collective (XIX calls on a certain "we," XXXVI a plural, familiar "you"), and both resemble avant-garde declarations of war against the dominant discourse and its use of the aesthetic both to mask and to perpetuate its own interests. In keeping with the poem's manifesto-like tone, the third stanza of XXXVI goes on to enjoin this plural "you" to action: "Intervenid en el conflicto de puntas que se disputan / en las más toriondas de justas / el salto por el ojo de la aguja!" [Intervene in the conflict of disputing points / in the ruttiest of jousts / the leap through the eye of the needle!]. A key clarification needs to be made concerning the relation between proscription ("Rehusad") and injunction ("Intervenid"). Whereas I earlier suggested that "harmony" functions as a metapoetic trope of the culturalist project, offering the aesthetic as compensation for the failures and dissymmetries of modernization, I would now like to propose that we consider this figure as the index of an ethical moment. In the reading I am proposing, "harmony" and "symmetry" are names for a certain attempt to calculate and regulate the uncertainty that arises as we come into contact with others or with the unknown. (I am reading "en la más torionda de las justas" both as an echo of the first stanza's trope of encounter and strife—"enfrentados a las ganadas"—and as a subtle allusion to the question of justice introduced in the first stanza under the eschatological figure of the eye of the needle [*justas* denotes "jousts," but also contains the word *justa* or "just"].) What must be refused, if we follow the link I am suggesting, is any calculative thinking that claims to resolve, programmatically and in advance, the aporetic nature of decision. The metaphysics of presence is itself the double/duplicitous security against which Vallejo warns us: its primary objective is to dissolve the always singular impasse that attends decision, and it does so through the implementation of repeatable concepts. Metaphysics is the search for a guarantee concerning what constitutes the best and most desirable course of action, and thus it would radically suspend or annul the undecidability that makes for decision. We must not confuse what I am calling the undecidable with indifference or simple ignorance: undecidability is also one of the tonalities through which we open to others and to the unknown.

Our response to the manifesto, then, cannot be that of a Hegelian Beautiful Soul, which, faced with decision and knowing all of its options to be fraught with moral peril, shrinks from acting at all, preferring to maintain what it imagines to be its clear, unsullied conscience. Indeed, such a refusal would constitute one of the worst kinds of violence. To refuse the double/duplicitous ground of tradition is not to remain in one's ivory tower; it is necessarily to prepare oneself for intervention in the face of our own radical blindness. But here is the catch: what is to be undertaken is precisely beyond preparation insofar as it constitutes an unprecedented threshold. If Vallejo, having stripped away the metaphysical calculus that would reduce the decision to a moral or mathematical formula, attempts to think the ethicopolitical nature of the decision as a radical form of groundlessness, how then does he save himself from lapsing into a crude form of decisionism, according to which the good can never be known in advance and thus all that matters is the subjectivity of the one who must throw him or herself into the decision? One possible response to this question can be located in the tragic model offered by Schelling. For Vallejo, there is no such thing as undecidability without an attending, nonnegotiable urgency: if we must decide, it is because we have suddenly found ourselves without a moral road map, profoundly ignorant both of the eventual outcome of any particular choice and of the relative merits of all choices put together. Indeed, the urgency that issues from a decision—that we cannot be satisfied with endless deliberation, and that we must act *now*—is inseparable from the fact that the decision also resists calculative thinking, or is essentially unprecedented. If a proper course of action *could* in fact be discerned and guaranteed in advance through a sufficient force of reflection or speculation, then all exigency would immediately dissipate. There would no longer be a decision to be undertaken, but merely a rote and mechanical application of rules. As subjects, then, we are always already *implicated* by the structure of decision, and thus we cannot *not* decide. To attempt to recuse oneself or claim neutrality is itself a choice that falls within the framework of the decision. The sense of uncertainty that necessarily accompanies every decision cannot be explained, per decisionism, as simply an experience of our freedom as moral subjects (recall Kant's assertion in the second *Critique*: the fact that we experience anxiety before the decision is a signal that we have the freedom to choose good or evil, i.e., that we are neither mere cogs in a deterministic wheel nor absolute subjects in a world of moral relativism). Anxiety is at the same time a confrontation with our limits as subjects. As I have suggested above, the final line of the third stanza ("el salto por el ojo de la aguja!") is a recurrent trope that echoes the redemptive motif introduced in the first stanza. However, the intervening twenty-five lines have decisively suspended the transcendent register of Judeo-Christian eschatology. What is left, it seems to me, would require us to read this "salto" or leap as something akin to what Kierkegaard terms the moment of "madness" inherent to every decision: the leap into action is necessarily a suspension of theory and calculation, but to say that we must stop thinking in order to act is in no way to lessen the responsibility that marks us as subjects who decide. Indeed, as the tragic account of Oedipus indicates, responsibility necessarily *precedes* the conscious, intentional subject.[33]

Earlier I suggested that the Venus de Milo functions as an index for a considerable range of ideas about tradition and cultural transmission, and that Vallejo's use of this figure illustrates the manner in which *Trilce* engages with both the Latin Americanist and Western traditions. I now return to that assertion, which I would like to clarify by way of concluding this section. The poet's account of the Venus in the second stanza wavers between two conflicting descriptions: one is of an arm that has been sheared off, and the other of an arm that was never present to begin with: it is a "cercenado [lopped off], increado [increate, or of divine origin and thus not created] / brazo." We can now begin to hear in a different way the earlier suggestion that the statue functions like a signifier. The standard culturalist view of the Venus de Milo, I have suggested, assigns it a function akin to that of the phallus: the work of art is an exemplar of truth, knowledge or permanence, which it preserves from the forgetting and errancy of history. Vallejo, on the other hand, proposes a different relation between the statue and potentiality. The double affirmation concerning the lost or increate arm invites us to see the statue as a potens. For Vallejo, the relation between the work of art and truth is not based on anything that the statue might have preserved, conveyed, or reflected of antiquity. Permanence is not the ground of truth, but rather its death. What the statue reveals or illuminates is how truth emerges from the relation or double movement between presence and absence, or between emergence and retreat. The presentation of truth cannot be separated from the possibility of loss or oblivion. If the statue is like a vessel, it is not because of what it preserves, but rather because its contours give shape to a lacuna or a void, while at the same time inviting us to fill this hollow in. The potens is like an invitation, but it is also an enigmatic call that cannot be grasped in its entirety: the "lopped-off," "increate" arm both flashes and retreats before our eyes. Our tendency to speak of the Venus's arms as "absent" thus belies the more radical nature of the potens, which remains irreducible to any given present or presence. Or, if one likes, the potens is *both* presence and absence *and* it is neither: in its withdrawal from presence and being, the potens "is" what makes time and place for presence. As an absent metonym of the statue itself, the increate arm *is not* to the extent that *it gives*. I will treat this enigmatic relation between presence or "presencing" and absence at greater length in the final section of this chapter, when I turn to a discussion of the political as event.

The Venus de Milo thus offers an insightful index for Latin

Americanist cultural production. This statue accommodates two incommensurate positions or attitudes, one of which views modernity's task as that of capturing, reproducing and perfecting the knowledge and spirit of the ancients, while the other views modernity as a time of groundless translation, a time whose limits—and possibilities—are inscribed by an experience of radical loss or absence. The statue assumes the function of a cultural signifier, although saying this is not to reduce everything to language: it is precisely a signifier of the *failure of signification*, of the signifier's inability to signify itself. There can be no One—no idea or *eidos*—prior to its translation into the many. This is also to say: no truth without the possibility of loss, displacement, or transformation. For Vallejo, these seeming constraints on cultural transmission also bear the positive conditions for the emergence of a Latin Americanist poetics that would seek its possibilities in what the culturalist tradition passes over in silence. As a potens, and in distinction from the filial and patriarchal potestas, the statue both unveils and conceals a bastard power, a potentiality that *is not yet* (not One, not of the Father or the eidos), and which the poet names in the final stanza: "¡Ceded al nuevo impar / potente de orfandad" [Make way for the new impure / potency of orphanhood].[34] Vallejo's poetry thus gives impetus to a thought of power in relation to what would appear to be power's limiting conditions: it is a power that is at once odd or uneven [*impar*], impotent [*im . . . potente*], and orphaned. In other words, it is precisely through these indices of the improper, of the dirty secret of the filial and patriarchal tradition, that Vallejo attempts to think historicity and the emergence of truth.

The Remains of the Future: on Messianism and the Apocalypse of Revelation

I have argued in this chapter that the past, and in particular the problem of its symbolization, constitutes a key site for poetic reflection in *Trilce*. In the final section, I will suggest that a question of *future* time is also highly pertinent to Vallejo's work. Poetic consideration of the future establishes a messianic tone which in turn evokes, among other things, a long history of resistance to colonial domination in the Andes.[35] At the same time, an important distinction separates *Trilce* from "messianic" narratives such as Valcárcel's *Tempestad en los Andes*. Whereas Valcárcel's text seeks to render imaginable the emancipation of an indigenous subject, Vallejo's poetry is concerned with the problem of how to think, anticipate or imagine the future when the future may well precisely resist thinking. Vallejo's poetry suspends the commonplace determination of the future as a mere continuation or extension of the present, and seeks in the future a twofold thought of apocalypse: the future as imminent overturning or revolution, as radical suspension of the present order; and the future as revelation, as the arrival or return of that order that would redeem the present in its fallen state. However, this poetic reflection on futurity and its messianic promise is in turn complicated by a thought of alterity, or by a notion of the future as radically unpresentable: futurity is not just "different" from the present, it is also that which presentation destroys. Vallejo's poetry thus attempts to distinguish futurity—as opening, offering or arrival—from the calculative thought of a present-to-come, no matter how redemptive it may be. Whatever emancipatory and redemptive value the future might be said to hold in store for us, it also marks a lingering impossibility that haunts every thought of the actual, every hope of a better day to come. My remarks in this section will focus primarily on a reading of poem XXXVIII ("Este cristal aguarda ser sorbido" [This cristal waits to be sipped]), which touches on the theological and political dimensions of this question of the future. I begin, though, with a few words about the history of messianic discourse in the Andes.

As Frank Graziano notes in *The Millennial New World*, projects of resistance in colonial and postcolonial Latin America have frequently borrowed symbolic material from the eschatological narratives of Catholicism in order to affirm a radical break with the dominant (colonial or republican) regime of signification. Somewhat ironically, perhaps, these appropriations often contest one of the principle ideological projects associated with Catholicism in Latin America: the attempt to impose a single language, religion, and political horizon in the region. I will say more about this "irony" momentarily. First, a brief account of the historical context is in order. Messianic narratives often begin by making reference to the arrival of the Spanish *conquistadors* and the institution of the colonial regime, associating these events with the death or flight of the gods that ruled over the pre-Columbian worlds. In a number of cases, the advent of the colonial regime is registered as a catastrophic collapse of time itself, and as inaugurating a timeless time of mute suffering.[36] But the use of messianic narratives to symbolize the apocalyptic rupture brought about by colonialism is mirrored by a parallel intent, which seeks in messianism the symbolic instruments needed to invoke and awaken a newly constituted indigenous political subject.[37] This "revelatory" dimension of messianism plays an important role in the thinking of prominent twentieth-century indigenists such as Mariátegui and Luis Válcarcel.

In the Western tradition, the connection between societal catastrophe and the notion that the gods have abandoned this world, has more than once served to define the experience of modernity as tragic. For the ancient Greeks it is *hubris*, or the human tendency to overstep our bounds and identify too much with the gods, that leads to tragedy's monstrous coupling of incommensurable orders. For modernity, meanwhile, it is the endless retreat of the divine that defines our time as tragic: that the gods are never done absenting themselves means that the gaping wound left behind cannot readily be filled or healed. Both the radical indigenism of Valcárcel and the poetic discourse of Vallejo display what we could tragic conceptions of Peruvian modernity.[38] Jean-Pierre Vernant's account of tragedy, which I have discussed in earlier chapters, proves a useful theoretical framework for discussing Peruvian modernity. For Vernant, Greek tragedy is distinguished by its particular way of representing conflict between different epochs (more than just a chronologico-historical period, an epoch is also defined by a distinct "mood," which in turn helps to configure a particular way of making sense of the world). In this sense, the tragic work constitutes a kind of historical palimpsest, inscribed and informed by discrete epochal moods or attunements (for instance: the time of heroism and conflict between the gods, and the time of human statecraft and democracy) whose logics are at first glance fundamentally incompatible. Tragedy is an attempt to symbolize a traumatic breech in history, a wound that would otherwise fail to appear as such—or that would return as part of the real rather than appearing in the symbolic framework of collective memory.

As I have already suggested, the complex history of messianic discourse in Latin America points to a similar thought of epochal rift. At the same time, the use of messianic discourse—which has its origin in theological tradition—for political ends also tends to produce a tension between conflicting symbolic registers. The result is frequently a paradoxical text in which distinct levels of meaning and signification compete with and distort one another's message.

The presence of messianism in cultural texts associated with resistance to (neo)colonial domination suggests two aims that are not necessarily compatible with one another. On the one hand, the terms of messianism would seem to indicate a limit for any possible politics. Strictly speaking, there could be no politics of messianism insofar as the latter's utopian core anticipates the end of all earthly concerns. Messianism prepares for the divine institution of a full society on earth, or a time and place without conflict, strife, or division. And so the end of messianism, were it to be realized, would effectively dissolve the social antagonism that provides the material and affective basis for radical and contestatory politics.[39] On the other hand, it is clear that the "translation" of this eschatological discourse into Latin America has often served as a catalyst for projects that do possess an important political objective. Messianic narratives provide a common locus of counterinterpellation for indigenous or popular sectors, and seeks a radical transformation of what can be imagined at the level of political praxis and the state.

Valcárcel's *Tempestad en los Andes* (1928) presents an emancipatory project grounded in the messianic motifs of apocalypse and resurrection. For Valcárcel, the task of indigenism is not reformist but revolutionary and redemptive. Indigenism cannot be satisfied with a more just or democratic incorporation of indigenous sectors into the state. Instead, the first step in any true emancipation of the indigenous subject must be the absolute suspension of the state mechanism itself. What interests me in the context of this chapter, however, is the way in which the *Tempestad* narratives envision language as a potentially sovereign site for emancipation. With this link between language and politics in mind, let us now turn briefly to Valcarcel's text, through which I hope to underscore both the common ground and the differences between Vallejo's poetry and radical indigenism.

Valcárcel presents language—understood in a broad sense: not only the language of man but also the archaic language of nature—as a seal of "divine violence," or as harboring a revolutionary force that could potentially shatter the postcolonial order and initiate a radical clearing of this order's ontological ground. I am interested in how this conception of language in its *pragmatic* dimension—and by this I mean the signifier as it opens onto transformation as well as communication—can help to shed light on the political potentiality of Vallejo's poetry. In the eponymous essay "Tempestad en los Andes," Valcárcel thematizes this emancipatory potential as a passage from the prematurity of infancy (the Latin *infans* denotes one who is unable to speak) to a speaking relation:

> Su alma infantil, de primate anacrónico, no se emancipaba del miedo ancestral. Poblada estaba para él la noche de poderosos enemigos.
> El murmullo del viento era la ininteligible voz de monstruo nocturno.
> Una vez, sintiose con valor sereno y se puso a escuchar el murmullo del viento. Estaba solo, completamente solo, en plenas tinieblas, se podía imaginar aún no llegado al mundo, en el materno claustro, así debía ser de oscuro.
> Articulábanse las voces dispersas del viento de la medianoche. Escuchando, en silencio, concentrada toda el alma en percibir distintamente el mensaje misterioso, intuyó el desconocido lenguaje. Sí, era la invitación a la libertad en las sombras (31).[40]

> [His infantile soul—that anachronistic primate—could not free itself from ancestral fear. For him the night was filled with powerful enemies.
> The murmuring of the wind was the unintelligible voice of a nocturnal monster.
> Once, he felt in himself a serene valor, and he began to listen to the murmur of the wind. He was alone, all alone, in the darkest of nights. So dark was it that he imagined himself still in the maternal cloister, not yet having emerged into the world.
> The midnight wind's disparate voices joined together. Listening in silence, his soul concentrated on that mysterious message. At last he divined the unknown language. Yes, it was an invitation to freedom that resided in the shadows.]

It is the distant and mysterious language of nature that affords the emancipatory possibility that indigenism seeks. It is the convergence and "articulation" of nature's disparate "voices" that provides the hegemonic link sought by Peruvian indigenism. It is this strange murmuring that can somehow bring the subject to discover its truth—both an awareness of domination and a conviction concerning the possibility of freedom—where previously it had only encountered alienation. As an apotheosis of a populist indigenous subject, Valcárcel's text invites us to consider the origin of the subject as an experience with language. The text literally performs the interpellative procedure that it claims to recount: where it pretends to describe the attentive listening and patient deliberation of the *campesino*, it in fact reveals the retroactive structure of choice and agency. The subject, with whose "voice" the narrative is suddenly found to be in complete identification in the final phrase ("Sí"), is

4: THE CATASTROPHE OF MODERNITY

literally *called forth* through nature's "mysterious message." The subject is summoned to be the destination of this oracular missive. The final words, "Sí, era la invitación a la libertad en las sombras," function both as a constative description (yes, there it is: the invitation to freedom in nature) and as the performative countersignature of a subject (the one who says "yes"), prior to which there can be no emancipation. This countersign is the affirmation on the basis of which an invitation will have become what it already is. Its punctual appearance is already a redoubling of a prior, silent "yes," and thus a co-originary affirmation of the subject in and through language. It is the "yes" on the basis of which there will have been a subject.

Valcárcel's attention to what I am calling the pragmatics of the word has the perhaps unintended effect of opening to a different thought of language, one that would constitute a limit for any populist politics. This populist manifesto is haunted by an unforeseen experience with language as irreducible to any descriptive or communicative theory. The "invitation," which Valcárcel presents as a form of divine (law-shattering and redemptive) violence, is the opening of language's own enigmatic demand, echoing to the subject an obligation that precedes any knowledge of to what or to whom this debt is owed. And thus this allegory of emancipation proves to be incommensurable with populism's supposition of a collective subject whose positivity would be reflected or instantiated by a leader. I am not interested in arguing that the political scope of Valcárcel's project has unwittingly relinquished its urgency to a series of linguistic or philosophical questions, nor is it my claim that theory alone can sufficiently account for what is at stake here. What I am suggesting is that the resolute and decisive manner of the text's political engagement is complicated by the crucial importance of language to the text's inquiry. Through its invitation, language opens to or reveals a kind of political possibility, albeit one that Valcárcel himself may not be prepared to acknowledge.

Language in its "revolutionary" potential, which Valcárcel's text both solicits *and* seeks to secure and control as law-giving capacity, as a language of naming, marks both an inaugural moment and a limit for the indigenist projects of the early twentieth century. And while a number of similar concerns can be located in Vallejo's works, *Trilce* in particular displays another dimension of what might be termed the poetics of messianism. One important distinction between Valcárcel's and Vallejo's texts can be described as the difference between messianism put to work for a populist politics and the "unpopular" poetics of *Trilce*—which, while by no means comparable to the antipopular conservatism of Borges, is relentless in its attempt to mark the limits of every institutionalization of the political. While Valcárcel is interested in mobilizing the pragmatic dimension of language for a revolutionary cultural and political project, the reflection on language in *Trilce* reveals a catastrophic moment that is at least implicit in every messianism. The thought of poetic language as avatar of divine truth is but one side of a coin, whose reverse side bears the thought that the letter might not arrive, or that its destination includes in advance the possibility of its errancy or its oblivion. *That the letter might not arrive* is, as Barbara Johnson has shown, already part of its "destination," its circulation in the radical errancy of the symbolic.[41] Vallejo's poetry is an interrogation of the signifier as both avatar of divine revelation and as radical errancy or the withdrawal of the divine. In the words of *Trilce*'s XII, it is a reflection on language as "[un] proyectil que no sé dónde irá a caer. . . . Chasquido de moscón que muere" [a projectile that will fall I know not where. . . . Click of a dying fly], where "chasquido" [click] also suggests *chasqui* [Quechua for messenger].

Poem XXXVIII ("Este cristal aguarda ser sorbido") is informed by a messianic tone that, at first glance, seeks an overtly political determination of the eschatological figures of apocalypse and revelation. Instead of identifying bread and wine with the body of Christ, the poem speaks of the proper recipient of the Eucharist as a "mouth to come" [*boca venidera*]. The poem appears to suspend the transubstantial ground of the Catholic rite and, at the same time, curiously reintroduces a certain thought of transcendence at the level of the contingent and the finite. It is not God in the form of Spirit that is brought forth through shared ritual; what is in fact anticipated or awaited in these repetitive acts is a community without communion. The result, I will suggest, is a thought of a communism to come, which nonetheless reveals important differences with classical Marxian theories of revolution and class struggle. However, these distinctions also call into question the basic assumption I have just put forth, i.e., that Vallejo effects a rather easy transition from the domain of religion to that of revolutionary politics. And so it will be precisely the aporetic incompatibility of the theological and the political that interests me here: that is, of how for Vallejo the question of revolution or political emancipation is approached via one of the most traditional discourses in the history of Latin America. For the author of *Trilce*, the possibility of revolution would seem to hinge necessarily on a question of faith. I will now perform a brief and partial reading of the poem (the reservations staked out earlier concerning hermeneutic approaches to *Trilce* are still in effect), and along the way will attempt to indicate how, as a Latin Americanist text, this poem offers a new way of thinking about—but not necessarily a *theory* of—political praxis and poiēsis.

The principle object of poetic consideration is what the poet terms a *cristal* [a pane of glass or crystal] that, at varying points in the poem, is assigned both inanimate and animate qualities. In my view, it is not of primary importance to determine exactly what the cristal "is," what it stands for or metaphorizes. As has already been suggested, such an approach to *Trilce* is doomed to encounter more frustration than rewards. The important point, it seems to me, is to map the various interpretive possibilities put into play by this poetic object, together with the relations—and limits—that emerge between discrete interpretations.

In the first stanza the cristal is described both as a vessel ("Este cristal aguarda ser sorbido") and as bread ("Este cristal es pan" [This crystal is bread]). And thus we clearly have to do with a scene of Catholic communion, where the cristal stands in for both aspects of the Eucharist, both wine and bread as the blood and flesh of Christ. Let us note, parenthetically, that in assuming this function the cristal is definitely *not* just a metaphor. If we are to take the Catholic ritual seriously, we must not think of bread and wine as "symbolizing" the body of Christ in the same way that, in literature for example, an owl might be a metaphor for wisdom or a house might represent the human soul. Messianism knows nothing of substitution. In its mysterious logic, the ritual of communion insists that these contingent objects, this wafer and that glass of wine, precisely *are* the body of the Son. To see why this is the case, let us consider that traditional literary exegesis would take this poetic relation between the cristal and the Eucharist as a tropological point of departure that potentially mobilizes various thematic aspects of communion within the poem. The mystery of transubstantiation would only tell half the story: in reading the poem we would also need to account for faith and the community of believers, while further addressing the crucial function of spirit as the "glue" that holds the community together. As the ground of community, spirit is not exactly what philosophers would term a transcendental: it is not "out there," waiting to be discovered or put to work. It *is* only when and where there is a community of believers who actively engage with a certain set of practices and rituals. The constitutive function of ritual for faith and community provides one way of understanding the requirement that we take the Eucharist "literally": unless we act *as if* the Messiah's arrival were imminent, there could be no faith, no community, and no revelation.

Let me now briefly address the question of faith, which will provide a key term for discussing the possible relation between the theological and the political in Vallejo's poetry.[42] Faith, as it functions in the Judeo-Christian tradition, names a certain relation between the believer(s) and what is strictly unpresentable. Faith does not accede to the standards of truth stipulated by other discourses (science, for instance), which would demand of faith that it make its findings available for all to scrutinize. Indeed, faith is only what it is—and not some other form of knowledge—insofar as its object is not (yet) present. The absolute certainty or conviction that is faith is precisely irreducible to the scientific mode of truth, whose ground is presentation. Scientific certainty, were it applicable to the realm of the divine, would render faith null and void. Thus, as Pascal suggests, one does not first need something called "faith" in order to participate (in good faith, let me add) in the community of believers: on the contrary, it is not until one acts (and again, this is to act *as if* one were a believer) that one can begin to call oneself a believer. Faith *is* only when and where a shared activity is undertaken.

Returning now to the first stanza, we also encounter here a term that complicates the thematic development of Catholic communion in the poem. The recipient of the Eucharist is not a living, breathing member of the community; it is what the poet calls a "boca venidera" [mouth-to-come]. Two implications are worth noting here. First, this recipient appears to invert the idea of transcendence presupposed by the Catholic ritual: rather than a community of mortals who are brought together and uplifted in their anticipation of the imminent arrival of the Son, we have here a (transubstantial) object that awaits the arrival of its proper recipient, the one mortal mouth (to come) that will know how to receive it. The mouth-to-come will not be just any mouth: it will be both "sin dientes" [without teeth] and "no desdentada" [literally, not de-toothed; but in "desdentada" we can also see and hear "desdén" or disdain: so the mouth is toothless but not disdained? I will say more about this possible interpretation below]. This strange and spectral prophecy of a mouth-to-come-without-teeth casts a different light on the material components of the Eucharist: the reference to "pan no venido todavía" that follows cannot help but introduce the thought of material deprivation, suffering and starvation. Thus, if the boca venidera inverts the finite/transcendent relation by attributing a messianic futurity to the mouth—or, by metonymic extension, to a certain form of community—then the final line of the first stanza ("Este cristal es pan no venido todavía" [This crystal is bread that has not yet arrived]) appears to resubstantialize the ideal notion of transubstantiation, returning to bread its concrete, alimentary function. Does this ironic displacement of the transubstantial mystery signal a critique in the same vein as the Second Treatise of the *Lazarillo de Tormes*, in which the Eucharist provides a literary forum for exposing the miserliness of the church and its failure to meet its responsibility to the lower classes? Does the tropology of transubstantiation in fact give way to an image of social antagonism—and hence possibly open the door to a different thought of communion, or a communism to come? Let us move on, noting that these questions are posed but not answered in the first stanza.

The second and third stanzas further complicate both of the readings—the theological and the political—that I have been developing up to this point. The middle stanzas establish a tension between two animated and quasi-anthropomorphic images of the cristal, both of which are presented in the conditional form of "if one did x, the cristal would respond with y." One of these images is that of the impassioned cristal offering itself to the world. In the third and fourth lines, it is suddenly animated through a poetic play on the vocabulary of sugar processing, with "se melaría" [*melar* can mean to boil down the juice of sugar cane to a syrupy consistency] and "la horma" [the mold into which the syrup is poured to make sugar loaves] also comprising an image of ejaculation. Then, in the fourth and fifth lines, we encounter the cristal as a linguistic entity, like those nouns that—a strange and wonderful turn of phrase—"se adjetivan de brindarse" [roughly, that offer themselves as adjectives]. There is no doubt much to say about this distinction and the passage it implies between substantive language and adjectival language, between a language of essences (*ser*) and a language of becoming (*estar*), and between language as constatation and language as offering.

The other aspect is of the cristal withdrawing from the world, or "no [darse] por ninguno de sus costados" [that does not yield on any of its faces]. In the same lines, the poet begins to speak of love. It is the love proper to those concerned ones who find the cristal in its withdrawn solitude, "triste individuo / incoloro" [sad, colorless / individual]. But, the poet advises, rather than seek to draw the cristal out of its solitude, the lovers must relinquish it if they wish to free it: "lo enviarían por amor, / por pasado y a lo más por futuro" [they would send it for love, / to the past and at the most to the future]. In this phrase, "por" can mean both "for the sake of" [*por amor*] and "toward" or "to" [*por pasado, por futuro*]. This redoubling underscores the ethical demand of love for Vallejo. Love makes itself known to us as obligatedness, in the sense that it does not allow us to remain passive witnesses to the other's suffering. But this responsibility is not easily relinquished through intervention, since love does not justify an attempt to "save" the other according to the image of our own subjectivity—although similar humanistic formulas have been used to legitimate geopolitical interventions for more than five hundred years. The trope that provides the measure for Vallejo's conception of love—"lo enviarían por amor"—is neither the autorestitutive redemption of humanism nor the false security of the Beautiful Soul. The encounter with the other always calls for a decision: "enviar" [to send] requires that we get our hands caught in its web.[43] Any encounter worthy of the name is necessarily unprecedented and singular. The encounter provides no ethical road map that would allow us to weigh and calculate the consequences of a decision in advance. No encounter and no *envío* [sending] without an irreducible vestige of uncalculability. And, of course, we cannot elude this ethical bind simply by recusing ourselves: no decision is already a manner of having decided. What does it mean, then, that the poet counsels the lovers to send the cristal "to the past" or "to the future"? Past or future of what or of whom? These two temporalities would seem to impose a certain limit upon the restitutive ideal of restoring the other to wholeness or presence. What would it mean to send or give the other *to the future*? What is it to give (to) the future?

In the final lines of the third stanza we encounter another reference to the mouth-to-come, only this time it is a "boca ve- / nidera que ya tendrá dientes" [mouth to / come that will already have teeth].[44] What are we to make of this projected transformation of the mouth-to-come, from "sin dientes" to "ya tendrá dientes"?

Does the presence of "teeth" reflect a change at the ontological level—a transformation of substance or a "transubstantiation"—in which domination and subalternity are evacuated and replaced with agency and emancipation? Perhaps this transformation could be read through the following general question concerning subalternity and hegemony: would it be possible to constitute a social field (society, community, etc.) that would fully dissolve and put an end to subalternity? Or would any hegemonic politics, no matter how democratic or popular, necessarily reproduce subalternity through its own particular logic of exclusion? Is hegemony conceivable without exclusion, or is hegemony itself based on radical or a priori exclusion? If the poem can be said to offer a response to this question, I would argue that the answer must be both "yes" (there must be a form of hegemony that would not reproduce subalternity) and "no" (there is no form of hegemony that does not reproduce subalternity).

I say "yes" because, in light of the final stanza's reference to "[marcharse] ahora a formar las izquierdas" [going off the form the lefts], the poem clearly anticipates a political approach to the aporetic structure of the decision. The poem partakes in an effort to imagine or to render conceivable a certain community or communism, one that would coincide with the emergence of a subject where previously there was only domination and subalternity. The "boca venidera" is not just an individual or singular mouth, but also a metonym of the collective or whole. The horizon of this community-to-come is strictly messianic in the sense that there is no place *within* the present and its established order from which one could think and direct the complete dissolution of subalternity. Every *available* site for thinking has always already been co-opted by the dominant discourse and its own constitutive exclusions. And so poetry must undertake the impossible: it must produce such a site for praxis ex nihilo, as an act of poiēsis. Perhaps it is poem XXXVI that best captures this utopian poetico-political project. I am thinking of the lines "Rehusad la simetría a buen seguro. / Intervenid en el conflicto de puntas que se disputan." Vallejo's poetry is thus the radical antithesis of the revolutionary vanguard. For Vallejo, the question of messianism emerges precisely through the awareness that there can be no revolutionary subject per se: there is no universal, omniscient ground from which the revolution could be directed and its just end guaranteed in advance; revolution as such presupposes the radical suspension of all subjectivity and all ground. Reiterating the fact that every decision necessarily contains its own "undecidable" kernel (no symmetry presents itself between knowledge and decision) does not free us from the obligation to decide or intervene. What is the right or ethically correct choice? How will my decision be received? What will it lead to? Not knowing does not eliminate our responsibility to the decision itself. The notion of hegemony, at least as it has been discussed by Laclau and Mouffe, is one possible response to this aporia: hegemony reaffirms the necessity of *articulation* (of conceiving or negotiating new links with others) in the face of undecidability.

But the poem's response to the above question would also be "no" insofar as the poetic vision of XXXVIII seems to point to something quite different from the classical Marxian conception of emancipation. The poem can no doubt be read as partaking in an effort to transform the horizon of what is thinkable and imaginable under the heading of politics. But this transformative project, in which poetry both unmasks and remakes the collective imaginary, does not ground itself in a claim to *know*—or at least not in any traditional form of rational, systematized knowledge. Unlike the revolutionary vanguard, it does not presuppose a self-present subject that would extend its own positivity to the rest of the newly constituted social field. The other name that the poet offers for the emancipatory "las izquierdas" is "los nuevos Menos" [the new Less/Minus]: in other words, it is decidedly not the old vanguard subject, the subject supposed to know because "its sufferings are [not particular but] universal."[45] Similarly, I suspect that Vallejo would hesitate over the term "emancipation," which for him would still retain too much onto-theological baggage to be able to function as an effective discursive or political strategy. If Vallejo's poetry were to name the demand that calls this subject into being (and he does not), perhaps the term would be "dignity"—I am reading "no desdentada" (stanza 1, line 3) as "no longer disdained," no longer the detritus that is excluded from the symbolic.

In the final line of the poem there is an echo of the aporia I have been discussing. The phrase "Déjenlo solo no más" [loosely translated, "Leave it alone and that's it"; literally, "Leave it alone (and) no more"] could be heard to recall Christ's warning to Mary Magdelene, "noli me tangere." Only here, the prohibition against contact with alterity or death might well insist upon a limit for reading ("noli me legere"). But the insertion of the pleonastic negative ("no más") at the end of this final injunction provides the re-mark of an irreducible vestige of uncertainty concerning the relation to alterity. Grammatically speaking, this phrase is a redundant reiteration of the proscription "déjenlo solo," a veritable end-of-story (it could be translated "and that's it") that would punctuate the ethical constraint. But in reiterating the prohibition on coming into contact with alterity—a limit beyond which knowledge shall not seek to grasp the other, and beyond which poetry must not attempt to speak of or for the other—poetry already says too much. "Déjenlo solo no más" can also be heard, if one reads it to the letter, as "Leave it alone no more." Here the poem says what it did not mean (to say), what it had not intended for the public eye: it foretells the lifting of the divine prohibition against mimesis, the collapse of the sublime ground of the aesthetic in its turning from the divine. It is my position that this textual bind does not simply play itself out in an aesthetic debate between representation and prohibition: it also points to the political domain of the decision. The ambiguity inscribed by the pleonastic "no más" reveals a paradoxical endeavor at work in *Trilce*: the text seeks to repeat the event of the political, or simultaneously to catch sight of and to restitute an *event* whose time has either already passed or not yet come, an event that can only be registered as a missed encounter with what fails to take place in any institutionalization of time and place.[46]

This *already/not yet* character of the event and its arrival—and this is also essentially the aporia over which tragic mourning labors—informs the messianic inflection of Vallejo's poetry. The political, for Vallejo, coincides with a radical suspension of the transcendental realm. It marks a necessary deferral—the postponement of all (aesthetic and eschatological) judgment—that is the condition of possibility for acting in the world. But in undertaking any decision, do we not inevitably postulate the ethical resolution of the aporia? Do we not act as if there were a knowable law waiting to reveal itself? In this sense, every decision (and thus every politics) finds itself indebted to a question of faith that is irreducible to politics.

Like many of the poems in *Trilce*, XXXVIII could be read as a consideration of aporetic incompatibility: in this case, between theory, knowledge and calculation on the one hand, and action on the other; between politics and religion; and perhaps even between poetry itself and alterity. In each case, this incompatibility is aporetic because the two sides or moments belong to incommensurable orders *and* they prove to be equally necessary. Poetry, then, would reveal what we could call the tragedy of the political: an attempt to symbolize the opening or the chance encounter through which a given time and place takes shape and is defined. The reference to tragedy is relevant insofar as the origin—qua emergence or opening—is always already lost: it cannot itself be said to have taken place on any institutional ground. Tragic attunement, in this broad sense, seeks—albeit impossibly—the revelation of what presentation destroys.

The political, in the sense that I am using the term, both *does* and *does not* take place. It is an event that signals an irreversible transformation of our world, an event whose emergence inaugurates a new measure or horizon. Nonetheless, the event "itself" (if we could even assign it such a self-identity) could not be fully grasped and understood by either the old measure or the new. The event is precisely the measureless origin of measure itself, the origin whose disappearance will become measure. Poem XXXVIII testifies to a certain hesitation in the face of the event: it describes a pause between prohibition and injunction, between the ethical limit placed on representation and a demand whose urgency indicates that we are always already entangled in a relation to the other. In this way, poetry is a remembrance of the event (or the political) qua opening and absent cause or potens. This opening is both the condition of possibility and the limit of any politics. And it means that our desire for certainty in the face of decision—or for the assurance that this or that choice represents the ethically correct one—is also a desire for the end of the political: such certainty, were it in fact possible, would only serve to entomb any encounter worthy of the name. It would cause any opening to the other to collapse into the institutionalized, standardized space of the Same. The political *as possibility* only emerges where politics in its programmatic, institutionalized and calculative form begins to waver. Let us recall once again the injunction of XXXVI, "Rehusad . . . la seguridad dupla de la Armonía": the poetic renunciation of "harmony" is an attempt to destabilize this institutionalized ground of (false) certitude, and thereby to recall what has been foreclosed in each and every foundation of the law. In this interpretive key, the messianic cadence of Vallejo's text ("listen to me!") is also a kind of mourning: it marks a fall from the sublime purity of silence, and it acts out or re-marks the death of harmony and the retreat of the event.

It should not be surprising, then, that the messianic tone of Vallejo's text also reveals an antimessianic tendency within it. Or, more precisely, it discovers a profoundly nonmessianic moment at the very heart of its attempt to free the political from its calculated, institutional death. As Vallejo will later assert in the context of his so-called "conversion" to Marxism, "the revolutionary intellectual displaces the messianic formula, saying: 'my reign is of this world'" (*Arte y revolución*, 14). A similar thought is audible in many of the poems of *Trilce*. Messianic tone presents a limit for theoretical systematicity, as an index of faith that points to an unpresentable kernel within every mode of presentation. But the messianic register is itself marked by a limit it shares with political praxis. *Trilce* signals the need for praxis both to remember and to relinquish (or to mourn) the singular. It suggests that we must renounce the desire for absolute certainty in undertaking any decision, but at the same time it affirms the irreducible difference that divides any political act from itself (and the thought of this difference necessarily distinguishes Vallejo's poetics from decisionism). In Vallejo's terms, the origin of the act as instantiation of a political project *is* this state of being divided: between our responsibility to a demand or call that precedes and summons the subject, and the finite existence in which relation takes place. That these two faces cannot be made to coincide in theory or in practice constitutes the tragic sense *and* the only hope for politics in *Trilce*.

5
Heterotopic Memory and the Narration of Disaster in Piglia

> Somebody does something that nobody understands, an act that exceeds the experience of everyone. The duration of that act is but an instant; it belongs to the pure character of life. The act is not narrative, but it is the one thing that it makes sense to narrate.
> —Ricardo Piglia, "En otro país"

> The social only exists as the vain attempt to institute that impossible object: society. Utopia is the essence of any communication and social practice.
> —Ernesto Laclau, *New Reflections on the Revolution of Our Time*

THE NOVEL-LENGTH WORKS OF RICARDO PIGLIA CONSTITUTE AN IMportant intervention in contemporary debates concerning the relation between narrative representation and history, and form a sustained attempt to think the possibilities that remain for literature in our time. *Respiración artificial* (1980) and *La ciudad ausente* (1992) are explorations of narrative as fundamental to any determination of *a* time, and of the community named in this phrase "*our* time." These two novels straddle an epochal division in the Argentine tradition, formed by the 1976 to 1982 military dictatorship and the subsequent transition to market-driven democracy. Piglia's writing can be understood as an attempt to close the gaping personal and societal wounds left by these events. At the same time, the metaliterary perspective that emerges repeatedly in Piglia's text—or, more specifically, the ways in which the text reflects on the act of narration itself—points to a general heading, of epistemological and ontological concern, that cannot be fully subsumed within the national context of both novels. The broader order of literary inquiry here responds to what, following Maurice Blanchot, I will term "disaster." Piglia's writing approaches and seeks insight into an event that exceeds or eludes conventional cognitive and epistemological mechanisms, an event that renders inoperative both the epistemological *and* the ontological systems in which experience is traditionally inscribed and registered.[1] The magnitude of disaster, as an event that destroys the very possibility of recording it, not only creates problems for determining the specificity of historical experience (its meaning, its when, where, how, and why), but likewise signals an ontological problem: the radical doubt surrounding the event (*Did* it happen? *Is* it *still* happening?) also entails a crisis for truth itself.

In the wake of the Holocaust, literature has become the site of seemingly antithetical demands whose torsion threatens the very ground of modern aesthetics. Following the occurrence of unthinkable horror, literature is at once marked by the shadow of its own impossibility (Adorno's declaration that poetry after Auschwitz is "barbaric") *and* it is charged with being the sole remaining possibility for world-building (the German poet Paul Celan's assertion that following the Holocaust *only* poetry can be written). This contradictory judgment has little to do with epistemological boundaries (what is or is not representable); it marks the appearance of an ethical limit, and it impacts our consideration of what ought to be the limits of art or aesthetics. And thus the contradiction is not necessarily resolvable. Instead, these conflicting imperatives together give evidence of the radical transformation that *disaster* imposes on artistic representation. Literary production in our time is situated alongside a void that it can neither fill, seize and make its own, nor renounce once and for all. Narrative returns to a past that continues to leave its mark on the present and yet remains in need of further articulation in order to "take place" or become meaningful in a historical sense. However, literature is also aware of the possibility that it may not be adequate to the twofold task of articulating the past in a meaningful way while also respecting the specific limits that the event introduces into language. The frequent allusions to "the unnameable" and "the unspeakable" in Piglia's work suggest that to situate disaster within a chronology and a chain of repeatable signs is to misrecognize its truth: the temporality and texture of narrative enables us to forget the sense of immeasurableness and unpreparedness that characterizes certain experiences during the dictatorship period. The artistic forms with which the Western tradition has generally sought to make sense out an event that otherwise exceeds human understanding ("the sublime," "the tragic") cannot help but usher in previously established codes of comprehension and valuation. In other words, traditional artistic representations of societal catastrophe risk reintroducing epistemological ciphers that the event itself radically forecloses.

Piglia's writing is a reflection on history as horizon for thinking, or as historicity. In the absence of historicity, there can be no insight into the past, nor can there be a thought of the future as anything but a mere extension of the present. It is historicity, in other words, that contains the possibility of thinking *difference* or *rupture* in any given present, at any given moment. In the postdictatorship, however, both the Right and the Left have tended to reduce history to teleological and quasi-apocalyptic terms. Transition is equated with the "end of history," or with the postulated exhaustion not only of the political paradigms of previous generations, but likewise of the very possibility of signifying contingency and social antagonism.[2] The equation of the nation-state's future with a postulated "end of history" would mean: 1) the foreclosure of the political, understood as the conditions in which hegemonic processes take place, as opposed to the tendential completion of hegemony under one particular-universal position or signifier; and 2) the inauguration of a new epoch in which politics would receive its essential bearing as an administrative task. The idea of politics as praxis, as a transformation of the world that in turn implicates and changes the subject or agent itself, would therefore have been supplanted by a paradigm of navigation in which the completeness or self-identity of the subject lies beyond any possibility for thinking or questioning.

While it is extremely difficult to refrain from placing any text in a determinate sociopolitical, historical and aesthetic context, the reader's temptation to historicize Piglia's narrative, or to situate the text within a particular moment in history, only obscures a more fundamental problem. The paradoxical nature of Piglia's text, as Idelber Avelar and others have suggested, lies in the fact that the (perhaps unavoidable) question of context or referentiality cannot be settled without taking into account the ways in which Piglia's writing brings the narrative process into confrontation with its own limits. Referentiality, or the question of what the story is "about," cannot be freed from the specter of the impossibility of narration, or from the *uncertain* possibility of its own failure: before we can say anything about "when" and "where" Piglia's novels are situated, we must read them as accounts of the possibility or impossibility of telling stories.[3] The dual question of narrative and its (partial or impending) failure recurs throughout Piglia's oeuvre in the manner of an undecidable point of contention between the literary and the metaliterary. On one hand, his work endeavors to trace and delimit what I will call a certain history of the Argentine imaginary, or to map a cultural-production process that has historically tended to project the image of the nation as a unified whole, and to incorporate and institutionalize the very limits of the nation-state (and thereby annihilate them as limits and as openings). However, the critique of this colonization of limits by the state at times comes very close to an uncanny reproduction of the very phenomenon it would seek to comment on and contain. With *La ciudad ausente* in particular, it becomes increasingly difficult to distinguish between the critique of the dream of a total history and the construction of a total history through critique. I am not interested in presenting this interpretive problem as a shortcoming of the author or of his text. Instead, I propose that it be considered as a dimension of the very problem Piglia is grappling with: of the dual necessity and impossibility of an adequate representation of the real.

The Tragic Sense of History: Utopia, Dictatorship, and Fragmentation

Respiración artificial (1980), Piglia's novel of the dictatorship, begins with an oracular question: "¿Hay una historia?" [Is there a/ one history, a/one story?]. Given the paucity of contextual reference in the novel, together with the interpretive opacity that prevails throughout the narrative, one might suspect that the only possible answer would be "no." Instead of telling the story of dictatorship in way that would restore coherency and consistency to this time of terror and uncertainty, Piglia's text submerges us in an experience of blindness, disorientation, and circular paths without exits. Rather than submitting dictatorship to representation, it implicates the reader in a space that, by virtue of what does not come into view, precisely reproduces an aspect of the former experience. The catastrophe of history cannot be told but only repeated. This is at least one possible reading of Piglia's dictatorship novel. A closer examination of the myriad *relatos* [relations or juridical accounts], however, offers a slightly different key in which to hear the book's liminal question. Seen as a collection of fragmentary stories or histories, *Respiración artificial* engages the reader in a kind of historical detective work, in which multiple relatos are assembled from distinct times and places in the Argentine tradition. Among the many narrators are three writers of letters: Enrique Ossorio, an exiled liberal writing in the mid-nineteenth century; Marcelo Maggi, a victim of "internal exile" during the 1970s in Entre Ríos; and Emilio Renzi, the nephew of Maggi, currently reading his uncle's letters in Buenos Aires. For each letter writer there is a corresponding recipient or reader who must also struggle with the absence that accompanies the text, the absence of the sender himself. These missives are thus both placeholders and signs affirming that the origin—the author and his context or lived experience—has retreated or (been) disappeared from the symbolic community in which the letter first becomes legible. The multiple relatos that comprise *Respiración artificial* are bound together not as a single, unified History, but instead as partial histories. And as ruins or fragments, they may share certain borders with one another, but they do not together comprise a whole. Like Sarmiento and other exiled liberals, Ossorio seeks to combat exile during Rosas's authoritarian rule by addressing his letters or journal entries to a utopian vision of the nation. Ossorio's utopia is not a spatial configuration; he does not imagine an Ushuaia, a place located at the extreme circumference of the known world. It is instead a future date [*cita*: appointment or citation], a time in which the liberal ideal of the nation, will have become both legible and legal. Ossorio assigns this time the seemingly arbitrary date of 1979, which is also presumably the year in which Renzi is reading the journal entries. Renzi is likewise unable to comprehend the meaning of his own historical moment; and the reader is only indirectly made aware that it is the time of the most recent military dictatorship. Renzi thus turns to the century-old missives of Ossorio, through which he seeks insight into his own obscure present. But no unifying force emerges that could assign a single meaning or destiny to Ossorio's and Renzi's relatos. Instead, in pointing to the partial, broken historias, the work holds out the hope that insight might be found *between* these fragments of the whole, and within the condition of transcendental "blindness" that they share. Meanwhile, the fact that Ossorio's future "utopia" will have been the terror of el Proceso suggests that if one time represents the hope of another, the one also constitutes the other's limit.

The hermeneutic strategy underlying this hope of historical redemption is based on a fundamentally tragic attitude, in the sense described by J. P. Vernant in his reading of *Oedipus Rex*.[4] For Vernant, the tragic polemos is not only a synchronic clash between warring antagonists, but is likewise a site of diachronic conflict: tragedy is the conjunction or superimposition in one moment and in a single character of distinct epochs and their irreconcilable attunements, codes, and logics. Through the unfolding of the *pragma* [action], which requires interpretive work to begin anew at various points in the drama, tragedy evinces the unraveling of *ethos* [character] as an index of overdetermination. The pragma inscribes on the ethos multiple and seemingly irreconcilable senses. The tragedy of Oedipus, then, is that we must see him implicated in the opposing worlds of the mythos and history: he is both king *and* criminal, both master hermeneut *and* patricide. He is all of these at the "same" time, but his presence testifies to the fact that we cannot be in both "times" at once: in tragedy, the crime necessarily belongs to the structure of the unconscious. Each of these activities or dispositions *mark* Oedipus; his identity *is* precisely the paradoxical conjunction of these conflicting assignations.

We can take the tragic sense of *Respiración artificial* a step further by turning briefly to Walter Benjamin's notion of the "dialectical image," and to what Benjamin calls the specific time of its legibility.[5] The image, drawn from a prior time (what Benjamin calls "the Then") as a piece or fragment of that past, offers itself as legible to and in another time ("the Now"). It flashes before the Now with fleeting exigency, as what will only have been legible *now*. In so doing, however, the image also transforms the time in which it is read—if in fact it is read. This "other time" to which the image offers itself—the Now, which is suddenly confronted with its own "internal" difference—can only *become* what it already *is* by producing an interpretation or a reexamination of the Then, or by finding the Then *in* the Now. This back-and-forth movement that determines and alters the meaning of each particular is the hallmark of dialectical interpretation. Should the Now fail in its (self)transformative task, it risks lapsing back into the self-enclosed blindness of myth.

Tragic hermeneutics thus also provides a figure for the work's worst nightmare: that the traces of disaster had already been inscribed, at some point in the utopian history of modernization, as the present's ineluctable destiny. From Ossorio's perspective, this disastrous possibility means that the letters he addresses to the future will not have arrived—at least not for the long-awaited realization of the nineteenth-century Argentine imaginary—but will instead find their final destination in the dystopian collapse of this dream. Piglia's writing seems to suggest that the passage from the whole (Work, History, Nation) to the fragment (ruin or partial history) is marked by a profound irreversibility: while we can well imagine the Whole as the sum of discrete parts, we cannot begin with fragments and then work our way back to the idea of the Whole. The irreversibility of this passage can be understood in the context of interpretive insight (a question of reading) or in the context of epochal attunement (a question of historicity). Just as one cannot "break" a fragment ("broken" is already as broken as can be), the fragment presents itself as irreducible to all combinatory and recuperative measures: its existence cancels the very notion of the whole. In piecing together these partial historias through theoretical reflection, the text thereby indicates the hope (the condition of possibility) and the limit (the impossibility) of historical knowledge. The possibility of speaking thoughtfully in the wake of societal disaster is seemingly offered only in another historia; but the passage between historical narratives also underlines the very constraint it seeks to overcome: not only is the object of narrative desire here a logical impossibility, but it is also, as we shall see per Tardewski's law, prohibited.

Through reference to Walter Benjamin's work on baroque *Trauerspiel* or "mourning play," Idelber Avelar suggests that the consideration of history in *Respiración artificial* is governed by allegory. The rules of allegory mandate that, if the novel is a consideration dictatorship and its consequences for history, then the content of its relatos will be anything but *plena dictadura* [full-fledged dictatorship].[6] An important instance of allegorical circumlocution can be found in Tardewski's narrative. Tardewski, a Polish immigrant who fled Europe shortly before World War II, recounts the stunning discovery he made forty years ago as a doctoral student in England. While conducting research for his dissertation on "The Pre-Socratics in Heidegger," he uncovered evidence of a previously unknown encounter between Franz Kafka and Adolf Hitler in Prague during the 1920s.[7] The literary author whose work ranks among the most renowned accounts of modern alienation and terror is thus found to have come into direct contact with the intellectual author of the twentieth century's most infamous disaster. Furthermore, Tardewski's byzantine relato proposes a perverse link between the Enlightenment as "civilizing" project and Nazism as a "cleansing" process. It is on the basis of a common grapheme ("Hi-"), shared by Hitler and the Greek thinker Hippias, that Tardewski makes his serendipitous discovery in a Cambridge library. And thus the topic of his investigation, which investigates the German reinterpretation of Greek culture as one of modernity's defining projects, also points to a considerably less fortuitous connection between the height of Western philosophical thinking and the event that is the final death knell of the Enlightenment project. One could no doubt link this conjunction in Piglia's text to Heidegger's own brief complicity with National Socialism in the early 1930s (although the 1989 publication of Víctor Farías's *Heidegger and Nazism*, which first disclosed the full extent of Heidegger's participation in National Socialism, in fact postdates *Respiración artificial* by almost a decade). But a more compelling account of this "chance" discovery is offered by Brett Levinson, who notes that the common grapheme ("Hi-") is in Spanish also a homophone for a sign of pain ("ay"). The horrifying conjunction between the Enlightenment project and Nazism thus circles around a lacuna in representation itself: Tardewski's research stumbles across a signifier that does not correspond to any experience that could be repeated or shared. The signifier ("Hi-" or "ay") stands in for an experience for which there can be no adequate words—and hence no memory, no identification, no transmission, but only the experience of the limits of world.[8] Through the emergence of multiple interpretive possibilities, the signifier reveals its limits while also allowing us to see how the relato constitutes a kind of "unconscious," a space comprised of material fragments in which distinct meanings and assignations circulate and compete with one another.

The profound finitude of modern history reveals itself further in Tardewski's paraphrase of Ludwig Wittgenstein's famous aphorism, "Whereof one cannot speak, thereof one must remain silent" (Piglia, *Respiración artificial*, 271). The proscription has little to do with what is or is not representable per se—after all, if we cannot speak of something, why would it be necessary to counsel silence?—and more to do with a different kind of restraint. Tardewski's citation offers itself as a kind of verbal sepulcher: in affixing a "must not" to the impossibility that is already said to be in effect, the statement suggests that speech must find itself implicated in (or responsible *to* but not *for*) the gaps and silences for which it cannot render a complete account. Speech must thus become a kind of placeholder or tomb, guarding in silence a place for which there is no adequate sound or signifier. The question of the relato and its limits has direct implications for the discussion of the Argentine tradition and tragedy: the ethical silence Tardewski counsels would attempt to mark and hold in place a limit for narrative as a process of repetition, organization and memor(ial)ization. In contrast to the silence advocated here, to produce a heroic or memorializing narrative of el Proceso would in fact be to commit oneself to a far worse form of forgetting. The suspension of speech called for by Tardewski points to an ever-present question for literature: how to narrate the real in a manner that, while dissolving the paralyzing effects of psychic trauma, would also respect the gaps, silences, and contortions produced in the memory of these events? How to refrain from retrospectively normalizing the event, and thus avoid what Claude Lanzmann terms the "obscenity of understanding"?[9] How, that is, to discover or invent new literary or artistic forms and strategies that do not merely reproduce at a different level the same ideological and epistemological impasses of prior generations?

With Tardewski's relato, we have to do with a slightly different inflection of the structure of heteronomy discussed in the earlier chapter on Borges. Perhaps the aphoristic style of Piglia's short story "En otro país" (published in *Prisión perpetua*, 1988) offers the interpretive key in which Tardewski's story should be heard: "Lo más importante es lo que no se dice. Una historia que el narrador no comprende" [Most important is what one does not say: a history that the narrator himself does not understand] (Piglia, *Prisión perpetua*, 28). This statement offers a theory of literature itself: reading does not happen at the level of the narrator's or writer's intention, i.e., as the communication of information and meaning from writer to reader; rather, it takes place at those points of a story or history that exceeds the comprehension of the one who narrates. The "truth" of a history is to be found not in the subject's discourse (the meaning that he or she manipulates more or less at will) but in his or her *speech*—in what emerges through the slips, omissions and repetitions that occur in any narrative. The possibility that the truth of speech lies beyond what has already been understood prior to the speech act is relevant for my discussion of the ethical limits of narration. For one, the "fortuitousness" of Tardewski's discovery defies understanding: the common thread, the grapheme "Hi-," literally has no meaning in and of itself. Likewise, the connection he appears to be proposing, a link between the rational and emancipatory project of the Enlightenment and the ruination of this project's ideological basis, itself marks a limit for conceptual thinking. Tardewski's relato does not reflect or constitute an ideal unity between the subject of enunciation and the enunciated subject, as a certain idealist reading of tragedy would have it.[10] On the contrary, the story or history it articulates is one that it does not fully grasp, and which thus calls for more reading. While we could hear the aphorism just cited as implying that narration is itself an attempt to "come to terms" with an event that otherwise defies understanding, it is also possible to hear this statement as describing the relato as the *production* of a truth that alters the speaker: as an emergence of language that *implicates* the speaker from a point that falls outside of the cognitive and rational faculties of the subject.

Trauma and Affect: the Material Limits of Language in *La ciudad ausente*

Recent theoretical elaborations on the relation between trauma and narrative can be of help in examining Piglia's literary work as an intervention in national cultural production in Argentina. One of the most salient aspects of Cathy Caruth's investigations on trauma is her elaboration of the peculiar temporality of the traumatic event.[11] What Caruth describes, following Freud, as the "latency" of traumatic experience suggests that, at a certain level, the traumatic event is actually characterized by a *failure* to take place, while at another level it could be described as an event that never ceases to take place. With "nontraumatic" experiences, our cognitive processes function with the help of temporal metaphors that reinforce the idea of linear time: of "before," "during" and "after," of cause and effect, and so on. On the other hand, for one reason or another the basis of traumatic experience precisely resists or exceeds incorporation into temporal sequences and existing mnemonic threads. Trauma thus introduces a rift between the concrete materiality of the event, or the way in which the event inscribes itself in the unconscious history of the subject, and the partial or complete failure of the cognitive processes in their idealizing function, or the sense in which the event never takes place *for a subject*. Insofar as the event marks the subject from a point that exceeds or falls away from recognition, it is subject not to understanding but to "repetition" in the form of symptoms. The rift or lag-time between inscription and cognition constitutes the traumatic core of certain experiences. Trauma consists in the gap between inscription and the failure to recognize it, in the arrested or incomplete corroboration between the real and its incorporation into the symbolic world of the subject. An event that remains unrepresentable or inaccessible for the conscious subject need not be completely absent from memory as in amnesia and "recovered memory," however. On the contrary, it can also be overwhelmingly "present."

However, to affirm that Piglia's text manifests certain aspects of what Caruth and others have described as a crisis in narrative arising from traumatic experience is not to state that the author of *Respiración artificial/La ciudad ausente* is like a traumatized victim or witness. Nor does it necessarily mean that Piglia has taken up trauma and testimony as the themes or objects of his writing. On the contrary, it is to suggest that certain moments or facets of these literary texts cause the interpretive distinction between traumatic and nontraumatic discourse to begin to waver. This destabilizing effect can be identified in certain tonal dynamics of Piglia's writing. One such tonal element is found in a prevailing sense of anxiety or unease whose origin remains difficult to identify. In tone and cadence we encounter the possibility of both an emergent relation to the unknown, to the other (tone as imparting an appeal or a call) and of a work of delineation that functions as the zero degree of narrative itself: the cadence of speech, as *La ciudad ausente* never ceases to remind us, can also serve as structuring act, as a kind of ordering or "spacing" that allows correspondences and differences to become apparent.

In contrast to *Respiración artificial*, Piglia's second novel, *La ciudad ausente* (1992), is a consideration of the time of transition. The text explores the challenges and problems of narration in the course of a dual societal transformation, from dictatorship to democracy and from state economy to market economy. Akin to Piglia's earlier work, this novel provides a sketch of Argentine history as a dissemination of multiple relatos, only here a "translation machine" forms the center of the text's meditation on national history and cultural production. While the story it tells is that of the "return to normalcy," the narrative is in fact marked by an intensification of the disorienting effects found in *Respiración artificial*. The protagonist, Junior, is a marginal and peripatetic figure charged with solving a mystery: someone is trying to steal "la máquina" and thereby gain control of its production process. Junior is led to wander throughout Buenos Aires, following a series of clues that never seem to bring him any closer to resolving the story's central enigma. The myriad relatos of *La ciudad ausente*, many of which allude to the dictatorship period and to the gaps and disappearances that remain in its wake, establish a sense of foreboding and wariness without ever allowing us to categorize this mood as either paranoiac or as justifiably cautious:

> Todo era normal y a la vez el peligro se percibía en el aire, un leve murmullo de alarma, como si la ciudad estuviera a punto de ser bombardeada. En medio del horror, la vida cotidiana siempre prosigue y eso ha salvado la cordura de muchos. Se perciben los signos de la muerte y del terror, pero no hay visiones claras de una alteración de las costumbres. Los ómnibus paran en las esquinas, los negocios funcionan, algunas parejas se casan y hacen fiestas, no puede ser que esté pasando nada grave. Se ha invertido la sentencia de Heráclito, pensó Junior.

> [Everything was normal, and yet there was danger in the air: a soft murmur of alarm, as if the city were about to be bombarded. In the midst of horror, daily life always goes on, and this has preserved the sanity of countless people. One can sense the signs of death and terror, yet people show no sign of changing their daily rituals. The bus still stops at the corner, businesses are open, people get married and have parties—it can't be that something serious is about to happen. Heraclitus's maxim has been inverted, thought Junior] (*La ciudad ausente*, 88).

Above and beyond attention to the signified or the overt message, it is important to indicate what this passage *does not* say. Let us take note of the manner in which it "says" while at the same time avoiding saying. The indices of a banal daily existence provide a metaphorical framework in which traditional notions of communication and meaning are set to work: the economy of *negocios* [business] and the *ómnibus* [buses] are not only signs of daily activity or habit, they are metaphors of metaphor itself, of the transport of signification in its clockwork regularity. The tonal vacillation between normality and danger, however, warns that we have in fact to do with a simulacrum of normality, through which the traces of incredulity and disreality are faintly perceptible. The narrative warns that something is afoot or amiss. It points to an impending conspiracy or disaster that remains to be named or identified as such. It is the *tonal discord* of this passage that illustrates one important aspect of what I will call literary mourning. The exigency of mourning emerges as the need for a symbolic production that register the fact of loss under conditions for which historical memory is increasingly suspect.

The tonal dynamics at work in the passage cited above play a dual function for hermeneutics. Tone fixes a limit on the referential basis of interpretation, while at the same time acting as a signal, warning us against an imminent shock. The intensity and variation of tone conveys a different kind of "sense" from that of signification: while the latter is based on the transferential structure of metaphor, tonal registers manifest what could be described as the insistence of the untransferable in these processes of negation and signification. "Pitch" and "timbre" may well speak loudly and clearly, but they nonetheless bring forth a material dimension of language irreducible to the ideal registers of exchange and equivalency. The specific intensity of language in *La ciudad ausente* tends to run counter to and undermine the explicit message of quotidian normalcy, producing instead an anxious vacillation between the extremes of celebratory euphoria and depression. Tone introduces a subsidiary narrative here: it is through the differences, fluctuations and dissymmetries between tonal-semiotic and symbolic-semantic registers—and through the conflicting "senses" established therein—that the text attempts to relate an account for which all traditional narrative modes may be inadequate.[12] In "speechlessly" pointing toward a horror it cannot or will not name (this inability to name is part and parcel of the horror), the affective register tells the story of a literary attempt to escape or forestall disaster, the disaster of an unprepared encounter with the real.

Alongside tone or cadence, a consideration of "rhythm" also plays an important function in *La ciudad ausente*. Irreducible to processes of signification and ideation, rhythm likewise assists in shedding light on the role that narrative plays in traumatic experiences.[13] As a quasi-transcendental condition of possibility for temporality and consciousness, rhythm renders possible the experience of a particular event within a given time, yet it is impossible to encounter anything like "rhythm" in its pure, originary state. Rhythm cannot be said to exist prior to or outside of its playing out through syncopation. The term describes a retroactive process of identification in which repetition (or the process through which we experience a second and proceeding moments or beats, and are able to identify them as such) allows a certain regularity to take the place of random occurrence. As a mode of consciousness, the occurrence of rhythm has the character of always having begun already. By extending this retroactive temporality in the opposite direction, rhythmic sequence also has an anticipatory function: in poetry, for instance, a series of four consecutive iambs prepares the reader for another sequence of four. And, within certain limits of internal modification and mutability, rhythm also enables us to assimilate occurrences that could not have been predicted or expected: for instance, the irruption of the caesura in Greek tragedy's iambic trimeter. The origin of rhythm is thus contained within a hermeneutic and affective double movement (both consciousness and the body are "moved" in this ebb and flow between past, present and future), which continually reproduces temporality from a recurrent and discontinuous series of cuts. But if there is no such thing as pure rhythm, "rhythm" is nonetheless a continual object of interrogation in *La ciudad ausente*, from the marginal, subterranean and peripatetic existence of Junior (who experiences urban life in its propinquity and anonymity, according to the underground movements of the *subte* [metro] or the coming and going of the *ómnibus*) to the series of discontinuous and partial relatos produced by the textual apparatus, leading up to the linguistic utopia of the final relato. But there remains an important distinction between Piglia's narrative discourse and what is often conceived as the merely passive or repetitive nature of depressive or melancholic discourse. The thought of rhythm that informs a number of the relatos in *La ciudad ausente* underscores one important aim of Piglia's writing, which could be described as a retroactive attempt to produce the meaning of an event which has not yet taken place.[14]

In contrast to the idealizing function of signification, rhythm provides a "material" basis for the text to address the foundational role of the imaginary in Argentine society. I am alluding to what the text terms "las primeras historias" [the originary histories] (47–49): an array of narrative forms, scenes and mythologemes which, as the genetic code of national cultural production, constitute both a basis of memory and a *potens*, allowing for a nearly infinite production and modification of a few key metaphors. Piglia's text proposes that the nineteenth-century national imaginary in Argentina is situated in the romanticized image of train travel. This judgement, which could well be based on Dahlmann's journey to the south in "El Sur," also illustrates the position occupied by Borges in Piglia's conception of the Argentine tradition.[15] If, by way of this symbolic constellation, the nineteenth-century Argentine imaginary reveals its investment in romanticized notions of technology, exploration and modernization of the interior (the train is both a vehicle for experience or knowledge of the other and for economic exploitation), it is clear that late-twentieth-century experiences of dictatorship and globalization require a fundamentally different array of images. In attesting to the need for new symbolic material with which to elaborate new historical projects, Piglia's text also illustrates an important truth regarding the limits of the national imaginary: while the reproductive function of metaphor is crucial for any attempt to represent society as totality, at a certain point (and one might just as easily say: always to a certain degree) the constellation of metaphors and mythic fragments through which a society would constitute itself as One also mark the limit of every social sphere. The very need to repeat these "primeras historias" serves as an indication that they will never be made to say the Same. And thus the new histories that Piglia's work seeks will also be charged with avoiding the fatal identifications and misrecognitions of the past.

The Mechanics of Translation: Contrivances of Mourning and the State

En la isla no conocen la imagen de lo que está afuera y la categoría de extranjero no es estable. Piensan la patria según la lengua. ("La nación es un concepto lingüístico.") Los individuos pertenecen a la lengua que todos hablaban en el momento de nacer, pero ninguno sabe cuándo volverá a estar ahí. "Así surge en el mundo . . . algo que a todos se nos aparece en la infancia y donde todavía no ha estado nadie: la patria."

[On the island the image of the outside is unknown, and the category of the stranger is unstable. They think *patria* through language. ("The nation is a linguistic concept.") Each individual belongs to the language that was spoken at the time of his or her birth, but nobody knows when he or she will return to that first scene. "And so there emerges in the world . . . something that appears to each of us in our infancy, but in which none of us has ever set foot: the patria] (*La ciudad ausente*, 122).

The postmodern cliché in this passage—the nation as mere linguistic construct—masks a far more demanding thought: patria names an aporia that can neither be fully grasped in its positivity nor renounced as a mere ideological illusion or simulacrum. The nation is a shared "space"—the inverted commas suggesting that its basis is both of the concrete *and* of the imaginary—that presupposes the principle of fixed borders. Nation, in this sense, could perhaps be termed a discursive effect: its social consistency, its role in shaping the memories, imaginations and practices of its citizens, is the product of repeated and mutually reaffirming assignations. The contingent, more or less arbitrary nature of borders (or the fact that they are imposed by political will and custom—and that they therefore remain liable to shift—rather than the permanent effects of natural or divine law) is converted, through a process of repeated delimitation—of an inside and an outside, an us and a them, a proper and an improper—into a frontier: a natural, unimpeachable, and in a certain sense untraversable horizon. It is the naturalization of borders, or the forgetting of the difference between the contingency of the assignation and the essence it seems to name, that characterizes the essentialist dimension of twentieth-century Argentine nationalism. (Let us recall Borges' description of Juan Dahlmann's nationalist identification as an affective appropriation of certain material remainders, as well as a naturalization of borders.) Yet, with Piglia, the nation or patria is also said to be the *origin* of language itself. This entity gives birth to the very phenomenon of which it is said to be an effect. We do not choose the language into which we are born (rather, we might say that language chooses us), and yet linguistic usage is the basis on which every choice or identity becomes available *as a choice*. The idea of the patria as the unrecoverable decision *of* and *for* language is Piglia's attempt to mark a limit for nationalism: *la patria*, which every nationalism claims as its own rightful inheritance and property, is also radically incommensurable with ever social and political articulation. As a "place" that cannot be occupied or institutionalized ("donde todavía *no ha estado* nadie": let us note the untranslatable play between being [*estado* is the past participle of *estar* or "to be"] and the state [*el estado*]), the patria is another name for what Ernesto Laclau calls the impossibility of society. It is the inability of each and every hegemonic claim fully to suture or constitute the totality to which it aspires, or to make itself present at and thus fully institutionalize the origin of its own articulation. The naming of the patria thus evinces a kind of disjointure: it articulates a demand that has gone unfulfilled, or cites a debt that remains outstanding. For the traditions in which Piglia is working, it may be difficult to distinguish this account of the aporetic origin of nation from its utopian precedents in Echevarría, Sarmiento, Lugones, and others. Yet, while Piglia's texts continue to use the language of the utopian tradition, its also calls our attention to a profound dissymmetry in these acts of citation. In lieu of simple affirmations or negations of the tradition, this usage in fact generates a contradiction between the order cited and the act of citation itself. Piglia's text is haunted by an unmarked difference between content and mode, between what is said (frequently the language of tradition) and the way in which it is said (the disastrous rupture of tradition).

If one of the key interpretive threads of *Respiración artificial* is formed by the tragic hope of hermeneutic decipherment, it is perhaps a thought of translation that provides the central interpretive axis of *La ciudad ausente*. Through the dynamics of cultural translation, which involves the simultaneous reproduction and supplementation of tradition, literature sets itself a dual task: that of exposing and marking the limits of prior cultural configurations, as well as that of opening new spaces in which to think the future as potential difference, rather than as a mere continuation of the present. The text's central historical figure, Macedonio Fernández, is the author of *El museo de la novela de la eternidad*, a work that in fact is not a novel at all, but a seemingly endless chain of prologues to a hypothetical novel that never existed. The intertextual presence of Fernández lends support to Piglia's thesis on the improper origins of the Argentine tradition—and let us note that "impropriety" does *not* mean that the Argentine tradition is truly lacking anything that could be found in other traditions. It is the uncertain ontological status of Fernández's work—a prologue is a preliminary statement that precedes and sets the stage for the work itself; yet the prologue is often that which is written last of all—that offers insight into the mechanics and production of national cultural production as translation. The machine that is Macedonio Fernández's oeuvre functions as a metonym for the role played by national cultural production in securing the identificatory ground of the modern state: the work is at once a translation machine, a capitalist machine, a modernizing machine, a populist machine, a machine of surveillance and repression, and a mourning machine. In all of these senses, it is a cultural machination that produces the *idea* of the modern state, as distinct from the state's particular institution spaces. In referring to the "idea of the state" I am thinking of Althusser's notion of the interpolation of modern citizens, or the argument that the state mechanism functions primarily by generating *identification* between the subject and the state and its mandate. Interpolation, in other words, describes the operation of "consensus" rather than force and outright coercion. Also relevant here is David Lloyd and Paul Thomas's thesis that in postmonarchical societies "culture"—and particularly "literature"—have provided the ideal medium in which to carry out these interpolation processes. The line of thinking that links Althusser and Lloyd and Thomas roughly describes one avenue of reflection in Piglia's novel. At the same time, the text is also an attempt to think the limits of culture as a identificatory and representational mechanism, and a consideration of how literature might bear witness to the failure or noncompletion of interpolation. Let us note that the conjunction of the intertextual references to Fernández's *Novela del museo* as exemplar of cultural production mechanism and the discussion of patria as transcendental condition of signification also marks a limit for the immanentism of the posttheological (and perhaps poststatist) world order: a society that is totally *produced* can no longer experience its own origin as enigma or cause for questioning; and it can no longer conceive of its destiny as anything but a self-evident reproduction of sameness.

The *mekhanē* that is national culture links production and dissimulation, reproduction and displacement, while maintaining itself at the very edge of visibility. Piglia's attempt to think translation as a kind of "production" requires that we abandon conventional views of translation as the more or less adequate reproduction of an original. As a metaphor for national cultural production, the translation machine reminds us of the essentially finite nature of what it seeks to translate (the original). In absence of the finitude of its object, there could be no *trans*lation but only perfect copies and/or unrecognizable deviations. For Walter Benjamin, the object of translation is not simply to reiterate what was said in the language of the original, but rather to translate precisely what the original *is unable to say*. The limits of the original are experienced as a call for supplementation in which the original, in its fallen and dying tone, issues an appeal to and for another language. In the post-Babelian foreclosure of universal language, every particular language is confronted with its essential limitation, its innate and constitutive inability to say everything. And thus each language also attests to its need for supplementation through recourse to other languages. But, at the same time, these frontiers shared with others—as well as the graft, imports, tensions, and invasions that go with the territory—act to reproduce the very condition of having limits. The border, in other words, reintroduces the condition of finitude through translation and as the limit of translation: what does not and cannot translate is the border itself. Translation thus fails to fulfill the dream of absorbing the fragmented multiplicity of languages into one proper language. What resists exchange and transferal between languages is the necessity that attends the birth of translation: the call or the demand that constitutes the very condition of possibility for translation.

> Junior empezaba a entender. Al principio la máquina se equivoca. El error es el primer principio. La máquina disgrega 'espontaneamente' los elementos del cuento de Poe y los transforma en los núcleos potenciales de la ficción. Así había surgido la trama inicial. El mito de origen. Todas las historias venían de ahí. El sentido futuro de lo que estaba pasando dependía de ese relato sobre el otro y el porvenir.

> [Junior began to understand: the machine went astray from the beginning. Error is its first principle. The machine "spontaneously" broke Poe's story down into its basic elements, transforming them into potential seeds for new fables. This is how the first plot took shape. The myth of the origin. All of the histories came from the same place: the future sense of what was happening right now depended on an account of the other and of the future] (*La ciudad ausente*, 98).

For Piglia, translation also provides a transcultural weapon in the service of a parricidal assault upon the colonizing supremacy of the metropolitan original. In providing a theoretical key for reading the novel, the thought of translation underscores Argentine cultural production as a process of (mis)citation, errancy and apocrypha. Of course, it is only through Eurocentrism that the so-called "bad copies" of cultural production in the periphery can be said to confer (retroactively) on the originals the value of truth, authenticity, and propriety. Indeed, one ideological basis of Eurocentrism is precisely the postulated distinction between good and bad copies. But the critique of Eurocentrism, in turning the tables by determining Latin American literature as the true source of good copies of the Latin American real (in contrast to European bad copies or misrepresentations of this real), remains prisoner of the Eurocentric tropological ground. For Piglia, the critique of Eurocentrism must instead begin by exposing the disavowed limit of the good-versus-bad copies paradigm itself. Through (mis)citation and partial translations, cultural production at the "margins" of the Western tradition exposes the gaps, fissures, and inconsistencies that the nomination of "the original" would appear to deny. Citation thus functions as a kind of *overexposure* of the original, bringing out the limits that metropolitan culture would prefer to disown or mask. The effects of citation, in which usage precisely reveals the impossibility of the "ground" it would seem to redeploy, offers an interesting way of hearing Walter Benjamin's description of translation as "die Wehen des eigenen" [the suffering of one's own]. For Benjamin, translation entails confrontation with a language that one had previously thought to have mastered as familiar, proper, and so on: the language of the original, the mother tongue. Through translation, though, this language reveals a strange and estranging voice.

As we can now see, the description of the translation machine as "disgrega[r] 'espontaneamente'" is in fact an account of language itself. The metaliterary focus becomes increasingly apparent in the final relato, an extended reference to James Joyce's *Finnegans Wake*. The "literariness" of the concluding sequence should not be equated with the introduction of a postmodern cliché: this is not about a literary universe that has managed to incorporate and fictionalize its nonliterary outside. If literature has always been suspected of harboring colonizing designs upon the real, Piglia's text is a consideration of the ways in which literariness allows the real to emerge at the ecstatic limit of signification, or as the sudden and unexpected breakdown or rupture of the colonizing machine. And thus, while Piglia's novel offers us a certain literary echo of "il n'y a pas d'hors de texte," it also reminds us that what is called "textuality" or "literariness" is informed by concrete or material elements that cannot be captured by the idealizing and/or imaginary processes of signifying language without the engendering of an excess or remainder. In the final instance, the novel's reflection on its own literary condition destroys the claim of literature to have successfully fictionalized the real, or to have made the real accessible for knowledge and consumption through aesthetics. In reflecting on literature's participation in the consolidation of the modern nation-state, the novel also expresses a new awareness that arises as the traditional model of the state nears its exhaustion: that literature can no longer provide—if in fact it ever truly could—an epistemological or a political ground upon which to build, culturally or politically speaking. If the rhetorical and tropological dimensions of literature provide an important mechanism for meaning-producing processes and thus offer an ideal resource for the modern state, Piglia's text also demonstrates how the literary marks a limit for both aestheticized consumption and interpolation. Further support for this view can be found in the debt Piglia's writing owes to Jorge Luis Borges. As Borges has shown, literature is not in possession of the essence or timeless truth often attributed to it by culturalist Humanism: rather, its truth and its force lies in production and deferral, which together point to a meaning that is always yet to come. Literature never ceases to attest to the need for supplementation, for citation, translation, and rereading; and thus the path to literary truth must by necessity pass through errancy, unable to rule out at any point the possibility of future *mis*translation and *mis*reading.[16]

The phrase "El sentido futuro de lo que estaba pasando" in the passage cited above suggests that meaning is determined according to a pseudomessianic structure, in which the future and past are mutually implicated in the fashioning of meaning for the present. The possibility of meaning, that is, cannot be separated from its deferral and displacement between times. Meaning is always still to come, even when this means that it lies awaiting its discovery in the past. This textual figure of a meaning-to-come attests to the indeterminacy of the future (no one can say what the future will bring, nor can we see how it will interpret the present), but it also assigns the present to a kind of dependency upon the future as the deferral and irreducible difference of meaning: there could be no interpretation in the here and now, no production of meaning, without a concurrent generation of gaps and remainders—and hence of potentialities for future interpretive work. The future thus stamps each and every statement with the value of an oracular statement. At the same time, the veil separating the present from its possible future(s) could be conceived in terms of the responsibilities, demands, and exigencies that confront us every day, but for which we do not necessarily possess a name or an address. The present is thus informed by both a residue of insistent uncertainty or uncertain insistence, without which there could be no decision worthy of the name: our present becomes what it is—ours, and hence beyond substitution or exchange—by virtue of the urgency with which our decisions present themselves, by nature of an exigency that often precedes any certain as to whom or to what one finds oneself summoned or held accountable.

La ciudad ausente also invites us to read it as a novel of the Southern Cone transition. While *Respiración artificial* is engaged in problems of hermeneutics and history—and thus, at least in its formal conception, the novel remains decidedly modernist—the thematic framework of *La ciudad ausente* stages a conflict between warring imaginaries in which it becomes increasingly clear that the text has left open no possible outlet of escape. The hyperbolic proliferation of image and fantasy in the later novel is not only a commentary on actual conditions, at least not in the sense that the novel would claim to diagnose the end of history in the contemporary retreat of the political signifiers "utopia" and "revolution." Instead, and as has already been suggested in the earlier discussion of rhythm, the novel's staging of this metaliterary scene sets the stage for reconsidering the role that cultural production has traditionally played in securing the relative stability of the modern state. Piglia's text initiates this reexamination by laying bare the aesthetic ground of national identity as something resembling the zero-degree of history. It is in this sense that the text suggests that there is no exit from la(s) historia(s): the competing ideological narratives are not simply different from one another in a way that would leave them unrelated; rather, each reconstitutes the "núcleos potenciales" in a certain key or mood. The apocalyptic threat against which the narrative is mobilized—"no more *historias*"—would thus mean the culmination of an entire epoch of world history. As a "transitional" work, *La ciudad ausente* announces the end of the modern novel and the foreclosure of the utopian imaginary upon which this novelistic form is constructed. Or, more precisely, Piglia's novel announces the exhaustion of a certain framework of understanding literature and, in particular, the modern novel. It does so in part because the utopian tradition that was initiated with Echevarría and Sarmiento now reveals its dystopian kernel of truth: its having been based on an imaginary structure of opposition and mutual negation. Throughout this tradition, the being of one ideological pole is constituted as threatened by the appearance of the other, whose very existence poses problems for the former's imaginary unity-without-limits. The identity of one is thus secured—or so each pole thinks—through the visible and total annihilation of the other, and via the recognition that this negation would hypothetically confer upon the victor (but of course, what the one who has been annihilated precisely cannot do is recognize the other). It is this battleground of imaginaries that Piglia's text seek to delimit and abandon.

The transition from dictatorship to democracy, and from state economy to market economy, marks a transformation in both mode of production and available political forms.[17] But transition also—

and just as profoundly—entails the exhaustion or suspension of a certain determination of politics as such. It signals a shift in regime of signification, or of the particular mechanisms according to which meaning, values and even thinking itself take shape. For the Enlightenment tradition, the prevailing political systems headed by the sovereign or the modern state both draw their legitimacy from their seeming capacity to refer to a beyond, a transcendent point whose trace the system has nonetheless managed to incorporate and put to work. In this sense, the difference between the theological state and the secular state is merely a difference of degree: the sovereign receives his legitimacy as a stand-in for God, and the state justifies itself as the embodiment of Reason that sutures the radical division between culture and nature. In the time of "globalization," however, the sovereign and self-sufficient nature of the nation-state is thrown into doubt on a number of fronts: through the predominance of free trade, the emergence of transnational corporations and NGOs, and the increasing visibility of human rights groups whose influence extends beyond traditional national borders, as well as with a variety of local or regional discourses whose demands call attention to areas where the state has failed to maintain (the appearance of) social mediation. At the same time, the specter of the total commodification of nature signals the imminent collapse of very field of signification (culture/nature) in which the modern state is called into being. It is not that the state simply ceases to exist with "globalization," nor is its presence in certain social circumstances any less repressive than before. Instead, it is the transcendental principle of the state—as universal mediator—that has been shaken, perhaps irreparably, in recent decades. Transition thus signals the culmination of a certain epochal determination of history, which could be summarized as the narrative of the self-realization of a people, pueblo, or Volk by way of the nation-state. In light of these tectonic shifts and the "interregnum" or epochal suspension implied therein, the idea of culture—which for postindependence Latin America has always had the nation-state as its postulated end, and which is thus rigorously coterminous with the state: we cannot think one without the other—must itself undergo a serious and sustained reconsideration if its conceptualization within Latin Americanist thought is to avoid lapsing into merely reactive attempts to forestall the crisis of historical transformation.[18] Globalization calls for different ways of thinking about history, politics and culture—

but what? This question evinces epochal transition as a passage through irreducible uncertainty or even terror.

The retreat of the state in postdictatorship society forms one basis for understanding the shift between "estado" and "estado mental" in *La ciudad ausente* (see 144). As Foucault and others have shown, the modern state-form operates through the mechanisms of disciplinary and pedagogical institutions, in which subjects or citizens are produced through the inscription, repetition and memorization of laws and codes—all of which are based on an ontology of propriety versus impropriety, or the postulated difference between "productive" and "unproductive," "sane" and "insane," "citizen" or "legal" and "illegal," and so on. The designation of an "estado mental" in Piglia's text would appear to announce the ambivalent total fulfillment of this program, at which point the distinction between the state and its disciplinary institutions on one hand, and civil society and private life (the two spaces in which statist "discipline" is carried out) on the other hand, begins to mutate or disappear. Again, it is not that the state has simply been replaced by other mechanisms of discipline or control; rather, it is that civil society and private life themselves begin to assume the functions formerly entrusted to the state as a "third party" removed from civil society. The widely proclaimed diminishment or shrinking of the state thus serves to conceal the sense in which the state increasingly could be said to be everywhere. The "estado mental" names something resembling the Jamesonian theory of postmodernity: the sacred spaces that the Humanist tradition had always held to be off-limits to forces of political and economic domination—dreams, desires and the imagination—must today be acknowledged as having been transformed from sites of private reflection or poetic world creation into spaces where dominant ideological formations are unwittingly reproduced and fulfilled. Let us say that *La ciudad ausente* presents this total colonization of the imagination as a threat or a tendential phenomenon rather than as an accomplished truth. At the same time, Piglia's writing is also a ceaseless interrogation of language and cultural production as constituting a kind of "unconscious," or as forming spaces or hollows in which material elements or primary "signifiers" circulate and give rise to competing, partial representations. Yet, to pursue the psychoanalytic model one step further, none of these representatives could be said to succeed in closing the gap between itself and its unary signifier—whose atemporal origin is strictly irreducible to any given present—and thereby exhaust or close the field in its entirety. This extension of the unconscious from an individual to a collective basis would suggest that any colonization of the imaginary, such as those that accompany nation-building and globalization, also partakes in reproducing the limit of colonization as a process of incorporating and marketing difference. But of course these limits do not act on their own: they are instead the effects or byproducts of repeated reading and writing.

In juxtaposition to nearly two centuries of national cultural production, *La ciudad ausente* is an endeavor to work through a nearly interminable chain of cultural imaginaries. Through what seems an endless process of citation and rereading, the work seeks to expel an accumulation of calcified cultural signifiers and thereby release the present from the disastrous circulation of these remnants. The literary ritual in which *La ciudad ausente* is engaged hopes to transfer back to itself the specific quantity of energy that had been invested in the emergence of these cultural formations. These two tendencies together comprise a project that reveals aspects of what we could term a "literary mourning." But the competing logics of mourning also tend to produce conflict within the text. For one, Piglia's text manifests what we could term a refusal of mourning; or it marks a certain impossibility that haunts the work of mourning.[19] Yet this project also manifests a different tendency, one that would seem to run counter to the dyadic process just now described: the work seems to believe itself capable of delivering, through the functioning of a textual *mekhanē*, a metahistory of Argentine *historias*. The seductive logic of a literary metahistory is irreducible to any one *relato*, and is to be found rather in the strong tropology of narrative production itself: the work presents itself as having identified and incorporated the origin of all *historias*, and thereby appears to offer itself, or "literature" as such, as the metahistorical origin from which history could be reconstructed in its totality. There is a drive toward the total exhaustion of history in this text, which thus necessarily bears certain characteristics of the very terror it seeks to bracket and move beyond. Within the specific historical juncture of its production, Piglia's work manifests a confrontation with the most pressing limits of its own literary form. Amidst the crisis of the modern novel, this text performs an incorporation or an introjection of its own limit. The radical ambiguity of this gesture is displayed in a moment that entails the suspension of any possibility of deciding between self and other, the living and the dead, mourning

5: HETEROTOPIC MEMORY 247

and melancholia. It is at this site of apparent impasse, between the work (the labor) and the impossibility of the work (or of the principle of its completeness, which would also be the height of forgetting), that the paradoxical thought of literary mourning can be approached.

[Macedonio] había descubierto la existencia de los núcleos verbales que preservan el recuerdo, palabras que habían sido usadas y que traían a la memoria todo el dolor. Las estaba anulando de su vocabulario, trataba de suprimirlas y fundar una lengua privada que no tuviera ningún recuerdo adherido. Un lenguaje sin memoria."

[Macedonio had discovered the existence of the verbal nuclei of memory, words whose use also brought memory along with all of its pain. He was deleting these words from his vocabulary; he was trying to repress them and found a private language that would no longer have any memories attached. A language devoid of memory."] (148).

[Macedonio] concibió la idea de entrar en el recuerdo y quedarse ahí, en el recuerdo de ella. Porque la máquina el es *recuerdo* de Elena, es el relato que vuelve eterno como el río. . . . Meses y meses encerrado en el taller, reconstruyendo la voz de la memoria, los relatos del pasado, buscando restituir la forma frágil de un lenguaje perdido.

[Macedonio had the idea of entering into a memory and remaining there, in the memory of her. Because the machine is the *memory* of Elena, it is the account that becomes eternal like the river. . . . Months and months shut up in the workshop, reconstructing the voice of memory, the accounts of the past, seeking to restitute the fragile form of a lost language] (154).

The movement between expulsion and introjection, and between effacement and reinscription of memory, requires more commentary than space permits here. For one, a marked dissymmetry emerges within the presentation of memory itself, underscoring the difference between discrete mnemonic instances, images or fragments [*recuerdos*] and the faculty of memory itself [*memoria*]. This distinction offers a venue for exploring the tension between memory as affective register (as experience of longing, nostalgia, pain, etc.) and memory as resting place and placeholder of the beloved or as sepulcher. In the two passages cited above, the language of mourning reveals itself to be responsive and responsible to the other by way a call whose origin is always already receding. Mourning would capture and restitute the "forma frágil" of this call—the beloved's dying words—and thus safeguard it twice over: both from the oblivion of eternal silence and against the painful disaster of its unending return. Mourning takes shape as a confrontation with an aporia in the face of which there is neither exit nor retreat. It must thus preserve the call both against its loss and against the destructive effects of its unchecked return, and in both cases by adding something to the form it would protect. In order to give a just hearing to the other's dying speech—and justice here begins with the hearing that speech would receive on the threshold of its disappearance—the work of mourning must itself participate in a kind of second death: it must also be the mourning of language, of the dream of a self-identical or full speech, of a signifier that could fully account for itself without recourse to other signifiers. The aporetic nature of mourning can also be explored by way of the transition: as Piglia's novel suggests, transition is experienced both as an uncertain, indeterminate duration, and as the aftermath of a personal and collective loss whose extent remains difficult or impossible to measure. In many cases, the specific magnitude of the event and the loss attendant upon it includes the disruption or destruction of the very instruments and resources with which it would traditionally have been registered.[20] Transition thus introduces a profound dissymmetry into the mourning process. It compels us to rethink mourning beyond the possibility of either simply surpassing or simply remaining within the traumatic sphere of its lost object.

A tentative distinction can be drawn between Piglia's text and the utopian narratives it traces, collects and reproduces, by turning to the distinction between utopia and heterotopia that underlies Michel Foucault's analyses of discourse and history in *The Order of Things*. While utopia presupposes a closed system whose (non)existence has no essential bearing on its being (in essence, with utopia faith itself is enough), heterotopia names a system whose components, or particular moments, interrelations and significations, belong to an order or disparate orders radically incommensurate with the general truth expressed by the system. A heterotopia can only be constituted as a totality by exposing language to the destruction of its own reality effects (Foucault cites the famous example of Borges' Chinese Encyclopedia). We could pursue the traces of heterotopic effects in Piglia's text on the basis of the following supposition: that the conditions under which the text is produced include the suspension or near-complete displacement of the key terms and relations involved in the signification of a social or an aesthetic totality. I am thinking specifically of the relation Piglia's text assumes to the tradition of the modern novel—which, as Piglia himself has noted, is essentially a utopian tradition.[21] The text's painful awareness of the catastrophic history of its own discourse, together with the fact that it continues to speak it in a stammering voice, would constitute a heterotopic effect.

We can glimpse the traces of this epochal crisis in Piglia's work by turning once again to the crucial shift in interpretive registers between *Respiración artificial* and *La ciudad ausente*. This shift entails a movement between distinct logics and cultural indices, between the tragic tone of *Respiración artificial* and the repeated confrontation between imaginaries that informs *La ciudad ausente*. I have argued that the fundamental textual dynamic of *Respiración artificial* is tragic in that the text projects the possible opening of a new world through an aesthetic synthesis of mutually exclusive moments. For reasons that involve both aesthetic and ethical concerns, however, the tragic cipher of *Respiración artificial* should not confused with the very different idea of turning dictatorship itself into tragedy.[22] The tragic postulate in the latter scenario, which would amount to the claim that literature could accomplish some sort of aesthetic "recognition" or "reconciliation" between torturer and victim, would amount to the worst kind of aestheticism. To represent the military junta as "Creon" in relation to the victims' "Antigone" would yield not tragedy but farce. In the wake of dictatorship, the spirit of reconciliation that constitutes one of tragedy's fundamental moments could only function in profound ignorance of the incalculable, unsettling effects that this event continues to produce today.

It is my position that the tragic hope or promise of Piglia's dictatorship novel lies not in a potential reconciliation between Left and Right, or victims and perpetrators of terror, but rather in the possibility of elaborating a reflected relation between different generations in the Argentine tradition: between Enrique Ossorio, representative of the nineteenth-century utopian discourse of nation-building, and Marcelo Maggi, whose disappearance marks the collapse and annihilation of the Left in the 1970s, and thus signals the final exhaustion of utopian politics in Argentina. The longing for a tragic synthesis that would heal this newly opened epochal rift is imbedded in a hermeneutic work of deciphering that must begin by *assuming* the (non)relation between discrete histories that do not meet up in the end: "assuming" in the sense of taking this nonrelation as its own fundamental condition, and not as a contingency to be overcome. The great hope projected by Piglia's text is that the discrete and seemingly incommensurable historias of Ossorio and Maggi could at some level be made to function as symbolons vis-à-vis one another. The literary work would constitute itself through the mutual implication of discrete, partial historias, in which one time or historia is made to read another and perform a partial decoding of the other. In *La ciudad ausente*, on the other hand, the possibility of inaugurating a hermeneutics of fragmentary histories is replaced by a seemingly endless cycle of confrontation between competing imaginaries. The key motif, Macedonio Fernández's *El museo de la novela de la eternidad*, stages this eternal conflict between narratives vying for dominance in the cultural market: narratives of modernization, Peronism, capitalism, authoritarianism, exile, and resistance. In the transition as a time of interregnum, the old affective registers of fear and pity no longer provide sufficient impetus for coming to terms with societal catastrophe and terror. It might seem that Piglia's work has renounced the possibility of exiting from this interminable reproduction of warring imaginaries, and resigned itself to the reproduction of ideological fantasy. This is one possible reading, and the reverse face of a suggestion raised earlier: that while the text seeks to delimit or expose prior claims upon the totality of the nation, it also repeats the very crime it encounters elsewhere by pretending to deliver a total history of the nation. On the other hand, it is also possible to read this "flattening out" of Argentine history as what Lacan would term a *traversal* of the fantasy of the nation as self-identical, homogeneous totality, and likewise as an attempt to shatter the mutually reinforcing illusions of "true" and "false" national discourses. The work seeks to expose the imaginary remnants or kernel of fantasy at work in any signification of a whole, and thereby to mark the limit of every articulation of a unified society. In so doing, the work attests to the need for new narratives that would respond both to the experience of loss and to uncertainty regarding the future. The interpretive conflict between the return of fantasy and the traversal of fantasy, and between distinct expressions of nihilism and an ethical urgency, may well be unresolvable. Perhaps this aporetic experience of reading is akin to the discovery in mourning of an interminable travail, and of a demand that can be fully heard only through a repetition that would also bear tidings of its death.

Concluding Remarks: Modernity, Tragedy, and Disaster

In the central chapters of this project, we have seen how the tragic dynamic performs multiple functions in the national literary traditions of Argentina, Mexico, and Peru. If at times tragedy operates at the service of national unification projects (Sarmiento, Lugones), in other cases tragic aesthetics point to the ethical and political limits of these claims upon the All (Borges, Rulfo, and Vallejo, despite their many differences). These representations of the nation as tragic topos are necessarily topical endeavors: an experience of the tragic is not produced in a formulaic manner or through purely formal procedures, but on the contrary remains highly attentive to both the time and place of production *and* to what we could term the limits (or the unavowed contradictions) of any given time. Borges' treatment of Argentine modernity bears a tragic tone not because of the decisions undertaken by Dahlmann alone; rather, it becomes tragic through the juxtaposition and disjunction of multiple and conflicting temporalities and histories. The emergence of a tragic dimension in Vallejo's lyric poetry underscores an important historical distinction: the determination of modern thought as essentially tragic also gives shape to a distinctly modern view of tragedy. From this stems a strange thought of identity, of the modern subject as radically "unlike" itself—and as deriving the chance of its freedom from precisely this "difference." Yet, as Rulfo's text teaches us, a deconstruction of the national subject by way of a tragic turn does not alleviate the political exigencies stemming from inequality and domination, nor does it cancel out the need to act in the face of the unknowable. Finally, in discussing (post)dictatorship writing in the novels of Piglia, I have attempted to shed light on a crucial point, at once an epistemic rupture and an ideological shift, at which tragedy is no longer able to provide a compelling representation of violence and societal disaster. In *Respiración artificial* Piglia gives notice of this suspension, while suggesting that it is the Holocaust that will function as referential index for the experience of state terrorism in the Southern Cone. However, this transformation from tragedy to Holocaust is not an exchange of one cultural referent for another. Indeed, the "meaning" of this index of twentieth-century disaster is precisely its singular status as unexchangeable: what the Holocaust "means," if one can continue to use this language, is the possibility of the impossibility of reference. If there is an inherent risk in the literary move that underlies *Respiración artificial*, it is perhaps that of reinforcing the belief that we can identify something in particular (or something essential) that would set the Holocaust apart from all other disasters, something that would singularize it and thus convert what is unspeakable in it into a memorial.

The conviction that tragedy cannot provide the appropriate attunement for twentieth-century disasters recalls the seemingly contradictory assessments of Adorno and Celan regarding the fate of poetry in the wake of the Holocaust. Is it simply that we are too close to the genocidal and terrorist disasters of the twentieth-century to be able to conceive of them as tragedies, or to locate in them anything resembling a tragic thought or insight? (This would seem to be Geoffrey Hartman's position with regard to contemporary artistic representations of the Holocaust.) Or, on the other hand, do the specific political, social and technological configurations of these events in fact constitute a fatal rupture in the aesthetic tradition that begins with Classical Greek art, and thereby call for a radically new aesthetic basis for artistic representation? Does "disaster," as a possibility that belongs distinctively to our time, simply require a postponement of tragedy and its particular brand of symbolic production? Does it call for a deferral or lag time in which personal and collective memories can begin to heal? Or, on the contrary, does disaster in fact destroy the imaginary basis upon which the tragic mechanism depends?

Notes

INTRODUCTION

1. Among numerous commentaries on the "double bind" that both links modernity to classicism and prohibits the realization of this bond, see Lacoue-Labarthe, *Typography*.

2. On the role played by "culture" in the unification of Germany, see Lloyd and Thomas, *Culture and the State*, and Chytry, *Aesthetic State*.

3. Among the earliest examples of this view of literature as a formative space for national institutions can be found in Esteban Echeverría's *Dogma socialista*. For a discussion of the influence of German Idealism and Romanticism in the *Dogma* (and particularly the relation to Schiller's *Aesthetic Education*), see Leonor Fleming's introduction to Echeverría.

4. I discuss the prominence of writing in Sarmiento's discourse at greater length in chapter 2. On the relation between nation-building and literature, see Ludmer, *El genero gauchesco*.

5. Among the most influential treatments of the relation between philosophy and mimesis, see Derrida, *Dissemination*; Lacoue-Labarthe, *Typography*; and Rancière, *On the Shores of Politics*. For a different approach to mimesis and tragedy, which comes close to rejecting the philosophical dimensions of this problem, see Girard, *Violent and the Sacred*.

6. On the importance of tragedy for German Idealism, see Szondi, "Notion of the Tragic," Lacoue-Labarthe, *Typography,* and Chytry, *Aesthetic State*.

7. Fenves, "Topicality of Tone" in *Raising the Tone of Philosophy*.

CHAPTER 1. THE IDEA OF TRAGEDY

1. As quoted in Lacoue-Labarthe, "Caesura of the Speculative," in *Typography*, 215. The passage cited is from *Essay on the Tragic,* 1.

2. Thus Hegel speaks in the "Natural Law" essay of the absolute as the self-reflexive relation of an "eternal tragedy": "it eternally gives birth to itself into objectivity, submitting in this objective form to suffering and death, and rising from its ashes to glory" (Hegel, "Natural Law," 104). As Jacques Derrida suggests, the tragic character of this movement is underscored by the "absolutely double" nature of the movement (see *Glas*, left column, 102–3): that is, the absolute is at once forever going against itself, splitting away from itself, and rejoining itself in anticipation of an absolute "being-one" [*Einssein*]. A distinction, then, between tragedy and comedy: whereas comedy plays at the separation of the absolute from

its essence, reveling in the slackening of its form or the loosening of the bonds of meaning, tragedy enacts a rejoining and healing of the wound which the Absolute inflicts upon itself.

3. An attempt to theorize the aesthetic as both origin and mediation of the political constitutes the basis of Schiller's notion of the "Aesthetic State" (see *Aesthetic Education*). For recent discussions of Schiller's text and its relation both to German Idealism and its influence on nineteenth-century cultural production, see de Man, "Kant and Schiller," in *Aesthetic Ideology*; and Lloyd and Thomas, *Culture and the State*.

4. Hegel's most concise presentation of tragedy as mourning is found in the *Natural Law* essay. On the question of mourning in Hegel's thought, see Jacques Derrida's *Glas*. For a discussion of the specific intersection of tragedy and mourning in Hegel, see Beardsworth, "Aporia and Fantasm." On a related note, it should also be clear that Hegel's conception of tragedy would present considerable difficulties for a certain tradition of thinking about "the subject" (e.g., the "individual" posited by various forms of liberalism). The pragma of tragedy marks a thought of action as irreducible to any notion of rational choice; tragedy places decision prior to any possibility of a transcendental subject: "[Tragic heroes] act in accordance with a specific character, a specific pathos, for the simple reason that they *are* this character, this pathos. In such a case *there is no lack of decision and no choice*. The strength of these great characters consists precisely in this that they do not choose, but are entirely and absolutely just that which they will and achieve" (*Hegel on Tragedy,* 55; my emphasis). Hegel's insistence on the interrelation between tragic character, suffering and pragma should perhaps be interpreted as a response to Aristotle's attempt to distinguish between these registers, and a reply to Aristotle's assertion that the essence of tragedy lies in the dynamic pragma rather than in a fixed ethos or "character."

5. See the essays by Peter Fenves and Jacques Derrida in Fenves, *Raising the Tone of Philosophy*.

6. I would argue that Nietzsche's reading does not necessarily accomplish a true break with the Hegelian reading against which it moves: while Nietzsche rejects Hegel's and Schelling's association of tragedy with the emergence of a subject, his reading appears to be no less *systematic* than those of Hegel and Schelling.

7. There is an unmistakable gesture toward the aesthetic running throughout Heidegger's discussions of technē and history. This is not an "aestheticism," but rather an attempt to think everyday activity as a mode of creation—in the sense that we usually speak of artistic activity as "creative." It is not only the imagination that emerges in this dual question of agency or praxis and poiēsis, but moreover a fundamental relation between activity, language and desire, through which production always manifests *something more*, something in addition to and in departure from preconceived design. In Heidegger's essays on art, namely "The Thing" and "The Origin of the Work of Art," we see that this "something more" is in close proximity to the fashioning of a "void" that could be described as the origin of the work of art. The creative and ordering violence that is poiēsis could be termed "reciprocal," then, except that the violent relation in fact precedes and presides over the constitution of its parties. For a helpful discussion of the relation between praxis and aesthetics in Heidegger's thought, see Fynsk, "Between Ethics and Aesthetics."

8. We could also turn here to the decisive confrontation between Oedipus and Tiresias, in which the "double edge" is manifested through language itself, in which Oedipus' own words come back to haunt him. The king, after compelling Tiresias to name Laius' murderer, adamantly disputes the seer's account, dismissing it as a thinly veiled attack on the his sovereignty. Tiresias responds that the truth "with all its power lives within [him]," and that truth has taught itself to him through Oedipus' ill-advised and tyrannical use of force. Tiresias' prophetic response opens onto a catastrophic moment within the hermeneutic tradition of which Oedipus is an exemplary figure: the blind seer's speech suspends all proprietary claims upon the truth, collapsing the usual authorial relation in which speaker (or author or dictator) authenticates the content of the address. (O: "You, shameless— / aren't you appalled to start up such a story? / You think you can get away with this?" T: "I have already. / The truth with all its power lives inside me." O: "Who taught you for this? Not your prophet's trade [*technē*]." T: "You did, you forced me, twisted it out of me" (Sophocles, *Oedipus the King,* 179 [1.402–7]).

9. See in particular Derrida's "On a Newly Arisen Apocalyptic Tone in Philosophy," and the commentary by Peter Fenves, entitled "The Topicality of Tone," which accompanies this essay in Fenves, *Raising the Tone of Philosophy*.

10. The texts I will be drawing on include "The Caesura of the Speculative" and "Hölderlin and the Greeks" (both published in translation in *Typography*) and "The Scene is Primal" (translated in *The Subject of Philosophy*). However, the double foci of Greek tragedy and mimesis forms a current that runs through much of Lacoue-Labarthe's work, and the ramifications of this are a good deal more complicated than I am able to make clear here. A general survey of this double theme would have to address, among other instances, Lacoue-Labarthe's attempt to situate Heidegger—his thought and his politics—within this tradition of (de)negation, and consequently to determine the Holocaust in relation to "tragedy" (see Lacoue-Labarthe, *Heidegger, Art and Politics*). I will attempt to suggest some of the limits of such a gesture in my conclusion, although I will not do so in reference to Lacoue-Labarthe and Naziism but rather with respect to contemporary Argentine literature and the question of state terrorism. In so doing, I will point out a risk of conflation between "tragedy" (often functioning as a universal metaphor for disaster) and what I will be referring to as the traumatic character of certain twentieth-century disasters, and in particular a leveling of the important differences between epistemological and ethical stakes.

11. "Relieves" [*relève*] contains a thought of continuity between Aristotle and the speculative tradition, as it both recalls Derrida's translation of the Hegelian *Aufhebung* and provides one possible interpretation of the continuing operation of catharsis (of fear and compassion) in the dialectic. Incidentally, Aristotle can also be seen to perform some of the transferrals which Lacoue-Labarthe underlines in Schelling (though this in no way alters the general point regarding the double function of mimesis for speculative philosophy). For instance, Aristotle too seeks to restrict the cause or origin of the spectator's experience to an intellectual order: in aligning tragic drama's "cathartic" function with the action—and not character—he suggests that one should be able to experience tragedy's effects solely on the basis of having heard the plot. "To produce [the cathartic] effects by means of spectacle is less artful and requires lavish productions" (Aristotle, *Poetics,* 17). No doubt a long history of thinking about representation and violence could be traced as an ongoing reinterpretation of these lines.

12. While implicit in some of Freud's discussions of Oedipus, this transformation is specifically theorized in the lesser-known essay "Psychopathic Characters of the Stage" (*Standard Edition* 7, hereafter abbreviated *SE),* which also advances an important distinction between classical and modern tragic drama.

13. A reference to *Vorlust* appears in the final paragraph of the "Psychopathic Characters" essay. These concepts are developed at greater length in "Three Theories of Sexuality" (Freud, *SE*) and "Jokes and their Relation to the Unconscious" (*SE* 8).

14. Among recent discussions of Lacan's reading of the play, see Fynsk, "Between Ethics and Aesthetics" and Joan Copjec, "Tomb of Perseverance."

15. Among the existent tragedies of Aeschylus, Sophocles, and Euripedes, Lacan excludes only *Oedipus Rex* from this rule of "after the race is run." It would be of some interest to reexamine Lacan's comments on tragedy in relation to J. P. Vernant's notions of the epochal overdetermination and anachronistic character of Greek tragedy. Vernant's discussion of the peculiar discourse of the chorus is especially relevant in this regard: he suggests that the lamentations of the chorus would likely have been heard as archaic in fifth-century Athens. If the chorus represents, in Lacan's view, "those who are moved" by the action, what would it mean that tragedy's performance of its own "enjoyment" is registered in a characteristically belated tone?

16. Lacan, *Ethics of Psychoanalysis*, 112 (hereafter abbreviated *EP*). If I understand it correctly, this statement moves in various directions at once. For one, it suggests—via the "raising" of the "object"—that sublimation is not necessarily the evacuation or negation/elevation (*Aufhebung*) of a sexual content. On the contrary, it reveals a propensity toward provocation and rupture (the proximity of this passage to Lacan's discussion of Arnaud Daniel's "Domna Ena" poem suffices to indicate the limitations of the model of productive transformation, demonstrating how that which goes by the name sublimation at times produces a traumatic (re)encounter with precisely the Thing it is supposed to avoid). At the same time, the allusion to an erection draws extensively on Heidegger's meditations on the relation between aesthetic activity and what he designates as "world." Here, we could say, Lacan attempts to establish a link between Freudian and Heideggerian articulations of *das Ding*. For Heidegger, the work of art fulfills a dual function that is described in the neologism "e-rection," at once a kind of standing-out (the art work is much like "the signifier" or "the phallus" in Lacanian vocabulary) and an institutional or legislating function that gives shape and sense to its surroundings. The two senses of "e-rection" are thus formally akin: we could say that the work comprises its own formal self-consistency insofar as it teaches us how to relate to or "read" it.

17. Lacan's observations regarding what he insists is the nonnatural and nonoppositional difference between Creon and Antigone (in other words, it is a difference that cannot appear as such within the dialectic) seem indisputable. Nevertheless, I find somewhat surprising Lacan's implication that it is in the tragic hero or heroes themselves that speculative thinking would seek reconciliation. While this may be the conclusion that Aristotle's thought points to, the Hegelian and Schellingian theories of contradiction in fact demand something else entirely. It is Schelling's insistence upon the hero's excessive and enduring defiance and silence in the face of justice that in turn leads to the possibility of a certain recon-

ciliation—not between the tragic antagonists per se but within reason itself. This distinction does not invalidate Lacan's conclusions, but it does invite a renewal of this line of thinking with respect to *Antigone*. Lacan's argumentation would seem to be suggesting finally that an intellectual coming-to-terms with the position adopted by Antigone is not possible, i.e., that her image never allows our desire to recognize itself in her, but nor does it permit desire to rid itself of her and move on to more familiar reflections. There remains, however, the important question of the tragic figure: how, that is, does Antigone's presence in the tragedy help to shed light on the psychoanalytic scene? What kind of example, if any, does she provide for the psychoanalytic experience itself? Or, for that matter, what would it mean to treat Antigone's own brand of absolutism as exemplary? What lessons does analysis find in her adoption of a position "beyond the law" and "between two deaths"?

Chapter 2. Visages of the Other

1. The first concrete modern articulation of this aesthetic ideal can be found in Schiller's late eighteenth-century *Aesthetic Education*, and in particular concerning the notion of the "Aesthetic State." It is not until Matthew Arnold, writing almost a century later, however, that the entity known as "literature" comes to be regarded as the ideal aesthetic medium for social organization.

2. Shumway implies that Borges' writing promotes aesthetic autonomy in the place of, and as a substitute for social, economic and political emancipation. However, it should be clear how such aestheticism, were this in fact an accurate description of Borges' poetics (*concesso non dato*), could easily serve to conceal any number of political projects. As a critical category, therefore, the "apolitical" is a bit misleading: "apolitical-ness" is precisely a form of politics operating under the banner of neutrality.

3. Natalio Botana attributes the origin of Sarmiento's terminology to Enlightenment thinkers and historians such as Gibbon, Michelet, Guizot, and Thierry (see Halperí Danghi, *Sarmiento*, 103). A comprehensive summary of the impact of *Facundo* on Argentine cultural production is not feasible here.

4. My attention to problems of knowledge and perspective in the text is not meant to suggest that Sarmiento's text should be classified as a philosophical treatise. In fact, I would argue that the work defies classification in any established taxonomy, and thus reveals its own kind of literary "barbarism." At the same time, I believe that the philosophical topoi discussed here—or, more precisely, their literary presentation—constitutes a necessary and fundamental step in Sarmiento's nation-building project, which seeks to ground itself in a European narrative of Reason.

5. The full passage reads: "La inmensa extensión de país que está en sus extremos es enteramente despoblada, y ríos navegables posee que no ha surcado aún el frágil barquichuelo. El mal que aqueja a la República Argentina es la extensión; la soledad, el despoblado sin una habitación humana, son por lo general los límites incuestionables entre unas y otras provincias" ["The extremes of the country in its immensity are entirely unpopulated, and it has navigable rivers which even the smallest of boats has yet to breach. The evil that plagues the Argentine Republic

is its extension: between one province and the next lies nothing but solitude and wilderness, devoid of even a single human dwelling"] (Sarmiento, *Facundo*, 11). Later in *Facundo*, however, Sarmiento will offer an important distinction between Facundo Quiroga and Manuel Rosas as representatives of two kinds of "evil": while Quiroga is a *passionate* barbarian who draws the nation together (albeit under the sign of an uncivilized spirit), Rosas is a cold, *passionless* barbarian whom Sarmiento equates with the petrification of all national unity. In light of this difference, which will eventually be seen as the basis for presenting Facundo as a tragic hero of the barbaric epoch, it would seem that Sarmiento trades off between a Catholic conception of evil as lack of good (Rosas) and a Kantian notion of evil as substance (Facundo). Thus it could be said that Quiroga represents an attempt to think Argentine history in terms of a "radical evil," and to present Argentine existence as containing an excess that is irreducible to the totality of Western onto-theology, or which can only be *misrecognized* as lack or lapse.

6. Of course, the open immigration policy that remained in effect in Argentina during the second half of the nineteenth century and the first decade of the twentieth century had a practical basis as well. Modernization, which entailed both the development of Buenos Aires as urban center and the transformation of the interior into an agricultural-exporting region, required a good deal more labor power than the nation could provide in 1850. By 1910, however, the vast scale of Argentine immigration would be evident: in 1910, one-half of the country's population would be foreign born, and nearly 80 percent were immigrants or descendants of immigrants arrived since 1850 (Rock, *Argentina*, 166).

7. In Hegel's words, "Self-consciousness is the reflection out of the being of the world of sense and perception, and is essentially the return from otherness" (*Phenomenology of Spirit*, section B 4 ["Selbstbewußtsein: Die Wahrheit der Gewißhiet seiner selbst," section 167, 134; 105 in A.V. Miller's English language translation]). This *einheimische Reich* is the proximate space in which self-consciousness attempts to seize and know itself by approaching and grasping itself in and as the other—and this is to say, as Nature. Self-consciousness comes to know itself as the negation of what Hegel calls "sense-perception"—which is to say, as the Aufhebung of contingency, or, in Sarmiento's terms, as the overcoming of barbarism. "Otherness" should not be mistaken for a living, breathing other. Rather, it is a specular phantasm, a shadowy maximum point of extension and return in the self-projection of the Hegelian subject.

8. My use of the term "transculturation" may seem out of place here for a number of reasons. For one, the first Latin Americanist use of the term "transculturation" postdates Sarmiento by nearly half a century; and, with Fernando Ortiz and Angel Rama, the use of the term implies political orientations rather far removed from the racist and elitist ideology that underlies Sarmiento's thinking. These important differences notwithstanding, it seems to me that a formal continuity could be identified between, on the one hand, the transformations in Sarmiento's thinking following the writing of *Facundo* and the voyages to France and the United States, and the kinds of cultural reinterpretation called for by Ortiz and Rama on the other hand.

9. In later writings Sarmiento will prove to be one of the leading apologists for the state's genocidal war against Argentina's indigenous populations. He will attempt to justify these massacres by arguing that, unlike the gaucho—whose inte-

gration into the national labor force is celebrated in the "second part" of José Hernández's *Martín Fierro*—the Amerindian is utterly resistant to assimilation into "civilization," and must thus be eliminated as an impediment to nation-building.

10. See Jacques Lacan's discussion of the role of the "mirror" in the formation of subjective identity during infancy ("The Mirror Stage as Formative of the Function of the I as Revealed in Psychoanalytic Experience," *Ecrits*).

11. I am referring to the neoclassical appropriation of the Greek tradition, beginning with Winckelmann, Goethe, and Schiller, and specifically to Schiller's notion of the "Aesthetic State" (see his *Aesthetic Education*). The Weimar appropriation of classical culture was in turn highly influential in the formation of Echeverría's civic philosophy (see Leonor Fleming's introduction to the Cátedra edition of *El matadero/La cautiva*). For a discussion of the notion of the "aesthetic state" and its effects on political development in England and Western Europe, see Lloyd and Thomas, *Culture and the State,* and Chytry, *Aesthetic State*.

12. On the difference between Kantian and Schillerian aesthetic theories, see de Man, "Kant and Schiller," in *Aesthetic Ideology*.

13. The "advertencia" appeared in the first edition of *Facundo* but was suppressed by Sarmiento in subsequent editions. Ricardo Piglia discusses the relation between the political stakes and the literary impact of *Facundo* in an essay entitled "Sarmiento the Author" (Halperín Donghi, *Sarmiento*). He suggests that Sarmiento, in the course of his second exile from Argentina (1840–51), inaugurates the Argentine "tradition" of citation and misquotation made famous by Borges and others. This hypothesis is discussed at greater length in Piglia's first novel, *Respiración artificial*.

14. Due to spatial constraints, this discussion of Lugones as a key intellectual figure in Argentine nationalism cannot take into account an extensive body of poetic and prose writing, much of which would no doubt complicate this outline of nationalism. Again, my intention has not been to pit the writing of Lugones against that of Sarmiento, but rather to describe a general conflict within Argentine cultural production.

15. In her book-length study of the gauchesque, Josefina Ludmer provides ample evidence that the gauchesque has in fact repeatedly been appropriated for political purposes, and thus bears a long history of "sacrificial" readings: for instance, the genre's transformation of the gaucho from defiant outlaw to hero coincides with attempts to domesticate the interior and convert its inhabitants into citizens (see *El género gauchesco*).

16. Lugones likens what he calls the Argentine "vida épica" [epic life] to the Greek heroic epic, or rather he suggests that the gaucho poem be understood as the return or continuation of spirit of the classical tradition. In his reinterpretation of the gaucho poem as world-historical return, Lugones must ignore the fact that Greek heroism was only invented later, i.e., during the fifth century production of tragedy. The creation of a heroic tradition thus belongs precisely to a postheroic time (see J.P. Vernant's discussion of the relation between Ancient Greek tragedy and heroism in "Greek Tragedy." Likewise, the Spanish *romancero* and the Argentine gauchesque are forms that both celebrate and mark the death of a particular way of life. In fact, then, these inventions of tradition implicitly recognize that death is a necessary condition for the emergence of tradition.

17. My use of "material" here is meant to emphasize the distinction between *cantar* and the idealist understanding of *escribir*: if writing is understood by Sarmiento as a transcendent act, in the sense of calling upon and transcribing an order of *meaning* that bears no essential relation to the language itself, then *cantar*, according to Ludmer, is different in that its *truth* qua act is precisely irreducible to such an ideal order of signification, or to the meaning of the words themselves. The key distinction hinges on the difference between what is said and the effects produced by the act of speaking, which may or may not coincide with the meaning of the words themselves.

18. The collection of short stories entitled *La historia universal de la infamía* (1934), published five years prior to the publication of "Pierre Menard," could well unsettle the distinction between the "early" and "late" Borges. While I will not address any of those short stories here, my own reading is likewise interested in examining the (unthought?) relation between these two modalities of writing.

What, then, is involved in this critical distinction between the "early" and the "late" Borges? Borges gives an account of how he came to write what he terms *ficciones* in his "Autobiographical Essay." According to Rodríguez Monegal, the essay is a composite sketch taken from various sources, including interviews, prologues, and so on, later edited by Norman Thomas di Giovanni (see Monegal, *Ficcionario* 421). The essay was first published in English in the *New Yorker* (1970) and then republished as part of the third edition (1970) of the English-language translation of *El Aleph*. Only recently was it translated into Spanish, by Aníbal González (1999). Borges attributes his turn to short stories to an accident suffered on Christmas Eve of 1938. While going to pick up a family friend, he bumped into a door jamb, cutting his forehead. The wound became infected and Borges contracted septicemia. As he describes it, he then wavered between life and death for weeks, unable to speak. When he finally began to recover, his concern for what he calls his "mental integrity" prompted Borges to undertake a new mode of writing: "I had previously written quite a few poems and dozens of short reviews. I thought that if I tried to write a review now and failed, I'd be all through intellectually but that if I tried something I had never really done before and failed at that it wouldn't be so bad and might even prepare me for the final revelation" (*Aleph*, 243). What interests me in this self-assessment is the tension it makes manifest within the terms of writing: between a kind of deferral—it is as if Borges conceives of fiction writing as a way of avoiding confrontation with the horrific (the possibilities of aphasia, mortality and madness)—and what he names, without any further clarification, a "final revelation." Writing, then, is both a turning from and a grappling with the limits of language and understanding. Writing is marked simultaneously by a desire not to know and by the hope of an absolute knowledge or revelation to come.

19. Suffice it to mention the dramatic transformations in national discourse beginning in the years leading up to World War II, and continuing late into the 1940s. In the early 1930s, Lugones and others became increasingly sympathetic to fascist and antisemitic ideologies, which Borges on the other hand vehemently rejected. Then, in the early 1940s, the nationalist movement was effectively coopted by the populist regime of Juan Perón—with which Borges was equally antagonistic. Thus, to speculate: perhaps a relatively "innocent" interest on Borges' part, concerning a transcendent national mythos that had incidentally also informed the nationalist

project prior to 1930, must then—retroactively and decisively—be discredited as the avatar of national and global disaster. It seems possible that something akin to the general experience of horror with which the West has since regarded the events leading up to World War II—specifically, the thought of a profound and terrible complicity between the Enlightenment project and its fascist or racist other—might be at work in Borges' attempts to distance himself from the scene of the 1920s. This speculation is not to suggest that Borges at one point felt sympathy toward the fascist turn in Argentine cultural politics, but rather that such a terrible complicity (the logic of which is itself never far from the surface in Borgesian irony) is perhaps a good deal more "personal" than might otherwise have been suspected.

20. A remark by Sarlo concerning Borges' engagement of the philosophical tradition is relevant here. With Borges, she suggests, a philosopheme such as destiny ceases to function as an exogenous topic of discussion or analysis in what is otherwise a "literary" mode of presentation. Such a concept is stripped of the privilege it enjoys in the philosophical tradition—that of shaping the denouement without *exposing itself* in the process—and is converted into diegetic structure (see chapter 4 of Sarlo, *Writer on the Edge*, "Tropes of Fantastic Literature"). Borges' engagement with the philosophical tradition begins by exposing philosophy to a literariness with which it has a long history of antagonism. This pattern of metonymical inversion can be understood as a response to the peculiar status of philosophical thought in the Latin American tradition, in which there are few trained philosophers, and where the possibility of engaging seriously with philosophy must always confront the problems posed by working with partial translations.

21. As is often the case with Borges, it would seem that the proper name functions as an emblem of the story (the story that Dahlmann tells himself). Francisco Flores: "free" [the Latin *francus*, presumed to originally refer to the political freedom enjoyed by a conquering Germanic tribe, the Francs] and "flowers" [*flores*]. As a kind of organic metaphor for national spirit, the name recalls the nationalist elevation of the gauchesque to the level of national myth, or as what Borges elsewhere terms "the spontaneous poetry of the gauchos." But if the name Francisco Flores provides a cipher for reading Borges' text, what does it mean that Dahlmann's voluntaristic identification in fact breaks with the patriarchal tradition (if he were truly following tradition, he ought to identify with the paternal grandfather from whom he receives his surname, Dahlmann)? Does this "errant" identification merely reinforce our suspicions that Borges is parodying the nationalist project? Or does this slippage point to the "internal limit" of the filial tradition, something "within" the mechanics of the tradition that causes it to stumble or go astray? I will return to these questions as time and space permit.

22. With Doris Sommer's suggestion that the literature of nation-building can be read as the representation of an Eros, one could also read this missed encounter with the woman as attesting to a rupture in the discourse of national patrilineation. That is, Borges' text marks a disengagement with or rupture within the reproductive tropology of nineteenth-century literature. I thank Roberto Díaz for bringing this possibility to my attention.

23. The homology between blood and nationalism is complicated, however, by the parodic style of treatment. The narrative account of Dahlmann's treatment at the sanitarium is characterized by an extreme opacity or reticence, and thus invites us to wonder about the precise nature and etiology of his "septicemia." "Una

tarde, el médico habitual se presentó con un médico nuevo y lo condujeron a un sanatorio ... [Era] indispensable sacarle una radiografía. ... [En] cuanto llegó, lo desvistieron, le raparon la cabeza, lo sujetaron con metales a una camilla, lo iluminaron hasta la ceguera y el vértigo, lo auscultaron y un hombre enmascarado le clavó una aguja en el brazo" [One afternoon, the regular doctor came by with a new doctor, and they brought him to a clinic ... [T]hey would need to take an X-ray.... [As] soon as he arrived at the clinic, the undressed him, shaved his head, and strapped him down onto a gurney. They blinded him with bright lights until he became dizzy, they auscultated him, and then a masked man stuck a needle in his arm"] (196). This passage resembles certain European avant-garde critiques of modernization and its technologization of death, centered around the flâneur's perceived impossibility of retaining a relation to his or her's own mortality in the modern city (see, for instance, Rilke's *Notebooks*). Dahlmann's experience of urban modernity is one of alienation, which is only heightened by the abject anonymity of his encounter with death. At the same time, however, one also begins to suspect that the narrative's reticence is covering for the protagonist's imminent psychic collapse.

24. Let us recall that the railroad has traditionally been associated with colonialism and imperialism in Latin America, due both to the foreign capital (usually English) used to finance the development of railway systems and because of the obvious "metaphor" of constructing conduits between the metropolis and the periphery. However, in Borges' text the traditional references to the Argentine railroad as a metaphor of imperialism receives a somewhat different inflection. Apropos of Scalabrini's remarks, alluded to above, we might say that the nationalist complaint constitutes *in and of itself* the reciprocal direction that it describes as absent. In other words, Borges remarks on a littoral-to-rural movement which begins with porteño nationalism's projection of a South that never in fact existed. What this projection masks is nationalist resentment regarding a theft of jouissance: the British imperialist presence in Argentina deprives the porteño creole community of its own "right," i.e., to exploit the pampa and exterminate the region's indigenous populations. It is likewise conceivable that this passage from Buenos Aires to the South signals a reading (in the strong sense, of remarking on a repression at work in the constitution of a system of meaning) of the scenario envisioned by Sarmiento in *Facundo*.

25. The ontological distinction between polis and the rural is already well-established in Plato's *Gorgias*: the contingent space of the city—a political space and a port of entry, and thus doubly subject to disorder and contamination from outside—must be grounded in the essential values (the highest of which is permanence as such) of the country side. For a discussion of this relation between philosophy and politics see Rancière, *On the Shores of Politics*.

26. The question of an identity or connection between Enlightenment thought and fascism or totalitarianism could be located in any number of Borges' oeuvre. I am thinking specifically of "Deutsches Requiem" and "La lotería en Babilonia," which present thematic treatments of a possible intersection between Enlightenment and totalitarianism.

27. See Alazraki, "Lectura estructuralista de 'El Sur' de Borges," and Rodríguez-Luis, "La intención política en la obra de Borges."

28. See the addendum added in 1956 to the Prologue of the second half (*Artifi-*

cios) of *Ficciones*: "De 'El Sur', que es acaso mi mejor cuento, bástame prevenir que es posible leerlo como directa narración de hechos novelescos y también de otro modo" (Borges, *Ficciones,* 120; emphasis in the original) ["Of 'El Sur', which is perhaps my best story, suffice it to say that it is possible to read it both as a direct narration of novelistic facts, as well as in another way entirely"].

29. In speaking of desire in terms of "cause" and "object," I am presupposing the Lacanian distinction between the "object of desire" (which is purely imaginary) and the "object-cause of desire," or a phantom-like "object" that causes or motivates desire without itself appearing or being named within the metonymical chain of "desires." The psychoanalytic "object" is the (always already absent) origin of desire.

30. I owe this insight to Alberto Moreiras's article, *"Circulus vitiosus deus."*

31. A similar structure of overdetermination is observed by J. P. Vernant in his analyses of Greek tragedy (see in particular "Greek Tragedy."). For Vernant, tragedy is a transitional mode of artistic production that attempts to mediate between a receding ("epic" and heroic) world and an emerging world (which is dominated increasingly by political maneuvering and, notably, Athenian democracy). But tragic mimesis is also precisely what resists historicization: tragic action, carried out between two worlds, becomes intelligible simultaneously within each of these mutually exclusive symbolic domains, and is thus reducible to neither. There is no Greek conception of the "heroic" prior to tragedy's lamentation of its passing.

32. The question of the body also comes to the fore in an important and startling way in the sanitarium scene that follows. There, in a strange sense, the protagonist's body begins to function as a metonym for pain (the whole for the part, or rather for the fragment). The body becomes a frozen signifier, short-circuiting the possibility of self-reflexive knowledge. Only when this pain is given a name (not by Dahlmann but by the other, the one supposed to know) is Dahlmann able to recuperate his subjectivity as distinct from his illness: "En esos días, Dahlmann minuciosamente se odió; odió su identidad, sus necesidades corporales, su humillación, la barba que le erizaba la cara. Sufrió con estoicismo las curaciones, que eran muy dolorosas, pero cuando el cirujano le dijo que había estado a punto de morir de un septicemia, Dahlmann se echó a llorar, condolido de su destino. Las miserias físicas y la incesante previsión de las malas noches no le habían dejado pensar en algo tan abstracto como la muerte." ["During those days Dahlmann hated every atom in his body: he hated his identity, his physical necessities, the humiliations that were visited on him, the beard that covered his face. He suffered with stoicism the painful cures, but when the surgeon told him that he had been on the verge of dying from septicemia, Dahlmann burst into tears, in great sympathy with his own destiny. The physical miseries and the incessant sleepless nights had not allowed him to think of something so abstract as death"] (Ficciones, 197).

33. For a discussion of relation as finitude and exposure, see Nancy, *Inoperative Community.*

Chapter 3. *Exígele la nuestro*

1. Fuentes, *La nueva novela hispanoamericana*, 17. All translations are my own unless otherwise specified.

2. Recent cultural studies-based critiques of culturalism have contributed significantly to defining the parameters of this traditional understanding of literature and its role in shaping modern social and political spaces. For instance, David Lloyd and Paul Thomas's *Culture and the State* develops an important thesis on the political role of culture in modern Europe, arguing that literature plays a key role in the emergence of such modern sociopolitical categories as "citizen" and "society." In short, literature instructs us on how to be good citizens, teaching or conveying what is, at least by one account, the essence of modern citizenship: the desire to be represented by the state. Thus literature complements and even coincides with the emergence of the modern state as suturer of particular differences (of ethnicity, class, gender, etc.). Lloyd and Thomas locate the emergence of literature as the dominant medium for cultural production in Europe with the writings of Matthew Arnold. However, we can see the beginnings of a similar equation in Latin America with Bello's and Sarmiento's respective uses of poetry and the essay to consolidate specific visions of the modern nation-state.

3. If Fuentes's *La nueva novela* provides the most enthusiastic account of the classical influences in Rulfo's writing, it is perhaps because Fuentes is equally eager to situate Rulfo at the threshold of a *fully developed and secured* Latin American modernity. For Fuentes, Rulfo's oeuvre would constitute an affirmation of a certain series of historical continuities: between the classical and modern traditions, and likewise between the Mediterranean qua "cradle of civilization" and Latin America.

4. Allow me to anticipate here one of the key differences that emerges in Rulfo's cultural "borrowing." As we will see, *Pedro Páramo* represents a past that is both no longer present *and* not yet past, in the sense that it does not fit into a chronological, progressive model of history. The various forms of narration—including Juan Preciado's recounting of his journey to Comala as well as the myriad mnemonic fragments issuing from Comala's dead—do not simply articulate a particular time or set of experiences within a larger chronological progression; at the same time, these narrative acts also underscore the impossibility of fully integrating the past into a linear and progressive narrative. In this sense, peripeteia and anagnorisis do not perform the same function as in Greek tragedy: they do not point to an idea of "destiny" [*tukhē*] which, however obscure it may be, assigns a sense of necessity and interconnectedness to what are otherwise purely contingent, unconnected moments. Rulfo's project, then, use of tragic aesthetics to build an epistemological or empathetic bridge between disparate epochs in national (pre)history; in addition, it involves the difficulty of symbolizing a national trauma.

5. The studies of Rulfo's formal innovations are too numerous to list here. Among the most influential studies, however, are a group of relatively early readings: Carlos Blanco Aguinaga's "Realidad y estilo de Juan Rulfo," Hugo Rodríguez Alcalá's *El arte de Juan Rulfo*, and Nila Gutiérrez Marrone's *El estilo de Juan Rulfo*.

6. Fuentes' homage to Rulfo at the beginning of his study of the Latin American novel is frequently cited as proof of Rulfo's efforts to transplant the Western tradition into a local context or idiom. Fuentes suggests that Rulfo has set out to recreate Greek mythology in a Mexican context, and thus he casts the narrator of *Pedro Páramo* first as a young Telemachus in search of his father, and then as Oedipus/Orpheus, a lover/son hybrid; his mother as Jocasta/Eurydice; and so on.

Whatever Fuentes would like to affirm about the "ambiguity" of Mexican identity, his reading remains conventional in that it conceives of Rulfo as introducing a cultural translation strategy based on the identification and preservation of differences. I will suggest that Ángel Rama's thesis of transculturation, on the other hand, presents us with a somewhat more rigorous demand: it takes hold of a notion of "translation" in order to think culture as a site of *production*, rather than as a safeguarding of differences. The distinction between Fuentes and Rama could be described as an ontologizing of differences versus a difference that divides ontology from itself. Among other critics, John Brushwood has similarly described the Mexican tradition as an ongoing conflict between autochthonous and internationalist or universalist tendencies (see *Mexico in its Novel*).

7. Let us recall at the same time the distinction between "modernism" and "*modernismo*," insofar as the latter refers to an historical period whose specificity is exceeded by Paz's commentary. On the contrary, Paz is referring to an array or conjunction of literary movements or tendencies, or perhaps even to a literary attitude that lays claim both to the autonomy of literary aesthetics (vis-à-vis political and economic forces) and to a capacity for renewal through poetic expression.

8. See in particular *Los hijos del limo*, where Paz describes literary modernism as a freedom of form and as a poetic use of analogy. While I am singling out Paz here, it should be noted that similar suppositions about the compensatory value of literature for history are implicit—despite some pronounced ideological differences—in a wide variety of twentieth-century Latin American literary discourses.

9. We can now state that Brushwood's distinction between autochthony and internationalism is not simply one model among many. It is a thesis on the nature of culture itself: a given form of expression belongs either to the Western tradition (and, by extension, to the European claim upon this tradition as its own), or it belongs to an "other" tradition (which, in Latin America, is frequently conceived as a recovered or an invented tradition, an indigenous or nascent autochthonous tradition). What this either/or thesis neglects is that the very notion of the *Other (of) tradition*—or the *Other (of) culture*, since autochthony is in many cases another name for "nature"—is itself a perpetual by-product of European culture. Every attempt to conceptualize or verify the existence of "the Western tradition"—of a self-identity expressing itself as *the* tradition—has invariably begun by positing an Other: a difference that must either be overcome or recovered. Rulfo's writing provides us critical leverage with which to engage this perpetual slippage within the determination of tradition and culture. What remains to be determined is whether or not the turn or suspension afforded by Rulfo's text can be said to contain something productive rather than a merely "subjective" (as Carlos Blanco Aguinaga describes it) or "negative" (in Neil Larsen's view) value.

10. The exact circumstances in which the narrator finds himself at the beginning of the novella are never specified in terms of a specific time and place. One possible interpretation, however, is that Juan Preciado and his mother have journeyed from Comala to Mexico City, thus mirroring the route followed by so many during the first half of the twentieth century, from rural, agrarian life to urban impoverishment.

11. García Canclini gives a number of brilliant accounts of the "invention of tradition" as it dually implicates national identity and state power in postrevolutionary Mexico (see especially his *Culturas híbridas*). In its self-appointed role as

guardian, organizer, and purveyor of "tradition," the state projects the existence of a unified and timeless expression. But the exemplifications of "tradition" found in state-sponsored museums in fact produces the semblance of a cultural ground that did not previously exist—at least not in the unified, continuous and self-comprehending way in which it is now presented. The relation between modernity and tradition also raises an important point regarding the cultural production process: the state does not confine its influence to those conditions under which cultural artifacts are gathered or produced, but also plays a role in the reception and distribution of these objects, i.e., to the ways in which they are organized and *re*presented. And thus—the crucial point—what is at stake in cultural production is not simply cultural artifacts, but *meaning itself.*

12. In a 8 July 1930 presidential address, Emilio Portes Gil illustrates this logic in a pseudo-Hegelian language, proclaiming the revolutionary state as a sanctuary for national and revolutionary spirit: "If we imagine the party as the originator of the people's social life; as the best agency where the primitive manifestations of the popular soul are perfected, then its existence will not be subject to the waxing and waning of militant politics, but will endure because it is founded upon the deep wellspring of the spirit" (as quoted in O'Malley, *Myth of the Revolution,* 16).

13. Castro Leal suggests that for writers such as Azuela and Augustín Yáñez, who are generally critical of the state's claim to represent the totality and truth of the national, literature functions as the "conscience" of the revolution. Literature is charged with producing a sustained critique of the entire history of (post)colonialism, including the political and cultural developments of the nineteenth century (Liberalism, the Porfirian oligarchy, and Positivism). The "fragmented" character of the postrevolutionary Mexican novel (the term is Carol D'Lugo's) can thus be viewed as a strategic device: through such a narrative strategy, postrevolutionary writing attempts to render visible the unavowed limits of the positivist claims upon the nation as an object of knowledge. Furthermore, the motifs of tragedy and sacrifice play an important function for postrevolutionary intellectuals operating under or in sympathy with the state. For José Vasconcelos and Octavio Paz, tragedy sheds light on a moment or a trait that, while necessary in its time, must nevertheless be transformed and overcome in order for modernity to take place. In *Ulises criollo*, his autobiographical account of the revolution, Vasconcelos criticizes the new interest in pre-Columbian iconography, arguing that modernity and national autonomy can only be achieved by submitting this violent past to a kind of cleansing ritual. The tropological appropriation of "sacrifice" as catachresis for revolutionary violence thus repeats itself in Vasconcelos's attempt to expunge this barbaric sign from the postrevolutionary symbolic order: "Every revolution has unleashed a savagery that threatens the European transplant carefully cultivated by mestizos and creoles . . . a [savage] atmosphere whose deepest layers are still Aztec. If Mexico is to assume a place among the civilized nations, it must first transform this underlying Aztec barbarism. As long as the masses remain uneducated, the system of human sacrifices will persist. The ancient, instinctual demand for blood has yet to be vanquished"] (my translation of the text quoted in Portal, *Proceso narrativa,* 155).

14. In his essay "Cuture and Political Power in Mexico," Roger Bartra attempts to mark the limit of the classical Marxian notion of ideology as a form of general deception, arguing that references to the state's use of force and coercion are un-

able to account for the process by which power is shaped and reproduced. For Bartra, national culture plays a dual function in the state's emergence as hegemonic force. On one hand, culture provides the ground upon which the state would rise above and reconcile class difference. At the same time, cultural production helps to cloak merely particular interests under the guise of shared and universal meanings, values and memories. Bartra's notion of national culture functions somewhat like the Freudian concept of the fetish, an imaginary object that would cover over (and cover for) a real difference or an imagined "lack." The fictional projection of national unity, along with or over against various mythopoietic figures (such as the melancholic peasant), has real and potentially divergent ramifications. One of the ironic notes of Bartra's study is found in reference to Rulfo, whose work is concerned with the demystification of "national culture," but which has also provided Mexican cultural production with one its most lasting and exemplary resources in the ongoing construction of this cultural ideology.

15. The formal sequence I am suggesting is a movement from allegory (in which the novella begins by insinuating itself as a traditional "allegory of ideas") to tragedy (in which the question of agency, as well as reflective and specular knowledge runs up against a limit and a crime from which it cannot detach itself) and back to allegory again (only this time as something closer to the twentieth century readings of allegory offered by Walter Benjamin (*Origin of German Trauerspiel*) and Paul de Man ("The Rhetoric of Temporality"). In its second manifestation, allegory marks the internal difference and play of signification, while also recalling the tone of mourning initiated in tragedy. I will discuss the function of allegory in Rulfo at greater length below.

16. See Hölderlin, *Essays and Letters on Theory*. I have discussed the idea of caesura in chapter 1.

17. I will discuss at greater length the specific character of this link between formal experimentation and historical rupture in the next section.

18. The value attributed to literature for the formation and stabilization of national culture is apparent not only in the essays of Octavio Paz, but likewise in the work of Alfonso Reyes (see in particular the essay "Discurso por Virgilio") and others of the *Ateneo* generation.

19. See Felman, "Literature and Psychoanalysis."

20. This double question of the event and its (non)relation to representation forms one of the major axes in postmetaphysical thinking, from Heidegger to Derrida and from Freud to Lacan.

21. See Benjamin, "Task of the Translator."

22. Although Rama does not refer explicitly to classical tragedy in this context, the sketch of an encounter between forces threatening one another's annihilation would seem to invite a reference to exactly what Hegel has in mind when he refers to the mediating and reconciling potential of tragedy. But while—from the vantage point of German Idealism at least—the reconciliation forged by Athena in Aeschylean tragedy inaugurates and legitimates the ideal form of the democratic state, it would be interesting to note—with Rulfo, and perhaps Rama as well—that the modern Latin American state represents something closer to a return of the repressed rather than a force of mediation.

23. It should be recalled that Rulfo himself was employed for a number of years in the Instituto Nacional Indigenista.

24. Such would seem to be the conclusion reached by Pratt, *Imperial Eyes*.

25. On the relation between aesthetics and (in)digestion, see Derrida, "Economimesis."

26. This is why transculturation is also an unworking of the concept of the unified or total work. The reflexive interpretation of *desgarramientos* suggests that literary symbolization in fact constitutes an endless and agonizing labor that would disrupt the semblance of seamless or natural transformations.

27. Rulfo contrasts this writing of the popular to his early, unpublished literary efforts, which he describes as "a bit academic" and "more or less false." As he puts it, the function of his mature work is to bear witness to and convey the oral character of local tradition and language: "the system I finally put in place, first with the short stories [*El llano en llamas*] and later in the novel, was to use the language of the people, the spoken language that I had heard my elders speaking, and which remains alive to this day" (Sommers, *La narrativa*, 18; my translation). The reference to speech and orality points to an important distinction between determinations of "culture": between an Enlightenment conception of culture as universal, or as pedagogically transferrable substance, and culture as a discrete and local phenomenon whose intelligibility to outsiders remains in question. Rulfo's attempts to clarify this difference, which he also defines as the difference between an "academic" exercise and a testimony based on lived (or heard) experience, invites precisely the misconception that Rama warns us away from: it encourages an idea of cultural mediation based on a Platonic model of good versus bad copies of an original. In order to see why classical mimesis is inadequate for what is at stake in these attempt to think cultural difference, we must pay close attention to a generic tension that arises between self-criticism and the literary works.

28. In reading Rulfo it is also helpful to bear in mind recent critiques of Rama, many of which have taken transculturation to task for to its alleged inability to account for the specificity of cultural difference. According to these critics, transculturation remains satisfied with what is in fact little more than a step back from the dominant discourses of nation-building and modernization. As Neil Larsen indicates, a transcultural text might serve to demystify dominant ideological constructions of subaltern life, but it stops short of producing a real interruption of the neocolonizing process. Or, what is worse, in declining to fill the ideological vacuum it creates, in refusing to posit a "concrete" subaltern experience in place of the mythic and imaginary one it dismantles, the transcultural text effectively if unintentionally replaces the state with the author as the purveyor and (with)holder of subaltern truth, as the cultural subject-supposed-to-know. "If the Rulfian-transcultural moment achieves the initial autonomy of mexicanidad from the rationalizing discourse that posits it in a gesture of colonizing contempt, the next step must be that in which the nation effect returns from its self-isolation to be reinvested with the discursivity of a postcolonial subject. Signifier and signified are to meet again on a ground that is not that of the cultural artifact but that of language itself as the very creative and fluid energy of the cultural" (Larsen, *Modernism and Hegemony*, 77).

I would like to suggest that Rulfo's text can in fact be read before *and* after Larsen's critique. Upon rereading, it would pose difficult questions about precisely the point Larsen takes for granted: the primacy of the metaphysical subject, or the need for an agent (in addition to agency) in postcolonial analysis. I do not see, to begin with, why the elaboration of this postcolonial subject must be carried out on precisely the ground that Rulfo has just left behind. Why, in other words, must this experience of the destitution of the subject (not to say the elimination of the question of the subject and its truth: rather the opposite) necessarily be reduced to a preparatory moment or a first step? Does this reduction not in fact beg the question concerning the *end(s)* of this postcolonial subject? Larsen's relinquishing of this question by equating the experience of destitution with a purely negative (and thus, in the final analysis, epiphenomenal) moment, would seem to have foreclosed any question of desire when it comes to agency—and it is precisely desire that, in my view, must be confronted once again here.

29. See Bartra, *Jaula de melancolía,* for a discussion of this Mexican social typology, *apretado* (an "uptight," or roughly speaking, a cosmopolitan snob) and *pelado,* which literally means "shorn one," and refers to a proletarian figure who appears in the wake of the revolution and modernization as an unacculturated transplant from rural to urban life. Bartra describes the pelado as an oximoronic "urban peasant."

30. See Bastos, "Clichés Lingüisticos y Ambigüedad en *Pedro Páramo*" for a detailed discussion of the semantic composition of this exchange.

31. Like other Romance languages, Spanish distinguishes between two types of knowledge, *saber* or learned, intellectual knowledge and *conocer* or conjectural, experiential knowledge. For the context of the novel, this distinction might be elaborated in terms of the difference between the nineteenth-century positivism and attempts following the revolution to formulate a nonpositivistic knowledge that would respond to the particularities of the Mexican scene.

32. The verb "malparir" is literally to miscarry; "nacer en un petate" or "being born on a straw mat" is a colloquialism to describe a bastard. Juan Preciado's response, "no me acuerdo," also echoes the (less frequent) meaning of *acordarse* as "to come to an agreement."

33. I have relied on Margaret Sayers Peden's translation for much of this passage.

34. My use of the term "allegory" here calls for some clarification. I do not mean to suggest that Rulfo offers us what would traditionally be termed an "allegory of ideas," in which one narrative level reflects or stands for another (typically in the form of a story that presents a certain moral idea). On the contrary, I mean "allegory" in the sense described by Walter Benjamin's *Origin of German Trauerspiel*: allegory as a reflection on the historical hollowing-out of the system of classical signs, and as a form in which language turns back upon itself to discover and reveal its own groundlessness. Perhaps the most poignant aspect of Benjamin's study of baroque allegory for Rulfo's work is the connection between allegory and mourning. For Benjamin, the baroque is an early reflection on modernity as an experience of radical destitution (the origin of modern secular society is experienced as what Hölderlin would call the turning of the gods), which includes the loss of the very language through we might have articulated it. The parallels (as well as the differences) between Benjamin's discussion of allegory and Rulfo's writing are plentiful and would make for an illuminating discussion. Due to limitations on space, I cannot undertake such a study here.

35. On the irreducible "spontaneity" that characterizes the Mexican Revolution, see Womack, *Zapata and the Mexican Revolution.*

36. We could also describe this difference as a distinction between *politics* (understood as the more or less organized field in which social and institutional relations are played out while coming into contact with institutional forces) and *the political* (the originary conditions and dynamics in and through which a social field such as the nation takes shape and is transformed). This difference would allow us to extend the motif of dissolution in Rulfo (a motif I will develop in greater detail below) beyond its obvious diagnostic point regarding the failure of revolution or reform. What if the tones of mourning and disillusion that govern much of Rulfo's work were to be weighed against an *originary loss* which, as loss, could also be construed as a constitutive moment of the political itself?

37. In this sense, the land is inscribed by an encounter between worlds: a collision between different systems of production and regimes of signification, in which conflict arises over a shared and disputed site or nexus. Thus, for instance, in both the Spanish colonial system and the pre-Columbian Amerindian systems, "the land" acts to organize a wide array of relations and meanings, giving shape to "home," "territory," "individual property," "community," "nation," "nature," "cultivation," "sustenance," "nature," etc.

38. For general discussions of land usage in Mexico during the nineteenth and twentieth centuries, see Bartra, *Caciquismo y poder político en el México rural*, and Joseph, *Everyday Forms of State Formation*. On the transformations in land tenure systems following the revolution, see also Aguilar Camín and Meyer, *In the Shadow of the Mexican Revolution*, and Womack, *Zapata and the Mexican Revolution*.

39. As Águilar Camín and Meyer have shown, the statist "reparto" program, ostensibly modeled on the demands of the radicalized peasantry in the South, was promoted as the beginning of a large-scale redistribution of the old latifundista estates (see Águilar Camín and Meyer, *In the Shadow of the Revolution*). These reform measures were in fact viewed by the triumphant faction as means to placate the radical elements in the constitutionalist coalition, while effectively consolidating the state's role as overseer through the creation of a new class of citizen: the modern property owner. Thus the value of the proper name—*reparto, ejido* (the small plots of redistributed land whose creation was optimistically regarded by the Zapata forces as the first step in a return to collective, communal ownership of land)—is co-opted so as to mask a shift from social revolution to political management. In the end, however, the name too must be discarded in order to consolidate the modernization process. Calles is said to have later characterized the ejido system as a "useless reminder of the pre-Hispanic past" (as quoted in Águilar Camín and Meyer, *In the Shadow of the Mexican Revolution*). On a similar note, John Womack describes the ambiguous relation between state and revolution in terms of a sacrificial logic: "however important [the] emergence [of revolutionary demands and signifiers], their defeat and subordination mattered more" (*Zapata and the Mexican Revolution*, 81–82).

40. For the overall purposes of my argument, I am glossing over an important distinction concerning periodization. The term "nation-building" usually refers to projects undertaken during the nineteenth century, some decades after the Wars of Independence. For Mexico, however, the 1910 to 1920 Revolution constitutes a new transition from an oligarchical, authoritarian regime to what is, at least in name, a popular democracy.

41. To state that modernity is only incompletely institutionalized in the periphery is not to suggest that it ever truly arrives anywhere. My principal concerns here are: 1) to identify the relative and contrasting representations of "modernities" in center and periphery, and later "First" and "Third" worlds, and 2) to examine the real effects produced by these purely symbolic differences. As noted by the dependency theorists, Latin America reveals a fatal flaw in the notion that the Third World should, given enough time, be able to repeat the steps taken by the First World during the eighteenth and nineteenth centuries. What Latin America lacks in this respect is precisely a second Latin America over against which it could "develop." Perhaps the truly radical thesis of dependency theory is just this: that Latin America is in fact already fully "developed," or that its "underdevelopment" manifests the reverse, disavowed of development itself.

42. Rulfo subjects the exchange process that organizes social relations under the sign of patriarchy in many societies to a subtle yet important shift: in arranging his own marriage, Pedro Páramo acts as if he were his own father. This displacement is not a substitution (metaphor) but rather a slippage (metonymy). If we read this passage according to the kinship structures described by structural anthropology, this act would constitute a kind of symbolic theft, appropriating a paternal decision and a patriarchal right that cannot itself be subjected to scrutiny. Of course, the emergence of the modern nation-state would call for the elimination of this "archaic" and "barbaric" patriarchal structure. Rulfo's text could thus be said to present the ironic, reverse side of the discourse of modernity: in lieu of the symbolic place of the father, whose name acts as guarantor of the marriage rite as pact between communities, it is the son himself who, without the semblance of legitimacy, draws up and affirms this contract. Within the context of the modern nation-state, the lifting of this archaic patriarchal constrain and the introduction of individual autonomy will prove to be immeasurably more repressive than the order it replaces.

43. This last statement, "La tierra no tiene divisiones," is remarkably similar to a statement Aguilar Camin attributes to the revolutionary caudillo Venustiano Carranza ("This business of dividing up the land is ridiculous": see Águilar Camín and Meyer, *In the Shadow of the Mexican Revolution*, 46–47). The constitutionalist forces led by Carranza ultimately turns against and triumphs over the popular factions of the revolutionary alliance, and is viewed by many as embodying the institutional corruption that eventually prevails over the popular movements generally associated with Zapata and, to a lesser degree, Pancho Villa.

44. The latinate *usufructo* refers, in Roman Law, to the right to enjoy the use of land owned by another, without impinging upon the other's entitlement (a sovereign, for example, enjoys usufruct rights over his subjects' land). After the Mexican Revolution, the state attempts to accommodate the radicalized Southern peasant movements by implementing a usufruct system in which the state first seizes the large land holdings of the elite [*latifundios*] and then—ostensibly to prevent counterrevolutionary reappropriations—declared itself the true proprietor, while granting individual rights to cultivate small *ejido* plots. The ironic juxtaposition here, of nobility-state-cacique as various instances of an enjoyment or an appropriation that is beyond the law, will expose this moment in the determination of right as an *obscene* one (as can perhaps already be heard in the exchange between Sedano and Torribio Aldrete, in which "usufructo" is colloquially shortened

to "usufruto" [*fruto*: fruit]). I rely to a certain extent on Sayers Peden's English-language translation of *Pedro Páramo* for my own translation of this passage. However, Peden renders Sedano's *usufruto* as "falsification of boundaries." And so while it correctly translates the meaning, it forcefully rejects the irruption of the improper, obscene basis upon which this property right is conceived.

45. According to González Boixo, the phrase "Sé que usted las puede" alludes, via the colloquial *poderlas*, to a certain undefined political influence or clientism. At the same time, the phrase also retains a radical emptiness, and should be heard as saying something like "I know you have what it takes." See Rulfo, *Pedro Páramo* (1993), 99 (note 75).

46. After perceiving the veiled insults in Aldrete's words, Sedano murders him. Incidentally, this sequence had already been announced proleptically when the narrator first arrived in Cómala and, while staying with Eduviges Dyada, he heard the wailing of Aldrete's ghost. This insertion also announces one of the important thematic issues in Rulfo's text: on the possibility or impossibility of testimony, or concerning an unabsolved testimonial debt: "¡Déjenme auque sea el derecho de pataleo que tienen los ahorcados!" ["You at least owe me a condemned man's right to a final word!"] (18). The excessive demand of testimony overlaps with, and cannot fully be extracted from the sense in which its particular truth has previously been suppressed or repressed. What remains to be spoken in testimony is the irreducible difference it promises to bring to speech. Equally important, in Rulfo's novella, are the tragic resonances this statement brings to bear on the narrator. This spectral declaration of the impossibility of giving a complete account of death in turn signals the impending revelation of an internal limit confronting the project of positive self-knowledge. Juan Preciado, who was born out of the grave of positivism, describes the ghost's words as producing a sublime and unfathomable vortex, into which his own consciousness is drawn and threatened with annihilation: "No, no era posible calcular la hondura del silencio que produjo aquel grito. Como si la tierra se hubiera vaciado de su aire. Ningún sonido; ni el del resuello, ni el del latir del corazón; como si se detuviera el mismo ruido de la conciencia" ["No, it was not possible to plumb the depths of the silence that followed that shout. It was as if the earth had expelled its air. No sound; not even of my breathing or the beating of my heart. It was as if the very sound of consciousness had been arrested"] (18).

47. Of course, one could also argue that the "murmurs" to which Juan Preciado alludes in telling Delores of his death simply indicate that he does not yet know how to listen, and that the second half of the novella is also about the narrator's true education, to be contrasted with the patriarchal knowledge he had sought in the beginning. While I do not dispute the validity of such a reading, I would argue that the myriad cognitive and semiotic distortions cannot be dismissed as a sign of the narrator's bad faith or ignorance.

48. I thank Carlos Riobó for pointing out the relevance of this passage in *Pedro Páramo* to me. In a 1982 interview, Rulfo describes the near-absence of indigenous characters in his writing in terms of an epistemological limit: "Nunca empleo a los indios porque para mí es imposible entrar y llegar a profundizar la mentalidad indígena" (Antonio Palacio, "Juan Rulfo: la revolución cubana desencadenó el 'boom' americano," *ABC*, 4 April 1982, 31; as cited in Rulfo, *Pedro Páramo* (1997), 156). Perhaps Rulfo's position could be summarized as a radical agnosticism with regard to "perspective" itself: there is no guarantee that the very naming

of an "other perspective" does not—qua perspective—already impose the very European constraints it would like to avoid.

49. Among the many discussions of temporality in Rulfo, see Cohn, "Wrinkle in Time," and Dixon, "Three Versions of *Pedro Páramo*."

50. A connection between signification and justice—and the impossibility thereof—underlies the entirety of Rulfo's text. In historical terms, the tropological movement described by the shooting stars recalls the crisis of the church in postcolonial Mexico. During the liberal reforms of 1857, the Catholic Church forfeited much of its land and political influence to the state. Following the revolution, the new state likewise adopts a strong antitheological position. The marginalization of the church culminates in the southern districts with the 1926 Cristero counterrevolution initiated by Catholic priests. The revolution's renewed attacks on the church suggests that the theological basis of rural, agrarian society remained relatively intact throughout the *Porfiriato*—or enough so, anyway, that its name could acquire a new contestatory political function during the final years of the revolution. For Rulfo, the proximity of tropological anamorphosis to the iconography of the church indicates both a critique of the church's function in rural society and a crisis in the very notion of transcendence.

51. We could take this passage to be emblematic of Rulfo's use of allegory. The correspondence between literary and metaliterary orders, or between the thematic treatment of justice, eschatology, and death on the one hand, and the myriad allusions to the literary mechanics of signification on the other, does not in the end lead to a reconfirmation of the transcendental status of literature, or of its standing apart from the social realities it is thought to reflect. Instead, the "thematic" issue of eschatological crisis—the prospect of the human soul's divergence from its rightful destination—in turn casts doubt on the capacity of literary language to hit its mark.

52. As I have already indicated, the narrator's "testimony" reveals a temporal regression that, unbeknownst to us, has already structured the first half of the work: we now learn that the entirety of Juan Preciado's "return" to Comala has been narrated from the grave. Julio Ortega notes that this scene creates a paradoxical conjunction of death and memory. It is as if the narrator had to die in order to enter into the pueblo's secret, the realm of fragmented, collective memory. Of course, one can read this "death" in many ways, and perhaps any interpretation of the text precisely hinges on what one makes of this mortal limit. If we interpret this as the "death" of a particular (Western, metaphysical, Eurocentric) conception of the subject, as I am tempted to do, then we would also need to adopt a different conception of memory in order to read the second half of the work: a thought of memory that no longer presupposes the existence of a *subjectum*, an underlying presence or permanence (consciousness, Spirit, etc.). Memory would not reaffirm an individual or collective subject, but would mark a kind of originary indebtedness in relation to language.

53. In Hans Holbein's painting *The Ambassadors*, for instance, anamorphosis points to the dissolution of the humanistic and worldly concerns or vanitas around the startling emergence of a death's head For a discussion of anamorphosis as it relates to representation and its limits, see Lacan, *Four Fundamental Concepts of Psycho-analysis*.

54. See Ortega Galinda, *Expresión y sentido de Juan Rulfo*, 149–66.

55. The first sentence in this passage is perhaps an allusion to another Jaliscan writer, Augustín Yáñez, whose *Al filo del agua* (1947) Rulfo has described as an important influence. Yáñez is one of the first postrevolutionary writers to attempt a departure from the naturalism that had governed the novela de la revolución through its first decades. Yáñez's novel is also one of the first works to address the problem of revolution from the perspective of agrarian society, in contrast to the pseudojournalistic narrative perspective popularized by Azuela, Luis Guzmán and others. As a meditation on desire and prohibition in rural Mexico, Yáñez's text no doubt resonates yet again in the passage in question, in which the narrator has just made love with the woman who is both Donis's sister and wife.

56. This topos of dissolution could be contextualized in any number of ways. We could begin, of course, with the cultural typology of dissimulation (see, for example, Ramos and Paz). At the same time, the destitute character of Comala can be readily attributed to the devastating effects of modernization and civil war on the social fabric of rural society. As Rulfo never ceases to remind us, the reparto program cloaks the state's massive abandonment of agrarian society. However, I am equally concerned here with what this tone of dissolution and disillusionment means for the consideration of transition as a problem of representation. In this respect, I maintain that Comala as a topos marks a fissure within the ontotheological determination of mimesis.

57. The generic use of the term testimonio was first suggested by Miguel Barnet in 1968 when he published the *Biografía de un cimarrón*, an autobiographical chronicle produced collaboratively by Barnet and a former Cuban slave. For a history of the testimonio mode, see Sklodowska, *Testimonio hispanoamericano*. For a sample of contemporary debates concerning *testimonio*, see Gugelberger, *Real Thing*.

58. Studies of the feminine figure in Rulfo's novella include Luisa Bastos and Malloy, "La Estrella Junto a la Luna," and Lorente-Murphy, "¿Cuál Era el Mundo de Susana San Juan?"

59. Compare to *Revelations* 12:1: "Apareció en el cielo una gran señal: una mujer vestida del sol y con la luna debajo de sus pies, y sobre su cabeza una corona de doce estrellas" [There appeared in the sky an enormous sign: a woman draped with the sun, with the moon beneath her feet, and her head adorned by a dozen stars].

60. A *bullón* is the metallic, ornamental knob or boss formerly placed on the cover of books, appearing to hold the book together and/or fasten it shut, figuratively guarding its threshold.

61. It would at the same time be possible to read this passage, including the cacique's final words ("Ésta es mi muerte"), as a total abstraction of death: such would be the extreme truth of caciquismo as economic, political and ontological project.

Chapter 4. The Catastrophe of Modernity

1. One well-known later example of how literature contributes to the elite's attempt to build a postindependence national hegemony is Ricardo Palma's massive collection of fables known as the *Tradiciones peruanas* (published between

1872 and 1906). The pedagogical project apparent in Palma's writing—consolidating a certain formal Spanish as the proper national tongue—is also an important step toward establishing the appearance of a consensual national unification, in which indigenous sectors would be regarded as more or less fully assimilated, etc. Subsequently, any deviation from the norms established by Palma's fables would appear either as an annoying, intransigent refusal to join in or as simply an inability to adapt. Cornejo describes Palma's project as "producing an image and a discourse that would dilute the contradictions marking the very idea of nation, and constructing homogeneous spaces to cover over a startlingly heterogeneous reality, with the goal of creating in and for language a possible national community" (*Formación* 111; all translations are my own unless otherwise specified). I will return to the terms "homogeneous" and "heterogeneous" in a moment.

2. The economic boom of the 1840s and 1850s, during which decades much of the Pacific coastal region was adapted to the export economy of Lima, was followed by a collapse of the global nitrate market for which Peru had been a primary supplier. By the early 1870s, the government was nearly bankrupt, and the modernized infrastructure had by and large been defaulted to British creditors. Meanwhile, the "War of the Pacific," a failed military engagement with Chile in the 1870s, led to the partial invasion of the country by Chilean forces and the near-total collapse of the creole government. For a synopsis of the economic and political events of this period, see Gootenberg, *Between Silver and Guano*.

3. Mirko Lauer uses the term "cultural indigenism" to describe idealized representations of the indigenous in the literature of the late nineteenth century (such as Palma's fables), as opposed to the political indigenism of Mariátegui, Valcarcel and others (Lauer, *Andes imaginanos*). In Lauer's view, to put it bluntly, cultural indigenism utilizes the representation of indigenous peoples and practices in order to maintain national consensus for an economic system that is founded upon the exclusion and domination of a large majority of indigenous peoples.

4. Mariátegui seems to suggest something similar when he asserts that the true intent of literary indigenism is not mimetic or restitutive in the traditional sense of recuperating a true perspective: "indigenist literature cannot give us a rigorously realist version of the Indian. It has to idealize and stylize him." (*Siete ensayos*, 313).

5. As Mariátegui notes, the Spanish colonial project differs from other European colonizing ventures in that it remains primarily a military conquest intent on acquiring land and gold, rather than an economic project interested in developing new external markets to help foster development in the metropolis. The consequences are far-reaching: in the case of Peru, the colonial experience never yields the structural basis of a modern economic (i.e. capitalist) system, and this in turn means that the indigenous populations—relatively "unintegrated" in comparison to many regions of Mexico—lack the means to construct a communal or class identity. Most importantly for Mariátegui, the presence of capitalist relations in Peru has not produced anything like the conditions of a free labor market. According to classical Marxism, this failure renders unthinkable any class-based revolution. The identification of the "theoretical impossibility" of revolution in Peru marks one of Mariátegui's major contributions to radical Latin Americanist thought. That is, he rejects the economism of traditional Marxian theory, suggesting that "mode of production" narratives are unable to account for the problem

of ethnicity and indigenism in Latin America. It is not unusual for critics to read Mariátegui's privileging of *el indio* as a kind of metaphorical substitution: indio really means campesino, which in turn allows for the formation of class consciousness in rural Peruvian society in a way that resembles the Russian peasantry. Yet it should be clear that this substitution of an ethnic index for a socioeconomic identity marks an important departure from orthodox Marxism.

6. The division of Vallejo's Peruvian oeuvre between local and internationalist perspectives corresponds with important transitions in the poet's residency: the first published collection of poems, *Los heraldos negros* (1918), was written during his provincial years in Santiago de Chuco and Trujillo, while many of the poems in *Trilce* (1922) were written after Vallejo's arrival in Lima. In this chapter I will only be discussing a handful of poems from *Trilce*, written and published in Peru prior to his permanent expatriation in Europe beginning in 1923. To my knowledge, a comparative analysis of both the Peruvian and European periods in Vallejo's career, and of the corresponding distinction between the poetry written prior to and following his "conversion" to Marxism, remains to be written.

7. While it is not at all clear how much access Vallejo would have had to so-called European avant-garde texts during the writing of *Trilce*, it is generally taken for granted that he was exposed at least to the "idea" of the avant garde by way of Latin American poets such as Herrera y Reissig and Valdelomar (whose publication of *Las voces múltiples* in 1918, according to André Coyné, first introduced pre-war European vanguard poetry to Peru: see Coyné's essay in Ortega, *Expresión y sentido de Juan Rulfo*, 20). On the positioning of Vallejo as avant-garde poet, see in particular Jean Franco's highly influential 1976 book-length study of Vallejo's poetic development, *César Vallejo*. Following Franco, some examples of readings that have adopted the interpretation of *Trilce* as avant-garde text are von Buelow, "César Vallejo," Hedrick, "Y Hembra es el Alma Mia," and McGwirk, *Latin American Literature*.

8. These hermeneutic problems have been discussed in von Buelow, "Vallejo's Venus de Milo and the Ruins of Language."

9. On mourning and its aporias, see Sigmund Freud, "Mourning and Melancholia." For a discussion of mourning in the context of Latin Americanist discourse, see Moreiras, *Tercer esapcio*.

10. See Freud's anecdote of the dream of the burning child in *The Intepretation of Dreams*. In this dream, which could be said to define the unsurpassable threshold of mourning, what has been missed is the alterity of the other (or, for Freud, his or her desire). For psychoanalysis, the missed encounter, insofar as it resists or exceeds the cognitive faculties of the subject, remains subject to the law of repetition: in Lacan's terms, what is foreclosed from the symbolic returns in—or as—the real.

11. Significantly, this phrase is preceded by a reference to the absence of any mother or lover: "O sin madre, sin amada" [Oh, without mother, without beloved]. And thus, while the poet does not specifically refer to lamentation, the redoubled absence of the beloved establishes a mood appropriate to the disposition of mourning.

12. For a discussion of Freudian and Lacanian conceptions of the subject, see Fink, *Lacanian Subject*.

13. While I am suggesting that the work of mourning is here situated within a

reflection on language, this is not to say that language constitutes the sole "meaning" of the text. In fact, it is just the opposite: the prominent place occupied by language in this poem makes it—language—irreducible to any economic or signifying function. In this regard, it is important that poetic reflection focuses on indices or sites often associated with affect rather than logic and metaphor: taste and eating, sound, lips, palate, etc.

14. See Leclaire, *Psychoanalyzing*.

15. This phrase, "arrastrando todavía / una trenza por cada letra del abecedario," evokes the image of a child just beginning to learn to spell. The *trenza* [braid, pleat or tress] perhaps implies the Quechua aide-memoire known as the *quipú*: an apparatus composed of various braided strings, each suspended at one end from an axial braid.

16. See Sicard, "Poetry of Vallejo."

17. In "Signification of the Phallus," Lacan describes love as "the gift of that which the Other does not have" (Ecrits, 286). For a discussion of time and the gift, see Jacques Derrida, *Given Time*.

18. In Spanish the interrogative phrase would typically be preceded by an inverted question mark and followed by a question mark. The query in stanza 4 shows neither punctuation, and is marked only by the accented interrogatives ("cuál," "qué" as opposed to "cual" and "que").

19. In the Spanish language the ambiguity I am describing is intensified by the grammatical structure of the sentence, in which the verb "quedar" [to remain, to be left over] need not be accompanied by a specified subject.

20. Is it not significant that it is the mother and not some other figure—such as the father or a priest—who holds the key to commonality-in-transcendence or transcendent community? Only the Mother can heal the wounds left open by the long history of conquest and colonialism; only the Mother can successfully realize what the postindependence state sets out and fails to accomplish: the interpellation of the Quechua-speaking masses. Or so it would seem. What does it mean, then, that in Vallejo's poetry the mother is seemingly always dead? Could it be that, as a particular manifestation of the Other to whom the interpellated subject finds itself responsible, the Mother is always already dead according to necessity?

21. See Bürger, *Theory of the Avant-Garde* and Mann, *Theory-Death of the Avant Garde*.

22. As I have already indicated, Franco also explores a connection in Vallejo's work between the critique of aesthetic modernity and a reconsideration of the epistemological horizons of Latin Americanist thinking, and specifically of the preeminence of Positivism throughout Latin America in the second half of the nineteenth century. Due to spatial limitations, I cannot address Vallejo's relation to Positivism in this study. However, much of what I will say about the poet's engagement with the ontotheological tradition would likewise hold for his views on Positivism.

23. Apart from matters of periodization (the Venus is known to have been sculpted during the Hellenic period, probably during the second century B.C.), little has been definitively established about either its creator or its early history—although there has been speculation that the statue may be one of the two Venuses reputed to have been sculpted by Praxiteles. Its modern history, however, also bears some interest for the central concerns of Vallejo's poetry. According to William Shreve's account, the statue was unearthed in 1820 on the Aegean island of Melos by a

certain peasant, who, the story goes, did not fail to recognize the financial implications of his discovery (see Shreve, *Venus de Milo*). The peasant proceeded to negotiate the sale of the statue to the French ambassador to Greece, who envisioned it as a gift to the French king. But, when the transaction was delayed, the peasant turned around and sold the statue to a local priest, who in turn planned to give it as a gift to a certain Turkish prince. The French ambassador learned of the double dealings, and sent an aide to the port of Melos just as the priest was loading the statue onto his ship. The French aide claimed ownership of the statue in the name of the crown, and when the priest refused to back down, the ambassador's representatives resorted to force in order to retrieve it. The statue was loaded onto a French vessel and transported to the Louvre, where it remains to this day. According to Shreve, one possible explanation for how the statue came to be missing both arms is that it was damaged during the struggle between the French and the Greek priest, and that in the Frenchmen's haste to secure the statue and set sail, the damaged arms were left behind. Whatever credence one gives this anecdote, it is clear that the statue's presence in the Louvre—and thus the exemplary position it occupies in the Western imaginary—cannot be divested from the long history of colonial expropriation on the part of the European powers.

24. I have discussed the problem of defining allegory—which is specifically *not* the traditional allegory of ideas—in the previous chapter. See also de Man, "Rhetoric of Temporality" in *Rhetoric: Romanticism,* and Benjamin, *Origins of German Tragic Drama,* 77.

25. On the distinction between "sense" and "meaning" see Nancy, *Sense of the World*.

26. For discussions of sex and gender in *Trilce,* see Franco, *César Vallejo,* von Buelow, "Cesar Vallejo," and Hedrick, "y Hembra es la Alma Mia." It would also be of interest to reexamine Franco's work on the problem of sexuality in Vallejo's poetry in the context of what Doris Sommer has discussed as the idealization of sex and marriage in the literature of nation-building, as a means of sublating class and ethnic conflict (Sommer, *Foundational Fictions*).

27. In a well-known poem, "Peregrin cazador de figuras," Eguren proposes a view of poetry as attempt to hunt down the secret essence behind the transitory forces of nature, an essence he names "the harmony of the mystery." Perhaps Eguren is in fact simply reiterating a standard reading of French Symbolism (see Baudelaire's "It is by way of poetry that the soul catches a glimpse of the splendors situated beyond the tomb"). But it should also be clear that the aesthetic notion of "harmony" provides an ideal ground for what I have described in the previous chapter as a compensatory modernism, an aesthetic that would mask or compensate for or "harmonize" the violence and inadequacies of modernization. It is interesting in this regard that a number of critics have sought to identify in Vallejo's own poetry a similar desire for "harmony." For instance, in a reading of *Trilce* LXXIII ("Ha triunfado otro ay. La verdad está allí" [Another "ay" has triumphed. The truth is there]), James Higgins declares that "The truth is found in this shout, because it is the experience of pain that enables the poet to grasp the secret harmony of life." My argument, of course, is that *Trilce* constitutes a radical displacement of "harmony" and "the beautiful" as foundational concepts of modern aesthetic ideology.

28. One could thus read this ambiguous phraseology as evoking what Lacan

would describe as the two sides of the fundamental patriarchal fantasy. First, the fiction that man possesses what woman lacks: the phallus as guarantor of truth, being, and power. Second, that woman *is* that which man fears that he lacks. Whereas every man seeks the phallus in order to mask or compensate for his real and perceived insufficiencies, woman does not desire the phallus. On the contrary, she *is* the phallus insofar as she compensates for her partner's real and perceived insufficiencies. Suffice it to recall the misogynistic saying, "Behind every great man is a woman."

29. On the intimate connection between the structure of opposition and the metaphysics of presence, see the work of Jacques Derrida, and in particular *Writing and Difference*.

30. The ambiguity is heightened by the use of the verb "manquear," which in colloquial speech can mean either "to be one-handed" or "to play the cripple." The grammatical sequence of the first line cited here ("Tú manqueas apenas pululando") likewise introduces a certain irreducible ambiguity: does "apenas" [hardly, scarcely] modify the verb "manquear" [you hardly lack anything] or the adverbial "pululando" [You are lacking, and scarcely pullulating]? The stakes, needless to say, are considerable, but the syntactical rules of Spanish do not allow us to decide one way or another.

31. Lacan, in a 1959 essay entitled "Sur la théorie du symbolisme d'Ernest Jones" (published in the French-language version of Lacan's *Écrits*; to my knowledge, the essay has not yet been translated into English), describes the phallus as "the signifier of the very loss that the subject suffers due to the fragmentation [*morcellement*] brought on by the signifier" (*Écrits*, 715). The phallus is an imaginary object in the sense that nobody truly possesses it. One can only simulate or feign it, or represent it to another's imagination—much in the way that Aristotle describes the most compelling representations of violence as being those that are represented *offstage*. But this does not mean that we can simply dismiss the phallus as a figment of our imagination. For Lacan, the phallus also corresponds to the constitutive gap in any signifying regime—that is, it also belongs to the real. We recall from Sausurre that no word or signifier can account for its own meaning without referring to another signifier; and this second signifier must in turn refer to a third signifier, and so on ad infinitum. It is this gap or lag time between the signifier and meaning that keeps signification going. The phallus, then, is the fiction of the one signifier that *is* able to elude this constraint and account for itself by itself.

32. The neologism "todaviiza" is an untranslatable combination of the adverb "todavía" [still, yet] and the verb ending "izar" [equivalent to the English "ize"].

33. I believe that the final two stanzas, which I will not discuss at length, would support this reading. In the penultimate stanza, after establishing the body—represented metonymically by "el meñique / demás el la siniestra" [the extra pinkie on my left hand]—as an index of existential finitude (and thereby further substantiating the suspension of transcendence initiated in the first stanza), the poet goes on to wonder about a possible "exit" from this prison house of finitude. But the only exit, he suggests, is "haciendo / la cuenta de que hoy es jueves" [pretending / that today is Thursday]: paradoxically, then, the only possible transcendence of finitude is to embrace it, or to act *as if* the symbolic in all of its contingency (or the arbitrary fact that we refer to this moment as "Thursday") were

in fact natural or necessary. One way of reading the short final stanza, as I have already suggested, can be found in the earlier references to a Latin Americanist *potens*, which in philosophical terms cannot easily be reduced to either "finitude" or "transcendence."

34. This evocation of an "impar / potente de la orfandad" recalls what poem VIII terms "el hifalto poder," or a thought of power that breaks with the filial, Platonic determination of truth as proximity to the eidos. "Hifalto," a Vallejan neologism, is a displaced echo of "hidalgo" or "hijo de algo" [one who is someone: a person of substance or of name].

35. For a discussion of messianism in Peru, and particularly as a phenomenon of transculturation, see Millones, *Mesianismo e idolotría en los Andes centrales* and Graziano, *Millennial New World.*

36. In a sixteenth-century text, written in Quechua and entitled *Apu Inca Atawallpaman*, the experience of the conquest as destruction of the Incan theological system is rendered allegorically, following the execution of the Incan ruler Atahualpa, as nature's refusal to accept the Inca's corpse, followed by the retreat of the sun and the withering of time. Spanish colonial domination coincides with the withdrawal of the gods, and as the conversion of nature from self-revealing to suffering: "And everything and everyone hides, disappears / suffering" (*Apu Inca Atawallpaman*, trans. José María Arguedas, *El Reverso* 181–86; as quoted in Wachtel, *Vision of the Vanquished,* 30).

37. One obvious example is the case of the popular nineteenth-century rebellion led by Antônio Conseilhero against the newly formed Brazilian Republic, recounted in Euclides da Cunha's *Rebellion in the Sertao* and fictionalized in Vargas Llosa's *La guerra del fin del mundo*. Another is what is commonly referred to in Peru as the *Inkarrí* myth, whose origins have been traced at least as far back as the eighteenth century. The *Inkarrí*, which tells of the death and eventual resurrection of "the last Inca" (the divinely appointed royalty who rule the Incan state), appears to recount and condense two separate historical events: the garroting of Atahualpa in 1533 by order of Pizarro, and the beheading of Túpac Amaru II in 1780 following his direction of an uprising against the Spanish colonial system. The narrative augurs the eventual liberation of the Andes, foretelling that there will come a time at which the Inca's head, which currently lies forgotten in the earth, will generate a new body and spring to life once again. For discussions of the *Inkarrí* and other messianic cultural texts, see Castro Klaren, "Dancing and the Sacred," Millones, "Mesianismo é idolotría" and *El retorno de las huacas,* and Wachtel, *Visions of the Vanquished.* The Quechua term *Pachacuti*, which links the *Inkarrí* narrative to that of *Taqui Onkoy,* presents a sentiment similar to the early Christian notion of "el mundo al revés," and yet it describes the complete overturning of the political and ideological system in which the latter conception is inscribed. Only in Latin America, we could say, can Catholicism provide the symbolic basis for revolutionary discourse.

38. As I will suggest, it is also important to acknowledge a difference between these two latter conceptions of the tragic, which involves a distinction between indigenism's use of a classical conception of the aesthetic as a unifying principle and Vallejo's attempt to think the withdrawal of the sacred as the horizon of modern poetry—that is, as both its limit and its condition of possibility. The emergence of a distinctly modern thought of tragedy in *Trilce* in fact signals the destruction of any form of cultural populism or compensatory cultural politics.

39. On the relation between antagonism and contestatory politics, see chapter 3 of Laclau and Mouffe, *Hegemony and Socialist Strategy*.

40. This passage, and in particular the phrase "en plenas tinieblas," appears to engage with one of the dominant justificatory images of the conquest, as providential illumination of a previously dark, faithless world. See, for instance, the famous description by the Inca Garcilaso of Christianity as a "morning star" over against a pre-Christian "darkest night" in book 1, chapter 15 of the *Comentarios reales de los Incas*.

41. Johnson, "Frame of Reference: Poe, Lacan, Derrida," in *Critical Difference*.

42. In his prologue to the *Tempestad*, Mariátegui suggests that the intelligibility of the indigenist project also has to do with a question of faith rather than with knowledge or calculation: the hopes, demands, and exigencies conveyed within indigenism's "advent of a new world" require a form of participation or engagement, in the absence of which the sayings of indigenist messianism are likely to appear as the fanciful prognostications of those who refuse to face reality. By the same token, radical indigenism is not concerned with representing the Indian "as he truly was or is." A restitution grounded in mimesis—no matter how faithful— would only serve to reaffirm the dominant position of mimesis as the only possible model for truth. Instead, indigenism should be seen as an attempt to produce a subject where before there was none. It seeks to overturn the colossal idea of history as teleological progression (an idea that gives shape to the colonizing discourse of Providentialism and various postcolonial nationalisms), and to clear a space for a future that is neither a mere extension of the present nor a transhistorical essence waiting to be recovered, but rather a time and place that must be produced.

43. Parenthetically, this term could easily provide a figure for the earlier discussion of faith: no faith prior to the envio, the act or submission whose destination is precisely unknowable.

44. The orthographic division of "venidera," with "ve-" appearing at the end of the sixth line and "nidera" at the beginning of the seventh, is a fairly common practice in *Trilce*. In Spanish, the pronunciation of "ve-" is indistinct from that of "be-" (Vallejo frequently exploits this phonetic identity as well). And thus the division of "venidera" also introduces, within the text, the difference between writing and orality.

45. See the introduction to Marx's "Contribution to the Critique of Hegel's *Philosophy of Right*" (Marx and Engels, *Marx-Engels Reader*, 64).

46. This relation between poetry and what I am calling the event is illustrated in poem XXXIII, which can be read as a prolonged reflection on the process of poetic insight and creation. Due to lack of space I cannot attempt a detailed analysis of that poem here. However, a refrain from the final stanza of XXXIII seems to touch on the disjunctive temporality of the event. Following three stanzas in which the poet gives consideration to his own solitude and the losses he has suffered, he appears to suggest that the true *cause* or *debt* to which poetry owes its existence is in fact an absent or lost cause that never actually took place: "No será lo que aún no haya venido, sino / lo que ha llegado y ya se ha ido" [It will not be that which has not yet come, but / that which has arrived and has departed]. What at first glance appears to be a distinction between futurity ("lo que aún no haya venido")

and the past ("lo que ha llegado") is in fact an account of the retroactive nature of causality: as a whole, the phrase describes the origin of poetic creation using the future perfect: *it will be . . . that which has already come and gone.* And so it renders an account of the work and its debts as a movement between times, pointing to an arrival that properly speaking belongs to neither time.

Chapter 5. Heterotopic Memory

1. See Blanchot, *Writing of the Disaster*. The latter formulation is a paraphrase of the argument of Jean-François Lyotard's *Heidegger and the "jews."* While there are important distinctions to be made between the respective scenes of which Blanchot and Piglia write (to wit: Blanchot's naming of "disaster" is situated within the historical context of the Holocaust, and thus relates to fascism, racism and genocide, whereas Piglia's writing responds both to military dictatorship and to the hegemonic triumph of neoliberalism in the postdictatorship), it is my argument that these two scenes share something like a common stake, which is perhaps best indicated by reference to the specter of the total technification of the planet, or the complete reduction of the world to the terms of technology and use-value. Of course, I am not suggesting that the question of technology can account for all that is at stake in thinking about the Holocaust or *El Proceso*.

2. By the "traditional" determination of political horizons in the Southern Cone, I am thinking both of "revolution" as the horizon for radical politics prior to 1976 and also, following the prevailing global trends of the Cold War, of the tendency of both the Left and the Right to represent national politics as an absolute bipartite division of the nation. The emergence of neoliberalism as a hegemonic economic and political discourse threatens—by virtue of presenting itself as the *only possible* version of democratic politics—to reduce to the order of absurdity all debate concerning alternatives to free-market capitalism. Regardless of one's position concerning the relative merits of the market, such a development would constitute a second societal disaster by virtue of its structural effects: what would be foreclosed in this reification of history is, among other things, the possibility of thinking itself.

3. Within a rapidly proliferating corpus of critical commentary on Piglia, at least three are concerned with the relation between narrative—and its limits—and historicity. See Colás, *Postmodernity in Latin America;* Avelar, "Cómo respiran los ausentes," and Levinson, "Trans(re)lations."

4. See in particular Vernant, "Greek Tragedy."

5. See Benjamin, Konvolut N, 3.1 For a discussion of Benjamin's dialectical image, see chapter 8 of Fynsk, *Language and Relation.*

6. The origin of "allegory" in Piglia's work is not Romantic allegory, in which A stands for B (e.g. Rosas's time as a stand-in for *el Proceso*), but Benjaminian allegory. That is, allegorical reflection stems from the secular knowledge that the transcendental realm has been radically foreclosed to human knowledge, and that earthly embodiments or representatives of the transcendental (Church, King, History, Party, Man) have been irreparably shattered as concepts. Whereas the Romantic idea of allegory is an attempt to restore these placeholders of the transcendental, Benjamin's conception of allegory is an attempt to reflect on finite

existence as such. Allegory does present one level of meaning as the substitute for another implicit meaning; more fundamentally, it is a consideration of the ways in which language both invites and ruins the substitution of metaphor and the transcendence of symbol.

7. The connection between dictatorship and Holocaust is also encoded in the references to Kafka, whose major work *The Trial* is translated into Spanish as *El proceso*.

8. For a discussion of pain (and particularly torture) as the destruction of "world," see Scarry, *Body in Pain*.

9. In Lanzmann's vocabulary, "understanding" refers specifically to a rational process of identifying causes and effects, opposing psychologies and ultimate truths—all of which flies in the face of the crucial factor of incomprehensibility which, for the victim or survivor, continues to constitute the real truth of the traumatic event. See Lanzman, "Obscenity of Understanding."

10. In "The Caesura of the Speculative" (*Typography*), Philippe Lacoue-Labarthe points to a crucial distinction between the speculative theorization of tragedy proposed by Hegel and Schelling and the speculative translations of tragedy realized by Hölderlin. The difference between the Hegelian/Schellingian and Hölderlinian attitudes amounts to two distinct understandings of tragedy as "work," as either governed by a dialectic that manages to account for all differences on the basis of its own resources (Hegel and Schelling), or as the *instantiation* of a kind of difference that is not subsequently subsumed by the tropological system of speculative dialectics (Hölderlin's notion of caesura, by virtue of which the beginning and end of tragedy do not "rhyme"). I have discussed this at greater length in the introduction.

11. Caruth draws much of her analysis of the temporality of trauma from Freud's observations of "shell-shocked" soldiers during World War I. See in particular Freud's essay "Remembering, Repeating, Working-Through." On the relation between traumatic experience and narration, see among others Caruth, *Unclaimed Experience;* , Langer, *Holocaust and the Literary Imagination*; Felman and Laub, *Testimony;* and van Alphen, *Caught by History*.

12. On the distinction between "symbolic" and "semiotic" registers of poetic language, see Kristeva, *Revolution in Poetic Language*.

13. On the relation between rhythm, cognition and representation, see Abraham, *Rhythms*.

14. This temporalizing function informs the relato "La Nena," the story of a girl who had lost the ability to form new experiences. In one important sense, la nena provides as a good a figure as any for the conditions of literary production in postdictatorship, late-capitalist society. It is important to note that her peculiar, traumatized discourse cannot be easily opposed to nontraumatized discourse as a juxtaposition of pathological and healthy symptoms. On the contrary, the elimination of pronouns and the gradual withering of substantives in her discourse precisely corresponds with her emotion world, and manifests an effort to invent a new language that could convey, reflect or work through this tortured experience. In a similar manner, the myriad pedagogical steps through which the father will lead her toward the possibility of new experiences (by exposing her to repetition in music and storytelling, he attempts to convey to her a notion of temporality, rhythm and syntax) are purely formal maneuvers that will serve as the new structuring principles of an open-ended relation between language and the real.

15. According to one of the characters in *Respiración artificial*, Borges' oeuvre strictly speaking belongs to the nineteenth century: somewhat ironically, the Borgesian text retroactively becomes part of the very tradition it brings to a close, while failing or refusing to become part of the twentieth century tradition—which, we might presume, would have required Borges to engage more directly with the emergence of populism and the Peronist state. For an opposing view of Borges' oeuvre, see Alberto Moreiras, "De-Narrativizing the Populist State Apparatus."

16. Of course, one could also take the repeated references to Joyce's text in a somewhat different direction. The somewhat-uneasy presence of *Finnegans Wake*, a monument to the literary aesthetic, in proximity to a discussion of dictatorship, exile, and disappearance grabs our attention by way of what it leaves unstated: that is, it could be said to raise the question of the impossibility of citation or translation when it comes to an event for which speech is either too unstable or too full to bear passage into another language or a different context.

17. If, in one sense, the transition is always yet to come or essentially open-ended (despite what the neoliberal discourse on the "end of history" would have one believe), it could also be argued that the transition has always already taken place. This is the position of Nelly Richard, among others: the real transition from state economy to market economy is not enacted in the transfer of power from the military juntas to liberal, civilian administrations, but is rather accomplished as a transcendental operation beginning with the military takeovers themselves. The ties between the military dictatorship and the economic elite, and the claim that dictatorship facilitates the massive accumulation of formerly nationalized wealth by these elite, is in some ways more evident in Chile than Argentine, where the dismantling of the state economy had not become a foregone conclusion until the Alfonsín administration.

18. I do not mean to imply that cultural analysis should therefore blindly or cynically embrace the historical transformations associated with globalization and the retreat of the modern state-form. It is exactly this either/or—resist or embrace—that I am trying to call into question. My point is that traditional points of reference such as "culture," "art," and "literature," which constitute the ideological basis of the prior world-historical system, cannot be subsequently offered as antidotes to the very transformation that is administering to their end—at least this cannot be done without lapsing into a profoundly reactive theoretical attitude. On this point, see chapter 8 of Moreiras's *Exhaustion of Difference*.

19. I am thinking not only of the topos of mourning in Piglia and other contemporary Argentine writers, but also of some of the important differences that have emerged in various critical discourses in the past decade or two. For instance, while Argentine critical thinking has often defined contemporary cultural practices in terms of memory, a prominent tendency in the Chilean postdictatorship has been a "melancholic" or "schizoid" discourse that would constitute itself as irreducible to any economy of mourning. What is being refused or critiqued here, I believe, has to do with a standard assessment of mourning as refortification of a damaged Ego, or, in even more superficial terms, as synonymous with the discourse of "closure" that has become ubiquitous today. On the question of mourning and dictatorship, see Moreiras, "Postdictadura y reforma del pensamiento," Richard, *Residuos y metáforas*, and Avelar, *Untimely Present*.

20. This could be said both of personal loss, insofar as the "disappearances"

associated with state-sponsored terrorism entailed the methodical annihilation of all traces of the crime, and of collective or communal loss, in that postdictatorship becomes synonymous with the eclipse of a prior generation of political signifiers (utopia, revolution). Concurrent with the absence of these political names, the very possibility of a political praxis appears increasingly to be giving way to a conception of politics as an administrative matter best performed by bureaucrats.

21. It is the thesis of *Respiración artificial* that the entire Argentine tradition, beginning with Sarmiento's *Facundo*, is organized by a political utopian desire. A utopian tropology is at work, *mutatis mutandis*, in both the modernizing discourse of liberalism and in the antimodern project of nationalism. Akin to Borges and Roberto Arlt (their important differences notwithstanding), Piglia's text both reiterates and explodes the utopian model, demonstrating how the utopian logic in fact conceals a more radical and dystopian truth.

22. Here we must recall the distinction between conventional references to "tragedy," as denoting an occurrence of the unexpected that precipitates catastrophe (of which El Proceso could certainly be an example), and a specialized reference to "tragedy" as presupposing an aesthetic reconciliation of catastrophe. It is with the latter definition that El Proceso constitutes a fundamental rupture.

Bibliography

Abraham, Nicolas. *Rhythms: On the Work, Translation and Psychoanalysis*. Stanford, Calif.: Stanford University Press, 1995.

Abrams, M. H. *The Mirror and the Lamp: Romantic Theory and the Critical Tradition*. New York: Norton, 1958.

Adamson, Joseph. *Wounded Fiction: Modern Poetry and Deconstruction*. New York: Garland, 1988.

Águilar Camín, Héctor, and Lorenzo Meyer. *In the Shadow of the Mexican Revolution*. Austin: University of Texas Press, 1993.

Alazraki, Jaime. *Critical Essays on Jorge Luis Borges*. Boston: G. K. Hall, 1987.

———. "Lectura estructuralista de 'El Sur' de Borges." *Escritura: Teoría y crítica literaria* 3 (1977): 109–19.

Aristotle. *Poetics*. Translated by Richard Janko. Indianapolis, Ind.: Hackett, 1987.

Avelar, Idelber. "Cómo respiran los ausentes: La narrativa de Ricardo Piglia." *MLN* 110 (1995): 416–32.

———. *The Untimely Present: Postdictatorial Latin American Fiction and the Task of Mourning*. Durham, N.C.: Duke University Press, 1999.

Balderston, Daniel. *Out of Context: Historical Reference and the Representation of Reality in Borges*. Durham, N.C.: Duke University Press, 1993.

Bartra, Roger. "Culture and Political Power in Mexico." Translated by Susana Casal-Sánchez. *Latin American Perspectives* (Spring 1989): 61–69.

———. *La jaula de melancolía: identidad y metamorfosis del mexicano*. Mexico: Grijalbo, 1996.

———, ed. *Caciquismo y poder político en el México rural*. Mexico: Siglo Ventiuno, 1975.

Bastos, María Luisa. "Cliches linguísticos y ambigüedad en *Pedro Páramo*." *Revista Iberoamericana* 44 (1978): 31–44.

Bastos, María Luisa, and Silvia Molloy. "La estrella junto a la luna: Variantes de la figura materna en Pedro Páramo." *MLN* 92 (1977): 246–68.

Beardsworth, Richard. "Aporia and Phantasm: Modern Law, the Tragic and Time." *Angelaki: Journal of the Theoretical Humanities* 4:1 (May 1999): 37–54.

Benjamin, Walter. "Konvolut N: Theoretics of Knowledge; Theory of Progress." Translated by Leigh Hafrey and Richard Sieburth. *The Philosophical Forum* 15:1–2 (1983): 1–40.

———. *The Origin of German Tragic Drama*. Translated by John Osborne. New York: Verso, 1977.

———. "The Task of the Translator." Translated by Harry Zohn. In *Illuminations*. New York: Harcourt Brace Jovanovich, 1968.

Blanchot, Maurice. *The Writing of the Disaster*. Translated by Ann Smock. Lincoln: University of Nebraska Press, 1986.

Blanco Aguinaga, Carlos. "Realidad y estilo en Juan Rulfo." In *La narrativa de Juan Rulfo: Interpretaciones criticas*. Edited by Joseph Sommers. Mexico: Secretária de Educación Pública, 1974.

Borges, Jorge Luis. "Autobiographical Essay." In *The Aleph*. Translated by Norman di Giovanni. New York: Dutton, 1972.

———. *Un ensayo autobiográfico*. Translated by Aníbal González. Barcelona: Editorial Galaxia Gutenberg, 1999.

———. "El escritor argentino y la tradición." In *Discusión*. Buenos Aires: Emecé, 1957.

———. *Obras completas*. 2 volumes. Buenos Aires: Emecé Editores, 1989

———. *El tamaño de mi esperanza*. Buenos Aires: Seix Barral, 1993.

———. "El Sur." In *Obras Completas*, volume 1: 525–30.

Borges, Jorge Luis and Emir Rodríguez Monegal. *Ficcionario: una antología de sus textos*. Mexico: Fondo de Cultura Económica, 1985.

Brushwood, John. *Mexico in its Novel: A Nation's Search for Identity*. Austin: University of Texas Press, 1966.

Bürger, Peter. *Theory of the Avant-Garde*. Translated by Michael Shaw. Minneapolis: University of Minnesota Press, 1984.

Caruth, Cathy. *Unclaimed Experience: Trauma, Narrative, and History*. Baltimore: The Johns Hopkins University Press, 1996.

———, ed. *Trauma: Explorations in Memory*. Baltimore: The Johns Hopkins University Press, 1995.

Castro Klaren, Sara. "Dancing and the Sacred in the Andes: From the Taqui-Onkoy to 'Rasu-Niti'." In *Dispositio: Revista americana de estudios comparados y culturales* 14:36–38 (1989): 169–85.

Castro Leal, Antonio. *La novela de la Revolución Mexicana*. Edición Aguilar, México, 1981.

Chytry, Joseph. *The Aesthetic State: A Quest in Modern German Thought*. Berkeley: University of California Press, 1989.

Colás, Santiago. *Postmodernity in Latin America: The Argentine Paradigm*. Durham: Duke University Press, 1994.

Copjec, Joan. *Read My Desire: Lacan Against the Historicists*. Cambridge: MIT Press, 1994.

———. "The Tomb of Perseverance." In *Giving Ground: The Politics of Propinquity*, edited by Joan Copjec and Michael Sorkin. New York: Verso, 1999.

Cornejo Polar, Antonio. *Escribir en el aire: ensayo sobre la heterogeneidad sociocultural en las literaturas andinas*. Lima: Editorial Horizontal, 1994.

———. *Formación de la tradición literaria en el Perú*. Lima: Centro de Estudios y Publicaciones, 1989.

Darío, Rubén. *Prosas profanas y otros poemas*. Madrid: Akal Ediciones, 1999.

de la Vega, Garcilaso. *Comentarios reales de los Incas*. Caracas: Biblioteca Ayacucho, 1976.

de Man, Paul. *Aesthetic Ideology*. Minneapolis: University of Minnesota Press, 1996.

———. *Allegories of Reading: Figural Language in Rousseau, Nietzsche, Rilke, and Proust*. New Haven: Yale University Press, 1979.

———."Autobiography as De-Facement." *MLN* 94 (1979): 919–30.

———. "The Rhetoric of Temporality." In *The Rhetoric of Romanticism*. New York: Columbia University Press, 1984.

Derrida, Jacques. *Dissemination*. Translated by Barbara Johnson. Chicago: University of Chicago Press, 1981.

———. "Economimesis." *Diacritics: A Review of Contemporary Criticism* 11:2 (June 1981): 2–25.

———. *Given Time: I. Counterfeit Money*. Translated by Peggy Kamuf. Chicago: University of Chicago Press, 1992.

———. *Glas*. Translated by John Leavy and Richard Rand. Lincoln: University of Nebraska Press, 1986.

———. *Margins of Philosophy*. Translated by Alan Bass. Chicago: University of Chicago Press, 1982.

———. "On a Newly Arisen Apocalyptic Tone in Philosophy." In *Raising the Tone of Philosophy*. Edited by Peter Fenves, translated by John Leavy. Baltimore: Johns Hopkins University Press, 1993.

———. "Signature, Event, Context." *Glyph* 1 (1977): 172–97.

———. "Violence and Metaphysics." In *Writing and Difference*. Translated by Alan Bass. Chicago: University of Chicago Press, 1978.

Dixon, Paul. *Reversible Readings: Ambiguity in Four Modern Latin American Novels*. Tuscaloosa: University of Alabama Press, 1985.D'Lugo, Carol. *The Fragmented Novel in Mexico: The Politics of Form*. Austin: University of Texas Press, 1997.

Echevarría, Esteban. *El matadero*. Introduction by Leonor Fleming. Madrid: Cátedra, 1993.

Felman, Shoshana. "Literature and Psychoanalysis: The Question of Reading: Otherwise." Yale French Studies 55–56 (1977): 4–10.

Felman, Shoshara, and Dori Laub. *Testimony: Crises of Witnessing in Literature, Psychoanalysis, and History*. New York: Routledge, 1992.

Fenves, Peter, ed. *Raising the Tone of Philosophy*. Baltimore: Johns Hopkins University Press, 1993.

Ferrari, Américo. *El universo poético de César Vallejo*. Carácas: Monte Ávila, 1972.

Fink, Bruce. *The Lacanian Subject: Between Language and Jouissance*. Princeton: Princeton University Press, 1995.

Flores, Angel. *Aproximaciones a César Vallejo*. 2 volumes. New York: Latin American Publishing Co., 1971.

Flores Galindo, Alberto. *Europa y el país de los incas: La utopía andina*. Lima: Instituto de Apoyo Agrario, 1986.

Franco, Jean. *César Vallejo: The Dialectics of Poetry and Silence*. New York: Cambridge University Press, 1976.

Freud, Sigmund. *The Standard Edition of the Complete Psychological Works (SE)*. Translated by James Strachey. 23 volumes. London: Hogarth Press, 1953–74.

———. *The Interpretation of Dreams*. In *SE*, volumes 4–5.

———. "Mourning and Melancholia." In *SE*, volume 14: 237–58.

———. "Remembering, Repeating, Working-Through." In *SE*, volume 12: 147–56.

Fuentes, Carlos. *La nueva novela hispanoamericana*. Mexico: Joaquin Mortiz, 1976.

Fynsk, Christopher. *Heidegger: Thought and Historicity*. Ithaca: Cornell University Press, 1993.

———. "Between Ethics and Aesthetics," *L'Esprit Créateur* 35:3 (Fall 1995): 80–87.

———. *Language and Relation: . . . That There is Language*. Stanford, Calif.: Stanford University Press, 1996.

García Canclini, Néstor. *Culturas híbridas: estrategias para entrar y salir de la modernidad*. Mexico: Grijalbo, 1989.

Girard, René. *Violence and the Sacred*. Translated by Patrick Gregory. Baltimore: Johns Hopkins University Press, 1977.

González Echevarría, Roberto. *Myth and Archive: A Theory of Latin American Narrative*. Cambridge: Cambridge University Press, 1990.

Gootenberg, Paul. *Between Silver and Guano: Commerical Policy and the State in Post-independence Peru*. Princeton: Princeton University Press, 1989.

Graziano, Frank. *The Millennial New World*. New York: Oxford University Press, 1999.

Gugelberger, Georg. *The Real Thing: Testimonial Discourse and Latin America*. Durham, N.C.: Duke University Press, 1998.

Gutiérrez Marrone, Nila. *El estilo de Juan Rulfo: estudio lingüístico*. Jamaica, N.Y.: Bilingual Press, 1978.

Halperín Donghi, Tulio. *El espejo de la historia: problemas argentinos y perspectivas hispanoamericanas*. Buenos Aires: Editorial Sudamericana, 1987.

Halperín Dorghi, Tulio, et al., eds. *Sarmiento: Author of a Nation*. Berkeley: University of California Press, 1994.

Hedrick, Tace. "Y Hembra es la Alma Mía: Stumbling Over the Female Body in César Vallejo's *Trilce*." *Latin American Literary Review* 22:43 (Jan.–June 1994): 51–66.

Hegel, G. W. F. *Hegel on Tragedy*. Edited by Anne and Henry Paolucci. Smyrna, De.: Griffon House, 2001.

———. *Natural Law: The Scientific Ways of Treating Natural Law, Its Place in Moral Philosophy, and its Relation to the Positive Sciences of Law*. Translated by T. M. Knox. Philadelphia: University of Pennsylvania Press, 1975.

———. *Phenomenology of Spirit*. Translated by A. V. Miller. New York: Oxford University Press, 1977.

Heidegger, Martin. *Early Greek Thinking*. Translated by David Ferrell Krell and Frank Capuzzi. New York: Harper, 1975.

———. *An Introduction to Metaphysics*. Translated by Ralph Manheim. New Haven: Yale University Press, 1959.

———. *On the Way to Language*. Translated by Peter Hertz. New York: Harper, 1971.

Higgins, James. On the Socialism of Vallejo," in Sharman, ed. *The Poetry and Poetry of César Vallejo*. Lewiston, Maine: Edwin Mellen Press, 1997.

Hölderlin, Friedrich. *Essays and Letters on Theory*. Translated by Thomas Pfäu. Albany: SUNY Press, 1988.

———. *Sämtliche Werke*. Grosse Stuttgarter Ausgabe. Edited by Friedrich Beissner. Stuttgart: Kohlhammer, 1943–85.

Johnson, Barbara. *The Critical Difference: Essays in the Contemporary Rhetoric of Reading*. Baltimore: Johns Hopkins University Press, 1980.

Joseph, Gilbert, et al., eds. *Everyday Forms of State Formation: Revolution and the Negotiation of Rule in Modern Mexico*. Durham, N.C.: Duke University Press, 1994.

Kadir, Djelal. *Columbus and the Ends of the Earth: Europe's Prophetic Rhetoric as Conquering Ideology*. Berkeley: University of California Press, 1992.

Kafka, Franz. *The Trial*. Translated by Edwin and Willa Muir. New York: Knopf, 1992.

Kant, Immanuel. *Critique of Judgment*. Translated by Werner Pluhar. Indianapolis: Hackett Publishing, 1987.

———. *Religion Within the Limits of Reason Alone*. Translated by Theodore Greene. New York: Harper, 1960.

Kristeva, Julia. *Revolution in Poetic Language*. Translated by Margaret Waller. New York: Columbia University Press, 1984.

Lacan, Jacques. *Écrits*. Paris: Éditions du Seuil, 1966.

———. *Écrits*. Translated by Alan Sheridan. New York: Norton, 1977.

———. *The Ethics of Psychoanalysis*. Translated by Dennis Porter. New York: Norton, 1992.

———. *The Four Fundamental Concepts of Psycho-analysis*. Translated by Alan Sheridan. New York: Norton, 1978.

———. "Sur la théorie du symbolisme d'Ernest Jones." In *Écrits*. Paris: Éditions du Seuil, 1966.

Laclau, Ernesto. *New Reflections on the Revolution of Our Time*. New York: Verso, 1990.

Laclau, Ernesto, Judith Butler, and Slavoj Žižek. *Contingency, Hegemony, Universality: Contemporary Dialogues on the Left*. New York: Verso, 2000.

Laclau, Ernesto, and Chantal Mouffe. *Hegemony & Socialist Strategy: Towards a Radical Democratic Politics*. NewYork: Verso, 1985.

Lacoue-Labarthe, Philippe. *Heidegger, Art and Politics: The Fiction of the Political*. Translated by Chris Turner. Cambridge, Mass.: Basil Blackwell, 1990.

———. *Poetry as Experience*. Translated by Andrea Tarnowski. Stanford, Calif.: Stanford University Press, 1999.

———. "The Scene is Primal." In *The Subject of Philosophy*. Translated by Karen McPherson. Minneapolis: University of Minnesota Press, 1993.

———. *Typography*. Edited by Christopher Fynsk. Cambridge: Harvard University Press, 1989.

Lacoue-Labartle, Philippe, and Jean-Luc Nancy, eds. *Les fins de l'homme: A partir du travail de Jacques Derrida*. Paris: Galilée, 1981.

Langer, Lawrence. *The Holocaust and the Literary Imagination*. New Haven: Yale University Press, 1975.

Lanzmann, Claude. "The Obscenity of Understanding: An Evening with Claude Lanzmann." In Caruth, *Trauma: Explorations in Memory*. Baltimore: Johns Hopkins University Press, 1995.

Laplanch, J., and J. B. Pontalis. *The Language of Psycho-Analysis*. Translated by Donald Nicholson-Smith. New York: Norton, 1973.

Larsen, Neil. *Modernism and Hegemony: A Materialist Critique of Aesthetic Agencies*. Minneapolis: University of Minnesota Press, 1990.

Lauer, Mirko. *Andes imaginarios: Discursos del indigenismo-2*. Cuzco, Peru: Sur Casa de Estudios de Socialismo, 1997.

Leclaire, Serge. *Psychoanalyzing: On the Order of the Unconscious and the Practice of the Letter*. Translated by Peggy Kamuf. Stanford, Calif.: Stanford University Press, 1998.

Levinson, Brett. "Trans(re)lations: Dictatorship, Disaster and the 'Literary Politics' of Piglia's *Respiración artificial*." *Latin American Literary Review* 25:49 (Jan.–June 1997): 91–120.

Lloyd, Peter, and Paul Thomas. *Culture and the State*. New York: Routledge, 1998.

Lorente-Murphy, Silvia. "¿Cuál era el mundo de Susana San Juan?" *Confluencia: Revista Hispanica de Cultura y Literatura* 7: 2 (Spring 1992): 147–55.

Ludmer, Josefina. *El género gauchesco: un tratado sobre la patria*. Buenos Aires: Editorial Sudamericano, 1988.

Lugones, Leopoldo. *La guerra gaucha*. Buenos Aires: Ediciones Centurión, 1962.

———. *El payador*. Buenos Aires: Ediciones Centurión, 1961.

Lyotard, Jean-François. *Heidegger and "the jews."* Translated by Andreas Michel and Mark Roberts. Minneapolis: University of Minnesota Press, 1990.

Mann, Paul. *Theory-Death of the Avant-Garde*. Bloomington: Indiana University Press, 1991.

Mariátegui, José Carlos. *Siete ensayos de interpretación de la realidad peruana*. Caracas: Biblioteca Ayacucho, 1979.

Marx, Karl, and Friedrich Engels. *The Marx-Engels Reader*. Edited by Robert C. Tucker. New York: Norton, 1978.

McDuffie, Keith. "The Poetic Vision of César Vallejo in *Los Heraldos Negros* and *Trilce*." Ph.D. diss., University of Pittsburgh, 1969.

McGuirk, Bernard. *Latin American Literature: Symptoms, Risks and Strategies of Post-Structuralist Criticism*. New York: Routledge, 1997.

Meyer, Jean. *The Christiero Rebellion: The Mexican People Between Church and*

State, 1926–1929. Translated by Richard Southern. New York: Cambridge University Press, 1976.

Millones, Luis. *Mesianismo e idolotría en los Andes Centrales.* Buenos Aires: Fundación Simón Rodríguez, 1989.

———, ed. *El retorno de las huacas: estudios y documentos sobre el Taki Onqoy.* Lima: Instituto de Estudios Peruanos, 1990.

Moreiras, Alberto. "Borges y Estela Canto: la sombra de una dedicatoria." *Journal of Interdisciplinary Literary Studies* 5:1 (1993): 131–446.

———. "*Circulus vitiosus deus*: Borges y el fin de la memoria." *Siglo 20/20th Century* 9:1–2 (1992): 111–33.

———. "De-Narrativizing the Populist State Apparatus: Borges' 'La lotería en Babilonia'." In *Jorge Luis Borges: Thought and Knowledge in the 20th Century*, edited by Alfonso de Toro. Frankfurt: Vervuert, 1999.

———. *The Exhaustion of Difference: The Politics of Latin American Cultural Studies.* Durham, N.C.: Duke University Press, 2002.

———. "Global Fragments: A Second Latinamericanism." *The Cultures of Globalization*, edited by Frederic Jameson. Durham: Duke University Press, 1998.

———. "Postdictadura y reforma del pensamiento." *Revista de Crítica Cultural* 7 (1993): 26–35.

———. *Tercer espacio: literatura y duelo en América latina.* Santiago: Universidad Arcis, 1999.

———. "Transculturación y pérdida del sentido." *Nuevo Texto Critico* 3:6 (1990): 105–19.

Nancy, Jean Luc. *Birth to Presence.* Translated by Brian Holmes, et al. Stanford, Calif.: Stanford University Press, 1993.

———. *The Inoperative Community.* Edited by Peter Conner, translated by Peter Conner et al. Minneapolis: University of Minnesota Press, 1991.

———. *The Sense of the World.* Translated by Jeffrey Librett. Minneapolis: University of Minnesota Press, 1997.

Neale-Silva, Eduardo. *César Vallejo en su fase trílcica.* Madison: University of Wisconsin Press, 1975.

Neruda, Pablo. *Las alturas de Macchu Picchu.* Santiago: Librería Neira, 1948.

O'Malley, Ilene. *The Myth of the Revolution: Hero Cults and the Institutionalization of the Mexican State, 1920–1940.* New York: Greenwood Press, 1986.

Ortega Galindo, Luis. *Expresión y sentido de Juan Rulfo.* Madrid: J. Porrúa Turanzas, 1984.

Palma, Ricardo. *Tradiciones peruanas completas.* Madrid: Aguilar, 1964.

Paoli, Roberto. "César Vallejo y el expresionismo poético." *Mundi: Filosofía/Crítica/Literatura* 3:6 (Nov. 1989): 18–27.

Paz, Octavio. *Los hijos del limo.* Barcelona: Seix Barral, 1974.

———. *Laberinto de soledad.* Mexico: Fondo de Cultura Económica, 1959.

Pease, Franklin. *El dios creador andino.* Lima: Mosca Azul Editoriales, 1973.

Piglia, Ricardo. "En otro país." In *Prisión Perpetua.* Buenos Aires: Editorial Sudamericana, 1988.

———. *La ciudad ausente*. Buenos Aires: Seix Barral, 1992.

———. *Respiración artificial*. Buenos Aires: Editorial Pomaire, 1980.

Portal, Marta. *Proceso narrativo de la revolución mexicana*. Madrid: Cultura Hispánica, 1977.

Pratt, Mary Louise. *Imperial Eyes: Travel Writing and Transculturation*. New York: Routledge, 1992.

Rama, Ángel. *Transculturación narrativa en América Latina*. Mexico: Siglo Ventiuno Editores, 1982.

Rancière, Jacques. *On the Shores of Politics*. Translated by Liz Heron. New York: Verso, 1995.

Reyes, Alfonso. "Discurso por virgilio." In *Tentativas y orientaciones*. Mexico: Editorial Nuevo Mundo, 1944.

Richard, Nelly. *Residuos y metáforas: ensayos de crítica cultural sobre el Chile de la Transición*. Santiago: Editorial Cuarto Propio, 1998.

Rilke, Rainer Maria. *The Notebooks of Malte Laurids Brigge*. Translated by Stephen Mitchell. New York: Random House, 1983.

Rock, David. *Argentina: 1516–1982: From Spanish Colonization to the Falklands War*. Berkeley: University of California Press, 1985.

———. *Authoritarian Argentina: The Nationalist Movement, Its History and Its Impact*. Berkeley: University of California Press, 1993.

Rodríguez Alcalá, Hugo. *El arte de Juan Rulfo: historias de vivos y difuntos*. Mexico: Instituto Nacional de Bellas Artes, 1965.

Rodríguez Monegal, Emir. *Borges por él mismo*. Caracas: Monte Avilas Editores, 1980.

Rodríguez Monegal, Emir, Jorge Luis Borges. *Ficcionario: una antología de sus textos*. Mexico: Fondo de Cultura Económica, 1985.

Rodríguez-Luis, Julio. "La intención política en la obra de Borges: Hacia una visión de conjunto." *Cuadernos Hispanoamericanos* 361–66 (1980): 170–98.

Roffé, Reina. *Juan Rulfo: Autobiografía armada*. Buenos Aires: Corregidor, 1973.

Rowe, William. "Pain as a Cultural Sign in the Poetry of César Vallejo." In Sharman, *Poetry and Poetry of César Vallejo*. Lewiston, Maine: Edwin Mellen Press, 1997.

Rulfo, Juan. *El llano en llamas*. Mexico: Fondo de Cultura Económica, 1953.

———. *Pedro Páramo*. Madrid: Cátedra, 1993.

———. *Pedro Páramo*. Translated by Margaret Sayers Peden. New York: Grove, 1994.

Sarlo, Beatriz. *Jorge Luis Borges: A Writer on the Edge*. New York: Verso, 1993.

Sarmiento, Domingo Faustino. *Facundo: civilizacion y barbarie*. New York: Colección Hispánica, 1961.

———. *Recuerdos de provincia*. Buenos Aires: Editorial Universitaria, 1960.

Scarry, Elaine. *The Body in Pain: The Making and Unmaking of the World*. New York: Oxford University Press, 1985.

Schelling, F. W. J. "Philosophical Letters on Dogmatism." In *The Unconditional in*

Human Knowledge: *Four Early Essays, 1794–1796*. Translated by Fritz Marti. Lewisburg: Bucknell University Press, 1980.

Schiller, Friedrich. *On the Aesthetic Education of Man*. Oxford: Clarendon Press, 1967.

Sharman, Adam, ed. *The Poetry and Poetics of César Vallejo: The Fourth Angle of the Circle*. Lewiston, Maine: Edwin Mellen Press, 1997.

Shreve, William Price. *The Venus de Milo: Its Discovery, The Theories Concerning It, Its Subsequent History*. Boston: Shreve, Crump and Low, 1878.

Shumway, Nicolas. *The Invention of Argentina*. Berkeley: University of California Press, 1991.

Sicard, Alain. "The Poetry of Vallejo: 'Orfandad de orfandades.'" In Sharman, *Poetry and Poetry of César Vallejo*. Lewiston, Maine: Edwin Mellen Press, 1997.

Sklodowska, Elzbieta. *Testimonio hispanoamericano: historia, teoría, poética*. New York: Peter Lang, 1992.

Sommer, Doris. *Foundational Fictions: The National Romances of Latin America*. Berkeley: University of California Press, 1991.

Sommers, Joseph, ed. *La narrativa de Juan Rulfo: Interpretaciones críticas*. Mexico: SepSetentas, 1974.

Sophocles. *Oedipus the King*. In *Thee Theban Plays*. Translated by Robert Fagles. New York: Penguin, 1982.

Szondi, Peter. *An Essay on the Tragic*. Translated by Paul Fleming. Stanford, Calif.: Stanford University Press, 2002.

———. "The Notion of the Tragic in Schelling, Hölderlin, and Hegel." In *On Textual Understanding and Other Essays*. Translated by Harvey Mendelsohn. Minneapolis: University of Minnesota Press, 1986.

Valcárcel, Luis. *Tempestad en los andes*. Lima: Populibros Peruanos, nd.

Vallejo, César. *Arte y revolución*. Lima: Mosca Azul Editores, 1973.

———. *The Complete Posthumous Poetry*. Introduction by Clayton Eshleman, translated by Eshleman and José Rubia Barcia. Berkeley: University of California Press, 1978.

———. *Los heraldos negros*. Buenos Aires: Editorial Losada, 1961.

———. *Obra poética completa*. Caracas: Biblioteca Ayacucho, 1979.

———. *Trilce*. Translated by Clayton Eshleman. New York: Marsilio, 1992.

———. *Trilce*. Translated by Próspero Saíz. *Abraxas* 38–39 (1990): 5–63.

van Alphen, Ernst. *Caught by History: Holocaust Effects in Contemporary Art, Literature, and Theory*. Stanford, Calif.: Stanford University Press, 1997.

Vasconcelos, José. *Ulises criollo*. Mexico: Editorial Jus, 1964.

Vernant, Jean-Pierre. "Greek Tragedy: Problems of Interpretation." In *The Structuralist Controversy*, edited by Richard Macksey and Eugenio Donato. Baltimore: Johns Hopkins University Press, 1970.

von Buelow, Christiane. "César Vallejo: Allegory and the Dialectic of Enlightenment." Ph.D. diss, Stanford University,1984.

———. "Vallejo's Venus de Milo and the Ruins of Language." PMLA 104:1 (Jan. 1989): 41–52.

Wachtel, Nathan. *The Vision of the Vanquished: The Spanish Conquest of Peru through Indian Eyes*. Translated by Ben and Sian Reynolds. New York: Barnes and Noble, 1977.

Womack, John. *Zapata and the Mexican Revolution*. New York: Knopf, 1969.

Yáñez, Augustín. *Al filo del agua*. Mexico: Editorial Porrúa, 1947.

Index

Adorno, Theodor, 223, 252
affect, 18, 22, 29, 153–54, 158, 162, 178, 234, 235, 247, 250, 277 n. 13
Alberdi, Rafael, 58
allegory: and ideology, 80, 81; and modernity, 102–4, 228; and nation, 25, 84, 111, 130–31
alterity, 20, 47, 78, 88, 92, 147, 159, 184, 207, 218–19
Althusser, Louis, 83, 238–39; and interpellation, 62, 83, 166, 184–85
anagnorisis, 26, 48, 158
anamorphosis, 151–54
aporia, 12, 28, 104, 112, 115, 137, 162, 171, 175–77, 203, 212, 217–19, 236, 237, 248, 250,
Argentina: "Civilization and Barbarism" debate, 24, 25, 55–61, 64, 66–69, 93; Conquest of the Desert, 69, 77; immigration, 56–58, 65, 68, 73, 76; modernization, 24, 54, 58, 65, 68, 71, 73–74, 76, 78, 84, 93; nation-building, 13, 14, 24, 53, 56–66, 69, 73, 84, 246, 249; nationalism, 24, 25, 54–56, 65–69, 77–81, 237; State terrorism, 28, 29, 225, 226, 228, 233, 245–52
Arguedas, José María, 28, 119, 170
Aristotle, 15, 30, 48, 49, 153, 158. *See also* anagnorisis; catharsis; peripeteia
aura, 190
Avelar, Idelber, 22, 224, 228
avant-garde, 27, 163–64, 169–71, 186–88, 191, 202
Azuela, Mariano, 25, 106, 107

Bartra, Roger, 135
Bastos, María Luisa, 269 n. 30
Beardsworth, Richard, 254 n. 4

Bello, Andrés, 11
Benjamin, Walter: allegory, 150, 228, 269 n. 34; aura, 190; dialectical image, 159, 227; translation, 120, 239, 241
Blanchot, Maurice, 222
Boom novel, 11, 25, 98, 147
Borges, Jorge Luis: allegory: 25, 80–81, 84; critique of nationalism, 25, 39, 53, 55, 71, 74–89, 93; decision, 55, 75, 83–85, 88, 93, 95–97; "early" vs. "late" Borges, 71–74; errancy: 65, 75, 81, 83, 86, 93, 97; *las orillas*, 72, 87; patria, 65, 67–9, 95; poesía gauchesca, 54, 66–72, 75, 81–82, 95, 261 n. 21; temporality: 85, 91–92, 96; tragedy, 25, 54, 73–75, 78, 81, 84, 85, 88, 91; works: "Autobiographical Essay," 87–88; "Biografía de Tadeo Isidoro Cruz," 70; "El fin," 70; "Funes el memorioso," 92; "Pierre Menard, autor del Quijote," 71, 95; "El Sur," 74–97; "El tamaño de mi esperanza," 73
Brushwood, John, 265 nn. 6 and 9
Bürger, Peter, 27, 186

caciquismo. *See under* Mexico
caesura, 37, 113, 197, 235
Carranza, Venustiano, 271 n. 43
Caruth, Cathy, 231–32
Castro Leal, Antonio, 106, 266 n.13
catastrophe, 11, 17, 28–29, 32, 46, 62, 80, 90, 93, 103, 169, 171, 208, 224–25, 250
catharsis, 40, 48, 49, 255 n. 11
Celan, Paul, 223, 252
Cervantes, Miguel de la: *Don Quijote de la Mancha*, 77

INDEX

ciudad ausente, La (Piglia), 225, 231–50
Civil Society, 16, 40, 43–47, 245, 295
"Civilization and Barbarism," 24, 25, 55–61, 64, 66–69, 93, 107
Cohn, Deborah, 273 n. 49
colonialism, 19, 100, 105, 118–19, 123, 162, 165, 167–68, 171, 208, 262 n. 24, 266 n. 13, 277 n. 20
Copjec, Joan, 256 n. 14
Cornejo Polar, Antonio, 21, 164–68
cosmopolitanism, 19, 56, 65, 72, 80, 103, 117, 121, 125, 127, 129, 169, 176
Cultural Studies, 11, 13, 23, 186

Darío, Rubén, 11, 188, 189, 201–2
de Man, Paul, 22, 143, 259 n. 12, 267 n. 15
deconstruction, 16–18, 25, 30, 113–15, 251
Derrida, Jacques, 16, 43–47, 97, 98; and tragedy, 43–47
Descartes, René, 39, 59, 169, 176
dialectical image, 159, 227
dictatorship: comparisons to Holocaust, 223; State terrorism, 28, 251; and transition to market economy, 29, 222, 232, 243
dikē, 32, 33, 42
disaster, 28, 223, 227–28, 233–34, 251–52, 258
Dixon, Paul, 273 n. 49

Echeverría, Esteban, 11, 237, 243, 253 n. 3
Eguren, José María, 278 n. 27
Eurocentrism, 17, 25, 58, 60, 65–66, 99, 118–20, 123, 201, 240

Facundo (Sarmiento), 11, 13, 24, 54, 56–65
Farías, Victor, 229
Felman, Shoshana, 117, 283 n. 11
Fenves, Peter, 19, 254 n. 5
Fernández, Macedonio, 238, 247, 250
fetishism, 81, 193, 199
Fink, Bruce, 276 n. 12
Foucault, Michel, 245, 248

Franco, Jean, 169, 186, 188, 191
Freud, Sigmund, 18, 48–50, 174, 231, 276 n. 10; and tragedy, 48. *See also* affect; fetishism; mourning; psychoanalysis; trauma
Fuentes, Carlos, 25, 98–99, 101–2
Fukuyama, Francis, 53
Fynsk, Christopher, 254 n. 7, 256 n. 14, 282 n. 5

García Canclini, Néstor, 21, 105, 135
García Márquez, Gabriel, 98
gaucho, 19, 24, 57–58, 67, 69–70, 86–87, 93–96
German Idealism, 30, 38, 40, 47
Girard, René, 38
González, Aníbal, 260 n. 18
González Echevarría, Roberto, 21
Graziano, Frank, 207

Hartman, Geoffrey, 252
Hegel, G. F. W., 15–16, 18, 30, 32, 24–26, 38, 41, 43–44, 46, 57–58, 79, 84, 94, 116, 138, 169, 203; and *Aufhebung*, 34, 43, 88; and Beautiful Soul, 203, 216; and tragedy, 30–32, 43–44
Heidegger, Martin, 15, 34, 39–43, 47, 50–51, 169, 229; and ontotheology, 22, 34, 59, 149, 155, 164, 169, 176, 193, 195, 210; and technicity, 174; and tragedy, 39–43
hegemony, 55, 60, 63, 70, 135, 146, 157, 165–66, 180, 210, 217–18, 224, 237; and subalternity, 217–18
heterogeneity, 19, 21, 164, 166–67, 170–71
heteronomy, 25, 34, 78, 230
heterotopia, 29, 159, 248–49
Hölderlin, Friedrich, 30–31, 34–38, 113, 146, 161–62, 168–69, 196–97; and caesura, 37, 113, 197, 235
Holocaust, 28, 223, 251, 252, 255 n. 10
hybridity, 135

ideology, 196; aesthetic ideology, 63, 183, 186–87, 192–93; extirpación de ideologías, 196
Inca Garcilaso, 281 n. 40

indigenism. *See under* Perú
interpellation, 62, 83, 166, 184–85

Joseph, Gilbert, 270 n. 38
Joyce, James, 241

Kafka, Franz, 228
Kant, Immanuel, 63, 87, 204
Kristeva, Julia, 283 n. 12

Lacan, Jacques, 16, 49–52, 87–90, 198, 250; jouissance, 49, 68, 78, 136, 142, 192, 198; the imaginary, 49–50, 76, 78, 81, 120, 165–66, 182, 185, 198–99, 218, 225, 228, 235–37, 241, 243, 246, 250, 252; the name of the Father, 111, 116, 138, 160, 185, 206; the phallus, 197–200, 205; the symbolic, 37, 89, 91–93, 109, 138, 141, 144, 147, 160, 165, 177, 179, 185, 192, 207–8, 212, 218, 226, 232, 234–36, 252; the real, 58, 80, 87, 90, 91, 93, 96, 175, 183, 192, 200, 208, 225, 230, 232, 234, 241; and tragedy, 49–52
Lacoue-Labarthe, Philippe, 16; and tragedy, 47–49
Laclau, Ernesto, 136, 218, 237
Langer, Lawrence, 283 n. 11
Lanzmann, Claude, 230
Larsen, Neil, 265 n. 9, 268 n. 28
Latin American Boom novel, 11, 25, 98, 147
Lazarillo de Tormes, 215
Lauer, Mirko, 275 n. 3
Leclaire, Serge, 179
Levinson, Brett, 229
literature: as compensatory measure, 13, 23, 25, 68, 83, 86, 103–4, 187–88, 202–3; as pedagogical device, 11, 13–14, 32; and restitution, 145–48, 156; and testimonio, 23, 26, 155–57
llano en llamas, El (Rulfo), 98, 117, 152
Lorente Murphy, Silvia, 274 n. 58
Ludmer, Josefina, 21, 69–71, 95
Lugones, Leopoldo, 24–25, 54, 65–69, 72, 75, 82, 237, 251
Lyotard, Jean-François, 282 n. 1

Malloy, Silvia, 274 n. 58
Mariátegui, José Carlos, 28, 164, 167–68, 170, 208, 281 n. 42
Martín Fierro (Hernández), 66
Marxism, 173, 192, 212, 218, 221
melancholia, 22, 91, 125, 157, 235, 247, 284 n. 19
mestizaje, 27, 57, 148, 165–66
Mexican muralism, 106
Mexico: caciquismo, 111, 114, 131–44, 149–52, 157–60, 274 n. 61; La Chingada myth, 130; 1926–1929 Cristero counter-revolution, 108, 131, 273 n. 50; Instituto Nacional Indigenista, 267 n. 23; land reform (reparto), 134, 274 n. 56; modernization, 25–26, 101–03, 109, 111, 116–18, 121, 129, 131–32, 135–36, 144, 146, 148, 155, 158; Porfiriato, 106, 108, 119, 132, 134; Post-revolutionary state, 99–108, 127, 131, 134, 146; 1910–1920 Revolution, 19, 25, 26, 100–108, 110–11, 118–19, 124, 126–27, 131–34, 140, 142, 144, 149, 152; usufruct (rights to land usage), 140–41
Millones, Luis: 280 nn. 35 and 37
mood, 12, 18, 22, 38, 84, 90, 152–53, 162–63, 208, 233, 243
Moreiras, Alberto, 20–22, 127, 263 n. 30, 276 n. 9, 284 nn. 15, 18, and 19
mourning, 19, 22–23, 28–29, 32, 37–38, 40, 46, 91, 107, 162–63, 168, 172–79, 181–85, 219–20, 228, 233–34, 238, 267 n. 15, 269 n. 34; and impossibility of mourning, 29, 162, 173–78, 182, 184–85, 248, 250; as introjection and expulsion, 22, 174–75, 177, 246–47

Nancy, Jean-Luc, 263 n. 33, 278 n. 25
nation-building, 11–21, 24, 53, 57–66, 69, 73, 84, 101, 109, 118, 127, 162, 166, 195, 246, 249
nation-state, 11, 13, 18–21, 26, 31–32, 46, 50–51, 53–55, 59–60, 62–67, 69–70, 79, 99–101, 113–14, 117, 119–20, 123, 133, 137, 139, 140, 142, 148, 152, 162–66, 169–70,

180–81, 185–86, 192, 196, 209, 224–25, 238; and state economy, 29, 232, 243; and transition to market economy, 29, 99, 187, 222, 232, 243
naturalism, 98, 101–2, 126
Nazism, 229, 255n. 10
Neale-Silva, Eduardo, 176
Neruda, Pablo, 155, 156
Nietzsche, Friedrich, 15, 36, 48; and tragedy, 38, 39
nomos, 32, 50
novel of the Mexican Revolution, 106, 108

1001 Nights, The, 78, 80, 86
Ortega, Julio, 273n. 52
Ortega Galindo, Luis, 273n. 54
Ortiz, Fernando, 119

Palma, Ricardo, 27, 274n. 1
Paré, Luisa, 135
Paz, Octavio, 11, 13, 25, 102–06, 108, 117, 119, 130, 158; and compensatory modernism, 103
Pedro Páramo (Rulfo), 100–106
peripeteia, 37, 75, 112–13, 142, 195
Perú: Inkarrí myth, 280n. 37; modernization, 27, 165, 171, 180, 186–88, 193, 195, 203; indigenism, 165, 166, 170, 208–11; Taqui Onkoy dance, 280n. 37; Twantinsuyu, 168; 1879–1883 War of the Pacific, 275n. 2
Piglia, Ricardo: allegory, 228; aporetics of decision, 237, 242, 251; *La ciudad ausente*, 225, 231–50; errancy, 240, 242; mourning, 228, 233–34, 238, 246–48; patria, 236, 239; *Prisión perpetua*, 230; *Respiración artificial*, 222, 225–31, 242–43, 249; rhythm, 234–35; tragedy, 28–29, 227, 230–31, 235, 238, 249, 251–52; trauma, 231.
Plato, 15, 39, 47–48, 53, 186, 199, 201, 262n. 25; and mimesis: 15, 119, 155–56, 201
poiēsis, 63, 122, 124, 168, 213, 217
Portal, Marta, 266n. 13
Positivism, 266n. 13, 269n. 31, 272n. 46, 277n. 22

Postcoloniality, 123, 145, 148, 164–65, 168, 171, 180, 185, 207, 209
Pratt, Mary Louise, 268n. 24
prosopopeia, 155–56
Psychoanalysis, 16, 22, 30, 48–50, 52, 173, 245, 257

Rama, Ángel, 117, 119–23, 126, 166, 184
Ramos, Julio, 21
Ramos, Samuel, 106
Rancière, Jacques, 253n. 5, 262n. 25
realism, 170, 275n. 4
regionalist novel, 25, 99, 101–2, 117–18, 122, 124
Respiración artificial (Piglia), 222, 225–31, 242–43, 249
Reyes, Alfonso, 106, 267n. 18
rhythm, 23, 37, 113, 124, 178, 188, 234–35, 243. *See also* caesura
Richard, Nelly, 284nn. 17 and 19
Rilke, Rainer Maria, 262n. 23
Rock, David, 65, 77
Rodríguez Monegal, Emir, 260n. 18
Rodríguez Alcalá, Hugo, 264n. 5
Rodríguez-Luis, Julio, 262n. 27
Roffé, Reina, 125
Rosas, Juan Manuel, 60, 64, 226, 258n. 5
Rulfo, Juan: allegory, 102–04, 111, 114, 122, 130–31; anamorphosis, 151, 154; caciquismo, 137–44; deterritorialization, 127, 133; decision: 113, 115; errancy, 104, 109, 112, 121, 150; language and finitude, 26, 112–13, 120, 122, 146, 149, 151–60; *El llano en llamas*, 98, 117, 152; the maternal, 113–16; national identity, 26, 104, 106, 108–10, 113–15, 130, 142, 148, 156; *Pedro Páramo*, 100–60; representation of "indigenous mentality," 147, 148; suspended temporality, 118, 135, 137, 145, 148–49, 159; transculturation, 117, 119–26; la tierra, 131, 134, 139, 143, 153, 184; tragedy, 26, 100–02, 104, 107, 110–14, 122, 130, 145, 146, 148, 157–59; voz popular, 121, 124–27

Sarlo, Beatriz, 21, 71–72, 75
Sarmiento, Domingo, 13, 67, 68, 226, 237, 243, 251; "civilization and barbarism," 24–25, 54–58, 61–63, 69, 93, 107, 167; Eurocentrism, 58–59; *Facundo*, 11, 13, 24, 54, 56–65; and the United States, 59
Sayers Peden, Margaret, 269 n. 33, 273 n. 44
Sausurre, Ferdinand de, 279 n.31
Scalabrini Ortiz, Raúl, 68, 262 n. 24
Scarry, Elaine, 283 n. 8
Schelling, F. W. J., 15, 30–35, 38, 48, 84, 176, 204, 256 n. 17
Schiller, Friedrich, 63
Shumway, Nicolas, 53, 55
Sicard, Alaine, 180
Sklodowska, Elzbieta, 274 n. 57
Sommer, Doris, 261 n. 22, 278 n. 26
Sommers, Joseph, 124
Sophocles: *Oedipus Rex*, 33–35, 37, 104, 137, 204, 227, 255 n. 8; *Oedipus at Colonus*, 35; *Antigone*: 40–43, 46, 49–52, 55, 88–89, 249
State terrorism. *See under* Argentina
subalternity, 26, 28, 69, 71, 101, 103, 119, 127, 145–47, 159, 166–67, 176, 180, 185, 217
sublimation, 49–50, 88, 159, 185, 195
sublime, 62, 88, 92, 111, 159–60, 188, 219, 220, 224
"El Sur" (Borges), 74–97
Szondi, Peter, 30

technē, 40, 42, 173
Tempest, The (Shakespeare) 79
testimonio, 23, 26, 155–56
testimony, 26, 111–12, 146, 151, 154–60, 184, 232, 272 n. 46
tone, 12–14, 18, 19, 23, 32, 38–39, 44–46, 67, 71, 84, 98, 101, 116, 127, 153, 157, 161–64, 172–73, 175, 182, 196, 202, 206, 212, 220–21, 232, 234, 239, 249, 251
tragedy: and anagnorisis, 26, 48, 158, 264 n. 4; in the work of Borges, 25, 54, 73–75, 78, 81, 84–85, 88, 91; and caesura, 37, 113, 197, 235; and catharsis, 40, 48–49, 255 n. 11; as counter-foundational trope, 35–52; in the work of Derrida, 43–47; as foundational trope, 31–34, 38–43; in the work of Freud, 48; in the work of Hegel, 30–32, 43–44; in the work of Heidegger, 39–43; in the work of Hölderlin, 34–38, 46; in the work of Lacan, 49–52; in the work of Lacoue-Labarthe, 47–49; in the work of Nietzsche, 38–39; and peripeteia, 37, 75, 112–13, 142, 195; in the work of Piglia, 28–29, 227, 230–31, 235, 238, 249, 251, 252; in the work of Rulfo, 26, 100–102, 104, 107, 110–14, 122, 130, 145–46, 148, 157–59; in the work of Schelling, 32–34; and symbolic collapse, 14, 29, 55, 86, 88, 90, 118, 122, 137, 150, 207, 219–20, 228, 244, 249, 262 n. 23; tragic attunement, 11, 12, 38, 161, 173, 195, 196, 220, 228, 252; in the work of Vallejo, 26–28, 161–64, 168–69, 176, 195–97, 200, 204, 208, 219–21
transculturation, 59, 117, 119–26, 265 n. 6, 268 n. 28, 280 n. 35
trauma, 15, 28, 229, 94, 96, 108, 139, 160, 176, 178, 188, 192, 198, 208, 230–32, 234, 248, 283 nn. 9 and 14
Trilce (Vallejo), 170–221

Valcárcel, Luis: *Tempestad en los andes*, 209–12
Valdelomar, Abraham, 188
Vallejo, César: allegory, 211; aporia of decision, 163, 174, 202–4, 216–21; aura, treatment of, 27, 190; the beautiful, 187–88; Catholicism, 163, 200, 207, 212–14, 219, 221; conversion to Marxism, 276 n. 6; disjunctive temporality, 172, 190, 223, 281 n. 46; errancy, 191, 198, 201, 205, 212; ekphrasis, 188–90; harmony, 188, 192–93, 195, 202–3, 220; the maternal, 173, 176–85; messianism, 163–64, 206–9, 211–15, 217, 219–21; mourning, 162–63, 168–69, 171–85, 219–21; orphanhood, 178–80, 185,

206; tragedy, 26–28, 161–64, 168–69, 173, 176, 195–97, 200, 204, 208, 219–21; transculturation, 166, 184–85, 197, 202. Works: *Arte y revolución*, 221; *Los heraldos negros*, 169–70; *Trilce*, 170–221; "I," 173–74; "XIX," 202; "XXIII," 173, 177–84; "XXVIII," 176–78; "XXIII," 175–76; "XXXVI," 188–206, 217, 220; "XXXVIII," 207, 212–21; "LXXV," 175
van Alphen, Ernst, 283n. 11

Vasconcelos, José, 106, 266n. 13
Venus de Milo, 188–90, 197–205
Vernant, Jean-Pierre, 208, 227, 256n. 15, 259n. 16, 263n. 31, 282n. 4
von Buelow, Christiane, 276nn. 7 and 8

Wittgenstein, Ludwig, 90, 229
Womack, John, 269n. 35, 270nn. 38 and 39

Yáñez, Augustín, 25, 266n. 13, 274n. 55